Jazz Consciousness

PAUL AUSTERLITZ

Jazz Consciousness

MUSIC, RACE, AND HUMANITY

WESLEYAN UNIVERSITY PRESS

Middletown, Connecticut

Published by Wesleyan University Press, Middletown, CT 06459

www.wesleyan.edu/wespress

5 4 3 2 1

Library of Congress Cataloging-in-Publication Data

Austerlitz, Paul–
Jazz consciousness: music, race, and humanity / Paul Austerlitz.
    p.   cm. — (Music/culture)
Includes videography and discography (p.   ), bibliographical
references (p.   ), and index.
ISBN-13: 978–0–8195–6781–9 (cloth: alk. paper)
ISBN-10: 0–8195–6781–7 (cloth: alk. paper)
ISBN-13: 978–0–8195–6782–6 (pbk: alk. paper)
ISBN-10: 0–8195–6782–5 (pbk: alk. paper)
1. Jazz — Social aspects. 2. Jazz — History and criticism.
I. Title. II. Series.
ML3918.J39A97 2005
781.65'089 — dc22   2005010561

The author gratefully acknowledges permission to reproduce the following:

Sections of chapter 2 previously published in "Mambo Kings to West African Textiles"
Copyright © Frances Aparicio
From: *Musical Migrations*
By: Frances Aparicio
Reprinted with permission of Palgrave Macmillan

Sections of chapter 4 previously published in "Dominican Jazz in the
Black Atlantic Soundscape," *Black Music Research Journal* vol. 18, no. 1/2,
by permission of the Center for Black Music Research, Columbia College Chicago;
and "The Jazz Tinge in Dominican Music," *Ethnomusicology* Volume 44/2 (2000),
by permission of the Society for Ethnomusicology.

Contents

~~~

Color plates follow page 40.
Photographs follow page 94.

Acknowledgments

⁓⁓⁓⁓

An Akan proverb states that "the family is a force" and, indeed, it has been only been with the support of my extended family of colleagues and friends that I have been able to complete this book. At Wesleyan University Press, I am especially grateful to Suzanna Tamminen, editor-in-chief, and Robert Walser, editor of the Music/Culture Series. Funds supporting research were provided by the Fulbright Foundation, the Wenner-Gren Foundation for Anthropological Research, the American-Scandinavian Foundation, the Finlandia Foundation, and the Watson Center for International Studies at Brown University. Many colleagues, friends, and students read drafts of this book, providing valuable feedback. I am particularly indebted to Teresa Nemeth, whose editing greatly improved the clarity and readability of the text. Scott Currie, Mindy Keskinen, Meki Nzewi, David Yih, Ferdinand Jones, Alan Saul, Shanna Lorenz, Raúl Fernández, Lise Waxer, Steven Rabson, and Eric Charry played important roles in helping me hone my thinking. Robert Farris Thompson, Michael S. Harper, Kwaku Kwaakye Obeng, David Carp, Lewis Gordon, Chris Washburne, Lina Fruzzetti, Rebecca Miller, Judith Becker, James Campbell, Danielle Georges, Kimasi Browne, Dominique Cyrille, Tuomas Nevanlinna, Hannu Saha, Timo Leisiö, Vesa Kurkela, and Jari Muikku also provided advice and encouragement. Many students, including Katherine Brucher, Roshan Samtani, Kera Washington, Liam McGrenahan, Alan Williams, Liz Scheps, Paige McGinley, Jason McGill, and Adam Pogoff helped me cultivate this book. Leonardo Acosta, Max Salazar, Luc Delannoy, Pauli Hallman, Pekka Gronow, Keiko Morishita, and Markku Salo aided me in the field, while John Storm Roberts, Ruth Glasser, Ira Berger, and Anthony Brown helped me obtain oral historical data. I am indebted to Paul Karting, Henry Medina, Susan Dopp, Rick Britto, Bill Johnston, and Ken Carpenter for their generous help with photographs, art, and figures. Many musicians gave their time and wisdom; first and foremost among them is Milford Graves. Mario Grillo, Ray Santos, Delfín Pérez, José Madera, Jr., and Louis Bauzo provided assistance with my research on Machito. The Dominican and Finnish musicians I am most indebted to include Tavito Vásquez, Mario Rivera, Joseíto Mateo, Julito Figueroa, Crispín Fernández, Tony Vicioso, Edwin Lora, Rafaelito Roman, Rafaelito Mirabal, Juan Luis Guerra, Julio Alberto Hernández, Antonio Lora, Pavín Tolentino, Agustín Pichardo, Heikki Syrjänen, and Pekka Westerholm.

I also want to salute the Yorùbá *òrìṣà* Ẹlẹ́gbá by quoting a song:

> O Bara wá yọ,
> Ẹ̀ké e,
> Èṣù Ọ̀dàrà,
> Ọmọ yàlàwá'nà
> Mámà ké'ní irawo e.
>
> Vital force who comes to deliver [us],
> Forked Stick,
> Èṣù, performer of wonders,
> Child that separates, splits, and divides the road,
> May you not cut the initiates' mat of goodness.*

*Mason 1992: 69; my lineation.

Introduction

Percussionist Milford Graves maintains that the music he plays is "directly linked to African music." But he also proclaims, "I do not deal with music that has any ethnic classification. I deal with human music." Such positions are not uncommon: African American jazz players often assert black ownership of their art while declaring that it is universal or promoting it as a generically North American form. Pianist Billy Taylor, for example, espouses the idea that jazz is "America's music" but also champions its provenance in African American culture.[1] And while Duke Ellington said that he played "Negro music," he also insisted that his art is "international."[2] The fluidity of these perspectives evince a nuanced vision, a high comfort level with the natural complexity of our multifarious world: the major innovators of jazz have been black, but the music is played and enjoyed by U.S. citizens of all backgrounds, and indeed, by people the world over.[3]

In the introductory essay of his seminal 1903 book *The Souls of Black Folk,* W. E. B. Du Bois argued that "double consciousness," a dual identity based in the black in-group and to the larger mainstream, characterizes African American culture:

[T]he Negro is sort of a seventh son, born with a veil, and gifted with *second sight* in this American world. . . . It is a peculiar sensation, this *double-consciousness.* . . . One ever senses his two-ness,—an American, a Negro: two souls, two thoughts, two unreconciled strivings; two *warring* ideals in one dark body, whose dogged strength alone keeps it from being torn asunder.[4]

Of course, all people have multiple identities; it is natural to identify with different groups at different times. Race is only one aspect of African American identity, and people who happen to be black identify themselves according to many affiliations, ranging from gender to occupation and social class. But because race is a determinant factor in American life, it holds a prominent position in African American identity. For this reason, Du Bois's concept of doubleness has became a central trope of African American studies, inspiring variegated interpretations.[5] This book uses Du Bois's insight as a springboard for thinking about jazz from an ethnomusicological perspective.[6]

Focusing on the ethnographic documentation of music, *ethnomusicology* interprets musical styles in their cultural contexts, looking at "music *as* culture."[7] The task of an ethnomusicological study is to describe and document a musical type in its context, to interpret a *music culture.* What is the music culture of jazz? Is it the U.S. mainstream or the African American in-group? Of course, it is both. Moreover, because jazz is now performed by people of all ethnicities all over the world, its lessons have become relevant to people everywhere. I thus use the term *jazz consciousness* to situate the music in the overlapping contexts of the United States, the African diaspora, and the larger world.[8]

Spiritual Striving

The separate but interrelated essays in this book look at jazz through three large lenses as follows: (1) as an art that is intimately tied to national identity in the United States; (2) as a type of music that is inextricable from its African-influenced base; and (3) as a major current of transnational culture.[9] These perspectives are interrelated, and inevitably, they overlap. The truism that "jazz is America's music" is problematic for several reasons. First, it fails to recognize that the music's major innovators have been *African* American; in a land that has marginalized blacks, this fact must be noted. Moreover, the statement that "jazz is America's music" ignores the fact that this hemisphere includes South and Central America as well as North America, and that the United States is itself home to Latino as well as Anglo cultures.[10] Jazz has long partaken of both, and this book pays special attention to Latin tinges[11] in the music. At the same time, jazz is indeed an important North American music that can teach us much about the United States.

The perspectives in this book are further related because, as Paul Gilroy points out, the African diaspora is a transnational phenomenon that is part and parcel of occidental civilization: the labor and expressive forms of blacks have been central to the economic and cultural development of Western modernity.[12] As Gilroy's seminal book, *The Black Atlantic: Modernity and Double Consciousness,* shows, "the experiences of black people . . . [are] a part of the abstract modernity."[13] Similarly, Duke Ellington affirmed that African Americans were fundamental to "building America. . . .

Working building America into the most powerful nation in the world. . . . The foundation of the United States rests on the sweat of my people."[14] While it has been integral to the development of the United States and Western modernity, African American culture has also been marginalized. This marginalization has manifested itself in slavery and segregation, and today, in subtle, day-to-day forms of racial profiling. The story of the strife attendant to the five-hundred-year legacy of the forced migration of Africans to the Americas is inextricable from jazz consciousness.

Doubleness developed through force of necessity, through confronting the extreme vicissitudes of a troubled world. As Du Bois writes, while doubleness offers insights that amount to "second sight," it is also tantamount to an internal "war."[15] A speech attributed to the Ethiopian emperor Haile Selassie, and immortalized in Bob Marley's reggae song "War," eloquently states that as long as human relations are fraught with injustice, the world will be in a state of war: "Until the philosophy which holds one race superior and another inferior is finally and permanently abandoned, everywhere is war."[16] The anthropologist Melville Herskovits discussed a "myth of the Negro past" that is central to this strife. This myth erroneously posited that blacks living in the diaspora had lost contact with their ancestral traditions. Herskovits refuted this myth, meticulously documenting African influences in the Americas, which he called "Africanisms" or African "survivals," and he developed the concept of *syncretism,* the blending of elements from two cultures (in this case, African and European).[17] Herskovits discussed the discord inherent to this journey. He noted that while Haitians worship their ancestral African spirits, they sometimes feel guilty about it afterward, developing a "socialized ambivalence" as a result of ritual "possession by the gods of his [African] ancestors . . . despite his strict Catholic upbringing. . . ." His "desire to understand and worship the gods of his ancestors" is followed by "remorse after having done this."[18] Herskovits's colleague Erika Bourguignon argues that while syncretism "helps to present a complete picture of the universe . . . ambivalence is essentially disruptive not only to a harmonious world-view, but even to successful self-identification."[19] Similarly, the Martinican psychiatrist and anticolonialist Frantz Fanon noted that colonized and enslaved people often internalize hegemonic perspectives that cause feelings of ambivalence. He stressed, however, that this disruption is a natural reaction to societal rupture, that it is a manifestation of the larger problems of colonialism and racism.[20]

Ambivalence is a natural reaction to the contradictions that all sensitive people face, and I believe that it is by honestly confronting and working through internal contradictions that we grow. Invocations of double or split consciousness had already been made when Du Bois presented his concept of doubleness. The American philosopher Ralph Waldo Emerson called the unreconciled conflict between spiritual and mundane experience "double consciousness" in his 1843 published lecture, "The Transcendentalist."[21] Goethe also grappled with questions of spiritual duality.[22] Du Bois was certainly aware of, and was likely influenced by, both these invocations. Moreover, his Harvard professor, William James, was carefully considering the nature of consciousness during the period that Du Bois studied with him.[23] James was a psychologist, philosopher, and scholar of religion. In his work as a psychologist, James, like many of his colleagues, was interested in states of "split" personality.[24] It is James's work on religion, however, that resonates most powerfully with the concept of jazz consciousness as developed in this book. In *The Varieties of Religious Experience,* James contrasted two kinds of spiritual seekers. One type has a "'once-born' type of consciousness, developing straight and natural, with no element of morbid compunction or crisis." The other type, by contrast, is acutely aware of evil and has a "divided self" that must undergo a "process of unification" and be "twice-born."[25] Saint Augustine, for example, was a tortured soul who was torn between his carnal desires and his spiritual path.[26] James, however, sees this type of ambivalence as a good thing: he argues that it is through grappling with adversity that we learn and grow. Augustine and other tortured "divided selves" eventually resolve their crises, moving on to higher planes of existence. While this resolution can take many forms (it need not be religious) James calls it "conversion" and describes it as "the process . . . by which the self hitherto divided, and consciously wrong inferior and unhappy, becomes unified and consciously right superior and happy."[27] Similarly, Du Bois writes that doubleness engenders a "longing to attain self-conscious manhood, to merge his double self into a better and truer self." This merging of the black self and the generically American self negates neither of its components, instead giving rise to a higher consciousness characterized by "second sight." Du Bois was not a particularly religious man; significantly, however, the essay in which he articulates the concept of doubleness is entitled "Of Our Spiritual Strivings" and, as Du Bois's biographer David Levering Lewis asserts, it is "profoundly mystical."[28]

The concept of consciousness suggests a valuable—and provocative—way to look at music evocative of the new wave of "consciousness studies"; while this burgeoning field is related to neuroscience, it is also emphatically humanistic and several of its major figures are philosophers as well as scientists.[29] This book, however, does not treat the neuroscience of music, nor does it consider music in relation to altered states of consciousness. Instead, calling upon Du Bois's thinking, it invokes the concept of consciousness in a humanistic sense, as a trope that can help us understand music, culture, and identity. Consciousness implies awareness, mind-set, worldview. Musical consciousness is different from other forms of consciousness because musical experience makes us aware and mindful in ways that nonmusical experience does not. At the same time, musical experience cannot be separated from other experience; while it issues from a particular backdrop, music can inform, and even influence, other aspects of life—musical consciousness is an active agent in culture.[30] Even thinking about music or possessing a worldview that is informed by musical experiences is musical consciousness. Of course, musical consciousness is ineffable; it is impossible to describe it in words. But precisely because it speaks its own language, music can tell stories that otherwise go untold. One of the hallmarks of musical consciousness is that it can unite things that are separated in nonmusical reality. For example, despite racial segregation, musicians such as Duke Ellington seamlessly integrated European influences and African-derived traditions. Musicologist Christopher Small celebrates music's ability to reconcile competing currents of culture and identity. He writes that music can

articulate and reveal to us some of our deepest values. . . . All human beings carry around with themselves any number of contradictions and paradoxes, and we need not worry ourselves too much by that (I am comforted also by Walt Whitman's superbly confident "Do I contradict myself? Very well, I contradict myself!"). [In the musical experience] we have a tool by means of which our real concepts of ideal relationships can be articulated, those contradictions can be reconciled, and the integrity of the person can be affirmed, explored, and celebrated.[31]

The spiritual striving of double consciousness has manifested itself in various musical movements, some based in the black in-group and others reaching out to the wider world. Graham Lock's aptly titled *Blutopia* elucidates blues-based utopian projects instigated by African American musicians.[32] On one hand, these musicians have responded to the "war" of doubleness by turning inward and focusing on the in-group. This trend has manifested itself in various forms of utopian black nationalism. Jazz projects celebrating black identity range from Duke Ellington's many compositions devoted to telling the story of his people, to Afro-Cuban jazz, and the "new black music" (or "avant-garde") of the 1960s. At the same time, musicians have cultivated an extraordinary openness; developing during the Harlem Renaissance and civil rights movements, the consciousness of the jazz community has articulated an aesthetic of inclusivity and an ethos of ecumenicity. By melding many different influences, ranging from the blues to North American popular song, from European art music to Indian raga, from samba to hip-hop, jazz creates an expansive space. The experience of playing, listening, or dancing to jazz—and even feeling its lingering effects after the sound has stopped—manifests a holism that reconfigures the mind-set.

Planetary Humanism

The historian Eric Hobsbawm wrote that as early as 1958, the "extraordinary expansion" of jazz had "practically no cultural parallel for speed and scope," adding that at that time there was "probably no major city in the world where someone is not playing a record of Louis Armstrong or Charlie Parker."[33] The diffusion of jazz gained impetus from the growing influence of the United States that followed the two world wars, and the music both followed and promoted U.S. hegemony around the world. At the same time, issuing from African American culture rather than the dominant Euro-American culture, jazz was often seen as a counterforce to U.S. hegemony. This broadness of meaning allowed for multifarious interpretations, some of which are elucidated in this book. Other African-influenced styles, ranging from salsa to reggae and rap, continued to spread around the world in the late twentieth century and came to dominate the world stage to the extent that black musics have become the musical lingua franca of our times.[34]

Because jazz is diffused around the world, it can be said to be a global music.[35] The concept of *globalism,* however, is often used indiscriminately, in ways that overlook the many differences between various transnational phenomena. Ethnomusicologist Thomas Turino uses the term *cosmopolitan* to refer to "objects, ideas, and cultural positions that are widely diffused throughout the world and yet are specific to certain portions of the populations within given countries."[36] Much so-called global culture takes place within geographically dispersed "cosmopolitan" communities that, while traversing large geographic areas, are nevertheless insular groups in their own right. Moreover, cosmopolitan communities are different than diasporas because cosmopolitan groups lack a shared place of origin: while a particular cosmopolitan group may privilege a specific location, its members do not share a native land.[37] While many cosmopolitans belong to the middle or upper classes, Turino's usage of the term does not require this.[38] Extending around the world, the jazz community is cosmopolitan: while jazz originated in the United States, members of the transnational jazz community can be natives of almost any land, and while many of them belong to the middle or upper classes, they can belong to any social class.

Cosmopolitans often invoke notions of universalism, for example, saying that they are "citizens of the world."[39] Jazz bassist Cecil McBee, for example, states that music is "a universal language. . . . I've had people around the world understand what I was saying from my heart musically. . . . That's a very powerful force and you must appreciate it."[40] Musicians also invoke more radical views about musical universalism. Milford Graves, for example, says that the "basic stuff of life is solely of one family. Music is part of us as human folks, and no one can claim ethnic ownership of music." Ethnomusicologists are sometimes uneasy with the concept of universalism: indeed, the tenet of the field, that music can only be fully understood in its cultural context, refutes the truism that "music is a universal language." But musicians have wisdom to offer and their views are worth trying to grasp; as McBee says, we should try to understand the power of their universalistic vision. Cultural relativism is a powerful lens through which to appreciate the world's musical diversity. Developing the theory of cultural relativism in anthropology during the early twentieth century, Franz Boas proposed that each human culture should be studied on its own terms. To illustrate his position, he noted that while outside observers might look at an indigenous musical instrument as a sound-producing medium, insiders might see it as the "outcome of religious conceptions," or a means to "invoke or drive away spirits."[41] Evaluating non-Western cultures according to Western standards— standards that have been touted as "universal"—can lead to ethnocentric judgments. This, however, does not mean that human beings share nothing across lines of culture, nor does it mean that all universalist discourse is ethnocentric. A venerable line of thinking in structuralist linguistics and anthropology points to deep-lying structures of the human mind that cut across cultural boundaries. Ethnomusicologist Judith Becker has recently argued that the time has come for us to transcend a dualistic, either/or approach to the question of relativism versus universalism, that we need to "accept that paradox . . . that we cannot do without either perspective."[42]

Paul Gilroy points out that, developing in a context that has denied their humanity, people of color have been forced to ponder the question, What constitutes humanity? In many cases, they have responded by invoking what he calls "planetary humanism" or "strategic universalism":[43]

Yearning to be free, that is, to be free of "race" and racism, has provided enduring foundations for the resolutely utopian aspirations to which a racially coded world gave rise among the subordinated, immiserated, and colonized.[44]

Pointing to the fact that all people are fundamentally the same does not betray ignorance of the valuable lessons of cultural relativism; instead, it is a powerful strategy to counter the dehumanization of racism. Gilroy is influenced by Frantz Fanon, who, while espousing militant resistance to colonialism, made a "call for the institution of an anti-colonial and nonracial universalism,"[45] proclaiming that

I, the man of color, want only this: . . . that the enslavement of man by man cease forever. . . . That it be possible to discover and love man, whoever he may be. . . . The Negro is not. Any more than the white man. . . . I want the world to recognize, with me, the open door of every consciousness."[46]

The holistic aesthetic of jazz, its propensity to incorporate any and all outside elements, is a musical manifestation of this utopian universalism.

A *creative tension* resulting from African Americans' equivocal position both within and without Western modernity speaks eloquently to the contradictions that all people face. This book argues that jazz creates a virtual space where we can confront, learn from, and even heal the contradictions resulting from social rupture. Developing through force of necessity in a context of inhumanity, in a state of "war," the inclusivity of jazz works with conflict and ambivalence to arrive at "second sight." Issuing from African American culture, this consciousness enriches all folks "in this American world," as well as around the planet.[47]

A Scholar-Musician's Journey

This book speaks from the perspective of my personal journey, visiting spaces that I have inhabited as a scholar and a musician.[48] My musical experiences have played important roles in shaping my concept of what it means to be a citizen of this country, of *las Américas,* and of the world. Born in Finland to Finnish and Romanian parents, I moved to New York City at one year of age but maintained close contact with my Finnish kin. My father was a German-speaking Jew born in Romania who migrated to the United States in 1939. Both my parents were academics and amateur musicians. They inspired in me a love for learning and the arts, introducing me to the joys of mental reflection and to European classical music. Like many whites, I adored African American music, playing and listening to rock, blues, and jazz, as well as European sounds, as a child and teen. I entered Bennington College at the age of eighteen, majoring in its Black Music division, which had been founded by trumpeter Bill Dixon and focused on so-called free jazz, or, as Dixon called it, "black music." I was inspired by this vital movement, learning to improvise on saxophone, clarinet, and bass clarinet.

Coming from an immigrant background, straddling my European and North American selves and struggling with my own identity, I was attracted to the broadness of meaning in the music of artists such as Duke Ellington, Charlie Parker, and John Coltrane. I loved both blues and Western classical music and was delighted to discover that jazz availed itself of *all* influences. I was also attracted to the politically progressive milieu of the jazz community and became committed to working to heal social divisions in interracial settings. Perhaps most important, I was deeply touched by the depth of expression—indeed, the spirituality—that I encountered in the music of visionaries such as Coltrane. Without losing my love for European classical music or rejecting my European background, I came to identify with African American music. By playing and listening to jazz, I cultivated a consciousness that helped negotiate my own ambivalences, my own spiritual striving.

Milford Graves was on the faculty at Bennington and influenced me to study non-Western musics generally and African-influenced musics in particular. His course called "The Influence of Music" planted in me an abiding curiosity about the *efficacy* of music, a drive to understand the ways that music can affect the mind and body. Studying with Graves established a life direction for me to the extent that many of the ethnomusicological and creative perspectives that I later developed were, often unconsciously, influenced by him. As this book unfolded, even before I decided to include a chapter on Graves, I noticed that many of my ideas were uncannily similar to his. Graves is thus a fitting subject for the last chapter; the perspectives offered there dovetail with ideas developed earlier in the book.

After graduating from Bennington I returned to New York and played Latin jazz, merengue, and salsa, trying to learn all I could about the African-influenced musics that Graves had introduced me to. I became committed to Latino culture, learning to speak Spanish and moving to a Dominican neighborhood. My profile as a jazz and Latin music player, however, did not surpass that of a semiprofessional. I began to yearn for a more stable career, and calling upon the intellectualism that I had imbibed from my parents, enrolled in Wesleyan University's Ph.D. program in ethnomusicology.

When I began graduate school, my professor, David McAllester, a grand man of ethnomusicology and one of the founders of the field, once suggested that the central question of the discipline is, What is musical truth? Although McAllester was open to all manner of creative thinking, he, like many ethnomusicologists, has a strong background in anthropology. I learned that the primary method of conducting ethnomusicological research consisted of conducting in-depth, firsthand ethnographic research on a particular music culture. I eagerly applied my experiences with Latin music to my research, embarking upon a long-term historical-ethnographic study of Dominican merengue.[49] As I did so, it dawned on me that my previous immersion in the Dominican music culture of New York had been an unwitting enactment of the ethnographic method of research. Buttressed by my academic study, I continued playing in merengue bands and learning as much as I could about the music and the lifeways that surround it. I came to adore conducting fieldwork.

As I delved deeply into merengue and Afro-Caribbean culture, however, I began to feel estranged from my own background. Intrigued by my diligent study of their music, Dominican friends asked me about my Finnish musical heritage and I was ashamed to admit that I knew little about it. I realized that I had become so involved with other cultures that I had neglected to study my*self*. I embarked on a study of Finnish music to redress this deficiency. I was fascinated to discover that contemporary Finnish music is deeply influenced by African American music and that, like myself, many Finns have used jazz as a forum to negotiate their own identities and creativity, as a site of their own spiritual striving.

In addition to my long-term studies of Dominican and Finnish musics, I have engaged in smaller-scale exploratory research in Cuba, Haiti, Puerto Rico, and Brazil. I always brought my clarinet or saxophone with me into the field, and spent much fruitful time playing with musicians wherever I sojourned. I have been drawn to the rich constellation of African-derived religious practices, and have regularly attended Lucumí (or Santería), Vodou, and Candomblé ceremonies, not only in the Caribbean and Brazil, but also in the United States. While, as mentioned, this book does not discuss altered states of consciousness, my experiences in ritual settings have informed my thinking about the transformative power of *all* music. Moreover, the inner nourishment that I have imbibed in these settings has fed my development as an artist, scholar, and individual.

The term *participant-observation* was first used in sociology and anthropology to refer to field methods in which the researcher shares lifeways with informants (as opposed to relying on questionnaires and interviews).[50] In ethnomusicology, however, it usually refers to the valuable research method, advocated by Mantle Hood, in which the scholar becomes a performer of the music that he or she researches.[51] Despite the prevalence of this method, ethnomusicology has never overcome the Cartesian separation of theory and practice; Hood himself cautions students not to be seduced by playing music lest it distract them from "the sterner stuff of which academia is made."[52] While Hood's warning might apply to ethnomusicologists who perform music as amateurs, it does not apply to scholars such as myself, who play professionally. Musical performance, of course, is a highly demanding form of discourse that makes great demands on the intellect. My discussions with musicians often impress upon me that many artists are deep thinkers who have developed original philosophies informed by rich experiences and extensive travel. These cosmopolitan artist-intellectuals are similar to the "organic intellectuals" discussed by the Italian Marxist Antonio Gramsci.[53] As my musico-scholarly journey unfolded, my creative and academic pursuits melded, and performing became symbiotically related to my work as a scholar. My musicianly contacts with Dominican and Finnish players opened doors when I was conducting fieldwork, while my accomplishments as a scholar attracted the attention of accomplished musicians, opening not only research avenues but also opportunities to continue developing as an artist. Because I perform with professional musicians today, many of my academic colleagues assume that I was an established player prior to becoming an ethnomusicologist. Actually, the opposite is true: although I aspired to be a professional musician as a young man, it was only after I had matured as a scholar that my musicianship came to fruition.[54] The symbiosis of my development as a player and scholar has impressed upon me the extent to which musical thinking is scholarly and academic work is expressive.

Perspectives

I have been involved with jazz as a performing musician as well as a researcher throughout my life, but this book is the fruit of my engagement with it as a scholar. While the ideas presented here are based in current trends in academia, I sincerely hope that this book will reach beyond the ivory tower and speak to music fans, players, and readers from all walks of life. While my larger perspective is best communicated when the text is read from beginning to end, this book is a collection of separate essays, and readers might want to omit chapters or sections that do not speak to them. I invite you to interact with this book, to improvise your own personal engagement with it.

As jazz becomes entrenched in our institutions of higher education, academic interest in it grows. Significantly, the new wave of jazz studies reflects the holism of jazz: scholarly perspectives come from a wide variety of academic disciplines. It is not surprising that, as an African-influenced music that developed in the West, jazz is studied by both ethnomusicologists (who traditionally study non-Western musics),[55] and so-called historical musicologists (who study Western classical music).[56] Jazz studies have also attracted scholars from disparate fields such as film and gender studies,[57] and much recent scholarship looks at jazz as a transnational phenomenon.[58] Another important trend emanates from players' own writing and thinking.[59] This book applies ethnomusicological methods to jazz: it focuses on specific case studies and, whenever possible, employs original field research. It expands the usual ethnomusicological focus on a single culture to look at transnational currents by employing multilocale field research in several areas. Other than ethnomusicology, my principal academic background is in African American Studies, Latino Studies, and the study of nationalism and race. Most of my previous work has been in the study of popular music,[60] and I have benefited from the influence of British cultural studies and their focus on social class and power relations.[61] My perspectives are also informed by experiences as a performing musician. Combining ethnomusicology with performance, African American Studies, Latino Studies, critical race theory, and the study of nationalism, I aim for a scholarly perspective whose sum is greater than its disciplinary parts.

Extending the discussion of jazz consciousness presented in the introduction, chapter 1 looks at it in the context of the West as a whole and in the United States specifically, critically examining the truism that jazz is "America's music." It looks at the ways in which, struggling to survive in a context of unequal power relations, African Americans have improvised upon African and European musical influences to forge a holistic, inclusive musical consciousness that is central to national culture in the United States.[62]

Chapter 2 shifts focus to the African diaspora, looking at jazz in relation to other African-influenced forms, showing that in addition to the great diversity of African-influenced cultures, jazz and other diasporic forms foreground common process-oriented ways of music-making that are linked to dance and speech.[63] Chapter 2 also moves attention away from social processes and identity to aesthetics, invoking pictographic tools, synesthesia, kinesthesia, and metaphor to examine common elements in the efficacy of African-influenced musics, looking at the ways they make us *feel*. While this chapter is shorter than the others, it serves a crucial purpose by elucidating the African-based aspects of jazz and thus paving the way for the social and aesthetic issues that are discussed in chapters 3, 4, 5, and 6.

Treating the mutually enriching meeting of African American and Afro-Cuban cultures, chapter 3 presents a comprehensive study of the seminal New York–based Latin jazz band, Machito and his Afro-Cubans. As its name implies, this band promoted a self-conscious affirmation of pan-African solidarity. Significantly, while Machito was a foremost exponent of Cuban music, his band worked primarily in New York City and never played in Cuba. Moreover, for all its excellence as a Cuban dance band, I argue that the Machito band's greatest contribution was in the realm of jazz. It was thus a quintessential expression of U.S.-based Latino culture, demonstrating that Latino culture belongs to all people of the Americas, including those in the United States, and that it holds a central position in the history of jazz. The Machito band exemplified a sense of inclusivity atop its grounding in the pan-African and Latino spheres: it included musicians of all ethnicities and appealed to fans of all ethnicities in the Americas and beyond. Chapter 3 is the book's centerpiece and its longest chapter, exemplifying jazz consciousness in the United States, in all the Americas, in the pan-African arena, and in universalistic impulses.[64]

Chapter 4 considers jazz in the Dominican Republic, focusing on the blending of jazz with the Dominican "national music," merengue. Like the melding of Afro-Cuban music and jazz, the Dominican-jazz fusion was based in shared African-derived aesthetics. But while the architects of Afro-Cuban jazz were self-identified pan-Africanists and thus stood apart from U.S. hegemony, many Dominican jazz fans associate the music with the might of the United States.[65] Chapter 4 elucidates this central complexity of jazz consciousness. Chapter 5 recounts the history of jazz in Finland, where what locals call "rhythm-music" melded with local traditions.[66] It thus provides a valuable look at what happens when black music spreads outside the African diaspora.

At this point the text changes voice: chapter 6 is cowritten with the drummer Milford Graves, with Graves speaking in the first person. As a seminal influence on my work, Graves is a fitting subject for the book's final chapter. Graves decided to become a musician after hearing Machito's rhythm section at New York's Palladium Ballroom and, like many young African Americans, he was inspired by Cuban drummers' vital ties to a living African-based culture. Beginning his career performing Afro-Cuban music, Graves later took up the drum set and began playing freely improvised music (often called "avant-garde" or "free" jazz). Graves is internationally recognized for his original musical style, which he developed through his study of healing arts, and his computer-aided research on the sounds of the human heart.

The separate but interrelated essays in this book are linked by the application of Du Bois's concept of double consciousness to the study of jazz, arguing that "jazz consciousness" embodies an aesthetic of inclusion and an ethos of ecumenicity. It might seem romantic or naive for me, a white male, to make calls for racial inclusivity and musical universalism; after all, I have benefited from racial privilege and may lack the depth of experience to fully appreciate the nuances of race. This book, however, is no shallow call for "color-blindness" and it does not ignore unequal power relationships. On the contrary, its purpose is to elucidate the ways that musicians have responded to injustice. Artists such as Milford Graves are not naive about race, and it is precisely because of their acute awareness of the vicissitudes of life that they articulate a vision of pan-humanity. This vision, manifested in their music, has touched people all over the world and has been central to my own journey, my own quest for wholeness. This book is thus one European American scholar-musician's perspective on the spiritual striving of jazz consciousness. I share it in the hope that it will enrich others.

Jazz Consciousness

CHAPTER I

Jazz Consciousness in the United States

———

Eric Dolphy's bass clarinet speaks a guttural blues phrase, and Charles Mingus's bass intones an answer, but in another key. They continue their blues-based conversation, yelping, yelling their comments back and forth. There's an element of humor in the sound, but also a sense of urgency, and even tinges of anger. Is this modernist art or backstreet blues? It is both: the duo improvisation, based on the song "What Love?" immediately appeals to the ear, as it is based in the speech patterns of black English. But this is also modernist music, it is free improvisation.[1] As an embodiment of doubleness, inextricable from both African-influenced traditions and Western modernity, jazz spans barriers, creating a musical consciousness of inclusiveness. This chapter considers jazz in relation to national identity in the United States, arguing that the music's inclusive, creolized nature embodies the multiracial makeup of this country, but that unequal power relations emphatically color this creolization. After exploring the larger phenomenon of North American jazz consciousness, we will turn to its unique embodiment in multi-instrumentalist Eric Dolphy.

Strategic Universalism and the Music

But what is this thing called jazz?[2] As noted, Duke Ellington asked that we call his art "Negro music."[3] In fact, he spurned the word "jazz," saying that "jazz is only a word and really has no meaning. We stopped using it in 1943. To keep the whole thing clear, once and for all, I don't believe in categories of any kind."[4]

To what forces, social or musical, might Ellington have been reacting with this statement? And what purpose might a category serve? The words that we use to designate musical styles are integral to musical cultures, forming conceptual frames that permeate the musical experience. These frames are never used innocently; they always carry ideological baggage, they always embed aesthetic and social positions. Genres thus produce what the literary critic Hans Jauss calls "horizons of expectation."[5] W. C. Handy's most famous composition, for example, uses elements of vernacular African American music as well as the Argentine tango. His decision to call the piece "St. Louis Blues," however, frames our perception of it as black, North American, and rootsy.[6]

In his groundbreaking article "Constructing the Jazz Tradition," musicologist Scott DeVeaux shows that the notion of a "jazz tradition" developed as a social construct through time as musicians and critics sought cultural capital for the music. During this process, the boundaries of the genre were hotly debated.[7] As the music gained popularity, Euro-Americans appropriated it; economic control, in the hands of white club owners, record company executives, and promoters, resulted in the rise of white bandleaders and star musicians. Paul Whiteman was crowned "King Jazz" in spite of the fact the major innovators of the music were black. So we can see why Sidney Bechet would assert that jazz was "a name that white people have given to the music" and why Ellington would stress that this was indeed "Negro music."[8]

Some music critics in the 1930s and 1940s argued that New Orleans "hot jazz" could not evolve and that swing was not a form of jazz. Similar views surfaced with respect to bebop: the French critic Hughes Panassié believed that while bop was an important musical form, it was not jazz, because it had a different rhythmic structure than swing. Charlie Parker also noted bebop's divergence from swing, once saying that that this might mean that bop is a genre in its own right.[9] Beginning in the 1940s, the idea of an organic tradition, a tradition with internal innovations, arose.[10] Dizzy Gillespie fought to have bop accepted as jazz, believing that it would be beneficial to the new music to be housed under this umbrella concept. The idea of an organic, changing jazz tradition prevailed and the "jazz" epithet now refers to styles ranging from those innovated by Buddy Bolden to Ornette Coleman. Today, free improvisers and neoclassicists alike invoke "the tradition."

As we have seen, critics and audiences, as well as musicians, play roles in the process of genre formation.[11] And at some point, music-makers feel bound or limited by the categorizations. Many musicians, including Ellington, have rejected or remained ambivalent about them. When deejay Symphony Sid asked Charlie Parker to comment on the fusion of bebop with Afro-Cuban music, he said, "Bop is just a title . . . It's all still music."[12] Challenges to a reified jazz were made by Thelonious Monk, who once said that maybe jazz is "going to hell,"[13] and Miles Davis, who was quoted as saying that "jazz is dead."[14] Interestingly, Davis's provocative comment was consonant with the views of his critics, who excommunicated him from the jazz canon for his interest in R & B and forays into jazz-rock fusion. African American musicians associated with the Black Arts movement of the 1960s embraced the term "black music" for its links with other African American forms such as gospel and blues. They pointed out that these styles are all part of a larger black tradition. Drummer Beaver Harris, for example, said, "I prefer calling it Black Music because that way you have all your history to draw from."[15]

Feminists have drawn attention to the issue of marked and unmarked categories to the extent that the terms "man" and "he" no longer stand for humans in general (at least in academic writing). Black leaders similarly challenged the use of marked categories as referents for people of color; Malcolm X, for example, talked about the "so-called Negro." Trumpeter Bill Dixon notes that university music departments are usually devoted to European art music, an unmarked Ur-category that turns everything else into a hyphenated "other." Dixon founded a Black Music Division at Bennington College, pointing out that while it was called the Music Division, the college's other music department was in fact devoted to "white music."[16] Similarly, saxophonist Archie Shepp equated the word "jazz" with a racial slur, saying, "if we continue to call our music jazz, we must continue to be called niggers."[17] Ethnomusicology's challenge to Eurocentrism in the academy has had parallel repercussions. For example, Brown University's course Music 001, "Introduction to Music," was renamed "Introduction to Western Music" as awareness of non-Western styles grew.[18]

Many members of Chicago's Association for the Advancement of Creative Music (or AACM) advocated the term Great Black Music, while Anthony Braxton, also of the AACM, preferred the deracialized term "creative music" in keeping with his personal perspective, which combines black pride with avowed influences from European composers and white jazz players. The term "black classical music" also emerged in the 1970s and 1980s, as did the notion—popularized by pianist-educator Billy Taylor—that jazz is "America's classical music."[19] Its distance from racial politics and appropriation of the cachet associated with the "classics" made this concept attractive to many critics. This term thus played a significant role in gaining legitimacy for the music and increasing the style's cultural capital; as such, it aided musicians' interests. Today, the notion that jazz is America's classical music has commonsense appeal: most people agree that jazz shares much with other musics that are deemed "classical," such as the European concert repertoire. Both stress virtuosity, are performed by skilled professionals, and are meant primarily for listening. But, even as it clarifies some issues, calling jazz America's classical music raises new questions. As mentioned earlier, its divorcing of the music from its African American source is problematic. Moreover, for much of its history, jazz was dance music, not concert music. As musicologist Robert Walser shows, the idea of "classical music" is ill defined even with respect to the European concert repertory. One hallmark of classical musics, which applies to eighteenth-century European court music as well as many sub-Saharan repertories, is elite patronage. Other traits commonly ascribed to eighteenth- and nineteenth-century European classical music, such as the reliance on music notation and institutional training, developed in the twentieth century and do not apply to many of the so-called "classical masters": neither Bach nor Mozart, for example, studied in formal academies, and both were improvisers as well as composers.[20]

The road to today's notion that jazz is a type of classical music was paved by critics such as André Hodeir in the 1950s. Asking, "Where is jazz headed?" they answered that it was moving toward the classics, and they pointed to stylistic periods in the history of the music that resembled those of European classical music.[21] Although periodic schemes for jazz are now widely accepted, they are almost always skewed to the first half of the twentieth century and often neglect the last third of jazz history, from the 1970s to today.[22]

In current speech it is almost impossible to avoid the "j word." Adopting a Confucian middle ground that simultaneously accepts this term and affirms the African American basis of the music, some musicians who previously rejected the word returned to it in the 1990s, while continuing to acknowledge its problems. Rashied Ali stated that, to him, "the name, it really doesn't matter to me. As far as I'm concerned [the term] 'jazz' is cool . . . but we do know without a doubt that it is a Black art form that was discovered in this country."[23] Many of today's players often simply call what they play "the music," appropriating the unmarked category as their own in a subtle challenge to Euro-American musical hegemony.

As we have seen, genres, like all cultural artifacts, do not exist outside the power plays that are integral to social life. A reified notion of "jazz" may be a fabrication, an "invented tradition,"[24] but it is nevertheless a *real* fabrication, a real invention. Questioning the authenticity of invented traditions is moot because culture is always created by people; traditions are socially constructed by definition. The singer and pianist Les McCann cuts to the point when he asks, "Gotta make it real compared to what?"[25] Created by human beings, all culture is "invented," but this does not make it unreal.

In this sense of invention, genres are like race. Most people believe that there is a biological basis to race despite the fact that, biologically speaking, peoples' external appearances, the indices of "race," account for a minute amount of genetic information.[26] Moreover, the boundaries between the so-called races have changed through time, with some non-WASP groups categorized as nonwhite at various times in U.S. history. Still, race is a real factor in social interaction; in everyday experience, race is real. Race theorists Michael Omi and Howard Winant show that in spite of various "racial projects" that attempt to explain race in terms of ethnicity, nationalism, or social class, race remains a "central axis" of modern life.[27] For example, along with gender and age, a person's race is one of the things that most North Americans notice about each other upon meeting for the first time. Indeed, race is embedded in our psychological attitudes as well as our economic and social structures. While it would be ideal if we could be "color-blind," pointing out that race is a cultural artifact will not make it disappear. Similarly, while it would be ideal if the nomenclature of musical genres did not reflect social inequities, discourse about music cannot be separated from the unequal power relations that form the web of social life.

Paul Gilroy, however, argues that the social ills of our world are so acute that they demand a "radical response": we must "step away from the pious ritual in which we always agree that 'race' is invented but are then required to defer to its embeddedness."[28] The debates about the limits of so-called jazz as a genre constitute competing racial projects. In spite of a pervasive trend that treats black music as a marked category, African American musicians made repeated moves to break their art away from the confines of marginalization. The articulation of *non-racialism* is thus also a racial project: musicians' impulse to call jazz "the music," to put it in the unmarked category, is a real social force, a strategic invocation of universalism, a reaching out for "planetary humanism."[29]

Buscando América

Like races and genres, national identities are cultural formations; despite genuine feelings of patriotism, nation-states are "imagined communities."[30] Our prevailing notions of national identity issue from two separate, but often overlapping, types of nationalism. *Civic nationalism* (or Enlightenment nationalism) grew from the ideals of the French and U.S. Revolutions. It claims that one's national affiliation is conferred by virtue of citizenship in a particular state. *Cultural nationalism* (or romantic nationalism) was articulated by the eighteenth-century German philosopher Johann Gottfried Herder, who propagated the idea that the essence, or "genius," of each nation or ethnicity is expressed in its language and arts. While we usually use it to refer to sovereign states, the term *nation* originally referred to groups of people with shared histories, what we call races or ethnicities today.[31] In the wave of nationalism that swept Europe in the nineteenth century, patriots employed Herder's ideas in the creation of sovereign states that they claimed to be linked to particular ethnic entities. Nationalists searched for commonalities in folkways, language, history, and arts among groups that had previously felt little connection to one another. An assessment of the disparate populations that were united to form a single nation-state on the Italian peninsula in 1868 led one patriot to proclaim: "we have made Italy, now we must make Italians." A prominent Polish leader, faced with wide variance among factions, said, "It is the state which makes the nation and not the nation the state."[32]

National identities are thus strategically constructed: nation-states' populations are "ethnicized," they are represented *as if* they form natural communities. National myths, usually based on race or language, are reconstructed daily moving from present to past in propagation of "fictive ethnicities."[33] What is the fictive ethnicity of the United States, and what are its myths? As a "Land of the Free," founded as a republic on Enlightenment principles, the United States purports to follow the civic model of nationalism, which does not require citizens to belong to a particular ethnic group. But national identity in this country also follows the tenets of cultural nationalism: since the inception of the United States, northern European Protestants have held a privileged place. Native Americans, Asian Americans, African Americans, and, to a lesser extent, southern and eastern European immigrants have, at various times and in various ways, been excluded from full citizenship.

Insights provided by Juan Flores and others in Latino Studies demonstrate that "América" is a contested and troubled borderland: we are continually redefining what it means to be Native, Anglo, Latin, white, or black American. As salsa composer Rubén Blades puts it, we are perpetually "buscando América," we are always searching for, discovering, and inventing America.[34] The formation of national sentiment is thus an emergent, ongoing process: not only are nation-states socially constructed when they are founded, they are reinvented day in and day out, and we all play parts in the process. It is easy to deconstruct these processes and debunk nationalism. It is more challenging to examine these processes within ourselves. One day, after lecturing on Dominican and Finnish "fictive identities," I realized that my deepest motivation for discussing this subject was a search for my own identity as an American. Jazz has been an important arena for this quest for me and, I believe, for others in this land.

Conventional notions of U.S. national identity stress European-derived culture; in my elementary school, for example, I was taught to identify with the Pilgrims and (white) cowboys. In the university classes that I now teach, I often ask students who their forebears are. Inevitably, only a small minority are descendents of the English. A National Geographic map named "The Territorial Growth of the United States" could just as well be named "The Territorial Shrinking of Spanish North America," or, better, "Euro-American Usurpation of Native American Territory." As citizens of the United States, our fictive identity is determined by the dominant culture, not by the majority.

Europeans debated the humanity of "heathen" peoples of the conquered territories during the period of European expansion, and antiblack racism grew as an expedient way to justify colonialism and slavery. Notions about race that developed in the nineteenth century posited that each race had a fixed nature or essence. This *essentialism* was influenced by Herderian thinking; however, while Herder was a relativist who valued the contributions of all peoples, nineteenth-century thinking about race was ethnocentric. Evolutionist anthropology taught that Africans, Native Americans, and (interestingly) European peasants were "savages," while Asians were "barbarians" and the European elites were "civilized."[35] As popular interpretations of social Darwinism, the concepts of "high- and lowbrow" culture associated the high hominid brow with classical European traditions and the sloping brow of the ape with non-Western and vernacular traditions. Separation between "cultivated" and "folk" or "primitive" people was seen as the natural order of nature: each group had its place and should stay there. The "middlebrow" concept, coined in the 1920s, was originally a pejorative term for the mixing of high and low forms. Social class loomed as large as race in this discourse: the middlebrow straddling of class boundaries threatened the status quo, and press criticism of middlebrow culture was linked to antilabor sentiment. Critics argued that while middlebrows claimed to respect highbrow art, they actually corrupted it by producing half-caste bastards.[36] Euro-Americans were generally disinclined to regard black Americans as contributors to a national idiom, and it surprised them that European composers such as Antonín Dvořák, Igor Stravinsky, and Maurice Ravel saw black musics such as spirituals and jazz as quintessentially American. The Bohemian Antonín Dvořák commented in 1892, "In the negro melodies of America I discover all that is needed for a great and noble school of music. They are pathetic, tender, passionate, melancholy, solemn, religious, bold, merry, gay or what you will."[37] His Ninth Symphony, "From the New World," incorporates influence from black spirituals. Nevertheless, betraying a colonial mentality, arbiters of taste in the United States continued to look to Europe for models of high culture.[38]

As the folklorist and historian Lawrence Levine shows, in contrast to today's notion that jazz is "America's music," a cultural treasure, this art was considered decidedly un-American and decidedly un-"cultural" when it first rose in popularity.[39] An observer wrote the following about threats to national security in 1925: "We are headed for a smash in this country . . . our emotional instability is the product of immigration, automobiles, [and] jazz."[40] Emerging perspectives were influenced by growing contact with other parts of the world: there was a direct link between the budding field of psychology and primitivist notions of Africa and (Native) America. Early twentieth-century modernism, which developed in cosmopolitan centers such as Paris and (to a lesser extent) New York as a reaction to the traumas of industrialization, the Great War, and troubling new modes of thought raised by Freud and Einstein, conflated an uncertain future with a violent, primal past. In addition to indexing progress, the futuristic churning of machines hearkened backward to what was seen as the mindlessness of protohuman culture, and inward to the dark corners of the subconscious.

Essentialist ideas about an exotic blackness were rampant, and black music, combined with sinful vices such as alcohol, was believed to work in a mechanistic, contagious way to ignite sexuality. Many Euro-Americans considered black sexuality powerful in dangerous, as well as enticing, ways. White participation in jazz was characterized by contradiction and hypocrisy—a desire to partake, but a simultaneous fear and an impulse to remain separate. Dominant discourse feared that blackness would infect white women and the white race as a whole.[41] The barbaric practice of lynching African Americans was linked to this "fear of a black planet" (to invoke hip-hop group Public Enemy's song);[42] at thousands of lynchings that took place between 1882 and 1930, perpetrators repeatedly claimed that lynching was necessary to prevent rape.[43]

During World War II many African Americans only agreed to support the war effort after the articulation of a "double-V" philosophy, which called for victory on two fronts: the global fight against the Axis powers and the domestic fight against racism.[44] Dizzy Gillespie writes that, when he was drafted, he said this to the induction officers:

Well look, at this time, at this stage in my life here in the United States whose foot has been in my ass? The white man's foot has been in my ass hole buried up to his knee in my ass hole! . . . Now, you're speaking of the enemy, you're telling me that the German is the enemy. At this point, I can never remember having met a German. So, if you put me out there with a gun in my hand and tell me to shoot at the enemy, I'm liable to create a case of "mistaken identity," of who I might shoot.[45]

Gillespie claims that the officers concluded that he was mentally unstable and for this reason, deemed him ineligible for the draft.[46]

African American music had began to spread outward from the United States after the Great War, but it was not yet considered a national symbol. During and after World War II, however, the U.S. government found a purpose for jazz: the music was used to promote the reputation of the United States as an interracial, freewheeling society, to be contrasted with the intolerance of Germany; jazz was celebrated as a expression of "American freedom." The U.S. government instigated projects such as the Voice of America radio station, which beamed North American music and propaganda into the Eastern Bloc countries, and a 1955 *New York Times* article went so far as to proclaim that the "U.S. has [a] secret sonic weapon— jazz."[47] Jazz was promoted specifically in areas where the United States was susceptible to criticism for racism: the Iron Curtain countries, Africa, and the Middle East, where the State Department sponsored jazz musicians' tours. Dizzy Gillespie worked this circuit,[48] as did Louis Armstrong, who was portrayed as the quintessential cultural ambassador of the United States. Armstrong, however, cancelled his USSR tour after Governor Faubus blocked integration in Arkansas, saying that "the Negro has no country to call his own."[49]

During the postwar era, jazz's popularity grew in Europe and Asia; the embrace of it as a national symbol in the United States was intimately linked to the music's transnationalization. By the end of the twentieth century, most people in the United States acknowledged jazz as an invaluable national cultural resource. "Buscando América," seeking America, seems to have entailed leaving it and looking at it from outside. An annual jazz festival in Detroit is exciting because many top musicians hail from this city, one of the true cradles of African American music. Favorite sons often play at the event, creating a vital atmosphere as hometown musicians return. Ironically, however, the festival also derives much of its cachet from its links to a prominent jazz event in Europe: this is the Detroit–Montreux Festival.

Black Nationalism

Black nationalism and pan-Africanism developed in response to the exclusion of blacks from full citizenship in American lands. As Wilson Moses shows, while "color-blindness"[50] may be a laudable ideal, persistent segregation and subjugation have resulted in the articulation of black nationalism as "an expression of the impulse toward self-determination among Africans transplanted to the New World."[51] In a general sense, all in-group black institutions, such as African American churches and schools, exhibit a nationalist impulse. A more explicit nationalism has called for African Americans to repatriate Africa. The American Colonization Society was founded in 1816 to encourage free African Americans to repatriate Africa, and specifically, to move to Liberia, which was founded precisely for this purpose. The white promoters of this plan saw it as an effort to strengthen slavery by purging the United States of free blacks, but it also appealed to many African Americans. The influential black religious leader Alexander Crummell, for example, moved to Liberia and urged others to follow suit.

The black nationalist leader Marcus Garvey moved from his native Jamaica to Harlem in 1916, where he gained great popular support for his utopian vision of black economic self-help and "back to Africa" philosophy. Garvey headed the Universal Negro Improvement Association (UNIA), which had its headquarters in Harlem and chapters throughout the United States as well as in Latin America, the Caribbean, West Africa, and England. He also founded an all-black steamship company, the Black Star Line, to connect the various parts of the African diaspora. His vision proved larger than his business acumen, however, and the Black Star Line failed from a financial standpoint. It succeeded, however, in inspiring a sense of unity among masses of blacks around the world. Garvey was attuned to the roles of pomp and symbolism in nationalist movements, wearing ornate plumed hats at his Harlem processions and designing the pan-African flag of red, green, and black, which is still flown today.[52] Garvey is often quoted as maintaining that God (or Jesus) is black. His position, however, as expressed in the *Philosophy and Opinions of Marcus Garvey*, is more nuanced:

Our God has no color, yet it is human to see everything through one's own spectacles, and since the white people have seen their God through white spectacles, we have only now started out (late though it be) to see our God through our own spectacles. . . . We Negroes believe in . . . the One God of all ages. That is the God in whom we believe, but we shall worship Him through the spectacles of Ethiopia.[53]

While Garvey espoused black separatism, W. E. B. Du Bois operated in coalition with whites, working with the National Association for the Advancement of Colored People (NAACP) early in his career, and espousing socialism later. Du Bois was also, however, committed to pan-Africanism, organizing the first Pan-African Congress in 1919, which brought together African and Afro-diasporic leaders to promote African independence.[54] Later expressions of black nationalism included the work of the Nation of Islam and Malcolm X's philosophies.

Black nationalism has manifested itself musically in various ways. Duke Ellington's insistence that he played "Negro music," as well as his compositions dedicated to recounting African American history, was a kind of cultural nationalism. Bebop and its ally, Afro-Cuban jazz, were also self-consciously based in the black community and celebrated black achievement. Many jazz musicians' conversion to Islam expressed a nationalistic impulse. In the 1960s, musicians played an important role in the Black Arts movement: saxophonist Archie Shepp, for example, said that the new music of the 1960s was "an extension of the entire civil rights—Black Muslims—black nationalist movement that is taking place in America. That is fundamental to our music."[55] Black musicians took a stance away from the economic and political mainstream. Bill Dixon, for example, organized the October Revolution in Jazz in 1964, which stood as a challenge to the established jazz business, advocating that musicians take control of their economic destiny.[56] Musicians such as Sun Ra and Milford Graves bypassed record companies, putting out their own LPs. The Chicago-based Association for the Advancement of Creative Music, or AACM, was an avowedly black nationalist organization.[57] It set up programs to teach music to black teenagers, supporting themselves without recourse to granting agencies, arguing that accepting monies from established institutions would make them beholden to the corporate interests.[58] The idea was to create separate black organizations rather than to integrate into the white-dominated mainstream; for this reason, the AACM and Su Ra's band, for example, admitted only blacks.

Gilroy makes the important point that black nationalism can be as intolerant and authoritarian as any other type of nationalism. While motivated by an understandable disinclination to criticize an oppressed group, the tendency to avoid discussing this fact actually dehumanizes people of color by implying that the standards that apply to others do not apply to blacks: "susceptibility to the appeal of an authoritarian irrationalism has become part of what it means to be a modern person. To recognize that blacks are not . . . immune to this . . . is, perversely, to embrace our status as modern folks who can think and act for ourselves."[59]

Still, black nationalist impulses in jazz have often been tempered by a sense of doubleness. The multi-instrumentalist Rahsaan Roland Kirk was known for his striking ability to play two or even three wind instruments simultaneously. For example, he performed a medley of the popular song "Sentimental Journey" and a spiritual melody that Dvořák used in his Ninth Symphony, as a solo-duo on manzello and stritch.[60] Kirk alluded to both Garvey's black Jesus and Dvořák's spirituals in his spoken introduction to this medley on a live recording. Kirk shouted, "They say that Dvořák was a black man, but the white people say he was a white man!" A voice from the audience called out, "What do *you* say?" The answer: "I say I don't give a damn!"[61] Kirk delineated a double-edged perspective. By audaciously suggesting that the Bohemian composer Antonín Dvořák could be black, he intimated a black nationalist re-vision of history, he appropriated a European "great man" into the pan-African world. But by adding that he really didn't care about the matter, Kirk left himself open to universalism, he left himself open to pan-humanity. On another live recording, Kirk introduces his composition entitled "Blacknuss" as follows: "Now we are gathered here on the universe at this time, this particular time, to listen to the 36 black notes of the piano. There's 36 black notes and 52 white notes. We don't mean to eliminate nothing, but we're going to hear the black notes at this time, if you don't mind."[62]

Creolization and Power

Ralph Ellison once boldly asked, "What would America be like without Blacks?" He added that even being able to pose such an absurd question points to a "national pathology," a disunited state of America.[63] From the Constitution, which deemed blacks only ⅗ human,[64] to African repatriation schemes ranging from the American Colonization Society to Garveyism, the idea that this could be a black-free country has coexisted with the idea that it could be a country with freedom for blacks. And yet white America as we know it would not exist without African American influence: "Without the presence of Negro American style, our jokes, our tall tales, even our sports would be lacking in the turns, the sudden shocks, the swift changes of pace (all jazz-shaped) that . . . make life swing."[65] There would have been no slave economy and no Civil War, two tremendous historical forces that shaped who we are today. But consider also that Americans of all ethnicities use a vast and colorful repertoire of black-originated linguistic idioms and slang to articulate what we consider our unique North American character. We all dance with a distinctly African-influenced cadence, and we all sing with black inflection. Both black and white religious expression in the United States, as well as speech, incorporate African influences. The North American "mainstream" is not white; instead, it is the dialogue between various groups.[66] Albert Murray picked up Ellison's call, riffing that "American culture is . . . incontestably mulatto":[67]

[This] is a nation of multicolored people. There are white Americans so to speak and black Americans. But any fool can see that the white people are not really white, and that black people are not really black. They are all interrelated one way or another.[68]

He adds that immigrants who come to the United States immediately become American, which means they become "part backwoodsman and

Indian—and part Negro." Though they "finagle to become 'all-white' they actually become Omni-American, which means they are part Negro and part Indian."[69] While jazz issued from an African American source, whites have been full participants in its development since its inception. Indeed, many Euro-Americans, such as Bill Evans and Charlie Haden to cite only two, are seminal figures in the music. This is a creole country.

But American creolization is played out on an unequal playing field. A fundamental difference between whites and blacks in American music is that while whites have played what they wish, segregation kept black musicians behind fences. Today, it is easy to forget that African Americans did not have the choice of joining (all-white) symphony orchestras or Broadway pit bands for most of this country's history.[70] One great trumpeter, a child prodigy adept in classical music, aced his audition for the Detroit Symphony Orchestra as a teenager. Afterward, the conductor asked him to play "I Got Rhythm." He complied, playing brilliantly. The conductor informed him that while his Euro-classical music abilities were top-shelf, he should not pursue this field because, as a black man, he would face racial discrimination. The conductor felt that he was doing the teen musician a favor by providing realistic vocational counseling. While this musician acknowledges that the conductor's intentions were good, he remembers this as an experience of bitter racism.[71]

No matter how sincere whites' attraction to black culture, our forays into it always occur in a context of unequal power relations: as race theorist Eric Lott astutely puts it, "love and theft" go hand in hand in even the most well-meaning white participation in black culture.[72] Music has long been big business in the United States, and Amiri Baraka calls the continuing white appropriation of black music "the great music robbery," adding that African Americans have repeatedly responded to this trend by reappropriating their art, by creating new in-group styles that are (initially) out of reach to whites.[73] These, however, are soon appropriated, so a "cultural lag," in which white popular culture follows a generation or so behind black popular culture, ensues.[74] This, of course, does not mean that the history of black music is merely a series of responses to white appropriation; the music also developed according to in-group needs and creative impulses. Still, a dynamic of *stereotype and reappropriation,* as ethnomusicologist Charles Keil dubbed it, is central to musical change in the United States.[75] Blackface minstrelsy, the predominant form of popular entertainment in the nineteenth century, dehumanized African Americans by presenting demeaning stereotypes. But black performers walked through the door that opened as a result of this vogue, themselves gaining opportunity and fame as minstrel players. Neo-minstrel stereotypes were still prevalent at the turn of the twentieth century, but black musicians countered by creating the blues and jazz. When white swing bands commercially eclipsed the black ones, African Americans responded with bebop, and when whites took over the blues in the guise of rock 'n' roll, blacks created soul, then funk, then hip-hop.

Norman Mailer celebrated Beat Generation bohemians as "white Negroes," lauding their rejection of the "slow death by conformity" that bourgeois America sentences. He exoticized African Americans, writing of a "ménage à trois" among the bohemian, the juvenile delinquent, and the black man that had marijuana as the wedding ring and African American music as a cultural dowry. Mailer believed that blacks were free of the "sophisticated inhibitions of civilization," living instead in the moment, "for jazz is orgasm." He contended that blacks are hyperaware of American realities, and particularly attuned to the falseness of an ostensibly civilized culture that is based on racial subjugation. He argued that if African Americans were to attain equality under the law, they would become superior to whites. In this sense, his ideas are reminiscent of Du Bois's suggestion that double consciousness can provide "second sight." But while his intentions may have been good, ultimately, Mailer was simply appropriating elements of black culture to further his own agenda. Blind to the unequal power dynamic, he lost sight of his own stereotyping, his own neo-minstrelsy.[76] As cultural critic George Lipsitz has argued, whites' adopting of African American culture often issues from a sincere quest to become free of suffering; black music has provided whites with a powerful and legitimate critique of middle-class white America.[77] There is a fine line, however, between such a critique and endemic white exoticization of black culture. Awareness of this line is something we can only hope to increase.

The study of "whiteness" has recently enjoyed vogue among white academics.[78] Black thinkers, however, have been writing about it for some time. In his essay, "On Being 'White' . . . and Other Lies," James Baldwin notes that while whiteness is basic to mainstream identity in the United States, Americans' European forebears did not consider themselves "white." It was only when they came to the United States that they developed a sense of whiteness; this was the "price of the ticket" to American identity for European immigrants.[79] Similarly, Malcolm X once jokingly said that "nigger" is the first word that European immigrants learn when they come to the United States.[80] It has been important for immigrants to differentiate themselves from a marginalized group in order to set themselves up for success in white-dominated America. At the same time, many European immigrant musicians have been drawn to African American music and culture as a way of testing the cultural waters of a new land, as a way to Americanize themselves; paradoxically, identification with the reviled "other" has also been a way to construct whiteness. Al Jolson's blackface transformed him from Russian Jew to a white American. The Greek-American musician Johnny Otis, on the other hand, became so deeply involved in African American culture that he considers himself "black by persuasion," is accepted as such by the African American community, and is heralded as an important contributor to black music.[81] Unlike Jolson and Mailer, he lived in the black community and immersed himself in the whole of it rather than taking bits of it for his own ends.

Musical Consciousness Raising

After I had lectured about Du Boisian double consciousness one day, a white student in my class commented that if African Americans have double consciousness, many Euro-Americans must have "half consciousness," because—although we whites are often unaware of it—Euro-Americans are highly influenced by black culture. Her implication was not that whites are somehow culture-less but simply that many (well-meaning) Euro-Americans are only partially aware of the privileges that they enjoy and of the black influences in their culture. Du Bois himself once discussed the "Souls of White Folk," noting that many whites identify with their skin color to a point of dehumanizing themselves.[82] Masks of superiority are fitted with blinders, and unequal power relations demean all parties involved.

Frantz Fanon wrote that blacks are painfully conscious of race and racism: "since the racial drama is played out in the open, the black man has no time to 'make it unconscious.' The white man, on the other hand, succeeds in doing so to a certain extent."[83] He adds that white half-consciousness of racism is exacerbated when "a new element appears: guilt."[84] My own experiences bear this out: I have noticed that many whites, including myself at times, feel guilty about the racial inequities that permeate our society. While this feeling may be based in a laudable sensitivity and in good intentions, it often results in a breakdown of communication with African Americans. Good intentions alone cannot work through racial barriers. Bringing our true feelings about race to the surface in honest inter- and intraracial discussions, however, *can* expand consciousness. bell hooks advocates a resurgence of feminist *consciousness raising*, and her comments are as applicable to race as they are to gender. She points out that all parties suffer when any party is subjugated, and that everyone can benefit from consciousness raising:

Males as a group have and do benefit the most from patriarchy. . . . But those benefits have come with a price. In return for all the goodies men receive from patriarchy, they are required to dominate women, to exploit and oppress us, using violence if they must to keep patriarchy intact. Most men are disturbed by hatred and fear of women . . . we need consciousness raising groups . . . for all people, not just women, also men.[85]

Jazz and other forms of black music have played an important role in raising my own consciousness about what it means to be American and what it means to be a citizen of the world. Growing up in New York City in a European immigrant family during the tumultuous years of the 1960s and 1970s, I thought profoundly about my identity as a citizen of this country. I felt most at home here, and I adored African American music like Little Richard's rock 'n' roll and Charlie Parker's bebop. I also loved European classical music, but I did not identify with it, I did not feel that it was "my" music: as Ralph Ellison said, black music *is* American music. I was further drawn to black music in an effort to heal a bifurcation that I felt as a citizen of this shared land, in efforts to heal my "half-consciousness." The fault lines of U.S. culture, as manifested in the Vietnam War and black rights' struggles, disturbed me and led me to question the national myths of the United States. African American culture and music seemed to address the tough realities of life in a country split apart. I came to realize that I feel a great deal of ambivalence about my identity as an American. On the one hand, I naturally identify with the country in which I have always lived, whose culture and education have shaped me, and whose geography feels like home. On the other hand, I am repelled by the inhumanity of this country, by the violence of its foreign policies, and by the violence of its race relations. Playing jazz and other African-influenced musics in interracial settings put me into intimate contact with people whom I otherwise would not have known, engendering valuable social relationships that raised my consciousness. Jazz thus raised my consciousness, putting into perspective who I am as an individual, who I am as an American, and who I am as a citizen of the world. That is why Ray Charles's version of "America the Beautiful" speaks to me in a way that no other version of the song can: performed by a man who has lived the black experience and still sings of this land's beauty with utter sincerity in his inimitable blues style, it is supremely honest. It is supremely real.[86]

Jazz Consciousness

The Third Stream musical movement, initiated in the 1950s by the composer Gunther Schuller, was an effort to wed jazz with the European classical idiom. While the attempt was laudable, the results, at times, were stilted. After all, jazz has *always* been based in both black aesthetics and European influences. The blending of various "streams" is thus the norm in

African American culture. Distinguishing his stance from both the Third Stream approach and nationalist exclusionism, John Coltrane expressed interest in African, European, and all world cultures in an interview with the (white) black nationalist ideologue Frank Kofsky:

KOFSKY: Do the musicians who play in these newer styles look to Africa and Asia for some of their musical inspiration?

COLTRANE: I think so; I think they look all over. And inside . . .

KOFSKY: Do you think that the musicians are more interested in Africa and Asia than in Europe, as far as the music goes?

COLTRANE: Well, the musicians have been exposed to Europe, you see. So it's the other parts that they haven't been exposed to. Speaking for myself, at least, I'm trying to have a rounded education.[87]

Similarly, bell hooks writes that black poets "are capable of speaking in many voices . . . the Dunbar of a poem written in dialect was no more or less authentic than the Dunbar writing a sonnet."[88] For hooks, "It was listening to Duke Ellington, Louis Armstrong, and later, John Coltrane that impressed upon our consciousness a sense of versatility—they played all kinds of music, had multiple voices."[89]

Black music in the United States shares many characteristics with other African-influenced musics, which I shall elucidate in chapter 2. These include a kinesthetically based aurality, call-and-response patterning, and vocal inflections. Black Americans have improvised upon their African roots, blending them with European influences in an unabashedly inclusive way. The classic example of this is in religion. African cultures themselves have often displayed inclusiveness. Syncretism took place not only in the Americas, with the incorporation of European elements into Afro-Caribbean religions, but within Africa, where the proximity of various ethnicities made it common for people to incorporate influences from neighboring groups.[90] This approach was carried to the Americas. I have participated in several Vodou pilgrimages in Haiti in which invocations in front of Catholic churches played central roles. This inclusivity contrasts sharply with Christian doctrine (although not always with Christian practice); it would be difficult to imagine a Catholic priest making appeals to Vodou shrines! African American musicians' participation in European classical forms is a continuation of this strategy of comprehensiveness: hymns and African-derived elements were combined to create spirituals, the schottische and other European dance forms were African American-ized into ragtime, and North American popular songs became vehicles for bebop improvisation.

As mentioned earlier, Herskovits documented the "survivals" of African lifeways in the Americas, refuting the erroneous "myth of the Negro past" which had held that African influences had not survived in the Americas. He also noted that North American Africanisms are less acute than those in the Caribbean and Brazil.[91] In the United States, however, an African-based *style* survived even when languages and cosmologies were not passed down. African Americans have used extemporaneous creativity and improvisation to adapt African-based thought-forms in new settings. This process is well illustrated in language: while the vocabulary of black English, for example, derives from a European source, its syntax incorporates some elements derived from African languages. Likewise, black Christianity often preserves a clearly African *style* of worship. African Americanness has thus been a culture of shrewd improvisation based on all materials at hand.

Of course, the inclusiveness of jazz consciousness is not absolute. During most of its history, for example, the jazz community was not inclusive in terms of gender; until recently, female musicians were marginalized.[92] And as we saw, some black nationalist musical organizations admitted only African Americans. And while some African Americans espoused black nationalism, others, especially members of the middle class, embraced European-derived culture so fully that they lost touch with their own vernacular traditions. Sociologist E. Franklin Frazier argued that the black bourgeoisie is "without cultural roots either in the Negro world with which it refused to identify, or the white world which refuses to permit the black bourgeoisie to share its life."[93] Even W. E. B. Du Bois, who saw black spirituals as a cultural treasure, considered jazz and blues "degraded" music.[94]

While some bourgeois blacks were happy in this Europhilic world, others were not. Significantly, while many black jazz musicians have been middle class,[95] on the whole, they have represented exceptions to Frazier's valid point and successfully united their variegated influences: jazz players have mastered Euro-classical musical techniques within an African-influenced, creole aesthetic. Many of them played Euro-classical music at home or at school even if it was difficult or impossible to gain employment doing so during the period of legally mandated segregation. In response to the narrowness of white vision, these African American musicians developed a kind of musical "second sight," a sense for how to put something—music—back together that, perhaps, had never really been broken. For all the excellence of his forays into the realm of extended works composed for concert performance, Duke Ellington believed that for him, the path to creativity was not in the Euro-classical tradition. He asserted that

I'm not the offspring of a conservatory. I've avoided music schools and conservatories. I didn't want to be influenced away from what I felt inside. Back in 1915, 1920 when I was getting started in Washington, there were two schools of jazz. There were the disciplined jazz musicians who played exactly what was written. They had all the work. I got kicked out of a couple of those bands.

Then there was another group of musicians that didn't know music. Some of them could only play in one key. But they played precious things. I was in between . . . I wouldn't have been a good musician if I had gone to a conservatory and studied in the usual way.[96]

Since age fifteen, Willie Ruff studied the French horn, receiving an M.A. from Yale in 1954. Because U.S. orchestras generally did not hire people of color, he auditioned with conductor Erich Leinsdorf for a position on the Tel Aviv Philharmonic. Leinsdorf said that Ruff would be able to play in Israel, but that he wanted to help break down barriers of discrimination in the United States. He offered Ruff a position in the Buffalo Symphony Orchestra, saying,

I am certainly aware that positions in the professional orchestras in this country are not available to Negro artists. . . . I'm the director and conductor of the Buffalo Symphony Orchestra. I can definitely offer you a position in the horn section. It might be a more direct route to your later entry into another, larger American orchestra. The Tel Aviv position would also be good for you, and you would certainly be appreciated there regardless of race. There are no laws that would separate you from anyone else. I suggest you consider both these options.[97]

Ruff's choices, then, were to leave his homeland for Israel or to accept the Buffalo position, hoping that it would lead to a better job down the line. A third possibility was to play jazz. The advantage of the last choice was that he would be able to pursue improvisation and composition as well as the interpretation of Euro-classical music. Instead of replicating in the musical sphere the "one drop" rule for racial purity (which stipulates that even one drop of black blood makes a person non-white), Ruff embraced a path of musical inclusion. Ruff had begun to develop a fruitful jazz duo with pianist Ivory Mitchell. Mitchell was working with Lionel Hampton's band and convinced Ruff to join Hampton and develop the duo repertoire in their spare time.[98] Ruff contributed more to the history of American music as a member of the Ruff-Mitchell duo than he could have as the member of an orchestral horn section. He was enacting jazz consciousness, a virtual space of inclusiveness created out of necessity by musicians contending with an exclusionist society.

Charlie Parker was an avowed fan of Igor Stravinsky's music. Singer Sarah Vaughan, for example, said that Parker "used to sit on the bus or train with Stravinsky scores. And then he'd get on stage and play something from Stravinsky, but play it his way."[99] One night in the winter of 1951, opening a set at Birdland, the New York jazz club named after him, Charlie Parker saw Igor Stravinsky sitting in the audience. Parker responded by playing "Koko," a virtuosic tour de force customarily performed at break-neck speed. As he began his second chorus, Parker quoted the beginning of Stravinsky's *Firebird* ballet "as though it had always been there, a perfect fit," as an eyewitness put it. Stravinsky "roared in delight," spilling his drink.[100] While some critics, however, might laud jazz's aesthetic "integration" as an epitome of "American democracy," I argue that the inclusiveness of jazz is *atypical* of dominant trends in the United States, that it developed as a *counterforce* to racial polarization.

Improvisation itself is not uniquely African or African American; extemporaneous invention has long been integral to European concert music.[101] In 1639, for example, a music lover observed that Girolamo Frescobaldi's compositions are "witness to his genius, yet to judge of his profound learning, you must hear him improvise."[102] Bach's abilities as an improviser are well known, and improvisation was also integral to Mozart's displays as a child prodigy. According to some accounts, when Mozart auditioned Beethoven, it was only when he realized that the young musician was improvising that Mozart said that "he will make a noise in the world someday."[103] In a *Downbeat* interview, saxophonist Greg Osby and trumpeter Lester Bowie take the great trumpeter Wynton Marsalis to task. They point out that there is nothing new about jazz musicians playing Euro-classical music, as Marsalis does, but that black musicians have traditionally approached European traditions from a holistic perspective, combining them with African American vernacular traditions. If Marsalis were to meld his jazz and Euro-classical selves, if he brought his expertise as an improviser to bear on his mastery of the Baroque repertoire, for example, he would be innovating in the tradition of Ellington and Parker.[104] Marsalis's forays into Euro-classical music are important for their powerful implied critique of the historical exclusion of African Americans from professional activity in the world of Euro-classical music. Marsalis is remarkable for being able to build a successful recording career in this field as well as in jazz, and for legitimizing jazz and consequently winning it greater resources. Yet he is replicating the European tendency to exclude and categorize, to keep music in separate pieces that could have remained one whole. In this respect, he may exemplify holistic jazz consciousness less than does a figure like Eric Dolphy—whom we shall consider next.[105]

Dolphy's Consciousness

Eric Dolphy was born in Los Angeles in 1928. He was, of course, exposed to black vernacular music while growing up, but while a blues base underlies even his most modernist playing, Dolphy's main influences as a boy were from Western classical music. His biographers write that, according to people who grew up with him, "as a small child Eric showed great joy at the anticipation of attending . . . rehearsals and hearing the (church) choir's performances, which were not of the gospel variety, but included, for example, Handel's *Messiah*."[106] As a boy, Dolphy studied at Lloyd Reese's music school in Los Angeles. Charles Mingus was also a student of Reese, who had an important impact in the community. Dolphy started playing the clarinet and oboe as a child, the alto saxophone and bass clarinet as a teen, and later took up the flute. His early grounding in the Western classical idiom is underlined by the fact that while he was still in junior high school, Dolphy won a two-year scholarship to the University of California School of Music. Still, he did not lose touch with vernacular traditions, and also played in a Louis Jordan–style "jump" band in this period. Dolphy's first jazz influences were Duke Ellington and Coleman Hawkins, but he became a devotee of Charlie Parker already in high school and later once said that, for him, "Bird was *it*."[107] After graduating from high school, Dolphy performed with jazz groups in Los Angeles (including his own) and continued in the Euro-classical field, performing with the Tacoma Symphony Orchestra and studying at Los Angeles City College and the U.S. Naval School of Music.[108] In 1958 Dolphy began touring with Chico Hamilton's Third Stream–influenced group, and he later recorded with the Latin Jazz Quintet. Even before he left Los Angeles, Dolphy's catholic influences were intact; he had acquired a background in European classical music, a rooting in the style of Charlie Parker, and an interest in new musical trends.

Dolphy became aware of, and felt a rapport with, Ornette Coleman's work already during his early period:

Ornette was playing that way in 1954. I heard about him, and when I heard him play, he asked me if I liked his pieces and I said that I thought they sounded good. When he said that if someone played a chord, he heard another chord on that one, I knew what he was talking about, because I had been thinking of the same things.[109]

Dolphy also became friends and exchanged musical ideas with John Coltrane. Years later, Coltrane said that many of the innovations that he and Dolphy developed later in their careers began already in this period:

Eric and I have been talking music for quite a few years, since about 1954. We watched music. We always talked about it, discussed what was being done, down through the years, because we love music. What we're doing now was started a few years ago.[110]

That Dolphy was working on ideas associated with Coleman and Coltrane as early as 1954 belies goal-directed trajectories regarding the development of the music. Rather than following a linear progression of stylistic changes, Dolphy, like his colleagues Charles Mingus and Miles Davis, used all available resources; goal-directed periodic schemes do necessarily jibe with artists' musical journeys. In this light, it is notable that Lennie Tristano and Charles Mingus were already experimenting with collectively and freely improvised music by the late 1940s and 1950s.[111] Categories of genres and historical periods serve purposes in discussions of music and its development, but, like race, in the final analysis, they are artificial constructs. To really understand the music, we must consider that working musicians do not necessarily operate according to the categories' dictates. In 1959 Dolphy settled in New York City, working first at Minton's Playhouse and then with Charles Mingus. During this period Ornette Coleman was creating a sensation with his debut engagement at the Five Spot. According to Ted Curson, who was in Mingus's band with Dolphy at the time, Mingus took Dolphy and Curson into the car between sets at the Five Spot and said: "'Do you think you can play like that?' Of course we could. . . . Eric said OK. We rehearsed a bit, and soon we were playing that style."[112] Of course, as Mingus explained, he was not advocating wholesale imitation of Coleman. He saw, however, that the new trends demanded a move away from the established bebop language: "I'm not saying everyone's going to have to start playing like Coleman, but they're going to have to stop playing Bird."[113] Mingus's approach has implications for understanding the music in the last third of the twentieth century as the *coexistence* of various trends more than as the culmination of a linear periodic scheme.

Dolphy performed and recorded with Ornette Coleman, George Russell, John Coltrane, and his own groups (including one co-led by Booker Little). In fact, according to his biographers, Dolphy "seems to have played with nearly every jazz musician in sight."[114] Dolphy was also active in the fields of Third Stream and experimental European-derived concert music. With his double-edged backgrounds in Euro-classical music as well as black traditions, it was natural for him to participate in something like Third Stream. Unlike Schuller, however, he may not have needed to give it a title, since uniting "streams" is the norm in African American culture. In addition to working with Gunther Schuller on several occasions, Dolphy performed Edgard Varèse's difficult solo flute piece *Density 21.5* at the Ojai (California) Music Festival in 1962, which featured contemporary Euroclassical artists such as John Cage, Luciano Berio, and Cathy Berberian.[115]

In addition to his unique improvisatory style, one of Dolphy's most lasting contributions was his experimentation with instrumental tone-colors. His flute playing was innovative; with its high range and light timbre, the flute was a fitting vehicle for Dolphy's use of bitonality. His use of the bass clarinet as an improvising solo instrument was groundbreaking, bringing this instrument to the orchestral palette of contemporary improvised music. Writing about Ornette Coleman's historic *Free Jazz* record date, Dolphy's biographers note that his "bass clarinet work [is] . . . responsible for much of the excitement of the total sound. It is easy to understand why, from this record alone, this instrument gained popularity with the new wave of players."[116] In addition to playing the bass clarinet in standard settings, Dolphy used it in solo pieces and in duets with bassist Richard Davis and in tandem with Ron Carter's cello.

Dolphy also showed an interest in African and Indian musics, mentioning "the singing of pygmies" and Ravi Shankar as influences:

I've talked with Ravi Shankar and I see how we can incorporate their ideas . . . they call it Raga or scale and they'll play on one for twenty minutes . . . it's a challenge to play a long time on just one or two chords.[117]

The sounds of nature were yet another influence on Dolphy:

At home [in California] I used to play, and the birds always used to whistle with me. I would stop what I was working on and play with the birds. . . . Birds have notes in between our notes—you try to imitate something they do and like, maybe it's between F and F#, and you'll have to go up or come down on the pitch. It's really something! And so, when you get playing, this comes. You try to do some things on it.[118]

Dolphy connected his various influences, saying that "Indian music has something of the same quality [as bird songs]—different scales and quarter tones. I don't know how you label it, but it's pretty."[119] Dolphy's music is thus notable for traversing stylistic boundaries. Instead of ossifying various types of musical thinking into mutually exclusive camps, his approach was holistic, embracing bebop, the avant-garde, Euro-classical music, and other sounds. Gunther Schuller said this about Dolphy's catholic taste:

Eric was one of those rare musicians who loved and wanted to understand all music. His musical appetite was voracious, yet discriminating. It extended from jazz to the "classical" avant-garde and included, as well, an appreciation of his older jazz colleagues and predecessors. He was as interested in the complex surfaces of Xenakis, the quaint chaos of Ives, or the serial intricacies of Babbitt as in the soulful expressiveness of a Coleman Hawkins, the forceful "messages" of Charles Mingus, of the experiments of the "new thing."[120]

While this bold vision was making waves among players, many critics were not prepared to accept a manifestation of jazz consciousness so strong as Eric Dolphy's. One high-profile review, for example, stated that Dolphy and Coltrane's innovations were "horrifying" examples of "anti-jazz" that sounded like "gobbledygook."[121] To a certain extent, of course, this may have been an understandable reaction to innovations that were difficult to understand for their newness. But the failure to give the benefit of the doubt to master musicians such as Dolphy and Coltrane, perhaps due to the critics' sense of entitlement, amounted to a kind of "half-consciousness."

Because Coltrane's career was firmly established, he was able to weather the storm of negative press and keep working steadily. Dolphy, however, was not similarly entrenched in the music business, and he was soon having trouble finding work. He rejoined Mingus for a European tour in 1964, and before leaving, told the critic A. B. Spellman, "I'm on my way to Europe to live for a while. Why? Because I can get more work there playing my own music, and because if you try to do anything different in this country, people put you down for it."[122] Dolphy left Mingus during this tour to work in Paris, telling a German critic that "I'd like to stay in Europe, there is no race trouble."[123] Soon afterward, he died in Berlin of a heart attack caused by diabetes.

While it was marginalized, Dolphy's art embodied holistic musicality manifesting "planetary humanism." His story thus embodies both the tragedy of United States of America, its "war," as well as its unique vision, its "second sight."

As we have seen, genre, race, and nation are "invented traditions" that are strategically invoked to further particular agendas. In the same way, "planetary humanism" is an unabashedly strategic and utopian reaching-out for universalism. By usurping the unmarked category to refer to jazz and by appropriating Euro-classical influences, African American musicians seize power. This power manifests itself not only in ideas about music and in the musical experience, but even in the mind-set that remains when the sound stops. So while it cannot be divorced from the power-plays that permeate social life, jazz consciousness creates an aesthetic space that reconfigures the mind-set. Reed player Anthony Braxton articulates an overt vision of musical utopianism. He argues that "trans-African music" is a means of humanizing the world, a means of liberating all people.[124] While he developed in the black nationalist milieu of the AACM, Braxton espouses an inclusive approach that embraces Euro-classical music (especially Schoenberg) as well as the music of white jazzers (especially the saxophonists Warne Marsh and Paul Desmond). Braxton argues that, as survivors of slavery, African Americans have a special place in world culture, that the humanizing power of black music can liberate all people from the shackles of closed-mindedness.[125] Du Bois agreed that African Americans have "a contribution to make to civilization and humanity, which no other race can make."[126] Jazz consciousness is central to this contribution.

CHAPTER 2

Kente Cloth to Jazz
A Matrix of Sound

As Duke Ellington once said, "there is no more of an essentially African strain in the typical American Negro than there is an essentially French or Italian strain in the typical American of those ancestries."[1] The fact, however, that race is a social and not a biological reality does not mean that there is no cultural continuity between African-influenced cultures. Shifting attention away from the United States to the African diaspora, this chapter looks at jazz in relation to other African-influenced musics. My experiences as a performer of jazz, merengue, and salsa, my studies of Ghanaian music, and my attendance at Afro-Caribbean religious ceremonies have exposed me to many aesthetic parallels between the many modes of Afrodiasporic musicality.[2] I believe that scholars sometimes throw the baby out with the bathwater as academic fashions swing back and forth. Since the mid-twentieth century, we have moved from Herskovits's quantification of African "survivals" (those cultural influences that remained as Africans settled around the world) to a virulent study of the constructed strategies of social life. Current academic trends often eschew generalizing about the African diaspora lest they smack of essentialism. But as Paul Gilroy notes, despite a constructionist "orthodoxy" in academia that dismisses any "attempt to locate the cultural practices . . . that might connect blacks . . . as essentialism, . . . weighing the similarities and differences between black cultures remains an urgent concern."[3] Significantly, while Gilroy is not a specialist in music, he argues that music is especially useful in looking at "identity neither as a fixed essence nor as a vague and utterly contingent construction."[4] Understanding Africanisms is urgent for all people today because African-influenced cultural traditions are among the most deep-running characteristics of transnational modernity.[5]

Musical retentions and relations in the African diaspora are lifeways that, like language families, traverse time and space to form cultural continuities of long historical longevity and great geographic diffusion. Depending on one's perspective, one can focus on either similarities or differences between African-influenced cultures. Chapter 3, for example, highlights links between African-influenced cultures in the United States and Cuba, while chapter 4 contrasts the ways Afro-diasporic creativity is perceived in the United States and the Dominican Republic. Without arguing that the many African-influenced cultures are identical, this chapter looks at aesthetic links between jazz and other African-influenced musics. This approach necessitates a certain amount of generalizing, and I follow Ghanaian ethnomusicologist Kwabena Nketia's observation that African (and African-influenced) musics "form a network of distinct yet related traditions which overlap in certain aspects of style . . . and share common features. . . . These related musical traditions constitute a family."[6]

Attracting scholars from a wide array of academic disciplines, interdisciplinary research on music has blossomed in recent years. The excellence of musical scholarship produced by anthropologists and literary critics demonstrates that a background in musicology is by no means necessary for thinking about music. Coming from a performance background, however, I am often struck by the absence of attention to style and aesthetics in much academic writing about music. Verbal discourse, of course, is inherently disadvantaged when it comes to treating musical experience, which evades the boundaries of rhetoric. For this reason, I shall resort to other types of discourse, other modes of knowing. This chapter aims to capture the *feel* of African-influenced musics by using pictographic tools and appeals to synesthesia, kinesthesia, and metaphor.[7]

I now invite you to don differently hued spectacles, for we will change focus. Instead of looking at social life and power relations, we will muse on the musical experience.

Kente

One of the founders of the field of ethnomusicology, Charles Seeger, pointed out that musical knowing is not the same as verbal knowing, adding that there is no way out of this "linguo-centric predicament" except to acknowledge that it is inherent to the "musicological juncture."[8] He warned against assuming that a verbal medium can represent aural experience. He did not, however, advocate turning away from verbal discourse about music nor from other modes of musicological discourse such as notation and analysis. He made a distinction between *prescriptive notation,* which facilitates musical performance, and *descriptive notation,* an analytical tool that translates sound into a visual medium.[9] Even written texts about music are a type of descriptive notation: they represent music in a medium that is visual (as well as verbal). The purpose of descriptive notation is not to depict every aspect of a musical sound; this would only overload the senses with too much information. Instead, the objective of descriptive notation is to describe particular *aspects* of a sound. To this end, I will present several systems of musical notation as hermeneutic clues into Afro-diasporic aesthetics.[10]

European musical thinking organizes musical time according to numerical patterns called *meters.* Middle Eastern and South Asian notions of musical time also assign numbers to regularly occurring rhythmic patterns. Rural African and Caribbean musicians, however, do not customarily attach numerical values to music. Because much West African music[11] can be analyzed in terms of simultaneously occurring meters, African and Afro-Caribbean rhythms are often called "polymetric." However, Igbo ethnomusicologist and composer Meki Nzewi, whose insights are foregrounded in this chapter, argues that the notions of "polymetricity and polyrhythmicity are aberrations of African musical thought," that "do not apply to the feeling, motion, and relational organization implicit in African ensemble music relationships and structuring. Pursuing them results in shadow casting and impairment of perception."[12]

Ethnomusicologists James Koetting and Philip Harland developed the "Time Unit Box Notation System" (TUBS) to represent African musics visually. Representing a regular underlying pulse "at a level of precision heard by a trained observer," TUBS indicates each sound and silence as it occurs without reference to Western meter.[13] Like all systems of notation, TUBS is an abstraction: as I shall show later, the notion of a level of precision that a trained observer hears is a fiction. Still, it is a useful fiction. TUBS is depicted in rows of boxes, and each box represents a pulse. Empty boxes are silent, while boxes filled with dots or other symbols represent various sounds. *Kente notation* is an adaptation of a type of TUBS that fills the squares in with different colors, each color representing a particular sound.[14] The result bears an uncanny similarity to West African narrow-strip textiles. These textiles are pervasive throughout West Africa; kente cloth, their Ashanti variant, is known worldwide as a vital symbol of pan-African identity. Made on men's horizontal looms and consisting of variegated rectangular weft blocks, the strips are sewn together in ways that stagger the blocks to form juxtaposing patterns. Art historian Robert Farris Thompson relates the visual patterning of these textiles to diasporic musics, calling them "rhythmized . . . designs virtually to be scanned metrically, in

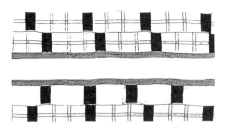

Figure 1. Asante narrow strip textiles

visual resonance with the famed off-beat phrasing of melodic accents of African and Afro-American music."[15] They are visual equivalents of Afro-diasporic musics: "as multiple meter distinguishes the traditional music of black Africa, emphatic multi-strip composition distinguishes the cloth of West Africa."[16] Compare the visual rhythms of the Asante cloth at figure 1 to the kente notation at figures 2, 4 and 6 (figures 3, 5, and 7 present the same music in conventional notation).

Nzewi charges that the Western "notion of rhythm as [a] statistical computation which can have independent structure . . . does not . . . belong to African philosophy and practice of music." He shows that African "drum playing is a process of deriving a rhythmic essence melodically, that is, as *melo-rhythm*."[17] (I shall employ this useful word in discussing African and African-based music throughout this chapter.) Even in European terms, the bifurcation of melody and rhythm is contradictory, as all melodies have duration as well as pitch. But the fact that, for example, the Ewe master drum *atsimewu* uses nine different sonorities, and that Latin jazz musician Giovanni Hidalgo can produce fifteen sounds from a single conga head, underscores the particular importance of sonority in African-based drumming.[18] The pervasive links between tone-based African speech and drumming, too, underline the forced nature of separating musical pitch from musical duration. My own performance experience with Caribbean rhythms has involved fixed-pitch (or so-called melodic) instruments:[19] the saxophone riffs, or *jaleos,* of Dominican merengue afford a colorful confluence of melody, timbre, and rhythm that lies at the heart of the music's vibrancy.[20] For all the beauty of their drumming, popular musics such as salsa, merengue, and *soucous*[21] foreground the fixed-pitch sounds of human voices, trumpet, saxophone, piano, and guitar. We usually think of jazz's "swing" or "groove" as an element of time, overlooking the fact that it relies on timbre and pitch as much as duration: this is what drummer Billy Higgins means when he says that "swing is not swing. Swing is the sound."[22] As we study African aesthetics, we find ourselves leaving behind the adage that the "jazz rhythm comes from Africa while its melody comes from Europe." Kente notation becomes useful, its colors synesthetically correlating with sonority to underscore the melodic color of rhythm.

Conversation

Responsorial structures underlie Afro-diasporic musics; call-and-response singing, the bedrock of Afro-diasporic music ranging from spirituals to Vodou songs and salsa, is perhaps the most obvious manifestation of this. Even the complex polyrhythms of African-based drumming are responsorial at their core. After recording Afro-Dominican *palos* drumming once during a field trip, I politely asked the lead musician if each player could demonstrate each drum alone; I wanted to record a separate track of each for purposes of transcription and analysis. His answer: "We cannot do that." Thinking that the drummer had misunderstood me, I repeated myself in respectful terms. He again said, "We cannot do that." I later realized that my request was perverse: playing one part alone is antithetical to the way that musicians hear the music.[23] Similarly, ethnomusicologist John Chernoff notes that while Western students of African drumming usually find it easier to play a pattern isolated from its ensemble context, the very idea of playing one part alone is foreign to the African sensibility:

We can think of this difference in sensibilities as the difference between conceiving a rhythm as something to "get with" or as something to "respond to." . . . [Chernoff's drumming teacher] Ibrahim [Abdulai] felt that isolated beating was meaningless without a second rhythm. . . . There was no conversation.[24]

Nzewi goes so far as to argue that the notion of "cross-rhythm," often used to explain African music, is "antithetical to African social and, therefore, ensemble philosophy" because "a community/family/team does not work together at cross purposes." As the Akan proverb states, "the extended family is a force." This does not imply that there is no tension in the sound. Instead, it shows that the tension is rooted in interdependence. Nzewi elaborates on this interesting nuance:

Motive as well as emotive suspense is generated when two entities tending to bounce into each other veer off. A *bounce-off* effect is generated. When anticipations that develop in motive or emotive relationships are not resolved or neutralized by actual contact there is energy tension, a suspension. But a merger, subsumption, or submersion of independence is avoided. In some African societies the bride price is never settled in full; in love there is more emotional intensity when resolution is not attained through marriage or physical consummation.[25]

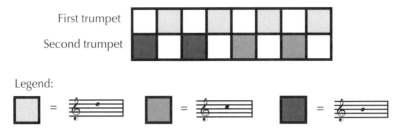

First trumpet

Second trumpet

Legend:

☐ = [musical staff notation] ☐ = [musical staff notation] ☐ = [musical staff notation]

Figure 2. Hockets in salsa: kente notation. See also color plate 1.

Melodies whose constituent notes are distributed between more than one fixed-pitch instrument or singer are called *hockets*. Hockets permeate BaAka (and other "pygmy") singing, much West African flute music, and are basic to *rara*, the one-note trumpet and percussion processional music of Haiti (rara is also endemic in the Dominican Republic, where it is called *gagá*).[26] As clear examples of bounce-off melo-rhythms, hockets are an appropriate place to begin looking at kente notation. Salsa arrangements occasionally use trumpet hockets in a technique called the *campana* (or bell).[27] Figures 2 and 3 present kente and conventional notation of two hocketing trumpets in a *mambo* (or instrumental interlude) in *salsero* Perico Ortiz's recording "Perico lo tiene."[28] As the figures' legends show, the colors of kente notation express specific pitches or sonorities; in figure 2, each color indicates a particular note played by a trumpet. The lighter the color, the higher the pitch, so the ability to read Western notation is not necessary for a passive reading of this visual correlate to the sound. The upper trumpet part repeats a note, leaving spaces that the lower trumpet part fills in. The resulting two-note melo-rhythms forge a different effect than the same pitches would create if produced on a single instrument: group coordination makes a crucial difference. As Chernoff puts it, "the notion of participation as a significant gesture of active effort" is a "contribution which gives life and meaning."[29]

Bb trumpet 1

Bb trumpet 2

Figure 3. Hockets in Salsa: conventional notation

The Body

As we saw in chapter 1, stereotyped views intimate that jazz works mechanistically, entering the body to ignite erotic desire. In the 1920s, for example, "hot rhythm" was portrayed as a dangerous social ill, a virus linked to a devilish sexuality that infected white bodies and minds.[30] The perversity of this exotification does not mean, however, that African-based musics are not linked to dance.[31] As Ghanaian ethnomusicologist Kofi Agawu affirms, West African "music is not prior to the dance. . . . [M]any misinterpretations of African rhythm and meter stem from a failure to observe the dance. To say that in the beginning dance and music were together . . . is not to exaggerate."[32]

The rhythms of Afro-diasporics musics are best understood in the context of related body movement. The Twi language of Ghana has no equivalent to the English word "music." The closest is *agorᴐ*, which denotes an aggregate of drumming, singing, and dance perhaps best translated as "dance theater."[33] Similarly, Caribbean genres such as salsa and merengue are dances as much as musics. For much of its history, jazz was danced, and its basis in body motion persists in later periods. Musicologist Gunther Schuller shows that the swing of jazz is based in body motion: it happens when the "listener inadvertently starts tapping his foot, snapping his fingers, moving his body or head to the beat of the music."[34] This finger-snapping swing is at the core of (Afro-) North American culture; it is basic to jazz, blues, gospel, rock, and hip-hop. Its upbeat or backbeat embodies a back-and-forth motion between aural and kinesthetic rhythms: finger-snapping body motion alternates with aural accents: the undulation gets into you, and it feels good!

Fanti master drummer Abraham Adzinyah talks about a "hidden rhythm" that he keeps in the back of his mind while improvising to the pattern, played on a bell (seen at figures 4 and 5).[35] In fact, this rhythm is only hidden aurally, for it is expressed in dance motion; we can thus also call it the dancers' *motor beat*.[36] Figures 4 and 5 combine the dancers' motor beat, the bell pattern, and a common drum rhythm (the *kagan* in Ewe agbekor music, the *okónkolo* in Afro-Cuban batá music, the *bula* in Haitian Vodou music).[37] Representing the motorbeat and the drum, the two lower lines express the bounce-off aesthetic: one can see the motor activity bouncing off the aural stimulation as dancers are lifted up by the drum rhythm and implanted in its wake. As the late, great Ewe drummer and dancer Freeman Donkor used to tell his students, drummers are "cheerleaders" for the dancers, encouraging them, spurring them on.[38] Figure 4 graphically displays where the timeline meets and veers off the other rhythms: it coincides with the motorbeat at the first and last occurrence of the motorbeat and coincides with both strokes of the

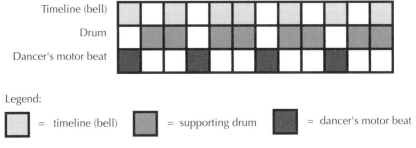

Legend:

    = timeline (bell)   = supporting drum   = dancer's motor beat

Figure 4. 12/8 rhythm: kente notation. See also color plate 2.

drum only at one point, the fifth and sixth squares. The rest of the time it veers around the drum. In resonance with the visual connections made by Thompson and Nzewi, ethnomusicologist Ruth Stone resorts to a visual metaphor in arguing that sound is best understood as a "*mosaic*." The structure of this complex polyrhythm, then, grows directly from responsorial participation, and its tone-color engenders shifting gestalts.[39]

To better understand this aesthetic, let us consider merengue (see figures 6 and 7). The patterns played by the double-headed tambora drum and saxophone and the movement of dancers' feet form dovetailing melo-rhythms. The most prominent percussive sound in merengue is a roll in the tambora's open tones, shown in the middle line of figures 6 and 7.[40] This roll leads into the dancers' motorbeat, shown in the bottom line, always bouncing off one motorbeat pulse and landing on the next. The tambora roll thus gives dancers a lift before implanting them. Typically articulated by electric bass as well as by tambora, the implanting beat is strong. Saxophones, however, tend to omit this motorbeat pulse and instead enter after it, as shown in the top line of figures 6 and 7. Typical saxophone jaleos echo the tambora roll pattern with a similar rhythm that begins immediately after the tambora's final stroke. In this way, the saxophones propel the dancers immediately after the

Figure 5. 12/8 rhythm: conventional notation

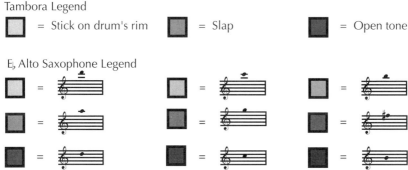

Figure 6. Merengue Jaleo I: kente notation. See also color plate 3.

tambora implants them.[41] Of twenty-four saxophone jaleos transcribed for a previous study, seventeen follow this pattern.[42]

Solo music is often showy and virtuosic. The objective, however, of much West African improvisation is to foment the larger event.[43] Dagomba drummer Ibrahim Abdulai told Chernoff that young players let their emotions get the better of them, playing "hot," but by showing off in this way they lose focus on the collectivity. Older, experienced drummers, on the other hand, improvise in ways that bring the collectivity together, keeping "cool."[44] Indeed, as Robert Farris Thompson shows, an "aesthetic of the cool" is a central ethos of African and African-influenced societies.[45] This issue came up in a disagreement that Jimi Hendrix had with English guitar virtuoso Eric Clapton. Clapton maintained that his masterful lead guitar playing was removed from that of the rhythm guitarist. By contrast, while he was an acknowledged virtuoso, Hendrix maintained that his style was rooted in the rhythm section, that his soloistic flights grew from his grounding as a team player.[46]

Even the complexities of bebop are based in a collectivist aesthetic. In bop drumming, the cymbal and high-hat maintain a groove while the snare and bass drums insert accented variations. Playing a role similar to that of the lead drum in West African and Afro-Caribbean drumming, the snare drum's staccato jabs and the bass drum's "bombs" add variety and keep the listener's ears perked without dominating them. The soloist provides another layer of improvisation, conversing with the drummer's groove, jabs, and bombs.[47]

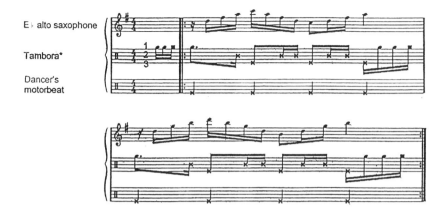

Figure 7. Merengue Jaleo I: conventional notation.

African American musicians in the United States sometimes extend the call-and-response aesthetic to solo performance. Blues musicians, for example, respond to their own singing with interjections played on the guitar. Charlie Parker could turn a single melodic line into a multifaceted sound. Dizzy Gillespie wrote that while he had been working on harmonic ideas similar to those of Parker when the two masters met, the saxophonist's rhythmic approach was new to him. By juxtaposing different kinds of accents—those based in harmony and melody—with those created through different kinds of attack or volume, Parker was able to weave a many-sided mosaic out of a single melodic line. The end of Parker's solo on "Mango Mangüé" (recorded with Machito and his Afro-Cubans), seen at figure 8, places melodic accents on unstressed beats juxtaposing them with accents implied by the harmonic progression. The line also emphasizes particular notes with techniques of tonguing. "Bird's time" thus uses material derived from the European system of musical harmony within an African-influenced aesthetic.[48]

Figure 8. Excerpt from Charlie Parker's solo on "Mango mangüé." Transcribed by Paul Austerlitz.

Mandala

In resonance with the fact that Africans do not attach numerical values to musical time, John Mbiti shows that "numerical calendars . . . do not exist in traditional African societies" and that "the linear concept of time . . . is practically foreign to African thinking."[49] Nzewi adds that unlike "Western statistical thought, . . . the African concept of time, including musical time, deriving from nature, . . . is cyclic."[50] Like mantras in Hindu meditation, musical cycles obliterate linear time. That most musical notation is displayed horizontally is at odds with this cyclicity: Seeger wrote that the "chain or stream" of linear music notation also distorts the reality of Euro-classical music, as sonic links are fused in the musical experience. [51] Circular notation circumvents this erroneous impression of linearity, expressing musical mantras in mandala form.[52] Figures 9, 10, and 11 transform the linear kente notation of figures 4, 5, and 6 into mandala notation. Circular scanning obfuscates the conceptual beginnings of each constituent element of the sound to create a hocketing mosaic, revealing an equivocal melo-rhythm that plays with the mind and body.

In performance, aural mandalas are not static: instead, they readjust and shift themselves constantly. Contemporary accordion-based (*típico;* typical, "authentic") merengue is a case in point: here, accordion and saxophone riffs interact with percussion and dance rhythms to create variegated qualities of aural, kinesthetic, and temporal experience. Witness the mandala notation of merengue at figures 10 and 11. In figure 10, saxophone and tambora sounds create a psychic space to engage dancers aurally, kinesthetically, and mentally: saxophone melo-rhythms bounce off the tambora roll, seducing body motion into complicity with the four-beat cycle. Without warning, musicians leap into figure 11. Dancers are seduced by the new

Inner circle: dancer's motor beat
Middle circle: supporting drum
Outer circle: time line (bell)

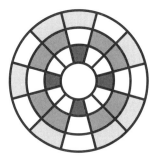

Legend:

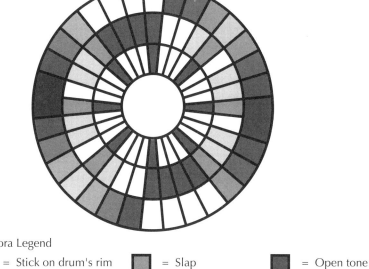

■ = timeline (bell) ■ = supporting drum ■ = dancer's motor beat

Figure 9. 12/8 rhythm: mandala notation. See also color plate 4.

Tambora Legend

□ = Stick on drum's rim ■ = Slap ■ = Open tone

E♭ Alto Saxophone Legend

Figure 10. Merengue Jaleo 1: mandala notation. See also color plate 5.

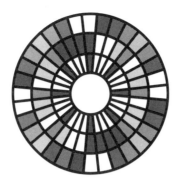

Tambora Legend

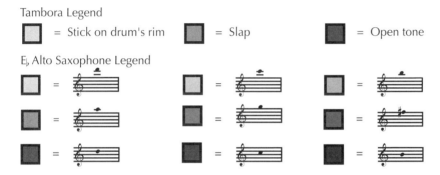

Figure 11. Merengue Jaleo II: mandala notation. See also color plate 6.

saxophone pattern, which is similar to the first one but articulates shorter patterns that bounce off every two, instead of every four, motorbeats. Dancers respond by intensifying their steps. Similarly, jazz musicians constantly shift and vary their melo-rhythms. Mandala notation provides a visual correlate to this life-wave, but its static nature cannot express music's ever-changing quality. So we must move on.

Microrhythm

We noted earlier that all forms of notation clarify some aspects of music but obscure others. In practice, musical time is not bounded by discrete units such as those expressed in conventional, TUBS, kente, or mandala notation. The basic time-divisions of jazz, swung eighth notes, are a most obvious example of this. Because they are of variable length it would be impossible to express them in these notational systems. Moreover, the very name of TUBS notation, "time unit box system," does not jibe with the responsorial aesthetic: as a closer look will show, while we often think of so-called rhythm as time measurement, it is perhaps better conceived in terms of tone, response, and movement, as a *quality,* rather than *quantity,* of experience.

Once, while discussing the West African figure at figures 3, 4, and 9 with Ghanaian master drummer Kwaku Kwaakye Obeng, I said that I love it because of its richness: I can divide it into two, three, four, six, and twelve. He responded that he agrees, but what about dividing it into five, seven, or nine? Numbers are irrelevant when one focuses on *response* rather than time-reckoning. In fact, the lead drum calls in Ewe and Vodou music often use asymmetrical patterns that would not fit on a twelve-part grid.

In jazz, the conversational aesthetic is expressed in microrhythmic push-pull between musicians. The "groove" is established primarily as a hookup between the bassist and drummer, and its profoundly social nature is underlined by the sound's being inextricable from the musicians' sensibilities. Saxophonist David Liebman explains that some excellent bass players refuse to play with equally good drummers simply because the two musicians have incompatible attitudes about the groove. Each musician must have a strong metronomic sense of pulse, but it is not a question of time-reckoning. Drummers and bassists adjust to each other: if the drummer plays ahead of the beat, the bassist may play slightly behind to compensate. Rather than issuing from metronomic accuracy, swing is the result of this interplay.[53] Musicians must have rapport, a willingness to enter into a conversation about the pulse. The drummer might play "on top," ahead of the beat, while the bassist plays "bottom," or behind the beat. What is important is that players willingly enter this game of push-pull, that they want to talk to each other.[54] The game implicates not only rhythm section players, but also improvising soloists, who develop personal, nuanced ways of placing eighth notes. The distinctiveness of a particular group's sense of swing derives from this interplay. Charles Mingus called this view of the beat "rotary perception": the beat is not located in any one spot.[55] Instead, it is like a circular target, and each player aims at it differently.

Ethnomusicologist-trombonist Chris Washburne discusses push-pull microrhythmic conversation in the music of salsa master Eddie Palmieri. Bells (mounted on the timbales drums) provide a "pocket pulse," on or near the center of the beat. Palmieri's piano plays ahead of the pulse, while the bass plays behind, balancing out the sound.[56] Bassist Rubén Rodríguez explains, "When I play with a pianist who pushes the tempo like Palmieri I try to pull back. If they play behind I have to push."[57] In soul music, Wilson Pickett's "Midnight Hour" derives much of its supreme tastiness from what the musicians who created it called a "delayed backbeat," which places beats 2 and 4 later than they would occur metronomically.[58]

Figure 12. Excerpt from John Coltrane's solo on "Oleo" transcribed by Paul Austerlitz.

Microrhythmic variation, of course, exists in European as well as African-based musics: the *notes inégales* of French Baroque style, for example, are similar to the swung eighth notes of jazz in their unequal divisions of time. The aesthetic use, however, of microrhythm is culture-bound: African-influenced aesthetics employ it responsorially, as part of the ethos of conversation and participation.[59]

Ethnomusicologist Charles Keil instigated groundbreaking work on the microrhythmic conversation of jazz using computer graphics to illustrate the push-pull of the bass-and-drums dance. Keil uses the term "Participant Discrepancies" (or PDs) to refer to microrhythms, microtones, and other musical elements that arise in the process of music-making. He celebrates their human quality and contrasts them with so-called "syntactic," or structural, aspects of music. The PD term, however, implies that musical process is somehow "discrepant" from another, more real matrix. As we have seen, the very distinction between participation and structure is forced at best, and a fallacy at worst, as complex polyrhythmic structures grow from the process of tonal and dance-based conversation.

At the same time, Keil's focus on the importance of in-the-moment musical participation is valuable. The excerpt from John Coltrane's solo on "Oleo" at figure 12 swings like mad.[60] At one point, Coltrane plays an idiomatically typical blues-based phrase, but places it non-idiomatically; in this sense it is a "mistake." Interestingly, he calls out with a grunt, "Ah!" as if to say, "Oh, I made a mistake, what will I do now, where will I go?" Significantly, this grunt falls squarely on the beat, recentering the sound and, it seems, Coltrane's concentration, because he then returns to swinging in the pocket. In some ways, this grunt is like the "hidden rhythm" mentioned in conjunction with Fanti drummer Adzinyah, earlier, and expressed in the bottom line of figures 4 and 5. It is also similar to what linguists call a "filled pause," an expression such as "um" or "uh" uttered by a speaker when she stops talking for a moment. Filled pauses give speakers time to think while keeping the listener's attention. Similarly, Coltrane's grunt helped him to stay in the groove while bringing his "mistake" into the flow.

Time

Visual art is static in time (even if it engages the eye in temporal play). Music, however, by definition, moves through time. But time is hard to fathom; as Saint Augustine put it, "When no one asks, I know what it is, but when I wish to explain it to someone who does ask, I don't know."[61] As noted, we often study musical time as a statistical calculation, but we often shirk from confronting it as lived experience. Philosopher Suzanne Langer contrasts the "sequence of actual happenings" (or "clock time") with non-durational "virtual time," maintaining that music evokes the latter.[62] Similarly, phenomenologist Alfred Schutz notes that humans experience many "provinces of meaning" or "levels of reality," that range from "the world of daily life" to theoretical contemplation, dreams, and various types of fantasy. He notes that Euro-classical music turns our attention away from the mundane world, suspending practical everyday concerns; he calls the transitions from one reality to another a "leap" or "shock." We "leap" from one state to another, for example, from not listening to music to listening, from dreaming to waking, or from playing with a child to watching news about the latest war on TV.[63] Schutz also contrasts "outer time" with "inner time," arguing that music is the "arrangement of tones in inner time."[64] Clock time and the notion of musical meter are quantitative perceptions, while inner time is a qualitative condition: the fact that two recordings of popular songs last about three minutes each is important to a radio deejay, but it is irrelevant to the listener.[65] You can "have a good time" without knowing "what time it is." We experience overlapping qualitative and quantitative perceptions of time when return trips seem to go faster than initial trips, and when time seems to speed up as we grow older. Bounce-off melo-rhythms can be analyzed in Western terms, according to time measurements or quantities of time, but in the aesthetic dimension, they create particular qualities of time.[66]

Qualitative shifts within a single performance of Afro-diasporic music resemble Schutz's "leaps," except that they occur within a single musical experience rather than marking transitions from nonmusical to musical experience.[67] Stone uses Schutz's ideas to elaborate on what she calls "moment time" among the Kpelle of Liberia. The Kpelle recognize, but do not emphasize, durational time: they are "cognizant of people growing old and time passing in the sense of 'outer' time [but] this dimension of time is simply not emphasized; rather, the Kpelle elaborate the present."[68] Nondurational "moment time" resembles Langer's "virtual time" and Schutz's "inner time." To the Kpelle, "life consists of a series of presents more distinguishable from one another through qualitative than quantitative differences."

Color Plate 1

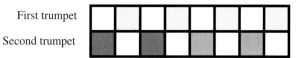

First trumpet

Second trumpet

Legend:

Color Plate 2

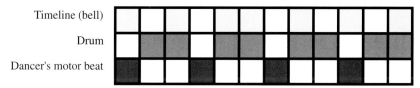

Timeline (bell)

Drum

Dancer's motor beat

Legend:

= timeline (bell)   = supporting drum   = dancer's motor beat

Color Plate 3

E♭ alto saxophone
Tambora
Dancer's motor beat

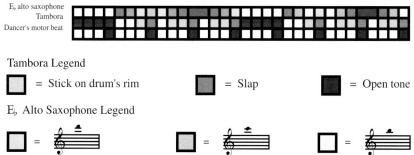

Tambora Legend

= Stick on drum's rim   = Slap   = Open tone

E♭ Alto Saxophone Legend

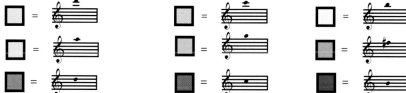

Color Plate 4

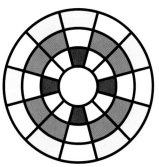

Inner circle: dancer's motor beat
Middle circle: supporting drum
Outer circle: time line (bell)

Legend:

☐ = timeline (bell)   ▨ = supporting drum   ▨ = dancer's motor beat

Color Plate 5

Color Plate 6

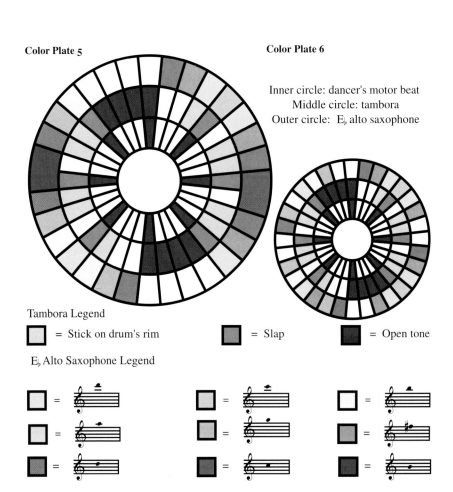

Inner circle: dancer's motor beat
Middle circle: tambora
Outer circle: E♭ alto saxophone

Tambora Legend

☐ = Stick on drum's rim   ▨ = Slap   ■ = Open tone

E♭ Alto Saxophone Legend

Kpelle music creates different qualities of the present: "Kpelle time is like a bubble in that while it is variably expandable, at some point it must cease to expand. At the point the bubble bursts, in a similar way the participants move to another present in time through a leap or a shock."[69]

I had the opportunity to participate in such activity myself when performing with Victor Waill's merengue band. Waill brought the momentum up gradually, bringing the dancers into a pulsating communal groove and keeping them inside it until they ached for a release. He then suddenly introduced a new rhythm or harmony, changing the feeling in the entire hall and giving the public an incredible lift: the bubble burst and the participants leapt into a new Now.[70] James Brown is a master of this type of transformation timing: Brown brings his band to the "bridge" (the second section of an arrangement) exactly when the listener-dancer aches for a change—the shock is a delicious gift.[71] Such shifts can be sudden. In his song "Sex Machine," Brown even teases the audience, asking bandmates, "Should I take them to the bridge?" before actually bestowing this gift.[72] But cycles of leaps and shocks can also be constant, ever changing. Bebop players, for example, constantly react to each other, creating a perpetually moving matrix of sound.

The jazz groove is viscerally pleasurable: one musician likens it to "soaking in a hot bathtub."[73] It can even take on a life of its own; when the band is swinging, a musician can feel as if "the instrument is playing itself."[74] Bassist Cecil McBee says that the groove is like a "wave,"[75] while drummer Michael Carvin likens it to a "trance" that brings on a feeling of "being out of yourself."[76] Other players go so far as to describe this aesthetic summit as a "spiritual" dimension, a transcendent plane whose "flow"[77] expands consciousness.

This flow issues from participation. Contrary to stereotypes that posit a mechanistic relation between music and the body, I am arguing that the mind-body link in Afro-diasporic aesthetics issues from engagement with the community. Instead of being an outside force or something that emanates from deep, dark inner recesses of the subconscious, melo-rhythmic undulation affects us because we are a part of it. It is our own human nature manifesting in a culturally encoded aesthetic whose source is in Africa and that has become the provenance of people all over the world.

CHAPTER 3

Machito and Mario Bauzá
Latin Jazz in the U.S. Mainstream

As we have seen, "buscando América," or looking for America, is central to jazz consciousness. This search, however, will be unsuccessful if it ignores the enormous Latino influence on music in the United States. The United States has long pertained to Latin America as well as Anglo America: the Southwest, California, and Florida, for example, were colonized by Spaniards before English-speakers arrived. Jazz composer Jelly Roll Morton argued that "Spanish tinges" were essential to jazz already in the early twentieth century.[1] Today, the United States is the fifth-largest Spanish-speaking country in the world, with a Latino population of more than 35 million, or 12.5 percent of the total.[2] Of the various manifestations of Latino culture in the United States, the mambo and Afro-Cuban jazz stand out for their relevance to *all* North Americans: even casual attention to twentieth-century popular culture (such as *I Love Lucy*) and to jazz history affirms that Cuban-influenced music has been at the forefront of both mainstream and modernist arts in the United States since the mid-twentieth century.

Latin America, of course, encompasses many strands ranging from Native American cultures to European, African, and Asian-derived strains, as well as all manner of mixings. Conventional wisdom about immigration to the United States holds that new arrivals eventually assimilate to the dominant Anglo-American culture. Because Spanish-speakers were present in North America prior to the arrival of Anglos, U.S. Latinos, especially in the Southwest and California, form a different kind of immigrant than do European and Asian arrivals. Moreover, while Latinos hail from many different countries, they share a language and thus form a variegated yet vast and united group that is integral to North American society.[3] Juan Flores's insights into the Puerto Rican experience in the U.S. mainland are applicable to other groups. He points out that the Latino experience has been a matter of neither "eventual accommodation nor 'cultural genocide'" but rather "a more intricate structuring of ethnicity. . . . Rather than being subsumed and repressed [Latino] . . . culture contributes . . . to a new amalgam."[4]

Latinos of African descent share ancestries with black North Americans, and encounters between them, which gained speed during the mid-twentieth century, were seminal moments in the history of the African diaspora. These encounters were marked by vital cultural cross-fertilization and attendant healing of wounds brought on by centuries of social rupture. Among the most influential Afro-Latin musicians to migrate to the United States was the black Cuban percussionist, singer, and dancer Chano Pozo, who collaborated with Dizzy Gillespie in the creation of Afro-Cuban jazz. Gillespie notes the rapport of two artists from different cultures within the African diaspora: Since Chano couldn't speak English, people always asked, "Well, how do you communicate?" "Deehee no peek pani, me no peek Angli, bo peek African," Chano would answer.[5]

Dizzy had been introduced to Afro-Cuban music through his close friendship with Mario Bauzá, the musical director of the Latin jazz and mambo band, Machito and his Afro-Cubans. Bauzá was a paramount exponent of overlapping Afro-diasporic, Latino, and U.S.-based manifestations of jazz consciousness. A black Cuban, his early background was in the fields of European classical and Cuban popular music. Drawn to jazz, he moved to the United States and worked his way up through the top swing bands. He developed a musical vision that united Afro-Cuban dance music with the techniques of the Harlem big bands and, in tandem with the singer Machito, founded Machito and his Afro-Cubans. The vital black renaissance that Bauzá and Machito witnessed in Harlem inspired them to re-examine their identities as black Cubans and forge their own brand of musical pan-Africanism. Their music combined Harlem jazz with the supremely dance-based aesthetic of Afro-Cuban popular music, thus connecting two centers of the African diaspora. Pride in African origins was apparent in the band's name, Machito and his *Afro*-Cubans, as well as in its foregrounding of black Cuban drumming. The presence of this group in the United States buttressed pan-African links, appealing to black North Americans. Machito once said that playing for dancers in Harlem "was exciting," because "it was black music, you didn't need to make no explanation to a black person."[6] He added that "the marriage of Cuban music with jazz was not a conventional union; it was a marriage of love."[7]

While Machito and his Afro-Cubans compared favorably to the top Cuban bands of their day, they were not the foremost exponent of Cuban dance music; while several of their recordings made hits in Cuba, Machito and his Afro-Cubans never once performed in their home country. Cuban musicologist Leonardo Acosta writes that Machito is "almost unknown" in Cuba but he is nevertheless more influential on the world stage than is the eminent Cuban composer Ernesto Lecuona.[8] While most Cuban dance music was influenced by North American music to some extent at midcentury, Machito and his Afro-Cubans was the only Cuban group whose style was steeped in jazz. For all its importance as a Cuban band, Machito and his Afro-Cubans' most remarkable contribution was as a North American institution.

Beginning in Cuba

Francisco Pérez (who later took the surname Grillo) was reportedly born to Rogelio Pérez and Marta Gutierrez de Pérez in a two-room *solar* (or compound apartment) in Havana on February 16, 1908, in the predominantly black barrio (neighborhood) of Jesus María. Francisco, who was called Macho by family and friends (and later, Machito by fans), was the oldest of six children. When he was ten years old, his father became successful in the grocery business, transporting food from docks to retail outlets. This was a poor Afro-Cuban neighborhood, but the Pérez family was better off than their neighbors, and Machito attended a private school; he was one of the only blacks there. Afro-Cuban cultural practices were deeply ingrained in the barrio. Drummers and dancers were heroes among local youth; Machito gave famed drummers free groceries simply because he respected their music so much.[9] Machito, whose grandmother was born in Africa, later remembered that "the Yorùbá religion or Santería . . . to us was like the Catholic religion" was to some whites: it was central to their worldview.

The religion that is usually known as Santería (because of its syncretic incorporation of Catholic saints; it is also called Lucumí) derives from the Yorùbá cultures of West Africa, employing spoken and sung liturgies in the Yorùbá language, Yorùbá musical instruments, and Yorùbá cosmology and divination. Three other primary African ethnic groups, whose cultures have been passed down in religious traditions, exist in Cuba. The Palo complex is based in the Kongo religions of Central Africa; the Arará religion derives from the Fon of Dahomey; and the Abacuá secret society comes from the Ejagham of southeastern Nigeria and southwestern Cameroon.[10] Afro-Cuban carnival music groups, or *comparsas,* betray many Kongo influences; their associated dance is, in fact, called the *conga.* *Rumba,* a form of street drumming and dance, uses drums that resemble those used in comparsas and that in Cuba are usually called *tumbadoras* (but which in the United States have been dubbed *congas*).

Life in the Pérez family was richly infused with music. An amateur singer, Machito's father enjoyed hiring top-flight popular musicians to play at his wife's birthday parties.[11] All the Pérez sisters sang, and for a period of time, they had their own son group.[12] The *son* is a syncretic Afro-Cuban popular dance music that emerged in eastern Cuba in the early twentieth century and soon spread to Havana. The classic son ensemble, the *sexteto,* gelled in the 1920s and consists of *tres* (a plucked lute with three double-course strings), guitar, string bass, maracas, claves (two wooden sticks which are struck together), and bongos (twin drums held between the knees and played with the hands). Sextetos were often augmented by a trumpet or cornet, making them *septetos.* While literally referring to the instrument mentioned above, the word *clave* also means "key," as in the key to a puzzle, and is used to designate the signature rhythmic structure of most Afro-Cuban music. Indeed, several permutations of the clave rhythm serve as deep structural elements of Cuban musics ranging from Santería songs to the rumba and son. The son clave underlies most Cuban popular dance music; see figure 13.[13]

Like the rest of his family, Machito sang, and as he was a baritone, he generally took the *segunda voz* ("second voice," or harmony) rather than melody. He loved to watch and listen at rehearsals of Havana's top son groups, marveling especially at the maraca players. He later remembered that they had such "control, fantastic. So I said that OK, I want to learn to do this. And I locked myself in my room, . . . and took the maracas," practicing day and night. "My mother thought I was crazy."[14] Machito also received instruction in solfège and flute.[15] He soon joined the top echelon of son musicians, debuting as a backup singer and maraca player with the Miguel Zavalle Sextet.[16] He attracted attention for his flair with the maracas, and when Ignacio Piñiero, the leader of the famed Septeto Nacional, heard him play in 1929, he asked Machito to replace their accompanying vocalist because the latter was not a good *maraquero.* Machito joined the great singer Maria Teresa Vera's Sexteto in 1930, and later that year substituted for the famed vocalist Antonio Machín with the Sexteto Aguabama.[17]

The music surrounding Machito in Cuba, which had been colonized by Spain, presents a contrast to music in the Anglo-dominated United States. The difference can be traced to the divergent development of race relations in the two countries. As part of a larger Afro-Asian-Iberian nexus, Spaniards were primed for social and musical interaction with Africans when the

Figure 13. 3-2 clave rhythm

two groups met in the Americas. Spaniards' previous exposure to Africa contrasts starkly with northern Europeans' geographic isolation, which inhibited the assimilation of African influences into English, Dutch, and French colonial culture. Spain was linked to the cosmopolitan world of Islam from 711 until the Moors were expelled in 1492 (interestingly, this is a longer period of time than the era of European domination in the Americas). Cultural ties between Africa, Asia, and Iberia were pervasive in the world of Islam. For example, Bilal, the Prophet Mohammed's *muezzin,* who composed the *Adhan,* or Islamic call to prayer, was a dark-complexioned African. Another influential Afro-Moslem musician was Ibrahim Ibn al-Mahdi (779–839), a master lutenist who was hailed as the greatest singer of his day. He was born in Baghdad, the son of an African slave mother and an aristocratic father, and he spent most of his life in Spain, where he founded an influential musical movement.[18]

Slavery existed on the Iberian Peninsula into modern times, and slave law, inherited from Roman precedents, persisted in Spain and Latin America. This law recognized slaves' humanity: slaves were seen as individuals who had lost their freedom through accidents of fate. The Iberian model of slavery thus contrasts sharply with the northern European one. Slaves had certain rights (for example, married slaves could not be separated against their will), and manumissions were considered good works by the Catholic Church. Slaves' conversion to Christianity was required in the Iberian colonies, while it was not in northern European colonies. Membership in the Christian community increased slaves' perceived humanity as contrasted with the "heathen" Moors and Jews (who had recently been expelled from Spain), as well as with those Native Americans who did not convert. Because the slaves' humanity was recognized, lifeways such as highly African-influenced religious rituals remained somewhat intact.

Contrasting this situation with the northern European colonies, where slaves were considered subhuman chattel, Frank Tannenbaum and others have argued that slavery was less brutal in the Iberian colonies than in the northern European colonies.[19] This "myth of racial democracy," however, is untenable. Cuban masters, for example, matter-of-factly discussed whether it was more advantageous to treat slaves well and hold them for many years, or to work them to death and replace them with new arrivals from Africa. Nevertheless, as the sociologist H. Hoetink puts it, the Iberian model did, in fact, streamline "social skill in everyday intercourse"[20] across racial lines. Hispanic colonists often recognized the offspring of their sexual unions with slaves as their own progeny, while Anglo colonists rarely did so. Afro-Cubans were thus able to nurture their own culture while simultaneously identifying closely with the Cuban mainstream. Their vibrant in-group allowed African-derived cultural traits to persist more strongly in Cuba than they did in the United States. Black religious traditions in North America betray an undeniable African style, but Afro-Cuban religions utilize African languages and cosmologies issuing from specific ethnic groups. So while it was possible for the African American sociologist E. Franklin Frazier to doubt the presence of Africanisms in North America in 1939, no one could ever have doubted their presence in Cuba.[21] In the United States, where offspring of liaisons between masters and slaves were rarely recognized by whites, and where many blacks were still denied the right to vote a century after abolition, African Americans developed a more separate in-group sense—and double-consciousness.[22]

In Cuba, Machito was steeped in a nurturing syncretic religious and musical culture. But he was not to stay; he would eventually begin to look outward to other parts of the African diaspora.

Machito's younger sister Graciela was born on August 23, 1915. She showed great musical talent as a child, and, like many girls, studied piano and solfège. Her predilection, however, was for singing popular songs. As Machito's musical career developed, he used his contacts with Havana's top musicians, recommending his sister to the famed all-woman band Sexteto Anacaona as a singer and clave player. So at the young age of sixteen, Graciela was already performing with one of Cuba's best groups; she stayed with Anacaona from 1933 to 1942. When she joined the band, Anacaona was a son group, but it later evolved into a *charanga* (an ensemble with violins, flute, and *timbales* [small tympani], and after that into a dance band with brass and reed instruments; Graciela even played the bass with Anacaona for a short period of time. In addition to the high profile that it enjoyed in Cuba, this group toured in Puerto Rico, Panama, and Venezuela.[23]

When Machito was nineteen years old his father moved to Pogoloti, a town just outside Havana. There, a boy began coming around the house to visit Graciela's and Machito's younger sister Estela, who was twelve. Hoping her elder brother would allow her to date the boy, Estela finessed an introduction: and so Machito met Mario Bauzá.

Mario Bauzá was born to Hilario and Dolores Bauzá on April 28, 1911, in the predominantly black barrio of Cayo Hueso, Havana.[24] His father, a cigar maker, was friendly with Arturo Andrade, a wealthy white military man with a respected position in the community, who lived in Pogoloti. Andrade became Mario's godfather and as he had no children, he asked Mario's father whether he could raise the child. The father consented and Mario moved in with his godparents. An amateur musician, Andrade taught solfège to children in the neighborhood in his spare time, without charging for his services. Mario picked up on these lessons by eavesdropping and surprised his godfather when, at about six years of age, he performed difficult solfège assignments perfectly. Andrade determined that Mario would receive a formal education in music from the best teachers available. The child's solfège instructor, however, imposed such a strict regimen that after six months Mario told his godfather that he wanted to stop. But his godfather said that he must continue. After studying solfège for two years, Mario began taking oboe lessons; because he disliked this instrument, however, he was allowed to switch to clarinet. The demanding practice schedule imposed upon the boy left little time for play; as Bauzá later remembered, it was just "study, study, study, study, study, so that I didn't have no kid's life."[25]

Bauzá's Euro-classical background contrasts markedly with Machito's grounding in Afro-Cuban popular music. At age sixteen, Bauzá was hired as the bass clarinetist of the Havana Symphony Orchestra.[26] In addition to working at this prestigious job, the young top-flight clarinetist was sought by dance bands, joining Antonio María Romeo's danzón group, one of the best in Havana. The danzón, while incorporating Afro-Cuban elements, occupies a spot closer to Spain on the continuum of African and European influences than does the son. It developed in the nineteenth century, when the Cuban *contradanza* incorporated Afro-Cuban tinges, and was performed by *orquestas típicas* comprised of wind instruments and timbales. Around 1920, the orquestas típicas gave way to *charangas francesas* (or simply *charangas*) consisting of violins, flute, and timbales. The danzón's simultaneous links to European classical forms and local African-influenced aesthetics made it appealing to a racial cross section of Cubans. Mario Bauzá's straddling of high- and lowbrow forms was not uncommon in the Latin Caribbean and, as we shall see, became a major determinant of his artistic vision.

Mario, well known in the area as an accomplished musician, met with Machito's brotherly approval and started dating Estela. Moreover, the two boys became fast friends, going to movies and baseball games together. They also reportedly started rehearsing a musical group for a projected tour to Panama. The tour never materialized, but the experiment was a watershed, marking the beginning of Bauzá and Machito's fertile musical association.[27]

The Color Question in the Two Americas

In 1927 the Victor Talking Machine Company hired Antonio María Romeu's group for a recording, and the entire band, including Mario Bauzá, traveled to New York City. During this period North American record companies generally recorded in the United States, even when the product was intended for sale abroad. Thus the teen prodigy was afforded the opportunity to see the Harlem Renaissance at its apex and to hear some of the top bands of the day. The musical excellence and innovations of these groups, compounded by their polished demeanor, impressed the young Cuban musician to no end; he later remembered thinking that "this is what I'm looking for."[28]

What had he been missing? With what had he been dissatisfied in Cuba? The innovative sound of jazz was one thing, and of course, Bauzá was attracted to the economic opportunities that were available in the United States. It also seems that he was attracted to a certain unaccustomed clarity in race relations. While black Cubans were more integrated into Cuban society than black North Americans were in the United States, the period of Bauzá's youth was racially charged. This in spite of the fact that, as elsewhere in Latin America, an ideology of racial democracy was promoted in Cuba. The father of Cuban independence, José Martí, espoused a color-blind Cubanness and worked closely with the mixed-race leader Antonio Maceo. But while Afro-Cubans fought valiantly against for Cuban independence, racial discrimination persisted in Cuba and the Martí/Maceo ideal of a Cuba for both whites and blacks never materialized. The ideology of a raceless Cuba, however, made it difficult for Afro-Cubans to maintain all-black organizations. This attitude extended to the realm of electoral politics. In 1908, Evaristo Estonoz and Pedro Ivonet founded the Partido Independiente de Color (Independent Party of Color), or PIC. The only black senator in Cuba, Martín Morúa Delgado, however, soon sponsored a law banning the institution of political parties based on race, making the PIC illegal and leading to its harassment. The PIC was especially popular in eastern Cuba, or Oriente, and in May 1912, a rebellion developed there. President José Miguel Gómez perpetrated a violent backlash later called La Guerrita del Doce (The little war of 1912) in which thousand of blacks and mixed-race Cubans were killed.[29]

The Afro-Cuban intellectual Bernardo Ruiz Suárez wrote a remarkable book entitled *The Color Question in the Two Americas* in 1922. Ruiz recognized that the position of U.S. blacks was worse than that of Cuban blacks, writing that while PIC leaders were "citizens dissatisfied with . . . the affairs of their country," U.S. blacks in 1922 were "not even [full-fledged] citizens of [their] country."[30] The thrust of his argument, however, was that while Latin American blacks "live in an atmosphere of apparent cordiality with the white race," Latin American whites conceal their prejudice, so that blacks become content with a hypocrisy of apparent racial equality. He opined that while "the pusillanimous and simple-minded" might prefer the Cuban ways, "strong and noble spirits" feel that the Anglo ways are better, because "they goad the black man into a . . . life of ideals which may in time be realized." North American blacks were brutally repressed around whites; away from whites, however, they founded their own schools, theaters, and churches.[31] Ruiz applauded the fact that black political movements, forbidden in Cuba, found fertile soil in the United States. His chapter entitled "City within a City" praises Harlem's thriving black community, lauding its attractive private homes, YMCA, public library, and exhibitions of black artists' work. Ruiz Suárez also marveled that African American subcultures such as the black Jews could openly parade in New York, while black organizations such as the Abacuá society were persecuted in Cuba.[32]

In spite of the fact that racial prejudice was stronger in the United States than in Cuba, it seems that for Bauzá, disenchanted with Cuba's myth of racial democracy, African American self-empowerment offered a refreshing mode of black empowerment. In later interviews, Bauzá said, "That's why I came to the United States; I feel so good as soon as I hit Harlem because I see all the Negroes, that they had everything."[33] This issue raises important methodological questions regarding oral historical data. These sentiments about race were expressed in interviews done well after Bauzá's arrival to the United States and it is thus possible that these views developed later, after Bauzá had become influenced by North American views of race. This lateness, however, does not invalidate them; it seems that in spite of virulent bigotry, the *clarity* of race relations in the United States appealed to Bauzá.[34]

Upon his return to Cuba after the Romeu recording session, Bauzá took up the alto saxophone and listened avidly to jazz broadcasts on short-wave radio from the United States; Ellington's Cotton Club performances made a special impression on him. He began to play the alto saxophone in dance bands at prestigious venues such as the Montmartre Cabaret, gaining notoriety on the Havana music scene for his proficiency in jazz.[35] The music he was playing, however, was not the jazz of Ellington and Basie but a jazz-influenced dance music, or, as he later put it, a kind of "simple jazz."[36] Beginning in about 1920, predominantly white Cuban groups had been playing North American dance music for elite Cubans and tourists in largely segregated venues, and by the end of the decade some of them were blending Cuban music with the North American styles. Parallel, then, to the "Latin tinge" in U.S. music, we can think of a *jazz tinge* in Latin music.[37] While Cuban jazz bands dominated recordings and toured internationally, they never gained the popularity of danzón and son groups. One of the most popular of these groups was Orquesta los Hermanos Castro, which played both jazz-tinged dance music and stylized son and conga numbers, gaining fame by accompanying singer Miguelito Valdés.[38] The jazz vogue in Cuba centered in the high society and, as mentioned, these groups were predominantly white. Although Bauzá was hired by Los Hermanos Castro, he consistently felt the sting of racial prejudice.

Ethnomusicologist Robin Moore elucidates an irony central to Cuban identity: in spite of a pervasive Euro-centrism, white Cubans have repeatedly adopted elements of Afro-Cuban culture as national symbols. But, utilizing the technique of stereotype and reappropriation, Afro-Cubans have repeatedly responded with ever more forceful assertions of their own identity. Influenced by Parisian primitivism and the Jazz Age, white Cuban nationalists appropriated Afro-Cuban expression into their vision of Cubanness in the 1920s. A conga craze took shape as stylized versions of the dance became popular in Havana ballrooms. From there, the conga traveled to Paris and New York. Stereotyped Afro-Cuban religious themes entered pop culture: singer Miguelito Valdés, for example, popularized "Babalú," a song named for a Yorùbá-Cuban spirit (but removed from authentic Afro-Cuban liturgical music).[39] Nationalist composers such as Amadeo Roldán and Alejandro García Caturla incorporated Afro-Cuban themes into their pieces. This stereotyping opened the door for Afro-Cubans to display open pride in their heritage: as stereotyped versions of African-based culture gained acceptability, black Cubans reappropriated their expression, asserting their culture even more forcefully. The famed son group Septeto Nacional, for example, referred to Santería in their "No juegues con los santos" ("Don't Fool Around with the Saints") and "Canto Lucumí" ("Lucumí Song"). Son lyrics also incorporated African-derived black slang such as *asere* and *chévere* (respectively, "friend" and "great" in the Carabalí language). These usages troubled many whites and middle-class blacks, but they empowered working-class blacks.[40]

In Havana, Bauzá played alto saxophone and clarinet in pianist Célido Curbelo's band. This group played much North American music but did not have a trumpet player who could play jazz. Bauzá determined to fill the trumpet chair, approaching Lázaro Herrera, the trumpeter in the famed Septeto Nacional, for lessons. Bauzá learned amazingly fast: after Herrera showed him the fingerings, several weeks of diligent practice, combined with his mastery of solfège, enabled Bauzá to become the band's trumpet soloist.[41] At the time, however, the trumpet was merely an experiment for Bauzá: he returned to the saxophone when he left Curbelo. Realizing that opportunities for playing jazz were limited in Havana, and inspired by his earlier visit to the United States, Bauzá decided to move to New York, to "improve" himself, to "reach the top," as he later said.[42] The decision was inspired not only by his quest for musical excellence, but also by the auspiciousness of the Harlem

Renaissance. Economic opportunities, of course, were available in New York. Added to this were racial issues: in spite of the ideology of a raceless society, Bauzá had lost several gigs in Havana to white musicians who were not of his high musical caliber.[43]

Music Stand Musicians

What connections awaited him in the United States? The jazz scene, of course, was flourishing in New York, and much of the music's inspiration had come from New Orleans. Race relations in New Orleans—a Caribbean city originally colonized by France and Spain—long conformed to the southern European rather than the northern European model. Large numbers of blacks and whites had entered the city from the Hispanophone and Francophone islands, bringing various African, Spanish, and French traditions to the rich musical stew that brewed there. Neo-African drumming and dance had a high profile at famed Sunday celebrations in the city's Congo Square during the nineteenth century. A vibrant mixed-race French creole musical subculture flourished, and as mentioned earlier, Jelly Roll Morton had argued that "Spanish tinges" were an essential ingredient of jazz. Several of Morton's compositions, such as "Mama 'Nita" and "Spanish Swat," betray this tinge. Links between Caribbean rhythms and ragtime are also notable, for example in Scott Joplin's "Solace Rag." New York stride piano, too, occasionally incorporated Latin elements; the music of the great Luckey Roberts stands out in this regard. By the 1910s, the Argentine tango, which had become a Parisian and cosmopolitan fad, was mixing in with the earlier Latin tinges. W. C. Handy visited Cuba in 1900 and expressed interest in local music. Moreover as mentioned in chapter 1, Handy used tango elements in his seminal composition "St. Louis Blues," the second copyrighted blues. Significantly, the tango was more prominent in mainstream U.S. popular culture at the time than was the blues, and Handy used the popularity of a Latin American genre—the tango—to promote the blues, which was then a new North American genre.[44]

Stereotyped versions of the son and conga reached the United States and France in the 1920s and 1930s; the son received the misnomer "rhumba" on the transnational stage. Justo "Don" Aziazpú's Havana Casino Orchestra made a splash in New York in 1930 with a "rhumba" (or son) called "El manicero" ("The Peanut Vendor"). The number was based on street vendors' cries, and Aziazpú's outfit performed it with authentic son instrumentation (even if it lacked the flavor of the classic black son septetos) while presenting a stage dance show of stereotypical Cuban street scenes. "The Peanut Vendor" became a big hit and was often recorded in the United States, most notably by Louis Armstrong and Duke Ellington. The salon conga incorporated rhythms from its street-level prototype: the well-known "pam-pam-pam-pam-pam—*kick*" choreography comes from Afro-Cuban carnival dance. Bandleader Xavier Cugat, born in Catalonia but raised in Cuba, emerged as the foremost exponent of "Americanized" Latin music in the 1930s. Openly admitting that "to succeed in America I gave the Americans a Latin music that had nothing authentic about it," Cugat believed that because North "Americans know nothing about Latin music . . . they have to be given music more for the eyes than the ears. Eighty percent visual, the rest aural."[45] His performances blended and diluted various Latin American strains into entertaining, flamboyant shows with attractive female singers, dance routines, and displays of instrumental virtuosity.

When Don Azpiazú's group left Cuba for New York City to make its above-mentioned 1930 hit, Bauzá (although he was not a member) joined the voyage, arriving on March 29. Because black musicians were barred from joining New York's musicians' union, Local 802, bandleader James Reese Europe had organized an alternate organization called the Clef Club, for which the Rhythm Club on 131st Street in Harlem served as an informal gathering place.[46] This was a private club for black musicians where members could relax, play pool or poker, or simply chat. It was also a valuable place to make professional contacts. Jam sessions were also held, and Bauzá remembers hearing Art Tatum play there. At the Rhythm Club, Bauzá met his Afro-Cuban compatriot, flutist Alberto Socarrás, who had come to the States in 1928. Socarrás was playing in a Broadway show called the Blackbirds; he already knew many of the best African American musicians in the city and was well placed to orient Bauzá.

Bauzá sat in at the Rhythm Club and was offered a job playing upscale private parties with the brilliant stride pianist Luckey Roberts, whose unique compositional style, as mentioned, displays a Latin tinge. Bauzá also worked on the short-run Broadway show *Fast and Furious* and with the formidable jazz violinist Leroy "Stuff" Smith. He soon landed a regular job with Noble Sissle's band. One of the top groups of the day, Sissle's group included top-flight musicians such as the great Sidney Bechet. As the featured artist, Bechet did not sit with the reed section; he played solos only. Details of decorum and appearance were of utmost importance in the classy Harlem venues, and Sissle inspected band members' uniforms before they were allowed to go on stage: collars had to be stiff, and patent leather shoes shined.[47] Soon after Bauzá joined, Sissle embarked upon a tour of Europe, but Bauzá remained in New York. He had come to the United States to participate in Harlem's vibrant music and culture, and even touring with such a great musician as Bechet was contrary to this objective. Bauzá went on to freelance around town, playing with Sam Wooding's band and, notably, Eubie Blake.[48]

Don Aziazpú's lead singer, Antonio Machín, had started his own quartet and was planning a recording session in New York, but he was in a bind: there were few musicians in the city who had mastered the Cuban son trumpet style. When Bauzá said that he would like to do the job, Machín was surprised: Bauzá was known as a saxophonist, not a trumpeter. While his first gig on trumpet in Cuba had been a short-lived experiment, this time Bauzá decided to take up the instrument seriously; he wanted to become a professional trumpeter. His motivation was based in his love of jazz: Louis Armstrong's towering influence had rendered the trumpet almost synonymous with hot improvisation. Bauzá later said that "I want[ed] to play like Louis Armstrong so bad I can taste it,"[49] adding that "I fell in love with the trumpet . . . so I started learning all his solos."[50] Bauzá gave up playing the saxophone for the time being, going so far as to give his alto to a friend.

Bauzá was asked to do a European tour with Ciro Rimac's Cuban vaudeville group as a trumpeter but again opted to remain in the jazz mecca, New York. Excited about playing jazz trumpet, he took a job as lead trumpeter with Hi Clark and his Missourians in spite of the fact that he considered it a "second-rate band." Clark was working at the famed Savoy Ballroom, where Chick Webb's fire-hot organization was the headlining act. Webb heard Bauzá play, and when a trumpet chair opened up in his band in 1933, he hired Bauzá. Although Bauzá sight-read the first gig proficiently, Webb asked him to come to a rehearsal after the show. When Bauzá arrived, he was surprised to see no one but himself and the bandleader. Webb told him that they were going to work together, one on one, that he would help the Cuban musician with jazz phrasing. Saying that "this was the greatest lesson that I ever had in my life,"[51] Bauzá later remembered that Webb told him to "'take such and such a number out.' I took the number out. He said, 'Play.' He said, 'Don't phrase like that.' So he used to hum to me the way he want me to phrase. I try. 'That's it, keep going—no—don't lose the idea; like that. Do it like this.'"[52] Accustomed to acing all musical tasks, Bauzá was discouraged, thinking that maybe jazz was not his calling. He told Webb that he was not the man for the job, but Webb countered that, no, "you got what I need, and I got what you need. . . . You play all the notes beautiful, but something about [it], is missing in there. If you listen to me, you're going to never regret it [sic]."[53] Bauzá was reading well, but he was not interpreting the music according to the African American aesthetic: he wasn't swinging in the jazz sense. Bauzá's formal training was an asset to Webb, and Webb knew that Bauzá wanted to play jazz, so it was a symbiotic union. This was not the first time that such a union played itself out in African American music; folklorist Ruth Glasser shows that black bandleaders, the most notable of whom was James Reese Europe, often used Latin-Caribbean players as "music stand musicians," because they were good readers.[54] Euro-classical training was more readily available to people of color in Cuba and Puerto Rico than it was to African Americans,[55] and a confluence of Euro-classical and Afro-Caribbean elements often characterized the musicality of Caribbean players. Webb made good use of Bauzá's musical training; within a year, he named Bauzá musical director of the band. For a youth who had traveled alone to a new country with hopes of playing a new music, this was a dream come true; he later remembered, "I flipped," thinking, "oh my goodness, I made it!"[56]

That Bauzá's skills were as a reader and interpreter—skills culled from his classical background—is underlined by the fact that Webb counseled him to stick to this forte. Although Bauzá loved Louis Armstrong and was learning to play in that style, Webb advised him to avoid emulating the great black improvisers. He later remembered Webb saying, "Don't try to do that hard stuff because you won't out-do them . . . those white trumpet players, when they play jazz, like Red Nichols, and you say you like it, they play around the melody. That's what I want you to do."[57] Indeed, while Bauzá was an architect of Afro-Cuban jazz, he was never known primarily as an improviser.

As the leader of one of the top black bands of the period, Webb was a competitor of Fletcher Henderson and Duke Ellington; his powerful drum-set playing, combined with top soloists and formidable arrangements,[58] made his group one of the swingingest in Harlem. Bauzá remembers battles of the bands between Webb and Benny Goodman at the Savoy, which he feels that Webb won. Webb recorded Bauzá's beautiful composition "Lona," which shows off Bauzá's pretty trumpet sound and his composing skills.[59] In addition to working with Webb, Bauzá made a great deal of extra money recording with New York Latin bands. [60] Earning more than the majority of his peers, Bauzá was a successful man. In 1936 Bauzá returned to Cuba to marry Estela, and two weeks later, returned with her to New York—but not before telling his Cuban friends about opportunities for blacks in his newly adopted city. Significantly, he encouraged Machito to begin saving money for the trip.[61]

Preparing a Wedding

In 1938 Bauzá had a disagreement with Webb's booking office which led to his leaving the band.[62] After a three-month stint with Don Redman and one month with Fletcher Henderson, Alberto Socarrás, whose band worked opposite Cab Calloway at the Cotton Club, recommended Bauzá to substitute for Doc Cheatham with Cab Calloway's band. This subbing led to a permanent job in 1939.[63] Calloway's was the most commercially successful black band of the period. Because he paid more than anyone else, Calloway was able to attract top players such as tenor saxophonist Chu Berry, bassist Milt Hinton, and drummer Cozy Cole. His emphasis on showmanship led to accusations of kowtowing to minstrel-tinged white taste, but Calloway had his own ways of maintaining self-respect. To avoid the indignities associated with traveling in the segregated South, for example, his group traveled by private rail car or charter bus; as one of his musicians put it, there was "no Jim-crow coach for Cab."[64] This philosophy of black self-help, perhaps inspired by Booker T. Washington, was consonant with Bauzá's attraction to the Harlem Renaissance: instead of looking to the white world for solutions, successful African Americans kept their dignity intact and their pocketbooks full by forging black institutions.

Bauzá had met John Birks "Dizzy" Gillespie a few years earlier when Gillespie was working with Teddy Hill opposite Webb at the Savoy Ballroom; Gillespie had jammed with Webb and had become friendly with Bauzá.[65] While many seasoned musicians of the day criticized Gillespie's modernistic playing, Bauzá was immediately attracted to the novel approach, sensing that Gillespie was destined to become a musical innovator. He thought that Gillespie would make a valuable addition to the Calloway band, going so far as to tell Calloway not only that he wanted Gillespie in the band, but that he believed that the band *needed* Gillespie.[66] To get his friend a foot in the door, Bauzá took a night off, asking Gillespie to substitute for him. Bauzá told trumpeter Lamar Wright to give Gillespie the lead part and to let him improvise.[67] He also coached Gillespie to play conservatively, saying "don't go overboard."[68] As it turned out, Gillespie's solo was an accompaniment to a Bill "Bojangles" Robinson's soft-shoe routine. He aced it, and when Calloway fired a trumpeter a few weeks later, he asked Gillespie to join up.[69] Gillespie became Bauzá's roommate and best friend in the band, and Bauzá remembers that Gillespie had already earned his nickname by playing the clown.[70] Gillespie attests that joining the Calloway band was an important career move for him, and ever thankful for Bauzá's guidance, he wrote that "Mario was like my father."[71]

It was during his stint with Calloway that Bauzá began to think about "marrying" Cuban music to jazz, as he put it. Remembering the lesson that Chick Webb had given him on jazz phrasing, it occurred to him that he could teach North Americans to phrase Cuban music idiomatically. Calloway's drummer Cozy Cole used to get bored between sets, and one day when he was sitting practicing on a drum pad in the dressing room, Bauzá said to him,

"Cozy, if I hum it to you some kind of rhythm do you think you can do it?" He said, "well, I'll try it." So I hummed something, and I said, "no, no not like that, like" [*hums a phrase*]. So I said, let me get hold of Dizzy. So I said, "Dizzy, put a mute in the trumpet. He's going to play some rhythm in there and I want you to play something jazz in there on top." So he start the phrase and I say "no, no, stop, stop. Cuban music, the metric of the Cuban music is clave . . . so put the phrasing from upbeat to the downbeat." So Dizzy start playing on top of that rhythm. I said this is it already, I know what to do now. All I got to do now is take the tune and dress it, voice wide like a jazz band, with the same harmony, the same voicing and instruments. That's how the Afro-Cuban jazz [was] born.[72]

Bauzá's idea was not merely to superimpose jazz solos over Cuban rhythms. Instead, he wanted the jazz elements to be rhythmically consonant with the deep structure of Cuban music: they should emphasize beats 1 and 3 instead of 2 and 4, and they should refer to the clave rhythm. Calloway recorded some Cuban pieces while Bauzá was in the band, but, as Bauzá noted, these were novelty numbers that did not capture the genuine feel of Cuban music. Still, Bauzá had conceived the idea that would later flower as a major innovation in American music.

In 1937 New York's top Latin bandleaders called a meeting to organize a protest against the musicians' union, Local 802: while Latin groups had found a niche in society clubs, they were generally denied top billing and used as "relief bands," filling in when featured acts took breaks. When he was invited to the meeting, Bauzá remembered the racial discrimination that he had faced when playing in the predominantly white Cuban bands before coming to the United States. Knowing that New York's light-skinned Latin bandleaders sometimes denied work to their dark-skinned compatriots, Bauzá later said that it "made him sick" that they were protesting discrimination when they themselves discriminated against Latinos of color.[73] In a tirade with which he later claimed to have ended the meeting, Bauzá reminded his compatriots that *his* home was in black bands whose musicianship was superior to that of the Latin relief bands. As the only dark-skinned musician at the gathering, he sarcastically asked why he had been invited, adding: "The reason why you people been classified like that [is] the musical standard you don't have. You people know where I am. But all the people in New York that look like me they don't have no chance because you don't use them so how the hell you going to call me and go demand something to the 802?"[74] Successful in the competitive world of top-shelf black bands, Bauzá had triumphed in the United States to the extent that he identified more closely with the black jazz scene than with the Latin music scene.

Machito arrived in New York in October 1937, staying with Mario and Estela in Harlem. Like his brother-in-law, Machito was awed by the accomplishments of the Harlem Renaissance, as he later remembered: "It was a fertile time, when everybody was thinking about improving themselves. The black North Americans who were living in Harlem had already established themselves there. . . . I went to the Savoy every night."[75] Machito was soon working with several New York Latin bands. While his musical experience in Cuba had been as a backup singer in small son groups, he now had the opportunity to sing lead vocals in large dance bands. He recorded with the Xavier Cugat and Noro Morales bands in 1938.[76] In 1939, Machito worked with Orquesta Siboney, and in the following year he took over its leadership for a job at a new midtown nightspot called Club Cuba. Though this was a short-lived gig, it is significant as his first experience as a bandleader in New York; the seeds of the Machito band were planted.[77] Bauzá and Machito decided to join forces, preparing a collaborative venture. Still working the lucrative Calloway job, Bauzá took charge of rehearsing Machito's musicians, preparing them for a debut.[78]

At the first rehearsal, Bauzá deemed that some of the players that Machito had chosen were not up to his standards, and he replaced them. Bauzá's objective was to create a top-shelf organization on the level of the legendary Harlem swing bands: a Latin band with the polish, decorum, and musical excellence of Calloway and Ellington. He wanted to create a group that would appeal to dancers, but that also could accompany shows. Sidemen remember Bauzá as an exacting bandleader, a "slave-driver" when it came to rehearsals; he was especially demanding about phrasing.[79] Because Bauzá wanted to blend Cuban rhythms with jazz phrasing, he needed musicians who were open to new ideas. For this reason he sought not only top musicians, but flexible musicians, musicians who were willing to be molded and work as a team. There were many excellent Latino players who could interpret Cuban music in New York, but in addition to Latino players, Bauzá used many African Americans. Machito explained:

On account they was American, they knew they got to learn how to get adjusted with us. . . . A Spanish guy would have said, "no, because I played with Coén, I played with Noro Morales, I played with Cugat." We don't want that. We want a guy who would pay attention to what we want. . . . There was a lot of musicians who could read, but . . . we were looking for people, for flexible people, that we could mold the way we want. . . . They don't supposed to be the best musician. The most flexible was the one we was looking for.[80]

In his later years, Bauzá explained that he approached his musicians in the same way that Webb had approached him, patiently teaching phrasing and interpretation, and that the musicians responded.[81]

As noted earlier, stereotyped Afro-Cuban culture had become popular among white Cubans. The Machito band rode the wave of these stereotypes, taking advantage of the aperture that they afforded into the limelight. They used this window of opportunity to display open pride in real Afro-Cuban culture: Machito and Bauzá determined to call the band Machito and his Afro-Cubans. Bauzá later said that some "people didn't want that title; the people say, why the 'Afro?' I said [that we used this name] because the music we represent come[s] from Africa, and we come from Africa."[82] Machito and Bauzá were articulating an overt ideology of pan-Africanism.

While Bauzá looked for flexible horn players, he tried to find the hottest drummers on the scene. The pianist and bassist needed to be well rounded, with a mastery of Cuban rhythms, jazz harmony, and sight-reading. The band started with five horn players and four rhythm section players.[83] The band's tenor saxophonist, José "Pin" Madera, arranged many of Machito's early hits, giving him an important place in forging the Afro-Cubans' early sound.[84] Bauzá once said that most New York Latin bands of the period were "hinky-dink" affairs that lacked the harmonic sophistication and virtuosity to which he had become accustomed with Webb and Calloway. Aiming for Machito and his Afro-Cubans to stand out from the crowd, he called on his contacts in the black swing world for arrangements, hiring arranger John Bartee, one of Calloway's arrangers. Because Bartee had no expertise in Cuban music, Bauzá worked closely with him: leaving the harmonization to the arranger, he provided what he called "blueprints" consisting of lead sheets augmented with instructions for introductions and, more important, bass parts, which were central to the band's style. Bauzá and Bartee sometimes stayed up until 3:00 and 4:00 A.M. preparing music on days prior to rehearsals. The jazz arrangements gave the band a modern flavor, which, as Bauzá later expressed, appealed to young people in the United States: "The sound is familiar to them, and it really moved them. It was a good combination."[85]

Machito and Bauzá found a good balance in their collaboration. For all Bauzá's importance, Machito's grounding in Afro-Cuban roots—his expertise as a son singer and maraquero—was a central attraction. Bauzá himself testified that his own background in Euro-classical music, the danzón, and jazz did not qualify him to discern the finer points of Afro-Cuban rhythms: "The danzón orchestra is a different metric . . . but the son and all that is clave." He added that Machito knew "that side of the music better than me. He used to show how important the clave was in the music." Machito thus determined whether arrangements written by North Americans adhered to the tenets of Afro-Cuban rhythm; Bauzá explained that Machito would caution him to "be careful with the clave in there: three and two [clave], not two and three [clave]."[86] Because the other Latin bands in the States at the time were stylistically removed from black Cuban roots, Bauzá went to far as to assert that Machito "brought the clave to the United States."[87]

Machito and his Afro-Cubans debuted at the Park Palace/Plaza Ballroom on 110th Street and Fifth Avenue on December 3, 1940.[88] Finishing his stint with Calloway at the time, Bauzá did not participate, joining the band several months later.[89] One musician who heard the band at this venue remembers that Bauzá

looked very professional, his whole attitude and everything, the way he walked, the way he spoke, and the way he tapped off the band. It was, this guy knew what he was doing, definitely. And the band sounded marvelous. . . . I hadn't seen that in a [New York] Latin band. I had seen that in. . . . Duke and Basie and the rest of the bands. But in a Latin band I had never seen that type of professionalism.[90]

Bauzá also wowed local musicians when he switched from trumpet to alto saxophone on boleros; he wanted a large, lush sound in the reeds for these.

Cuban singers often improvise, commenting on immediate contexts such as local people or events in their *inspiraciones* (inspirations, improvised lyrics). Machito developed a set of vocal improvisations into a song about *sopa de pichón*, or pigeon soup, at the Park Palace/Plaza.[91] This song has a double meaning, because "pichón" was slang for marijuana (or as Machito once poetically called it, "that particular happy cigarette").[92] Machito also explained that the piece was his first foray into songwriting and that its original version astutely paid homage to popular and powerful characters on the streets of Spanish Harlem:

[Before this,] I never composed anything in my life. Never wrote anything. . . . I said to [pianist] Frank Ayala "okay get a vamp in D" so he start: bam barambam bam bi—[and I sang] "tiene que tomarte una sopa de pichón" [you have to try pigeon soup], and then start to improvise lyrics. . . . I used to mention in my inspiration[s] all the tough guys in the neighborhood so that what [sic] became a hit.[93]

His use of slang and appeal to local big shots epitomized Machito's grounding in the grassroots barrio scene. In keeping with this down-home flavor, Machito pursued the culinary line in his other top number of the period, "La paella." Machito, in fact, was an excellent cook. He once told the story of this song's genesis: Federico Pagani, a close friend and Machito's promoter

was walking out of a restaurant and we were talking and I say, "Federico, how are you?" He said: "*Bueno*, I just had paella. Did you ever try paella before?" You know, I got insulted, I said, . . . "I know how to *make* paella. How you going to ask me if

I ever taste it, a paella?" So I went in the subway that particular day, that it was a matinee at La Conga, and I wrote "La paella" in the train.[94]

Machito's spontaneity was essential to his style:

[If we] played "La paella" now, and fifteen minutes from now, we played "La paella" again, . . . it is another bash, because [it] depend[s] on the atmosphere, the dance, the way I feel, the way the musicians feel. So this is not a machine or just a computer that you give it one information and it make a thousand cop[ies]; no, [with] my computer, you['re] going to have a different information every time that you hit the button.[95]

Paradoxically, most of the Harlem Latin bands used less percussion than did the high society Latin bands that played downtown and capitalized on flashy drumming displays.[96] The Machito group was thus innovative not only in its grounding in Harlem-style African American jazz but also in its foregrounding of authentic Afro-Cuban percussion, something that neither uptown nor downtown Latin bands were doing at the time. In addition to Machito's improvised lyrics, the band's formidable drummers, especially the bongó players, improvised a great deal, in the manner of the Cuban son sextets.

In addition to working at the Park Palace/Plaza, Machito and his Afro-Cubans played in other Harlem and Bronx, or "uptown," venues, often booking jobs through the Puerto Rican promoter Federico Pagani. Pagani rented a hall, leaving the bar profits to the house and taking the cover charge for the band. Because ballroom owners knew that Machito would attract a large crowd, they eagerly solicited his band. Its combination of new and *típico* (typical, authentic) elements was a hit with working-class Latinos; as Bauzá said, Machito was "the king uptown."[97]

Downtown and Around the Country

Machito and his Afro-Cubans had its first break downtown, a two-week matinee at the Beachcomber nightclub, in December 1941.[98] As a result, Jack Harris, the owner of an elite venue called La Conga on 51st Street and Broadway, heard about Machito and asked him to substitute for his house band, which was led by Anselmo Sacassas.[99] As we have seen, stereotyped versions of the son (called rhumba) and the conga line–dance were all the rage among Paris and New York socialites at the time. The clientele at La Conga consisted largely of affluent Jewish Americans.[100] The club featured a Latin band for dancing and a group led by the club's owner, Jack Harris, for accompanying dance shows and comedians.[101] Machito and his Afro-Cubans made a favorable impression on Harris and were offered a steady job at La Conga in 1942.[102]

While Harris's own band was competent to accompany shows, it was a small group that lacked an original style. Astute in the music business, Harris decided to disband his own group and feature two Latin bands. Machito and his Afro-Cubans became the headlining act, playing for shows and dancing, while José Curbelo's group acted as a relief band, filling for dancing when the Machito group took breaks.[103] Machito and his Afro-Cubans began the evening's entertainment, playing light supper music. They continued with a few dance numbers and then accompanied the show, which featured dancers and top comedians such as Jackie Gleason and Dean Martin. After this, Curbelo played for dancing, and then the two bands alternated sets for dancing. Bauzá had attained his goal of creating a band that, like the top Harlem groups, was both rooted in dance music and polished enough to accompany high-class shows:[104] "gutbucket, but sophisticated," as Ellington's music was said to be.

Until the early 1940s, use of the conga drum (or, as Cubans call it, the *tumbadora*) was confined to street rumba; it was not generally used in dance bands. Several bandleaders in Cuba, the most notable of whom was Arsenio Rodríguez, began to incorporate it in an affirmation of black Cuban culture in this period. The innovation caught on. The incorporation of the conga into dance bands meshed with the cosmopolitan conga line–dance fad. Prior to its use as a regular part of the percussion section, the *quinto,* a small conga drum, had been used as a sort of prop in stereotyped conga dance shows (Desi Arnaz used it while singing "Babalú" on *I Love Lucy*). Riding this stereotype, Machito and his Afro-Cubans first used the conga during their engagement at La Conga. They soon transcended the stereotype, however, by using the drum in the manner that had been innovated by Arsenio Rodríguez rather than as a stereotyped version of carnival drumming. Arsenio's addition of the conga drum to son instrumentation added a heaviness, a grounded funkiness that black Cubans loved. Machito and his Afro-Cubans was the first band in New York to employ this innovation on a regular basis.[105]

Machito was drafted in 1943 and the band was stuck for a vocalist. Bauzá hired one of the best Latino singers in New York, the Puerto Rican, Polito Galíndez. He also invited Machito's sister Graciela, who was working with the Anacaona band in Cuba, to join them in New York. Graciela was a fine singer, versed in up-tempo dance numbers as well as boleros. She was thus more versatile than Galíndez and Machito, who were not bolero specialists. Like her brother, Graciela was grounded in Afro-Cuban culture and had mastered the intricacies of clave; she had even played claves in the Anacaona band. Machito stayed in the Army for less than a year, receiving an honorable discharge after suffering an accident during target practice in basic training. When Machito returned, Graciela stayed as a second lead vocalist. Machito and his Afro-Cubans now had a sibling team of lead singers, each with an individual style.[106]

Graciela's most requested features were witty numbers such as "Juanita y José," which recounts neighborhood gossip, and "Esto es lo ultimo," renamed "¡Sí, Sí, No, No!" in the Machito version. "¡Sí, Sí!" features an introduction in which Graciela repeats "¡Sí! ¡No!" and other refrains, including "¡Que lo tengo en la chi-chi!" (I have something in my chi-chi!) in a sexy, provocative tone of voice. When the band recorded this song in Mexico, producers asked them to remove the "chi-chi" reference because in Mexico, this term refers to a woman's breasts. Graciela explained, however, that in Cuban Spanish, "chi-chi" is used by children to refer to the head; she had originally interjected the word into the song when her head was cold[107] after arriving at La Conga during New York's severe winter months. Still, the song's sexy subtext is undeniable: such double-entendres had long been a staple of Cuban popular music.[108]

In addition to its regular job at La Conga, the band was often asked to play at other venues, and by 1944 Machito and his Afro-Cubans were getting offers for more work than they could handle. When the Cuban singer Marcelino Guerra arrived in New York in 1944, Bauzá put together a new band for him, calling it The Second Afro-Cubans.[109] Machito sang a few numbers with them in the beginning as an endorsement, but Guerra was an excellent singer in his own right and New York's Cuban music aficionados were soon making favorable comparisons of the Second Afro-Cubans and Machito's band.[110] The Afro-Cubans played steadily at La Conga for three years. This was a triumph. Bauzá later remembered that some of New York's established white Latin bandleaders had predicted that Machito's emphasis on black Cuban roots would preclude acceptance in swanky white downtown venues: "people said that my band would not work below 96th Street, but after we subbed for Sacassas at La Conga, we stayed there three years."[111]

As a result of this exposure, Robbins Music Publishing began to publish Machito's songs and Decca Records offered the band a contract. "Sopa de pichón," "La paella," "Nagüe," and "Que vengan los rumberos" became hits not only in the U.S. Latin market, but also in Cuba. The band also recorded several sides accompanying singer Miguelito Valdés, including "Eco" (an Afro-son invoking liturgical themes) and "El botellero" (which later served as the basis for Machito's theme song "Tanga"; see below).[112] The Afro-Cubans' records with Valdés sold well in Latin America because of the singer's great popularity and the high quality of the U.S.–made discs. North American recordings came to Cuba independently of radio stations during this period and were often sold to proprietors of jukeboxes. The Machito sides became hits on Cuban victrolas, as jukeboxes were called in Cuba; a local deejay remembers that Machito was "*un victrolero por excelencia*" (a *victrolero* par exellence).[113] Machito also started broadcasting live, coast to coast, from La Conga in 1942, featuring music published by Robbins. The band also broadcast a *Saludos Amigos* radio show for armed forces from several ballrooms, aimed at raising morale among Latino troops.[114] In 1946, Machito was filmed playing "Tanga," "Tambo," and "Nagüe" for a movie starring Betty Reilly. This segment was not used in the final version of the movie, but it was released as a short and played at Latino community theaters.[115]

Just what was the relationship between Latin America and the United States during these years? The U.S. government's Good Neighbor Policy, instituted to promote good relations with Latin America, had long been in place but was largely ignored until FDR revived it during World War II in efforts to foment hemispheric solidarity. The policy's architects contracted Walt Disney to make animated films with Latin American themes. While they claimed at the time that this was "in no wise a propaganda project," memos released after the war reveal that they had requested a series of "direct propaganda films" intended to demonstrate "a warm feeling of interracial friendship and solidarity, counteracting the Axis propaganda about Uncle Sam's racial prejudices."[116] Disney produced the animated feature films *Saludos Amigos* in 1943 and *The Three Caballeros* in 1945. Despite good intentions, these, like other nonanimated Hollywood efforts, projected stereotyped images of domesticated, sensual Latin Americans. The films were hits in the United States, but while they enjoyed some popularity in Latin America, they often engendered resentment: *Argentine Nights,* for example, was reportedly "hooted off the screen" in Buenos Aires.[117]

The bandleader Xavier Cugat, the Cuban singer/actor Desi Arnaz, and the Brazilian singer Carmen Miranda emerged as the top stars of the Latin film explosion. The 1940 film *Too Many Girls,* starring Arnaz, was a mix of various Latin elements, including a bullfight and a scene in which microbes dance the conga. The 1946 *Cuban Pete* casts Arnaz as a bandleader in New York City; his later television show with Lucille Ball brought the Cuban bandleader character into American living rooms. Inspired by Miguelito Valdés's success with "Babalú," Arnaz cemented his fame on *I Love Lucy* by singing this song while playing a conga, gyrating, and letting his hair fall down over his face. The transplantation of Cuban stereotypes, already out of context in their own country (this song was written by a white Cuban and is not associated with Afro-Cuban religion), to the United States is doubly ironic and may be insulting to some practitioners of Afro-Cuban religion. Most Anglos, of course, have no idea that the word Babalú is Yorùbá and not Spanish, and that the drum played by Arnaz normally accompanies carnival songs, and not Babalú songs. The "Brazilian Bombshell" Carmen Miranda appeared in eight films from 1939 to 1944, achieving fame by dancing with bananas on her head. Her self-parody, however, made subversive readings possible, and a dynamic of reappropriation lurked beneath the stereotyped veneer.[118] As we have seen, black Cubans had also availed themselves of this dynamic of reappropriation: as stereotyped versions of their culture entered the Cuban mainstream, they had taken advantage of the limited acceptance to assert their own culture on their own terms. Operating in this way, Machito and Bauzá rode the wave of Latino stereotypes while remaining firmly entrenched in the Latino and black communities. While they clearly could not have entered the limelight had it not been for the Latin film and music explosion, and while they never shirked mass taste, Machito and his Afro-Cubans always presented themselves on their own terms and never pandered to racist stereotypes. As a result, they not only empowered themselves, but gave all Americans the gift of real Afro-Cuban culture.

Machito and his Afro-Cubans played at La Conga until December 1945, when promoter Phil Lander offered them a job at the Mocambo Club in Miami Beach. At first, Bauzá was leery about playing in the South especially when he discovered the Afro-Cubans would be the first black band ever to ever work at this venue. The fact that the group included musicians of varying complexions made things even more problematic; "mixed" bands were of course forbidden in the segregated South. To avoid racist harassment, Lander promoted the band as a Cuban band from *Cuba,* assuming that if all the musicians were believed to be Latin Americans, southern racists would tolerate the varying skin tones. Lander even provided bouncers (obtained through underworld connections, it was rumored) to deter any problems. In order to maintain the illusion that this was an all-Cuban band, the African American musicians had to refrain from speaking in public, lest racist audience members notice their perfect skills in English: Bauzá enacted even the charade of pretending to interpret for them![119] Once, overlooking the North American musicians, a local man pointed to the Latino bongó player, saying, "I know he ain't Cuban!" Bouncers removed the accusing gentleman from the club.[120] This scenario points to the peculiar North American construction of race: while the "one-drop rule" was strictly applied to Anglos in the segregated South, mixed-race Latinos were tolerated.

During their stint in Miami, Machito and Bauzá took a week off to vacation in Cuba (they did not, however, perform there).[121] After the Miami job, the band was invited to Los Angeles to perform at the Club

Brazil for thirteen weeks.[122] When they returned to the East Coast, they were offered a job at the Concord Hotel, a swanky, predominantly Jewish, summer resort in the Catskill Mountains. The Afro-Cubans were so well received there that they were invited back every summer for twenty seasons. As Machito's son Mario Grillo remembers, "for the ten weeks we were up at the Concord Hotel . . . up in what they call the Borscht Belt, the Jewish Alps, we used to call them as kids. They were very big on Latin music."[123] During the war years many musicians were drafted and it became difficult for Bauzá to find players. Requiring expertise in Afro-Cuban rhythms, jazz harmonies, and sight-reading, the piano spot was especially demanding and hard to fill. When pianist Joe Loco was drafted in 1944, Bauzá sent for René Hernández from Cuba. Hernández could not play right away because of New York's union rules, so his first job with the band was in Miami.[124] Hernández became one of the most important members of the Afro-Cubans, making an indelible mark on the band as both a pianist and arranger.

René Hernández

We often look to one great figure to represent musical trends, ignoring the fact that artistic tides naturally feed off interacting currents. It is regrettable that it is impossible to tell the story of the whole Machito family because essential data about the band's arrangers—the individuals who actually wrote most of the band's music—were never documented. Salsa bandleader Eddie Palmieri acknowledges the arranger's power, with the common saying "the pen is mightier than the sword."[125] Failing to receive credit for their work has often resulted in feelings of being cheated on the part of arrangers. Having borne the indignities of working as a ghostwriter (an arranger whose work is not acknowledged), Chico O'Farrill once said that the arranger is a "ghost of a ghost."[126] For this reason, I shall pay special attention to Machito's arrangers.

Alejandro René Hernández was born on June 3, 1914, in Cienfuegos, Cuba, to a musical family; his father was a bandleader and his brother was one of the top trumpeters in the country. René Hernández moved to Havana as a teen, developing into a fine pianist and writer, working with several top dance bands, most notably Julio Cueva's group.[127] Bauzá sent for him to replace pianist Joe Loco in 1945. Arriving in 1945, Hernández initially stayed with Bauzá in his apartment on Columbus Avenue between 106th and 107th Streets, where Bauzá lived until his passing. Arriving shortly prior to the Afro-Cubans' stint in Miami, Hernández debuted with the band there.[128]

Although he was hired as a pianist, Hernández soon became the band's principal arranger. Because of his expertise with Cuban rhythms, Hernández wrote most of the Afro-Cubans' dance music, while their other principal arranger, Chico O'Farrill, handled most of the boleros and pieces written for concert performance.[129] While Bauzá and Machito counseled North American arrangers about the exigencies of clave, they did not do so with Hernández; Bauzá said that he told Hernández, "I ain't going to tell you what to write, you write, that's all. I used to do that with Bartee and all those guys because they didn't know that work, no, but you, you do what you want."[130]

Hernández was a largely self-taught arranger whose sensitive ears guided his analysis of the new sounds he heard in New York; he absorbed the new jazz influences like a sponge.[131] He arrived in the United States at an auspicious time: 1945 was the height of the bebop revolution as well as the dawn of the mambo explosion. As arranger Ray Santos puts it, "you had like two revolutions going on at the same time, one in Afro-Cuban music and one going on in jazz, and they both like met head on and absorbed each other."[132] Santos remembers Hernández taking in the new influences.

[Once,] Machito's band . . . [was] . . . alternating with Bud Powell. So you know, René would be sitting next to him, watching his hands, you know, picking up on the harmonies and all that. Because René had great ears; yeah, he could pick up anything. [He had] good ears, plus he was creative, [he had] good tasty creativeness.[133]

Hernández was thus primed to expand the conventions of Cuban dance music.[134] He used a keen sense of critical judgment in his incorporation of jazz influences. Instead of indiscriminately incorporating all aspects of the new language, he filtered in particular aspects that he felt would mix best with Afro-Cuban music; he determined that some jazz elements would fit clave, while others would not.[135]

In Cuba, Hernández had been writing for smaller bands with perhaps two trumpets and three saxophones. With Machito, he was writing for a bigger group, and the larger orchestral palette stimulated his creativity. Most Cuban jazz-tinged dance bands[136] used four-part block harmony in the saxophones, but avoided the modernistic harmonies of bebop. As the Afro-Cubans grew in size, Hernández rewrote their arrangements, transferring them from the original three or four saxophones and two trumpet setup to four or five saxophones and four trumpets, using larger, more adventurous voicings.[137] Having a baritone saxophone, and a top-notch player in Leslie Johnakins, especially expanded the possibilities, making larger, more open voicings possible.[138]

Even more important than his inventiveness in harmony was Hernández's highly developed sense of the clave; Ray Santos opines that "he was like the most clave arranger I've ever come across."[139] Intricately hooked into the percussion section, the bass parts of Cuban dance music impart each arrangement with a characteristic "feel," or kinetic motion. This is the aesthetic that we explored in chapter 2: interlocking rhythm and pitch structures create cycles of rhythmic motion that incite movement and create particular qualities of time. Hernández was a master composer of bass parts, and Bauzá argued that his creativity with the bass was a crucial element distinguishing Hernández from his peer writers, who often employed standard bass lines.[140] Hernández often gave bass patterns to the baritone saxophone, a practice later used by many salsa arrangers.[141]

Another of Hernández's most impressive qualities was his ability to stay fresh, to continuously think of new ideas in spite of the large volume of work that he produced. In addition to arranging, Hernández composed many original pieces for the Afro-Cubans. His creativity was put to good use in the Machito band, for which he produced such diverse works as the percussion-driven vocal arrangements "Llora Timbero" and "Tumba el quinto," to smoother dancer-pleasing mambo compositions such as "Zambia," jazz-oriented material such as "Wild Jungle," and novelty numbers such as the pop-orientalist hits "Asia Minor" and "Oboe Mambo." Hernández was known to his friends as a cheerful person; Ray Santos says "you can actually hear this in his music: he's a happy writer, yeah. His arrangements, his riffs, everything sounds happy."[142] This exuberance is expressed in the catchy ease of "Zambia" and, combined with fiery syncopations and exuberant bopisms, in the innovative "Wild Jungle."

Hernández took advantage of his versatility by writing for several bands, emerging as the dominating force in New York Latin arranging in the 1940s and 1950s.[143] As Bauzá explains, Hernández created different styles for each group:

You [know], one thing about René, he had such a talented [way] that he [could] make arrangement[s] for each different artist in their own style. Because some guys, they just write the same way for everybody—not René. René write for Vicentico [Valdés], . . . it sounds like one way. [He] used to write for Panchito Rizet, was another world. Write for Machito, it was another world.[144]

Hernández's ability with the pen astounded his associates, who remember him writing at bars and in the subway.[145] He had an eccentric mode of operation: while most people in the music business rely on the telephone to get work, Hernández purposely set up his apartment on 76th Street near Riverside Drive without a telephone because calls distracted him. When people wanted to hire Hernández, they either contacted him through Bauzá, or simply approached him at gigs. He was in such demand that he did not need a telephone to get work.[146]

Hernández was also a formidable pianist; indeed, he was originally brought to the Afro-Cubans to be a sideman, not an arranger. While many pianists in New York could play Cuban dance music, Hernández's facility with Cuban rhythms, combined with his sight-reading skill, distinguished him from many of his peers. As a solo improviser, his playing was tasty and rhythmically clean, with tinges of jazz based in a solidly Cuban sound.[147] In 1965, Hernández left Machito to work with bandleader Tito Rodríguez, and when Rodríguez settled in Puerto Rico, Hernández followed him there.[148] Hernández's unique blend, which combined bebop with clave, was the core of the Machito band's contribution. Hernández succumbed to a heart attack in December 1977.[149]

Afro-Cuban Jazz

African American saxophonist Leslie Johnakins stands out among Machito's sidemen, acing the rhythmic baritone parts. At first, however, it was difficult; he remembers:

I got confused with the rhythm. I was used to having one drum, and here I joined a band with three drums: a conga drum, a bongó, plus timbales, and then there was a bass, and a piano. And you know, [with] the complicated rhythms of the Latin music, there's somebody hitting on every beat, and I didn't, couldn't find which beat was the one *I* was supposed to hit on [*laughs*]![150]

Johnakins's dedication to the band as a longtime member, combined with René Hernández's baritone-heavy arrangements, made a lasting contribution to the style and orchestration of Cuban dance music.[151] The use of a baritone saxophone was innovative for Cuban bands, which usually only used altos and tenor. The baritone changed the orchestral color and added a new way to intensify the bass part, which was often given prominence as the soul of the orchestral rhythm. In addition to his important contributions to ensemble work, Johnakins was often featured as a jazz soloist, holding forth on tunes such as "Mambo Inn," "Zambia," "Tanga," and "Hall of the Mambo King."[152] Because many of the Machito band's recordings feature guest soloists, the fact that Johnakins soloed so often in live performances is often overlooked.

Machito and his Afro-Cubans were adept at playing straight-ahead jazz as well as Cuban music; as early as the California job, they had played North American popular songs by ear when requested.[153] Timbales player

Ubaldo Nieto was adept at trap drums and on the Concord jobs, he played traps on North American music when the Anglo band that Machito alternated with was not able to play. Machito occasionally worked at Harlem's famed Apollo Theater, both as a featured act and behind established singers, once accompanying Billie Holiday and playing on Harry Belafonte's recording "Lean on Me."[154]

As Latin music caught on with Anglos, Latin bands began to record North American popular songs to the accompaniment of Cuban rhythms. Former Machito pianist Joe Loco started a band specializing in this style, gaining fame with Latinized versions of "Tenderly" and other songs. Machito participated in this trend, recording "Tea for Two," and an entire LP of Irving Berlin material. Recorded in 1949, Machito's best-selling record was a novelty number, "Asia Minor," which featured oboist Mitch Mitchell playing mock snake-charmer music. This success led to a follow-up called "Oboe Mambo," which was especially popular in Cuba.[155] Like Ellington's version of Grieg's *Peer Gynt Suite*, José Madera's arrangement of "Hall of the Mambo King" is a jazz-inflected take-off on the Norwegian composer's piece. "Hall of the Mambo King" exemplifies not only Madera's skillful writing, but Bauzá's genius as a bandleader: it juxtaposes sections featuring the swung eighth notes of jazz with sections featuring the even eighths and clave rhythms of Cuban music. Even in these so-called novelty numbers, then, the band exemplified musical innovation and excellence. Their success was also rooted in versatility. The Afro-Cubans were in tune with the various constituencies among their fans, playing several types of music; as Graciela put it, the band "knew how to please an audience."[156] The Machito group appealed to downtown as well as uptown audiences, effecting a reappropriation of Latin stereotypes that did not put anybody off, remaining faithful to roots-level aesthetics while gaining success in Anglo venues.

"Tanga"

In the early period, Machito and his Afro-Cubans' theme song, which they used to open and close sets, was Chano Pozo's composition "Nagüe." During their stint at La Conga, however, they adopted a new theme, "Tanga," which has been touted as the "first Afro-Cuban jazz composition."[157] "Tanga's" origin is controversial. An oft-told story recounts "Tanga's" purported genesis: while Machito was in the Army, during a break at La Conga, the band's pianist started playing a vamp from the introduction to "El botellero," a tune that the band had recorded with Miguelito Valdés. The bassist joined in and the resulting catchy sound caught Bauzá's ear. The next day, at the band's rehearsal at the Park Palace/Plaza,

Bauzá asked the pianist and bassist to replicate what they had done. Bauzá continued by aurally dictating horn parts to create a pyramidal texture with modernistic upper chordal extensions. He asked some of the band's African American musicians to play jazz solos over it. This was the realization of the experiments that Bauzá had effected with Gillespie and Cozy Cole in the Calloway band: a blend of Afro-Cuban rhythms and African American jazz improvisation.[158] Regarding the tune's name, Machito said that the Puerto Rican songwriter Pedro Flores heard an early performance, remarking that the sound was "as exciting as tanga," which he claimed to be an "African" word for marijuana.[159] When Machito returned from the service, he developed a set of improvised lyrics based on the interjection "¡Machito llegó!" (Machito is here!), which he inserted between chorus statements of "¡Tanga!" Machito often introduced the piece with the vocal interjection 'boru 'buya, a contraction of the Yorùbá-Cuban greeting ìbo rú di (ì) 'bo ye, which is bestowed upon the high priests of Santería, babalawos.[160] "Tanga's" melding of bebop with Afro-Cuban liturgical references crystallized Machito's vision of Afro-diasporic unity.

Bauzá published "Tanga" with Robbins Music,[161] but some charge that because others played important roles in its genesis, he did not have a legitimate claim to authorship. One longtime member band member believes that "Tanga" was the brainchild of Machito's saxophonist Johnny Nieto.[162] Strangely, in his many interviews, Bauzá never recounted the commonly told anecdote about "Tanga's" genesis, while Machito did. But according to this very story, Machito was not present when "Tanga" was created; he was in the Army. One thing, however, is clear: "Tanga" was forged aurally and collaboratively. Like many bandleaders in both Cuba and the United States, Bauzá worked by ear, adapting ideas from sidemen. Ray Santos remembers that "this was part of Machito's style, of Mario Bauzá's style: head arrangements: He'd dictate riffs to the brass, the saxophones right on the bandstand."[163] Duke Ellington also worked in this way, utilizing his musicians' ideas; muddy authorship comes with the territory of the aural tradition.

That "Tanga" was played strictly by ear presented problems when new musicians joined the band: each player knew what he was supposed to play but no one could teach new players their parts. As a result, Bauzá eventually asked René Hernández to notate the arrangement. Johnakins remembers:

as new men come in . . . we were beginning to have problems playing our own theme song. So [laughs], Mario had René write it down. And he even come to me and ask me, "At this spot what note were you playing? And what beat did you hit on when you just—" and I told him. And do you know, he put it down verbatim on paper.[164]

But the musicians were so accustomed to playing "Tanga" by ear that they were hard-pressed to capture its feeling from written music. Bauzá decided that it was best to continue playing it by ear:

We be looking at it on the paper, we couldn't play it [*laughs*]! It sounds unusual . . . [but] trying to play that, what is written, and still inject the feeling that you know you had over the years from playing it repetitiously—it didn't make it. So he just took the arrangement out of the book, threw it away, and said we'd do better without music![165]

Serving as the theme for Machito's live radio broadcasts from La Conga on radio station WOR, a large audience was exposed to "Tanga."[166] Although it includes a vocal section, "Tanga" is primarily an instrumental piece featuring improvised solos; the jazz sound no doubt contributed to its attraction to Anglos.[167]

We Both Speak African

Bauzá's aesthetic vision and the informal lessons on Cuban music that he had given Dizzy Gillespie in the Calloway band left a strong impression on Gillespie. He states in his memoirs that he had long wanted to incorporate Afro-Cuban percussion into his music, and when he started his own big band, "that was the first thing I thought of. I had to have a conga drummer."[168] He asked Bauzá to recommend someone, and Bauzá thought of conguero, singer, dancer, and composer Chano Pozo, who had recently arrived from Cuba.

A microcosm of the mutually enriching encounter between Afro-Cuban and African American musicians that took shape at midcentury, the Gillespie/Pozo collaboration had a lasting effect on North American music. Gillespie developed into an acknowledged expert and innovator in Cuban music, widely known and respected in Latin music circles. For his part, Pozo had a significant impact on jazz and other forms of North American music.[169] Luciano "Chano" Pozo y González was born on January 7, 1915, in the Pan con Timba barrio of Havana. He made a name for himself in Cuba as a composer of catchy popular songs, a bandleader, *conguero,* dancer, and consummate showman. Pozo founded the acclaimed carnival band (or comparsa) Los Dandys de Belén as well as a dance band, El Conjunto Azul. After arriving in New York in 1946 Pozo recorded with Miguelito Valdés and Machito in addition to his high-profile work with Gillespie. A somewhat wild character rumored to be active in underworld circles, Pozo was said to have wrecked a series of autos and to harbor in his body several gunshot slugs that he had received in Cuba.[170]

Pozo's songs made creative use of wordplay. Based in vocables, his "Paramparampampín" once won a carnival song contest, while "Blen, blen, blen" outlines the "three" part of the clave rhythm. His "Pin pin, cayó Berlin, pin pon cayó Japón" comments on the end of World War II (Pin pin falls Berlin, pin pan, falls Japan). Also informing his artistry was Pozo's involvement with Afro-Cuban religion and the Abacuá secret society. He was a fine dancer and a flashy showman, gaining attention with his drum/dance routines, which incorporated Afro-Cuban liturgical songs. As a conga player Pozo was noted for his creativity, but several experts have said that his abilities as a composer and showman surpassed his talents as a drummer.[171]

Pozo arrived in New York in May 1946 as a member of the Cacha and Pepe Vásquez dance team. Miguelito Valdés took this group to La Conga, where Machito and his Afro-Cubans were working, arranging for them to do an impromptu dance show. As Bauzá later remembered, Pozo was characteristically dapper, dressed in white, but was unable to dance because he was recovering from gunshot wounds. Instead of dancing, Pozo called on his indomitable charisma, sitting Pepe in a chair, putting a tablecloth around his neck and pretending to give him a haircut. Then Pepe started to dance with Cacha. This led to an engagement for the dance team at La Conga (although Pozo was unable to participate due to his wounds).[172]

Singer Miguelito Valdés and Pozo were close personal friends, Valdés acting as a guide (or as Bauzá put it, "a father") to Pozo in the United States. When Valdés left Pozo's side to honor an engagement in California he asked Bauzá to help his friend find work. Bauzá soon introduced Pozo to Gillespie, who asked the conguero to join his big band, which was preparing a debut at Carnegie Hall.[173] Gillespie's Carnegie Hall concert of September 29, 1947, was historic for many reasons. It featured Gillespie's innovative composition "Things to Come," aptly titled for its dissonant group-improvisation coda that foreshadows Sun Ra's later work. The concert also presented Pozo in the innovative "Afro-Cuban Drum Suite," a one-movement piece composed in several sections. The suite begins with Gillespie and Pozo in a duo improvisation that counterpoises fiery bebop lines over fluctuating conga rhythms, continues with an orchestrated section, and climaxes with Pozo singing, playing, and dancing Abacuá repertoire.[174]

Pozo also had an impact on Gillespie as a composer. While Gillespie's standard "A Night in Tunisia" was composed in 1942, he rewrote it, adding the well-known Latin-inflected bass line after Pozo introduced him to Cuban rhythms.[175] Collaborating with arranger Gil Fuller, Gillespie and Pozo coauthored "Manteca," which eventually became a Cubop anthem.

Its germ idea and A section was Pozo's brainchild, featuring an uncanny, catchy juxtaposition of bass, percussion, saxophone, and trumpet lines. Gillespie and Fuller added a jazzy bridge and claimed credit for the composition along with Pozo.[176] Pozo and Gillespie also coauthored the Cubop standards "Tin Tin Deo," and, with Fuller and George Russell, "Cubano Be, Cubano Bop." The static harmonies of Cuban music made their way into jazz through these compositions, influencing modal improvisation, which uses scales, rather than chords, as structural building blocks, and which became a standard technique in jazz beginning in the 1950s. "Cubana Be" is often cited as the first modal composition in jazz.[177]

The Gillespie/Pozo collaboration touched a primitivist nerve: jazz writer Marshall Stearns wrote that "Pozo crouched in the center of the stage and flailed a many-voiced conga drum with blistered hands" in Carnegie Hall.[178] To the in-group, however, the Gillespie/Pozo collaboration celebrated real—not stereotyped—African-based ties. Pozo gave Gillespie's sidemen informal lessons in Afro-Cuban music, handing out percussion instruments in the band bus, dictating rhythms and explaining how the parts fit together. He also taught Gillespie's musicians Afro-Cuban liturgical songs.[179] Gillespie, in fact, developed into a competent conga player as a result of these lessons, playing the drum himself in his later aggregations. Gillespie had long felt drawn to Africa, and even referred obliquely to anthropologist Melville Hersokvits's espousal of the study of Africanisms in his memoirs: "I've always felt polyrhythmic from a long way back. Maybe I'm one of those 'African survivals' that hung on after slavery."[180] He added:

A student of our music, if he goes back far enough, will find that the main source of our music is the music of Africa. The music of the Western Hemisphere . . . is primarily of African origin. . . . The Brazilian Africans created the samba, the West Indians created the calypso, the Cubans created the rhumba and various other rhythms, and my own is blues, spirituals. All of them were different and showed different characteristics. Yet they're together, so it was a natural thing for me to fall under the influence of these different rhythms.[181]

Just as working with black American musicians bolstered Bauzá's sense of himself as a black Cuban, exposure to Afro-Cuban traditions fostered Gillespie's search for his own African past.

Tragically, Chano Pozo was shot to death in 1948 in Harlem's Rio Café, possibly as a result of a dispute regarding a debt. As noted, the conga drum had been used only in carnival music and the rumba until the early 1940s, when it was incorporated in dance bands as a result of the influence of Arsenio Rodríguez. Pozo was innovative in bringing the conga to the fore as a solo instrument in the concert setting, and his short career thus had a lasting and vital influence: featuring conga drums in jazz, rock, and funk bands eventually became standard practice, a mainstay of North American music.[182]

Cubop Flights

The prominent bandleader Stan Kenton developed an interest in Afro-Cuban music, saying that "Rhythmically, the Cubans play the most exciting stuff. We won't copy them exactly, but we will copy some of their devices . . . And while we keep moving toward the Cubans rhythmically, they're moving toward us melodically. We both have a lot to learn."[183] Teaming up with Machito's percussion section and Bauzá in 1948, Kenton recorded his own arrangement of "The Peanut Vendor" ("El manicero") and, as a tribute to the Afro-Cubans, a tune called "Machito."[184] "The Peanut Vendor," recorded in December 1948 featured Carlos Vidal on conga, José Mangual on bongó, and Machito on maracas. The arrangement combines touches of Brazilian acoustic guitar played by Laurindo Almeida with the tune's catchy theme couched in exciting, dissonant harmonies.[185] Following the record date, Vidal joined Kenton's band as a featured soloist, fulfilling the role that Pozo played in Gillespie's band.[186] Bauzá applauded Kenton's efforts and enthusiastically participated in the project. He felt, however, that the result failed to capture the Afro-Cuban "nitty-gritty," going so far as to say that Kenton was essentially a "modern version of Paul Whiteman."[187] Still, Kenton's experiments were groundbreaking in their application of a bold new style of big band writing to Cuban rhythms.

Machito's jazz forays received favorable attention in *Downbeat* and *Metronome* magazines, and soon, the Afro-Cubans were playing at jazz venues such as the Royal Roost, Birdland, Bop City, the Clique, and the Apollo Theater. Jazz soloists such as Charlie Parker, Dexter Gordon, Zoot Sims, Brew Moore, Johnny Griffin, or Stan Getz often appeared with them.[188] Machito's percussionists José Mangual, Carlos Vidal, and Patato also sat in informally at bebop jam sessions in clubs such as the famed Minton's Playhouse. Bop musicians enjoyed having the drummers play with their groups as much as they enjoyed soloing with Machito.[189]

In 1948 Norman Granz decided to record Charlie Parker and tenorist Flip Phillips with Machito and his Afro-Cubans. A session was set up and Granz suggested that the band record "El manicero"; as the best-known Cuban song in the United States, this was a good choice from a business standpoint. Parker, however, felt that "El manicero"'s idiosyncratic syncopation, which outlines the clave-related cinquillo rhythm, would be difficult for him to negotiate. At first, Bauzá could not understand why this musical master would hesitate to play what most Cubans consider a bare-bones simple tune. Later, however, he realized that while the cinquillo is eminently hummable for Cubans, it embodies a subtle logic that is diffi-cult for non-Cubans to grasp; Bauzá thought highly of Parker for recog-nizing this.[190]

After agreeing not to record "El manicero," the band played a Graciela feature called "Mango mangüé." This piqued Parker's interest. After listen-ing, he played along with the arrangement. Machito remembers,

> We played ["Mango mangüé"] once, he says: "Play again." He put together his instrument and he played all through the arrangement, like he know that number for twenty years. . . . That fellow had a photograph[ic memory], a machine in his brain. . . . He was thinking ahead maybe ten, fifteen, twenty bars, with ideas.[191]

Parker, however, remained humble: Machito remembers him saying that "I could do better than that, let's play [it] again. . . . Forgive me."[192] In the first section of the recording, Parker paraphrases the melody, his character-istic improvisatory flights perfectly following the arrangement's twists and turns. In the second section, he solos over the tune's *montuno* (or vamp).

In addition to "Mango mangüé," this session produced "Okidoke," "Repetition," and "No Noise, Parts One and Two," arranged by John Bar-tee.[193] At one point during the session Parker improvised while bongó player Chino Pozo vocalized drum syllables.[194] This experiment was not recorded, but it served as the basis for a later recording called "Bucabú," which features tenor saxophonist Flip Phillips improvising while Machito's percussionists scatted Afro-Cuban drum patterns.[195] Parker later recorded two LPs, *South of the Border* and *Fiesta*, with Machito's rhythm section, fea-turing Brazilian as well as Cuban numbers.

On February 11, 1949, Machito and his Afro-Cubans played in a Norman Granz production at Carnegie Hall, sharing the stage with luminaries such as Duke Ellington and Lester Young. Slated to solo on "Tanga" with the band, the eminently unreliable Charlie Parker did not show up, so Granz substituted Sonny Stitt.[196] An LP called *The Jazz Scene*, presenting music by all the concert's participants (along with attractive photos of the bands), was released to commemorate the event. Machito and his Afro-Cubans' par-ticipation in this prestigious project demonstrates that their place in North American music had been recognized. Machito, for example, began to par-ticipate in Norman Granz's Jazz at the Philharmonic concert series. Granz wanted Machito's band to record a multimovement work for concert per-formance featuring guest soloists Charlie Parker and Flip Phillips. To com-pose an appropriate work, Granz enlisted a young Cuban arranger who was quickly ascending the New York jazz ranks: Chico O'Farrill.

Chico O'Farrill

Arturo "Chico" O'Farrill Theye was born in Havana on December 28, 1921, to well-to-do parents of Irish and German extraction; his father was an attorney in the employ of the government and the family owned land in the countryside. Many affluent Cubans sent their male children abroad for high school, and the O'Farrills had an extra incentive because their son played hooky habitually. They felt that a regimented environment would be beneficial for the boy, and he was sent to the Riverside Military Academy in Gainesville, Georgia. His roommates there enjoyed listening to the top dance bands of the day on the radio, and O'Farrill became a jazz fan. He took up the trumpet, and in his senior year wowed his friends by playing Bunny Berigan's solo on "Marie" verbatim. He also studied jazz writing on his own, arranging "Tuxedo Junction" for the school band. When Cab Calloway played in Gainesville, O'Farrill got wind that there was a Cuban in the band and met Mario Bauzá.

After graduating, O'Farrill returned to Cuba to fulfill his family's expectations that he follow in his father's footsteps and study law at the University of Havana. His heart, however, was in jazz. O'Farrill played weekend gigs with Cuban jazz-tinged dance bands, dedicating himself to music rather than his studies. He found a new circle of friends who were jazz lovers, listening to records with them in homes and going to jam sessions.[197]

While developing as an improviser, O'Farrill became more and more interested in writing. He began to take private composition lessons with the dean of Cuban arrangers, Félix Guerrero, who had also taught the pre-eminent Cuban bandleader, Pérez Prado. Guerrero himself had received training from Nadia Boulanger and had befriended the likes of Stravinsky and Gershwin.[198] O'Farrill became enamored of modernistic Euro-classical music, once saying that "one of my greatest influences was Stravinsky and his compositions Petrushka and the Rite of Spring."[199] He also became acquainted with the work of Cuban composers Amadeo Roldán and Alejandro García Caturla who, as mentioned earlier, had created an Afro-Cubanist style of concert music by blending black Cuban rhythms with modernist innovations. Influenced by this movement, O'Farrill began writing a jazz suite based on Afro-Cuban themes in 1945.[200]

O'Farrill wrote for Isidro Pérez's band, one of the most jazz-oriented groups in Cuba, gaining an opportunity to express his modernist bent by writing a modernist arrangement of "Deep Purple" in ¾ meter.[201] Noting that O'Farrill did not yet know about Bauzá's Cubop experiments at this time, music critic Luc Delannoy argues that O'Farrill is the "true creator of Cubop."[202] Isidro Pérez's band, however, had great difficulty in finding work; there was little demand for strongly jazz-influenced music in Cuba. O'Farrill moved to New York City, later saying that "going to New York was an act of rebellion"; he felt that "if this orquesta is not good enough for Cuba, Cuba is not good enough for me." A comparison of O'Farrill's and Bauzá's backgrounds and their statements regarding motivations for coming to the United States and their attractions to jazz is instructive. Both were versed in European classical music and interested in pursuing jazz as a career, and both were looking for economic opportunities. But while Bauzá was a working-class Afro-Cuban musician who linked jazz with black Cuban culture, O'Farrill was an upper-class white Cuban who initially saw many differences between jazz and traditional Cuban music.

As we saw with the help that Socarras gave Bauzá and Valdés gave Pozo, Cuban expatriate musicians often aided their countrymen upon arrival to New York: Bauzá helped orient O'Farrill. O'Farrill also became friends with the brilliant bop trumpeter Fats Navarro, a Florida native of partial Cuban descent, who introduced him to the bebop scene. For his part, Bauzá introduced O'Farrill to the bandleader Noro Morales and O'Farrill began writing for him. O'Farrill also gained employment ghostwriting for the formidable bebop arranger Walter Gil Fuller. Under this system, Fuller accepted more work than he could personally complete, meting out portions of arrangements to a stable of arrangers who worked for him. The ghostwriters were given specific instructions, for example, on the manner to harmonize specific passages. Working in this way, O'Farrill contributed to Gillespie's big band without receiving credit, working, for example, on the "Manteca" arrangement.[203]

Benny Goodman, savvy to twists and turns in the music business, formed a so-called "Bebop Band" in 1948. In the following year, hearing that Goodman planned to use Fuller's ghostwriting team, O'Farrill offered Goodman his "Undercurrent Blues" in efforts to avoid Fuller again taking credit for his work. Goodman was favorably impressed, not only consenting to record "Undercurrent Blues" but hiring O'Farrill as a staff arranger. This, of course, was a "dream come true" for the young writer, as he later remembered. Goodman is also responsible for bestowing the nickname "Chico" upon O'Farrill.[204] Goodman introduced O'Farrill to Stravinsky, a meeting that was memorable for the young arranger.[205] O'Farrill learned an important lesson from Goodman: influenced by Stan Kenton's "progressive jazz," he once wrote a modernist arrangement of "Goodnight Sweetheart" for Goodman. After hearing it the bandleader immediately said, "Chico, this is not the Kenton orchestra." O'Farrill learned that for an arranger it is always imperative to keep in mind for whom one is writing.

In spite of the fact that, under the influence of the Afro-Cubanist school of Cuban concert music, he had begun work on an Afro-Cuban suite in 1945, O'Farrill had never been inordinately interested in Cuban music. As he testified, Cuban dance rhythms only began to pique his interest after he "heard the Machito band." Machito's music was different than the traditional music that he knew in Cuba: "I came to New York and I heard the Machito orchestra and I was really surprised that this orchestra was so advanced. . . . I could say that for the first time I was really interested in Cuban music; I heard sounds that attracted me. I heard, you know, harmonies that were rich."[206] He added: "It was Afro-Cuban jazz. *Jazz:* that word was very important for me. Jazz, it was jazz. It was jazz-oriented. It was rich, rich as any form of jazz, and it was very aggressive; instrumentally it was rich too. That's what attracted me; otherwise I don't think that I would have been interested."[207]

Mario Bauzá asked O'Farrill to arrange several boleros for Graciela, and Norman Granz commissioned him to write an instrumental composition, "Gone City," for the Afro-Cubans to record. "Gone City" begins with a bebop flourish in the style of Dizzy Gillespie's big band and then buckles down into an Afro-Cuban bass line doubled in the baritone saxophone. O'Farrill let go with modernistic harmonies in his bolero arrangements for Graciela. For example, when the voice returns after an instrumental interlude in "Alma con alma," he injects a deceptive cadence before falling back to the tonic. Although she was an experienced singer, Graciela had not previously encountered such harmonies and found them so difficult that she once asked Bauzá to stop using O'Farrill's arrangements. Bauzá, however, convinced her to accustom herself to the style.[208] In general, Bauzá used O'Farrill for boleros and concert music; O'Farrill was not so sensitive to the clave as was Hernández. As Ray Santos put it, "René Hernández was a Cuban arranger with a jazz approach, and . . . Chico O'Farrill is a jazz arranger with a Cuban approach.[209] Still, O'Farrill wrote much danceable music, such as "Vaya Niña" and a version of "Carambola" that embeds polytonal chords in a clave base.

Norman Granz was impressed with O'Farrill's ability to merge new jazz trends with Cuban music, and when Afro-Cuban jazz became commercially viable, he commissioned O'Farrill to write an "Afro-Cuban Jazz Suite,"[210] that was recorded on the Clef label on December 21, 1950.[211] The suite is in five movements, each of which represents a different Afro-Cuban rhythm; the suite thus constitutes a compendium of Cuban musical styles. O'Farrill found it paradoxical that his best-known work is based on traditional Cuban genres, saying: "That's the irony of it: I was never an expert on Cuban music. What I did, for example, in that suite was purely instinctive; I never was an expert on Cuban music, frankly, and I never researched it, and I never paid too much attention to it really. They asked me, "write a suite, Chico," [so] I just wrote according to my best understanding, letting my jazz sensibility to guide me most of the time."[212]

After leaving the Afro-Cubans, O'Farrill did not cease to expand himself musically. In the early 1950s he embarked upon an ambitious course of private study and composed several extended works for concert performance. [213] In the mid-1970s O'Farrill began to write commercial music, composing Spanish-language jingles for companies such as McDonald's and doing arrangements for the likes of Ringo Starr and David Bowie. O'Farrill rarely wrote jazz-oriented material in this period, but after several years he returned to jazz to record two Grammy-nominated CDs. His *Carambola* CD includes a remake of the original Afro-Cuban Jazz Suite featuring the fiery tenor saxophonist soloist Mario Rivera (discussed in chapter 4), playing the part that Charlie Parker played in the original version of the suite.

Continuity and Divergence in the African Diaspora

As we have seen, Machito's innovations in Cubop were picked up by other bands. In 1957, promoters wanted Machito and his Afro-Cubans to record a new jazz-oriented LP to cement its high profile in this field. Its liner notes explained that the LP was named *Kenya* to commemorate the toppling of colonialism in Africa.[214] Recorded in December 1957 in the heart of Spanish Harlem at the Oddfellows Temple (which had a theater and a recording studio), *Kenya* features compositions and arrangements by René Hernández, A. K. Salim, and Ray Santos, as well as soloists altoist Cannonball Adderly and trumpeter Joe Newman. While the band rehearsed the charts prior to the session, the featured soloists did not; Santos remembers that the first takes of Cannonball's fantastically rhythmic solos "knocked everyone out," and that on following takes, he played equally good, but different solos.[215] Although he was hired as a guest artist and not a section man, Cannonball enjoyed playing with Machito so much that he asked to be allowed to lead the saxophone section on "Blues à la Machito."[216] Bauzá had met the African American arranger A. K. Salim in Paris, was impressed with his work, and asked him to participate in the project. As he had with Bartee, Bauzá provided Salim with bass lines and instructions on clave rhythms.[217] He wrote the arrangements that featured improvisation by guest soloists. René Hernández contributed exciting original Afro-Cuban jazz compositions, enlisting big-band's timbres and modernist harmonies within a percussion-soaked Afro-Cuban sensibility; his "Wild Jungle," for example, is an innovative work that cements

Hernández's place in the history of (pan-)American music. Bauzá took the African theme of the *Kenya* LP seriously, preparing for the project by consulting with the Nigerian bandleader Olatunji and looking for books on Kenya in the library (he later remembered finding material on "Swahili and Congo," but nothing on Kenya).[218]

As noted in chapter 2, the current academic vogue of stressing the strategic construction of social reality sometimes overlooks aesthetic common ground in the African diaspora; a central paradox of the diaspora is that while its parts diverge in many ways, they also share much. Issues of diasporic continuity and divergence come to a head in the critical reception of Cubop. John Storm Roberts writes that some of Charlie Parker's solos with Machito were not aesthetically successful, that his figures were sometimes out of sync with clave.[219] Experts such as Machito's arranger Ray Santos agree that some parts of the Parker/Machito *South of the Border* and *Fiesta* albums are rhythmically stilted.[220] For his part, Bauzá felt that Machito's guest soloists usually worked well with the band, but he cited a few notable exemptions: Harry "Sweets" Edison, for example, was hired as a soloist for Machito's Afro-Cuban Jazz Suite but excused himself, saying that "this is not my game."[221] Bauzá added that drummer Buddy Rich, who did record the suite, was not tuned in to the clave[222] and that Lee Konitz's first attempt to play with the Afro-Cubans ended abruptly because he was rhythmically not in sync. Konitz, however, later surpassed this stumbling block and joined Machito as a regular member.[223]

Ray Santos opines that while Parker's solos with Machito were occasionally out of clave in the sense that his figures do not refer literally to Cuban signature rhythms, the Machito/Parker collaboration was nevertheless supremely successful. The aborted "El manicero" session is interesting in this light. As mentioned, Parker refused to record this tune likely because it insistently emphasizes the clave rhythm in a way that is impossible to elide. Santos, Roberts, and most fans, however, agree that while the Bird flights in the "Mango mangüé" recording do not refer literally to clave, Parker was nevertheless rhythmically locked in.[224] As Chico O'Farrill put it, while Parker was humble as he faced Afro-Cuban music, "when you listen to it, you know it is *his* music."[225]

Mambo Time

During the 1950s, the mambo rose as a high-profile dance craze. Although it was associated largely with the Cuban bandleader Dámaso Pérez Prado, both the word "mambo" and its associated style existed prior to

Pérez Prado's rise. Of Kongo (Central African) origin, the term refers to liturgical songs in the Afro-Cuban Palo (or Kongo-derived) subculture.[226]

In 1938 the danzón group Arcaño y sus Maravillas recorded Orestes López's composition entitled "Mambo" with the usual charanga instrumentation of violins, flutes, and rhythm section.[227] López's "Mambo," however, dispensed with the sectional form and modulations typical to the danzón, consisting instead of a short introduction followed by a montuno (or vamp) overlaid with flute improvisations and a vocal chorus. Instead of outlining the cinquillo rhythm as is customary, the timbalero played a pulse on a mounted cowbell. Arcaño also incorporated the conga drum. Deemphasizing European melodies and employing rumba and son influences, Arcaño's "Mambo" reworked the danzón, Africanizing it, and labeling it "danzón de nuevo ritmo" (danzón with a new beat). Noting that this new style boils down to a montuno overlaid with improvised riffs, one observer called it "ordered anarchy."[228] Around the same time, bandleader Arsenio Rodríguez was innovating by incorporating influences from the Afro-Cuban Palo religion in his music, and, most significant, adding riff-based finales called mambos (or *diablos*, devils) to his arrangements.[229] Cubans soon began using the term *mambo* to refer to arrangements based on riff-montuno structures. This term remained in the lexicon of Cuban-based dance music, and today refers to instrumental interludes in salsa and merengue.

Cuban popular musicians and fans have a penchant for coining neologisms as trademarks for genres; as Acosta puts it, there is a "tendency to pigeonhole."[230] This often serves as a marketing strategy for new styles. Reception, however, is the final arbiter of such strategies: musical labels either catch on or they do not, according to popular taste.[231] Arcaño and Rodríguez's work aside, Cuban big band arrangers routinely based their work on saxophone and trumpet riffs in this period; as Acosta shows, the mambo style had been incubating among Cuban musicians in both Havana and New York for some time.[232] Acosta suggests that the first big band jazz style Cuban group to use montuno-riff mambo structures may have been Julio Cueva's group, for whom René Hernández was the writer.[233] Arrangers Bebo Valdés, El Niño Rivera, and Chico O'Farrill also wrote in this style in Cuba, and Machito's arrangements by José Madera and John Bartee from the early 1940s employed a riff-based sound. The New York mambo style—if not the name—thus clearly developed prior to Pérez Prado's rise.[234] Moreover, the "mambo" term was already catching on prior to Pérez Prado's rise; in addition to Arcaño and Rodríguez's usage, José Curbelo's "El rey del mambo" (featuring Tito Rodríguez on vocals) was released in New York in 1946,[235] and in 1947 Tito Rodríguez came out with a band called the Mambo Devils.[236] In response to Pérez Prado's claiming credit for the innovations that all these arrangers had created together, Bebo Valdés coined the term *batanga* in 1952 as a rival marketing label.[237]

Arranger and pianist Dámaso Pérez Prado was born in 1916 in Matanzas, Cuba, and moved to Havana when he was twenty-six to work in dance bands.[238] Like other young arrangers, he used a riff-based style in his writing for groups such as Orquesta Casino de la Playa.[239] Pérez Prado moved to Mexico in 1949, starting a band consisting of five trumpets, four saxophones, one trombone, piano, two congas, bass, bongó, and timbales. "Discovered" by music industry moguls in 1951, his widely distributed compositions "Mambo no. 5" and "Mambo, que rico el mambo" catapulted Pérez Prado to fame throughout the Americas.[240] A master orchestrater, he highlighted saxophone riffs punctuated by trumpets and a single trombone. His compositions, dubbed "mambos," often featured a vocal grunt that became his trademark. Pérez Prado is notable not only for his use of jazz-influenced big band riffs, but also for his mining of resources from European classical music: he incorporated Stravinskyan dissonances into his instrumental dance numbers while maintaining a witty quality that appealed to all; the eminent Cuban writer Alejo Carpentier thus called Pérez Prado a musical "humorist."[241] Astutely specializing in instrumental music with appeal to English- as well as Spanish-speakers, Pérez Prado made major inroads in the U.S. market, first making a splash in California. Dovetailing with the tango and conga vogues, the mambo came on to fertile ground. Moreover, a radio strike instituted by ASCAP in 1941 forced radio stations to turn away from many Anglo styles, and the demise of many swing bands created a demand for dance music.

A mambo craze was afoot. Magazines referred to its "high sex quotient" and "lids off demonic quality."[242] An article in *Ebony* proclaimed that "its impulses are primitive, its rhythms are frenetic, and it is called the mambo."[243] Tin Pan Alley tunesmiths began penning their own mambos; ten were released in October 1954 alone. Like the North American reworkings of the conga and rhumba, these, of course, were stereotypes. Perry Como's "Papa loves mambo" may have had little to do with Cuban music, but it still featured Pérez Prado's characteristic grunt.[244] As the mambo label gained currency and many Latin bandleaders began using it, Machito recorded an LP entitled *Mambo is Here to Stay* in 1950. Soon, the up-and-coming bandleader Tito Puente was crowned "King of the Mambo." In 1954, promoter George Goldner put together a "Mambo-USA" tour featuring Machito, Joe Loco's Quintet, and other assorted acts such as the "Arthur Murray Television Mambo Dancers."[245] Tastes in the mambo were allied to geographic region. Although the New York bands received airplay on the West Coast, Pérez Prado reigned there.[246] He arrived east in 1952 but New Yorkers preferred the percussion-heavy, jazz-soaked style of Machito and the other reigning bandleaders of the day, Tito Puente and Tito Rodríguez. During the 1950s a new dance craze, the cha-cha-chá, heated up, and perhaps because it was easier to execute than the mambo, it took the United States by storm. While most bands in Cuba used the danzón-derived (or charanga) instrumentation based in flute and violins, rather than the big band format, for playing cha-chas, New York bands catered to cha-cha dance steps within the rubric of the trumpet and saxophone big band sound.[247]

Multicultural Mambo

Located near the well-attended Arcadia and Roseland Ballrooms, the Alma Dance Studios at 53rd Street faced stiff competition in 1947. Hoping that Latin music would step up business, owner Tommy Martin hired Machito and his Afro-Cubans to play for Latin dances on Wednesday nights. Machito's friend Federico Pagani promoted the dances by distributing flyers uptown near subway exits, so some called the events "Subway Dances." Officially, the venue was dubbed the Blen Blen Blen Club after the popular Chano Pozo song. Machito and his Afro-Cubans headlined the bill, sharing it with other Latin dance bands. The Blen Blen Blen Club was a success. Graciela remembers that, once, the ballroom was so crowded that its coatroom quickly filled up. In spite of snowy weather, patrons checked outerwear down the block at a local restaurant, running back and forth between the dance hall and restaurant.[248]

With the notable exception of Machito's engagement at La Conga, Latin bands had previously worked as relief bands rather than as headlining attractions in downtown venues; it was unusual for downtown clubs to cater to black and Latino crowds. While the venue's owner, Tommy Martin, was happy with the Blen Blen Blen Club's success, he was worried that the preponderance of people of color would turn away white patrons. Impresario Federico Pagani remembers that as more and more blacks came to the dances, Martin said that they would "ruin my business." Pagani countered by pointing out that they were *good* business: "What do you want, the green or the black? If you want the green, you can have it . . . otherwise, throw them out of here."[249] Martin agreed, offering Machito and his Afro-Cubans a steady engagement. In the following year, Max Hyman bought the ballroom, renaming it the Palladium and featuring all Latin music.[250] The Palladium interior was attractive. There was a special section where single women sat, and dancers divided the floor into areas for virtuosi and novices.[251] The Palladium remained the number one spot for the mambo until it closed in 1966.[252]

A pattern developed whereby Wednesdays were dominated by whites, Fridays attracted a mixed crowd, and Saturdays attracted mainly Latinos. Sundays saw a mixed crowd with blacks predominating.[253] As Salazar remembers, Wednesdays attracted celebrities: "that would be the night you could see Marlon Brando, Sammy Davis, Jr., Harry Belafonte, Kim Novak, Hollywood personalities sitting in the audience there."[254] An emcee sometimes announced their presence to the crowd, shining a spotlight on them.[255]

Salazar claims that the New York mambo scene was remarkable for its lack of racial tension, saying that there was no feeling that particular groups were not welcome on particular nights and that as time went on, "everybody started going on these different dates: it wasn't black Sunday anymore or Hispanic Saturday and white Wednesday, forget it!" He adds that

during the late '50s and '60s, it was a lot of intermarriages because the music is what brought these dancers together at the Palladium Ballroom. Yeah, because what they did was when they got together at the Palladium, they got to find out that they were just alike, that people were like them. There were family [sic], they had married, they had children, they had rent problems. And the mambo is the things [sic] that really removed these barriers, by bringing these people together, because by bringing them to that dance-hall, they got to learn about each other. And realize there's not that much difference.[256]

African American mambo dancer Ernest Ensley remembers that he often went to predominantly white clubs in Brooklyn and did not have problems finding partners among white women.[257] Machito's assessment of race relations and the mambo culture may not be a total exaggeration: "That's where integration began."[258] Ray Santos, who left New York for Puerto Rico in 1966, was surprised to witness the city's ghettoization when he returned in 1984. While the mambo crowd had been a rich ethnic mix, most dances in New York in the 1980s catered to "either Latino crowds, or black crowds or Jewish crowds." With regard to Latin bands, "80 percent of the time they were playing to just Latino crowds, whereas before it was very spread out. . . . I missed that."[259]

The Primacy of Dance

As we have seen, the mambo (like other Afro-diasporic forms such as high-life, blues, and hip-hop) is dance as well as music. African American exhibition dancer Andrew Jerritt, who often danced at the Palladium, underlines the importance of dance to the Afro-Cubans when he testifies that Machito once told him that dance is the "book" upon which their music is based.[260]

New York's Latino youth, weaned on African American dance, fused the Lindy Hop with Cuban music, "dancing [as one would] to a swing band but . . . with Afro-Cuban rhythms," as Santos explains.[261] Or, as Mrs. Arthur Murray of dance school fame tritely put it, the mambo was "rhumba—with a jitterbug accent."[262] In addition to the Palladium, much of the vital mambo action was occurring in Spanish Harlem and Bronx venues.[263] Santos remembers that

[e]verybody up in the Bronx was saying that "well, if you want to see real dancing, you've got to go to the Palladium and watch the people dance." . . . They talked just as much about the dancing as the music. So I remember the first time I went to the Palladium, Tito Puente was doing a debut there that night with a three-trumpet conjunto. And I was just as impressed by the dancing as I was by the music. I'd like be listening to the music part of the time, but I couldn't keep my eyes off the dancers on the floor.[264]

Young dancers often practiced at home during the week, preparing steps to try out at the Palladium on Saturday night.

The best mambo dancers put on shows, or exhibition dances, at the Palladium and other venues. Prize money was negligble; dancers participated mainly because they enjoyed it.[265] Max Hyman and dance instructor Killer Joe acted as judges of the Palladium contests; a group of eight to ten couples participated regularly, and their dancing skills are legendary.[266] In a fascinating oral history, African American exhibition dancer Ernest Ensley recounts his life as a *mambero*. In addition to dancing, Ensley recorded bands at the Palladium, often carrying recording equipment in the subway in a timbales case. Because he danced in the Palladium shows, the ballroom's owner Max Hyman allowed Ensley to record any band he wished; even musicians who did not wish to be recorded could not protest because Hyman was the owner. Ensley's life as a mambero was a true labor of love: he often danced after a full day's work, returning home as late as 5:30 A.M., only to leave for work again as early as 8:00 or 9:00 A.M.! With Killer Joe as an informal manager, Ensley and other exhibition dancers brought their dance show on the road to Catskills resorts and as far afield as Mexico, Santo Domingo, Venezuela, and Africa.

Many of the Palladium exhibition dancers were African American, and many of the steps that mambo dancers developed later found their way into Motown and James Brown routines. Special activities were arranged for Wednesdays—traditionally an off-night for dancing—including free dance lessons at 8:00 P.M. and a dance contest at 11:00 P.M. The lessons provided an important service in encouraging patrons who were not expert dancers, and who might otherwise be shy, to take a spin on the floor. [267]

Frank "Killer Joe" Piro, an Italian American New Yorker who had excelled as a swing dancer in his teen years, started a small ballroom dance school near Times Square after World War II. Highly skilled at Latin steps, he won so many dance contests at the Palladium that he was hired to teach dancing there.[268] Underlining the Lindy-mambo connection is the fact that Killer Joe was originally a jitterbug; he shifted to the mambo when the swing era waned.[269] Ray Santos notes that Bauzá and Machito were strongly influenced by the Cuban bandleader Arsenio Rodríguez, remembering that Bauzá often called out to his percussionists: "Arsenio, Arsenio, pick up on Arsenio, I want you to play like Arsenio!"[270] With its emphasis on the conga drum, Rodríguez's percussion section used less improvisation than did the son septets, playing a steady and funky beat that black Cuban dancers loved. Adding the conga was like adding another bass; in fact, bassists even complained that this addition interfered with them. Significantly, the bass part in Cuban popular music derives largely from rhythms played on congas in rumba.[271] Santos remembers that Bauzá emphasized "real heavy percussion-oriented" material like "Barabaratiri" and the Arsenio Rodríguez composition "Llora timbero" at uptown venues: "That's where the band really excelled . . . . Bauzá always liked these fast, flashy flag-waving type arrangements where they'd blow any band away that was alternated with them [*sic*]."[272]

Machito's background, of course, was in the son, which is dance music. His sensitivity to the requirements of Latino partygoers complemented Bauzá's background in swing bands such as Webb's, which were masters at inspiring jitterbugs. The swing bands' riff-based style was a primary influence on both Machito and Pérez Prado. Bauzá and swing writer Edgar Sampson's cowritten hit, "Mambo Inn," often requested at Palladium dance contests, bears an uncanny similarity to the signature sound of riff-based swing bands such as Count Basie's.[273]

While Machito's repertoire had been fairly balanced between Afro-Cuban jazz and dance numbers in the late 1940s, the band gradually became more dance-oriented, developing a repertoire of 60 percent vocal dance music, 20 percent instrumental dance music, and 20 percent instrumental music meant for listening.[274] This may have been because a large number of Latinos entered the city in this period: many Puerto Ricans came due to a postwar slump in the island's economy, increasing the demand for Latin dance music in the city.[275]

A connection to dancers, integral to music throughout the African diaspora, was thus the pillar of the Machito aesthetic; while the band's most lasting contribution was in its bebop innovations, Machito and his

Afro-Cubans worked mainly as a dance band. And Machito's jazz influences were never at odds with dancers' requirements; the band combined bebop influences with dance rhythms, and even its bop experiments were grounded in the requirements of the dancing public.

In addition to stints at the Palladium and other predominantly Latin venues, Machito and his Afro-Cubans worked at the Savoy and Renaissance Ballrooms for predominantly black crowds. There they played their usual mambo repertoire, alternating with jazz and jump musicians including Arnett Cobb and Cootie Williams.[276] Johnakins remembers that when the Machito band first played at the Savoy, many of their Latino fans followed them to dance there, leaving the African American Savoy regulars watching on the sidelines. Gradually, however, the Savoy crowd learned to do Cuban dances: just as Johnakins and other North Americans learned to play Cuban music, black fans learned to dance the mambo.[277] Referring to the African American public, Machito remembers: "They was crazy about it. They was dancing [and] . . . it was exciting and you know, we was playing for black[s] and it was black music, so there was no—you didn't have to make no explanation to a black person about rhythm because they're born with rhythm; they come from where the rhythm comes from."[278]

In addition to the Latino and black dancers, many whites became proficient, and some became expert, at dancing the mambo; as Machito said, much of their public consisted of "a lot of [white] American[s] that know how to dance."[279] The group's base in the Latino and black communities did not distance it from Euro-American fans: during the 1950s, Latin dance music was at the forefront of mainstream pop culture in the United States. Martiniquan scholars Bernabé and Glissant, who espouse Caribbean cultural mixing, or *creolité,* provocatively state that while North Americans often eschew cultural mixing or creolization, the northeastern states, with their Jewish, Mediterranean, and Caribbean immigrant populations, approach a creolité.[280] Several white musicians became important in Latin dance music in the wake of Machito's influence, the most notable of whom is salsa bandleader Larry Harlow, whose promoters heralded him as "El Judío Maravilloso" (the marvelous Jew).[281]

While it was firmly rooted in African-based aesthetics, the magic of the mambo thus became available to everyone, regardless of ethnicity. The open magnanimity that Machito expressed in both his singing and his personality contributed much to the band's exuberant and inclusive air. As one musician remembers, even "in the most adverse circumstances," Machito "always had a wonderful smile for you and he always had something to share." The band's collaborativeness was based in this sharing spirit, which was "what Macho [Machito] was all about. Macho wasn't the center of attraction. *His whole band . . . was 'Machito.'*"[282] African American exhibition dancer Ernest Ensley notes that it says much about the United States that "here you have a music whose lyrics are in Spanish, unintelligible to the average American. Yet from the '40s through the '70s, it became an integral part of the American experience.[283]

Machito in the Mambo Soundscape

Bandleader, timbalero, and arranger Tito Puente organized a group in September 1949, debuting at the Palladium. He called the small combo, consisting of a rhythm section and three trumpets, the Piccadilly Boys (after *picadillo,* a dish of spiced chopped beef). A New Yorker of Puerto Rican descent, Puente exuded a charisma that struck a chord with the predominantly Puerto Rican crowds, and he quickly became a star. Puente soon abandoned the small-group format, putting together a big band and developing a winning formula that displayed his unabashed brand of musical excellence. A master showman and a virtuoso, Puente played exciting timbales solos on fast numbers and sensitive vibraphone obbligati on boleros. He was also a formidable arranger, forging a distinctly personal, flashy style of jazz-tinged Latin dance music. Puente had actually started out as a sideman with Machito, and he was influenced by René Hernández's innovations in arranging. The other rising star of the New York mambo was the Puerto Rican singer Tito Rodríguez, who started a band named the Mambo Devils in 1947. While Rodríguez eventually developed a style focusing on boleros, he made his early reputation singing in a manner influenced by Machito, often using similar syllables such as "no, no, no, no" in his improvisations.[284] Ray Santos, who played with Machito as well as Puente and Rodríguez, opines that the latter were "very good bands, [but] to me they were basically spin-offs off Machito, you know, the saxophone, trumpet concept of big band jazz" combined with Afro-Cuban rhythms.[285] By 1952, however, their novelty and, possibly, their appeal to the predominantly Puerto Rican Latino community in New York put Puente and Rodríguez ahead of Machito as the city's top mamberos. Machito even had trouble getting booked at the Palladium in one period.[286] The dominance of the two Titos ended by 1954, when Machito and his Afro-Cubans were again working regularly at the Palladium.[287]

Significantly, while Machito and his Afro-Cubans' recordings were popular in Cuba, the group never toured that country. By contrast, Pérez Prado, who was based in Mexico, did perform in his home country. Cuban deejay Manuel Villar, who was active at midcentury, believes that Machito's music was popular enough on the island, but that economic considerations impeded the viability of a tour: that the Cuban peso was on a par with the U.S. dollar made it more expensive to bring bands from the United States to Cuba than it was to bring bands from Mexico.[288] It is also true, however, that Cuban taste did not run toward the modernistic bebop that Mario Bauzá and Machito championed. And while Machito's singing was respected in Cuba, because he was a baritone, what Cubans call a "segunda voz" (second voice), Machito's voice was not what Cubans expected from a lead singer. Moreover, to make a name as a top band in Cuba, it was necessary to develop an original repertoire of songs not played by other bands; much of Machito's dance music, by contrast, consisted of covers of Cuban hits.[289] As a Cuban dance band, then, Machito and his Afro-Cubans did not surpass the work of top island groups such as the one led by singer Benny Moré, who made history with his hot band in the 1950s. Ray Santos feels that as far as dance bands go, bringing Machito's band to Cuba would have been like "taking coals to Newcastle . . . because as great as Machito's band was, they had some great bands in Cuba also. Benny Moré and the rhythm sections down there, forget it!"[290]

So while Machito and his Afro-Cubans worked primarily as a dance band and was respected and known in Cuba, its most original contribution was the melding of jazz with Cuban dance rhythms. This innovation could only have developed in New York. The very geography of the city's nightclubs, in fact, invited it: the Palladium and Birdland were situated within blocks of each other. The owners of the two venues had an informal agreement whereby musicians working at either club could enter the other one free of charge. Players could thus keep up on what the others were doing.[291] Machito's baritone saxophonist Johnakins remembers that "we used to go down to the Birdland when we were off the stand. And naturally they knew who we were and where we were coming from, and knew we weren't going to be there but a hot minute because we got to go back to work."[292]

Dance music in Cuba, from Pérez Prado's witticisms to Benny Moré's driving sound, all incorporated jazz elements but did not foreground bebop harmony and improvisation. Machito's band, on the other hand, used jazz musicians and jazz arrangers who were tuned to the latest North American innovations. As Mario Grillo puts it,

Benny Moré's band was based in Cuba and he was using Cuban musicians—the interpretation was very authentic, very Cuban, had some jazz influence but no *per se* jazz players. Whereas Machito was totally the opposite. He had guys writing who were writing for Benny Goodman, Count Basie and for Gene Krupa and then using musicians that were coming out of Count Basie and Gene Krupa and Stan Kenton's band, and coming in to play with the Machito orchestra. So then, they brought with them the feeling, the flavor, the ability to interpret the arrangements in that traditional big band jazz format. And I think that's really where the difference was: the arrangers and the personnel.[293]

It's clear that Cubans held the Machito band in high esteem.[294] But as Chico O'Farrill notes, Machito and his Afro-Cubans' emphasis on jazz was "simply too American, [too] Anglo-oriented" to make a splash in Cuba.[295]

The Later Years

In 1960 and 1961, Machito and his Afro-Cubans completed a three-month tour of Japan, where, like many visiting jazz luminaries, they received a regal reception. Cuban dance music had already made significant inroads in Japan: recordings by Machito, Pérez Prado, Cugat, and Puente were already known there. Graciela remembers that arriving at the airport, musicians were surprised to see a beautiful display of flowers and Machito LP covers. During press interviews, journalists told band members that they had already researched the history of the Afro-Cubans so they did not need to ask them about it. Instead, journalists just wanted to know whether their guests were enjoying the reception festivities.[296]

Back stateside, taste in Latin bands was turning to smaller aggregations, and Machito had difficulty finding work. Thinking that there might be more work in Puerto Rico, Machito brought a pared-down version of his group there in 1966. After eight months, however, they returned to New York. In the period that followed, the band only worked two to four nights a week. In addition to larger venues such as the Chateau Madrid and the Roseland Ballroom, they played for weddings and bar mitzvahs, and in hospitals and schools.[297] By the 1970s, only Pin Madera and Leslie Johnakins were left from the heyday of the band. Other seasoned Latin musicians such as saxophonist Chombo Silva and trumpeter Alfredo "Chocolate" Armanteros were now in the band,[298] while young players kept the group's youthful vigor intact.[299] In the early 1970s Machito began supplementing gigs with a job as a social worker, meeting with groups of senior citizens and drug addicts in the Latino community.[300]

On January 1, 1975, the Machito band performed Chico O'Farrill's brilliant composition "Oro, Incienso, y Mirra" (Gold, incense, and myrrh), featuring Dizzy Gillespie, at the first-ever jazz concert in Saint Patrick's Cathedral. The subsequent LP recording of this, *Three Afro-Cuban Jazz Moods,* featuring Clark Terry on trumpet, appeared on Granz's Pablo label. Including another master composition by O'Farrill entitled "Three Afro-Cuban Jazz Moods," it was nominated as a 1975 Grammy finalist in the jazz category, losing only to Ellington.[301]

In 1975 jazz promoter George Wien asked Machito to form an octet to work in Europe. Bauzá, however, felt that a small group would not ably present the band's style. Machito disagreed and split from Bauzá, doing the tour without his longtime associate.[302] Machito's Latin Jazz Octet, a stellar aggregation consisting of top New York Latin musicians,[303] played alongside jazz greats such as Charles Mingus and Roy Haynes at festivals in Paris and Berlin and, upon their return to the United States, at the Newport Jazz Festival.[304] This opened up the festival market for Machito, who re-formed his big band, this time without Bauzá and Graciela, featuring his son, Mario Grillo on timbales and his daughter Paula on vocals. More European tours followed, and the LP *Machito and his Big Band Salsa, 1982,* on the Dutch Timeless label, won the Grammy for Best Tropical Music.[305] The European jazz market was lucrative: fans throughout the world had heard Machito records but had never seen the band live. The band's new fans, however, differed from the Palladium mamboniks of the past; many of them were members of the hippie counterculture.

Back in the States, Machito began to receive accolades. The Latin Exchange Organization honored him with an event on March 13, 1980, and he received a letter from Jimmy Carter. On August 20, 1981, Machito's contributions to the City of New York were recognized by Mayor Koch on the steps of City Hall. Despite his estrangement from Machito, Mario Bauzá joined in honoring his longtime associate.[306] In 1984 Machito's ten-piece Latin Jazz Ensemble went on a European tour, and in London, Machito suffered a cardiac arrest and died of a cerebral hemorrhage in his sleep.[307]

Machito's son Mario Grillo, who was named after Mario Bauzá, had been sitting in with the Afro-Cubans since he was six years old, waging mock timbales battles with the likes of Tito Puente. He had joined the band as a full member at age fourteen and, became musical director in 1975.[308] Mario Grillo kept the band going after his father's death, calling it The Machito Orchestra and doing occasional concerts in Europe, Lincoln Center, and elsewhere.

Mario Bauzá and Graciela had left Machito and his Afro-Cubans in 1975 to start their own band. Long overshadowed by his coleader, Bauzá soon received the credit and the limelight that he deserved, releasing three critically acclaimed LPs, one of which was aptly named *This Is My Time.*[309]

Chico O'Farrill told me that "Mario Bauzá was visionary" in his decision to "bring those jazz people in front, you know, in the front line" to improvise over Cuban rhythms.[310] While there had been a long-standing Latin *tinge* in jazz, Machito and his Afro-Cubans forged a full-fledged union between Afro-Cuban and black North American music. Even the Cuban bandleader Alberto Socarras, who was active in New York prior to Machito and no stranger to jazz (he is credited with recording the first jazz flute solo ever), asserted that it never occurred to him to mix Cuban music and jazz because he thought of them as two separate things.[311]

Mainstream, commercialized versions of Latin American music clearly paved the way for Machito and his Afro-Cubans' rise to fame, but Machito transcended the stereotypes, staying true to Afro-Cuban aesthetics while entering the U.S. mainstream. Machito was thus a master of the stereotype-reappropriation dynamic, a master of turning negative clichés into positive energy. It is significant that the Machito band eschewed the most financially viable strands of North American popular culture, latching on to a relatively marginalized trend, bebop. Bauzá's embrace of this brand of black modernism was inspired by his twin commitment to pan-Africanism and musical innovation.

The encounter of black Cubans and black North Americans was a happy reunion of long-lost brothers and sisters: as Machito said, "our wedding of jazz with the rhythms of Cuban music was not a conventional union, it was a marriage of love."[312] This union proved fertile for African Americans as well as Afro-Cubans, as Dizzy Gillespie testified: the frontispiece to his memoirs presents "new lyrics" to Gillespie and Chano Pozo's composition "Manteca," that declare that African Americans will "never go back to Georgia," never go back to Jim Crow and the myth of the Negro past that tried to rob them of their history.[313]

While remaining ideologically based in the African diaspora, Machito and his Afro-Cubans included white musicians and appealed to a wide cross section of ethnicities. Their inclusive approach transcended genre boundaries as well as racial boundaries; Machito played for dancing, at jazz clubs, and in concert settings, combining barrio street smarts with the avant-garde. Moreover, the Machito band was an avowedly *regional* exponent of North American culture, as it was firmly grounded in New York City. While it toured the entire United States and, in later years, Europe and beyond, in its heyday the band worked almost exclusively in Manhattan and the Bronx.

As we have seen, the Machito band was the brainchild of Mario Bauzá. Still, some have exaggerated Bauzá's contributions, claiming that he was a master arranger, composer, or improviser. Aside from guiding his arrangers with instructions, however, Bauzá rarely or never wrote arrangements, and with the exception of pieces such as "Lona" and "Mambo Inn," he rarely composed.[314] And while Bauzá was enamored of jazz improvisation, he was aware of his limitations, remembering Chick Webb's admonition to avoid competing with master jazz soloists; while his few recorded improvisations are engaging, they do not represent his most important musical contributions.[315] Bauzá's grounding in European classical music was in line with the other New York Latinos who were "music stand musicians."[316]

Bauzá, however, took this forte to its highest level, not only proving himself a top-flight sideman, but using his interpretive skill to inform an integrated vision for a new aesthetic. His skills as an interpreter, acquired through solid training since childhood and honed through a decade of apprenticeship in the top black dance bands, made it possible for him to realize his ground-breaking vision of wedding Afro-Cuban music with jazz.

Conventional wisdom equates bebop with small ensembles. Musicologist Scott De Veaux, however, shows that the boppers' use of small groups was instigated as much by financial necessity as artistic purpose. Earl Hines's and Billy Eckstein's big bands were strongly oriented to bop, and Dizzy Gillespie aspired to keep his big band together throughout his career. But while they created some of the most artistically successful music of the twentieth century, the bebop big bands failed from a financial standpoint. Although it was not exclusively a bebop band, Machito and his Afro-Cubans had bop as one of its integral elements. In contrast to Hines's, Eckstein's, and Gillespie's aggregations, Machito kept working well after the demise of most swing bands. Its success issued from its simultaneous commitment to musical experimentation and the requirements of the dancing public, and because New York's Latino community continued to support live music after the era of big band jazz.

The marriage of Afro-Cuban music and jazz had a lasting effect. As we have seen, while North American musicians had a hard time coping with Cuban rhythms at first, these rhythms eventually came to permeate jazz as well as other types of North American music. Bauzá once said that "I used to get the complaints: [jazz soloists] said, but we cannot play with that guy banging on that bongó. They throw us off. They couldn't find the beat. . . . Little by little they get more, more, more into the thing. Now you call practically anybody, and everybody fall in—it don't bother nobody now."[317] "So evidently the marriage of the two things created a completely new, a new atmosphere."[318]

In 1957 Cuban President Fulgencia Batista put together a "50 Years of Cuban Music" reunion, bringing expatriate musicians home from various countries and putting them up in a luxury hotel. After the event, Francisco Fellové, the composer of "Mango Mangüé," which Charlie Parker had recorded with the Afro-Cubans, escorted Machito to the airport. Fellové asked Machito whether it was true that North Americans had become adept at dancing to Cuban music. Machito told him that indeed they had, and to emphasize his point, composed a song called "Bailan cha-cha-chá y guaguancó" (They dance the cha-cha-chá and guaguancó") in the airplane on the way back home to New York.[319]

Duke Ellington
Photo Credit: Paul Karting

Rahsaan Roland Kirk on reed instruments; with George Grüntz on piano and
Daniel Humair on drums. Amersfoort, Holland, 1963
Photo Credit: Paul Karting

Eric Dolphy
Photo Credit: Paul Karting, Henk Visser

Mario Bauzá (standing) with Chick Webb's Band, featuring Ella Fitzgerald, 1938
Photo Credit: Henry Medina Archives and Services

Machito, Graciela, and the Afro-Cubans, 1953
Photo Credit: Henry Medina Archives and Services

Mario Bauzá, René Hernández, and Machito
Photo Credit: Henry Medina Archives and Services

Tavito Vásquez
Photo Credit: Raymundo Vásquez

Mario Rivera
Photo Credit: Mario Rivera

Teppo Repo
Photo Credit: Folk Ways Archive,
the Dept. of Music Anthropology,
University of Tampere

The Ethno-boys: Heikki Syrjänen and
Pekka Westerholm
Photo Credit: Etnopojat

Edward Vesala
Photo Credit: Harri Aiho

Heikko Sarmanto
Photo Credit: Maarit Kytöharju

Milford Graves
Photo Credit: Bill Johnston

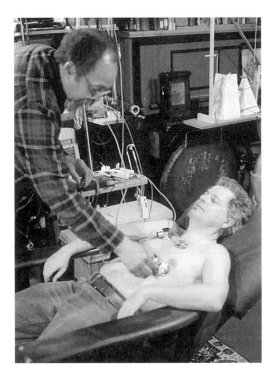

Milford Graves and
Paul Austerlitz, setting up
to record heart sounds
Photo Credit: Bill Johnston

During the 1950s mambo boom, rhythm and blues musicians availed themselves of Cuban influences; Johnny Otis even recorded "Mambo Boogie" with Machito's rhythm section in 1951.[320] Afro-Cubanisms were soon incorporated into the U.S. rhythmic vocabulary, musicians adapting these influences in creative ways. Even songs not categorized as "Latin" were often strongly influenced by Afro-Cuban rhythms; Elvis Presley's croonfests such as "It's Now or Never" and the doo-wop hit "Little Darling," for example, incorporate idiosyncratic reworkings of Cuban rhythms. The North American assimilation of Afro-Latin tinges gained momentum with the innovations of James Brown, disco, and hip-hop—all of which incorporated these influences.

The active agent in fusions between black musics from the United States and the Caribbean, of course, is their shared African base. In symbiotic union with similar African-derived traditions long present in the United States, Afro-Latinisms expanded the rhythmic palette of U.S. music to include straight eighth notes and clave-based syncopated rhythmic cells, especially in bass parts. Similar rhythmic cells had long been present in black North American culture, for example in "ham-bone" rhyme-songs and certain swing riffs (for example, the trumpet punctuations in arrangements such as "Jumpin' at the Woodside"), but their use was bolstered as a result of the Afro-Cuban infusion.[321]

Art Blakey took the Gillespie/Pozo experiments in a new directions, instigating collaborative Cuban/U.S. drumming sessions, as found in his *Orgy in Rhythm* LP. John Coltrane's drummer Elvin Jones listened to Afro-Cuban drumming and created an especially rich fusion.[322] Already in his early recordings with Coltrane, he adapted clave-soaked patterns to the ride cymbal in compositions such as "Mr. Knight," and his inspired drumming on the "Acknowledgement" movement on Coltrane's seminal *Love Supreme* LP is closely related to Afro-Cuban rhythms.[323] Jones, however, adapted these influences in such a way that, while musical analysis shows an Afro-Cuban link, the result is not coded as "Latin" by most listeners or musicians. Instead, like Machito and Bauzá's innovations, the sound suggests pan-African connections.

Latin jazz continued to grow at the end of the twentieth century. New York Puerto Ricans such as Jerry González developed their own brand of Latin jazz. Meanwhile, increased contact with Cuba and the arrival of Cuban masters such as saxophonist Paquito d'Rivera invigorated the U.S. Latin jazz scene. Touring Cuban musicians such as pianist Chucho Valdés and the rumba group Los Muñequitos de Matanzas increasingly performed in the United States. Significantly, several African American musicians with little previous recorded experience with Latin music, such as Steve Coleman, Roy Hargrove, and Don Byron made bold experiments in Cuban-tinged jazz.[324] European aggregations specializing in Afro-Cuban music also rose.[325]

Another pervasive Cuban influence on jazz and other forms of U.S. music was the use of static harmonies. North American popular music had traditionally utilized "common practice" chord progressions, but beginning in the 1950s, jazz and North American dance music increasingly used static harmonies. Jazz improvisation in this style was dubbed "modal improvisation" as it is confined to a single scale or mode, and this practice became extremely important in jazz. Its links, however, to Afro-Cuban music are rarely acknowledged; George Russell's "Cubano Be, Cubano Bop," for example, has been cited as the first modal jazz composition. Pianist/composer Horace Silver's signature modal style is influenced by both Latin music and, possibly, his native Cape Verdean traditions. Ray Santos remembers that at one time jazz musicians often asked Latin musicians, "Why do you stay on one chord so long?" but later, when Silver, Miles Davis, and other jazz innovators also "got modal," they understood.[326] This trend dovetailed with musicians' interest in Eastern musics, becoming part of the language of jazz as well as funk, disco, and hip-hop.

The genius of Machito and his Afro-Cubans lay largely in its collaborative nature. While Bauzá was responsible for many of the band's innovations, he never claimed to be a master of clave, acknowledging that the band's clave-logic came from Machito, Graciela, and the percussionists. The contribution of the band's many arrangers, most prominent of who were René Hernández and Chico O'Farrill, cannot be overestimated. Machito supplied his singing as well as his personable nature and attunedness to the barrio scene; his eminent sociability was at the heart of the band's aesthetic. Machito and his Afro-Cubans was a "family affair" (to invoke Sly Stone's soul hit) not only because Machito, Bauzá, and Graciela were related, but also because its style was based in an interactiveness that is central to Afro-diasporic arts. Just as responsorial rhythms were central to Machito's music, cooperation and collaboration were central to his band as a social institution. As the Akan proverb states, "the family is a force." While remaining firmly committed to its pan-African base, the Machito family welcomed people of all ethnicities: Jewish mamboniks, like the band's Harlem and Latino fans, inspired Bauzá and the band as much as their music inspired dancers; undulating body movement was the fulcrum of the Machito band, even when playing concert music.

Robert Farris Thompson argues that even when outwardly secular, Afro-Cuban music encodes an underlying spirituality that makes it "religious music in disguise":[327] it is no accident that the original meaning of the word "mambo" is a religious one. Machito and his Afro-Cubans' euphoric sound was thus a blessing that brought all ethnicities together in an avowedly New York–bred brand of inclusiveness. Traversing racial and ethnic divides, their pan-African vision pulled disparate constituencies together in a pan-American—and indeed, pan-human—family affair.

CHAPTER 4

Ambivalence and Creativity
The Jazz Tinge in Dominican Music

ᴍᴍ

Once, at a soiree in the Dominican Republic, the host introduced me to his other guests as a musician who plays *el jazz clásico*, "classic jazz." From his tone of voice, it was clear that this gentleman held jazz in high esteem. Happy to be complimented in this way, and happy to be in the company of people who shared my passion for music, I told my new friends about a recent experience at a weeklong Vodou ceremony in Haiti. The event had made a big impression on me as I had noticed many aesthetic parallels between jazz and Vodou music. I thought my friends would be interested in these links. I was wrong: they were taken aback, reacting with surprise, befuddlement, exasperation. They did *not* see Vodou in the same light that they saw "el jazz clásico." As I became more acquainted with the Dominican Republic, I discovered that a Hispanocentric ideology prevails there alongside of many vital African influences, effecting an acute case of the "socialized ambivalence" elucidated by Herskovits and discussed in the introduction.[1] I eventually became acquainted with the resulting complexities of Dominican jazz consciousness, and saxophonists Tavito Vásquez and Mario Rivera assumed particular significance as I explored the relationships between jazz and of Dominican music.

Merengue and Jazz in the Early Twentieth Century

The Dominican Republic's population is estimated at 80 percent mixed African and European, 15 percent black, and 5 percent white; Dominican sociologist Pérez Cabral aptly calls his country a "comunidad mulata," or mixed-race community.[2] The African element in this mix is cardinal; as the foremost Dominicanist ethnomusicologist, Martha Ellen

Davis, attests, the Republic "without doubt, should be considered an Afro-American nation—that is, a New World nation in which the African cultural influence figures prominently, if not predominantly."[3] Santo Domingo was a Spanish colony founded in 1493 by Columbus. Its western third was ceded to France in 1697, and Haiti was founded there in 1804 as the result of a successful slave uprising. Haitians entered the eastern part of the island in 1822, expelling the Spaniards and abolishing slavery. The light-complexioned Dominican ruling class looked disfavorably on this "Haitian occupation," and worked to expel the Haitians. They succeeded, and the Dominican Republic gained its independence in 1844. It is significant that the Dominican Republic gained its independence from Haiti and not from Spain: since 1844, the Dominican ruling class has propagated a Eurocentric notion of national identity.

After Spain's retreat as an imperial force and the rise of the United States as a world power, Dominicans became antagonistic about North American intervention but were also attracted to Yankee wealth and modernity. Dominican ambivalence took on a second life as U.S. neo-colonial domination of the country took hold. Indeed, as Frantz Fanon has shown, ambivalence is inherent to the colonial mind-set.[4] As we have seen, however, complex feelings engender multifaceted creativity. The prime determinants of Dominican adaptations of jazz are the rapport that Dominican musicians feel with jazz as a result of shared African-derived aesthetics on one hand, and the negotiation of mixed feelings resulting from neo-colonial attitudes on the other.

The music of the Dominican Republic reflects the country's Afro-Hispanic ethnicity. Neo-African forms, indispensable to rural religious ceremonies, predominate. These include *palos* and *salve* drumming[5] and a celebratory processional form called *gagá*, performed on one-note trumpets and percussion during Catholic Holy Week.[6] Less prevalent than these neo-African forms, European musics such as sung prayers called the a capella *salves sagradas* are also significant in the soundscape. Lying between the extremes of African and European influence is a large repertory of syncretic musics such as the *mangulina, bachata,* and merengue.[7]

Dating to the mid-nineteenth century, the earliest references to merengue describe it as a ballroom dance music related to the *danza*, which was related to the Cuban danzón and had developed from the stately *contradanza*. Merengue was distinguished by the fact that it was danced by independent couples (instead of in groups) and by Afro-Caribbean influences in the music as well as in an undulating motion of the hips. After a short heyday in Dominican ballrooms, it was rejected by Eurocentric elites because of its dance style, which was considered lewd, and because of its

African-influenced musical elements. The rural Dominican majority, however, adopted merengue and infused it with even more African influences. Merengue variants with various instrumentations developed in several areas of the Dominican Republic, but only the Cibao region's version gained prominence. By the early twentieth century, *merengue típico cibaeño* (Cibao-style folk merengue), performed on the *tambora* (a double-headed drum), the *güira* (a metal scraper), the button accordion, and the alto saxophone, was the top social dance in Cibao's countryside and barrios (lower-class urban neighborhoods).

The merengue accordion and saxophone style is based on ostinatos (or repeating riffs) called jaleos, which merge with tambora, güira, and dance rhythms in a typically African-influenced aesthetic, in the manner that was illustrated in chapter 2. In addition to playing jaleos, early merengue saxophonists improvised twisting lines in counterpoint with the accordion and tambora. As a Cibao native who had danced at many a merengue fiesta during the early twentieth century told me, saxophonists "used to embellish and play lots of scales and beautiful things: very beautiful. Their accompaniment went up, and down . . . it went out of the merengue yet stayed within the rhythm."[8] The similarity of this saxophone style to jazz improvisation begs the question of possible jazz influence on early merengue, but merengue groups incorporated saxophones prior to the period of U.S. influence in the Dominican Republic. Wind instruments were present in rural merengue already in the nineteenth century, and the saxophone was entrenched in the music by the second decade of the twentieth century.[9] The aesthetic link between early merengue and jazz, then, results from shared musical ingredients rather than from North American influences; both musics were spawned by the union of African and European sensibilities. The Dominican folklorist and composer Estéban Peña-Morell once turned the question of possible jazz influence on early merengue on its head by facetiously asking, "Did jazz originate in Santo Domingo?"[10]

A closer look at early merengue's stylistic history will illustrate the path that the mingling of African and European sensibilities took in the Dominican Republic. Emulating salon orquestas, which featured wind instruments, barrio merengue musicians occasionally incorporated a baritone horn into their groups. According to Cibao musicians who were active during the early twentieth century, the alto saxophone was first used in merengue only on occasions when a baritone player was not available.[11] Dominican composer Julio Alberto Hernández remembers that baritone horn players injected tinges of local, Afro-Caribbean flavor into the stately European-derived danza: "The baritone played a special role [in the danza]. It performed a rhythmic accompaniment. . . . They improvised típico rhythms, tropical rhythms, which had a certain character. . . . There were some excellent baritone players, with special embouchures. Often, people listened to the baritone rather than dance."[12]

Early merengue saxophone playing was thus based on the baritone style. Saxophonist Antonio Lora, who was active in the early twentieth century, explains that an approach more consonant with the percussive textures of the tambora and accordion soon emerged: "the saxophone was the best instrument . . . for típico music. The baritone sounded terrible; it sounded like a trombone. The saxophone . . . complemented the accordion better."[13] Hernández adds that the "saxophone accompaniment came from the danza. But since saxophones are more flexible than baritones. . . , well, they played lots of variations and pirouettes, up and down."[14] Pedro "Cacú" Lora and Avelino Vásquez were the first saxophonists to play merengue regularly and the architects of the original merengue saxophone style.

The Dominican Republic saw severe economic difficulties in the early twentieth century, and its European creditors threatened to send battleships to collect unpaid debts. President Woodrow Wilson found the possibility of a European military presence in the Caribbean unacceptable, and evoking Theodore Roosevelt's corollary to the Monroe Doctrine (which called for the United States to thwart European colonial presence in Latin America), ordered a U.S. invasion of the Dominican Republic on May 5, 1916. In the following year, the Marines established a military government that ruled the country until 1924. Dominicans did not take the U.S. occupation sitting down: rural populations waged a guerrilla war, while the urban upper classes mounted an international program of protest on the diplomatic front. These tactics were successful: they eventually forced the United States to "abandon the occupation."[15] Associated with the diplomatic campaign, the climate of cultural nationalism fomented the embrace of all things Dominican.

At the same time, however, many Dominicans were attracted to the North American popular culture that the Marines brought. These competing tendencies were at the crux of the occupation's musical repercussions. At the outset of the occupation, upper-class Dominicans had European tastes in music, rejecting both local, rustic Afro-Caribbean music and modernistic North American imports in favor of the waltz, polka, danza, and the danzón. The mood of resistance, however, likely played a role in inspiring composers in the Cibao city of Santiago de los Caballeros (Santiago of the gentlemen) to write Romantic nationalist art music based on merengue and other local forms. Influenced by this trend, the leader of the Cibao's top dance band, Juan Espínola, gained fame by performing refined, danza-like merengue arrangements for ballroom dancing.[16]

In 1921, Juan Pablo "Pavín" Tolentino founded Orquesta Bohemia, which soon displaced Espínola's group as the Cibao's premiere salon orquesta. Like Espínola, Tolentino started out specializing in the Cuban danzón, which called for two clarinets, cornet, baritone horn, string bass, and percussion. The growing popularity of North American music, however, manifested itself in the group's changing instrumentation: within a decade, Orquesta Bohemia had become a jazz band consisting of three saxophones (or clarinets), cornet, violin, baritone horn, tuba, banjo, trap drums, and percussion.[17] Pianist Luis Alberti brought a new group on the scene in 1928, and with the vogue for North American music in full tilt, he called it Jazz Band–Alberti.[18] Orquesta Bohemia and Alberti's groups vied for the position as the city's most authentic jazz voices; when Orquesta Bohemia added a banjo, Alberti had to get one too.[19]

As one can imagine, the jazz vogue did not meet a wholly favorable reaction in the face of anti-Yankee sentiment that reigned in the wake of the occupation: at one point, musicians had even "boycotted" the performance of North American music.[20] In 1933, Alberti got the original idea of taking the bite out of jazz's popularity by performing merengues with big band jazz instrumentation. Tolentino followed suit, reinforcing his regular band with a típico merengue group consisting of accordion, tambora, and güira.[21] The tambora, güira, and accordion were permanently incorporated into Alberti's and Tolentino's bands,[22] and merengue soon found a permanent, though small, place in the Cibao dance-band repertories; a practice of ending every ball with a merengue developed.[23] It was precisely the neo-colonial experience that had piqued the Cibao elites' interest in merengue; prior to the occupation, they had rejected local forms.

Some of típico saxophone pioneer Avelino Vásquez's younger relatives, who had been playing in Orquesta Bohemia, started their own group in 1932. Orquesta los Hermanos Vásquez (the Vásquez Brothers) soon became the number-one dance band of the region, and remained popular into the late 1940s. The street where many of the Vásquezes lived and where the band rehearsed came to be known as "La Calle Alegría" ("Happy Street"), because the band's rehearsals were so enjoyable that people gathered there to listen and dance. Orquesta los Hermanos Vásquez included several excellent saxophonists, who conducted innovative experiments in applying merengue accordion jaleos to the jazz band saxophone section. The composer Hernández wrote about the role of La Calle Alegría in the development of the merengue saxophone style: "The role of the saxophone in merengue acquired its traditional characteristics thanks to the contributions of celebrated popular musicians of Santiago [de los Caballeros], such as Pedro "Cacú" and the Vásquez family, who converted the alley known as

"Happy Street" into a quarry of saxophonistic gyrations that served as the model for the modern orchestration of our típico dance."[24] The fusion of the essence of merengue—saxophone jaleos—with jazz was the heart of the music's simultaneous link with local and cosmopolitan culture. It was also at the heart of the music's spicy danceability.

Meanwhile, barrio dwellers continued to dance to accordion-based merengue. Two types of merengue típico cibaeño were current in the early twentieth century: a sectional form with parts denominated *paseo, merengue,* and *jaleo,* and a one-part form called the *pambiche.*[25] While it is probable that both existed already before the U.S. occupation, the pambiche is often said to have originated during this period. As the story goes, U.S. Marines sometimes went to local fiestas but were unable to dance merengue correctly, combining fox-trot steps with merengue steps. Imitating the North Americans, Dominicans in the town of Puerto Plata created a dance step called "Yankee-style merengue" (*merengue estilo yanqui*) that was accompanied by a syncopated tambora rhythm. The new dance became associated with a song about a fabric called "Palm-Beach" (as in the Florida city).

Palm-Beach es mejor que dril,	Palm-Beach is better than drill,
Y es mejor que el casmir.	And it is better than cashmere;
Con él yo voy a fiestar,	I will celebrate with it,
Y con mi novia a bailar.[26]	And dance with my girlfriend.

The new style came to be called pambiche, a Dominicanization of the Americanism "Palm Beach:" just as the Palm Beach fabric was neither cashmere nor drill, the pambiche was neither fox trot nor merengue. The anecdote about the pambiche's origin turns occupation-era power relations on their head: Dominicans had a rough time contending with U.S. military might, but their superiority on the dance floor was unquestioned, and they even created a new genre out of the Marines' choreographic ineptness! [27]

Europhilism and Merengue Jazz

The Dominican dictator Rafael Trujillo rose to power in 1930. Although he himself was of mixed African and European extraction and his own grandmother was of Haitian descent, Trujillo espoused a racist idea of Dominicanness that excluded explicit links to Africa and Haiti from officially sanctioned national culture. Trujillo's attitudes about African and Haitian influences in the Dominican Republic reveal contradictions basic to Dominican culture. He persecuted Haitians, but was of partial Haitian descent himself. He instituted a law banning African-derived magico-religious practices such as Vodou, but was known to practice them himself.

Even today, such magico-religious practices are rarely discussed in the Dominican Republic in spite of their ubiquity. The extremity of Trujillo's anti-Haitianism was epitomized in his 1937 massacre of perhaps twelve thousand (or more) Haitians residing in the Dominican Republic.[28]

In spite of widespread antipathy to his brutal dictatorship, Trujillo, like other populist nationalists, had what one observer called "a sure grasp of those sensitive areas of national psychology": he knew how to motivate the masses through the use of "color and drama and spectacle."[29] Trujillo donned full-dress military uniforms, often complete with ornate ostrich-plumed hats (similar to those that Marcus Garvey wore), at formal occasions. He understood that folk culture can be a potent symbol of the nation-state. He had long been an avid social dancer, and determined that merengue cibaeño should be a national music. In 1936, Trujillo brought Luis Alberti's band, renamed Orquesta Presidente Trujillo, from Santiago to the capital city to play big band arrangements of merengue at high-society balls. All of the country's dance bands were required to perform newly composed merengues praising the dictator, and merengue became a staple of radio broadcasts. In keeping with the party line, scholars maintained that "Dominican folk music cannot be but a derivative of Spanish music,"[30] and Luis Alberti opined that "merengue has nothing to do with black or African rhythms."[31]

Other than Luis Alberti, the top exponent of "merengue tradicional," as jazz-tinged big band merengue was later dubbed, was Super Orquesta San José, featuring Joseito Mateo (the "King of Merengue") on vocals.[32] Mateo describes the impression that Luis Alberti's innovative fusion of rustic merengue and polished big band jazz made on young musicians:

Luis Alberti went straight to high society, because it was an elite band, sponsored by Trujillo. Trujillo had them play on the salons, and when we first saw them, they looked fine. And also, he was a great musician. This was another class of merengue; the musicians played better. That is, they respected musical conventions . . . such as crescendos, mordents, moderato; everything that [classical] music has. They did that, and it sounded beautiful.[33]

The jazz influences on the new merengue only furthered its association with cosmopolitan sophistication.

Trujillo sponsored a radio station called La Voz Dominicana (The Dominican voice), which specialized in live music performance. During the 1950s, the station employed more than ten musical ensembles, including several jazz-tinged Latin dance bands; típico merengue groups; a symphony orchestra; and groups specializing in Mexican mariachi music, the Argentine tango, and Trinidadian calypso.[34] Trumpeter Hector de León was acknowledged as the ringleader among jazz musicians at La Voz Dominicana;

as a colleague remembers, he "was the one that influenced that generation of [Dominican] musicians to get into jazz."[35] De León had gained exposure to the music while working in Venezuela[36] and developed an arranging style influenced by Stan Kenton. West Coast, or "cool" jazz, was better known in the Dominican Republic than was East Coast hard bop, probably because recordings of it were more readily available; artists such as Chet Baker and Al Cohn were popular among local musicians.[37] Hector de León's brother, alto saxophonist Choco de León, was also an adept jazz player, and was especially influenced by Art Pepper.[38] He is remembered for recording brilliant instrumental versions of traditional merengues with extended jazz-influenced solos that remain models for merengue-jazz fusions today.[39] By the 1950s, big band merengue arrangements often included improvised solos, often for trumpet backed up by the saxophone section playing jaleos.

In addition to jazz, other foreign musics gained favor in the 1950s, and all manner of fusions were made. When Mexican rancheras and Brazilian sambas became popular, Dominican bands recorded merengue versions of the foreign hits. An especially successful fusion of this sort was created by the young arranger Félix del Rosario; see the alto saxophone part of this arrangement (in del Rosario's own hand) in figure 14. His merengue version of "Skokiaan," a Zimbabwean song that had been popularized world-wide by Louis Armstrong under the title of "Happy Africa,"[40] combines elements of southern African music, big band jazz, and merengue. The arrangement commences with typical merengue tambora and güira rhythms embedded in a characteristic southern African I–IV–I–V chord progression, instead of the V–I progression typical to merengue. This progression continues throughout the arrangement. Played by an alto saxophone soloist, the melody calls for glissandos similar to those played by New Orleans clarinetists and alto saxophone stylists such as Johnny Hodges. Call and response between the band's brass and reed sections evoke similar effects of big band jazz. Outlining offbeat successions of diatonic arpeggios in a rhythm related to the Afro-Cuban (and pan-Caribbean) clave rhythm, the riff, or jaleo is often used in accordion-based merengue. While the African, jazz, and merengue elements each remain recognizable in the arrangement, their shared Afro-diasporic aesthetic forms a seamless union. The fact that the original "Skokiaan" was a *tsaba*—which David Coplan defines as a "syncretic style of African urban music blending African melody and rhythm, American swing, and Latin American" music[41]—further underlines the breadth of the cross-fertilization that was taking place. Félix del Rosario's "Skokiaan" demonstrates that at the same time that the dictator Trujillo was denying the African sources of merengue, Dominican musicians were alive to living links the diasporic soundscape; as Turino writes, "'Skokiaan' thus exemplifies the emergent, synthetic

Figure 14. "Skokiaan," alto saxophone part, arranged by Félix del Rosario, Félix del Rosarion's manuscript.

nature of cosmopolitanism, and jazz as a cosmopolitan genre, in a particularly clear way."[42]

Also coming to prominence in the 1950s was the single most important innovator of Dominican jazz, alto saxophonist Tavito Vásquez.[43] A nephew of the típico merengue saxophone pioneer Avelino Vásquez, he began to play professionally in 1940 with Santiago's Orquesta Hermanos Vásquez. Tavito Vásquez studied soprano saxophone and clarinet as well as alto saxophone, and he played North American music ("fox trot, boogie-woogie")

Figure 15. Excerpt from Tavito Vásquez's solo on "La manigua," transcribed by Tavito Vásquez; Tavito Vásquez's manuscript.

and classical music in addition to Cuban forms and merengue.[44] Vásquez moved to the capital city to work at La Voz Dominicana in 1947. There Vásquez played in Super Orquesta San José and led his own big band (called Orquesta Angelita) and típico merengue quartet (called Conjunto Alma Criolla, "The Creole Soul Band"). Until this time, the jazz elements in merengue had been in the instrumentation and arrangements. As Vásquez affirms, his innovation was to inject extended jazz improvisations into accordion-based and big band merengue: "I revolutionized merengue; this thing of [jazz] improvisation in merengue, I was the first one to do it."[45] He adds that this was "in the 1940's, during the same decade that Charlie Parker revolutionized jazz. . . . The 1940s were the decade of musical revolutions."[46] Coming from a típico merengue background and endowed with a sophisticated ear for jazz harmony, Vásquez was in a unique position to take the fusion of Dominican and North American musics to new heights; his solos evince a seamless amalgam of Afro-Latin and bebop sensibilities. In addition to making him an innovator of Dominican music, Vásquez's emotive tone, inventive harmonic sense, and original lines render him a jazz master by any standards. The LP *Tavito Vásquez y su Merengue-Jazz* presents standard merengue repertory reharmonized with jazz tinges by Vásquez and performed by a group consisting of alto saxophone, piano, bass, tambora, and güira.[47] Figure 15 is Vásquez's own transcription, in his own hand, of an excerpt from his improvisation on the merengue "La Manigua" from this LP.[48] Interestingly, the transcription's last phrase is rendered in two versions (the lower of the two is correct).

New Trends

After Trujillo was assassinated in 1961, the Dominican Republic opened to outside influences as never before. Bandleader Johnny Ventura and arranger Luis Pérez incorporated salsa elements and rock 'n' roll performance style into an exuberant, faster merengue that abandoned jazz band instrumentation in favor of a smaller "conjunto" (combo) format. Massive outmigration ensued in the decades that followed, and by 1990, an estimated 900,000 Dominicans—12 percent of the country's population—were living in New York City alone. Escalating transnational intercourse was reflected in merengue's continued assimilation of outside influences ranging from disco and rap to Haitian and South American sources. Access to the transnational Latin music markets gained new, non-Dominican audiences for merengue, which usurped salsa's position as the most-requested Latin Caribbean dance by the late 1970s. Trumpeter Wilfrido Vargas's band led the way in the "internationalization of merengue," as Dominicans called the music's boom.

Composer, arranger, and singer Juan Luis Guerra emerged as the most innovative merengue bandleader in the 1980s and 1990s. After studying jazz at Boston's Berklee College of Music, Guerra became influenced by the vocal quartet Manhattan Transfer and formed his own vocal quartet in 1984. The group's name, 4.40, reflects Guerra's schooled aesthetic: its music is to be sung perfectly tuned to the concert pitch of Euro-classical music, A at 440 cycles per second.[49] Guerra's music combines merengue with jazz and funk, and also includes touches of Latin American pop ballads, and sundry other musics such as soucous and flamenco: "Our main influence is, more than anything else, jazz. . . . Next to this, or along with it, is funk, [especially in the] trumpet rhythms, [which are combined] with the saxophone jaleos. We have an incredible mix: merengue saxophone and funk trumpets. A funk sound like Tower of Power's with an extremely Dominican rhythm."[50] As his statement reveals, jazz was close to Guerra's heart. His first LP, *Soplando* (Blowing), consists of jazz-influenced vocal arrangements in merengue, salsa, and samba rhythm, and features saxophone solos ("blowing") by Tavito Vásquez.[51] The innovative quality of this album did not attract the Dominican mass market, and Guerra soon began recording in a more dance-oriented idiom, but the high quality of his music did not diminish.

In spite of growing urbanization and modernization, accordion-based merengue remained vital in the 1970s, 1980s, and 1990s. While rural groups and those playing for tourists stuck to the traditional style, groups in the birthplace of merengue, Santiago de los Caballeros, developed a new form of típico merengue that added conga drums and electric bass to the traditional lineup of accordion, saxophone, tambora, and güira. These groups became more and more popular during the merengue boom, and today, they perform alongside top merengue bands in luxurious nightclubs throughout the Dominican Republic and in Dominican communities abroad. Because it is allied with both tradition and modernity, it is fitting to call this music *merengue típico moderno* (modern folk merengue).

Tavito Vásquez often sat in with típico moderno groups, especially those led by accordionists Rafaelito Román and El Ciego de Nagua (The blindman from Nagua, Bartólo Alvarado). Vásquez's impeccable bebop sensibility, couched in interlocking jaleos with the accordion, resulted in breathtaking performances that, lamentably, were never adequately recorded.[52] Although they lack Vásquez's jazz background, merengue típico moderno saxophonists perform inspired solos that often evince jazz-related characteristics. Contemporary accordion-based merengue exudes a wild exuberance that prompted the *New York Times* to call it an "avant-garde improvisational fest in Caribbean disguise."[53] The top saxophonists in this idiom are José el Calbo (formerly with El Ciego de Nagua and now the leader of his own group, La Artilería), and Oscar Peña (of Francisco Ulloa's group). A section of Peña's solo on Chachí Vásquez's composition "Los saxofones" is transcribed at figure 16. Played at breakneck speed, the intensity and momentum of this music privilege rhythm and texture, rather than the static tonic/dominant harmony, as determinants of improvisational choice. After an initial chromatic ascent, Peña plays a descending C major arpeggio over a D7 accompanying harmony landing on a C#, effecting a polytonal situation. He continues with a series of scales and diatonic arpeggios similar to those that Tavito Vásquez often employed; in contrast to Vásquez's precise, studied approach, however, Peña plays with wild abandon, manipulating the saxophone's timbre to create a texture rather than a melody, which cannot be adequately represented on conventional staff notation. The solo ends with a gesture contrasting the low range of the instrument with an extremely high note, far above what is considered the "legitimate" range of the saxophone. This type of playing brings to mind the music of the free jazz saxophonist Albert Ayler. Ayler often began his pieces with simple melodies and proceeded to manipulate the instrument's overtones, creating screaming textures instead of melodies. It is unlikely that Peña and Ayler influenced each other directly, but they

Figure 16. Excerpt from Oscar Peña's solo on Los saxofones," transcribed by Paul Austerlitz.

share an African-derived aesthetic in which use of growl and other manipu-lation of vocal and instrumental timbres is central. Milford Graves, who often played with Albert Ayler in the 1960s, once said that he and Ayler did not consider their music a "new thing" (as "free jazz" was called at the time), but rather an expression that calls upon the roots of African-based culture.

The importance of the saxophone in merengue may lie behind the fact that several of the foremost exponents of Dominican jazz are saxophonists. Following in the tradition of Tavito Vásquez, Félix del Rosario, and Choco de León, the Dominican saxophonists Crispín Fernández, Juan Colón, Carlito Estrada, and Mario Rivera emerged as major movers in Dominican jazz. Crispín Fernández, the first-call saxophonist for merengue recording sessions, leads a merengue-jazz group called Licuado that features Julito Figueroa on tambora and conga.[54] Juan Colón worked primarily in pop merengue; he was long Juan Luis Guerra's regular saxophonist. He completed an ambitious project conceived in honor of Tavito Vásquez, transcribing Vásquez's improvisations and harmonizing them for four saxophones, and recording them in arrangements that are interspersed with improvised solos.

A coterie of jazz musicians demonstrated an extraordinary commitment to jazz in spite of a paucity of performing opportunities formed in Santiago de los Caballeros in the 1980s and 1990s. Foremost among them is pianist-bandleader Rafaelito Mirabal, whose music evinces the influence of Pat Metheny. Mirabal has also ventured into merengue-jazz: his composition "Periblues," for example, combines fiery saxophone jaleos with blues chords changes. Often performing with Mirabal is alto and tenor saxophonist Carlito Estrada. Estrada is, in my estimation, the most inspired and authoritative jazz voice in the Dominican Republic today. He has developed a bold personal style of improvisation heavily influenced by tenorist Michael Brecker. As a native of the Cibao region, Estrada feels a rapport with típico merengue style, and occasionally plays with accordion-based merengue groups. Like other Dominican musicians working in noncommercial idioms, Estrada has sorely lacked recording opportunities, and he works primarily in hotel bands.[55]

Mario Rivera

Mario Rivera was born in the capital city of the Dominican Republic in 1939. As a child, he played tambora around the house, and as a teen, he began playing the oboe with a band associated with the fire department. He soon switched to soprano and then tenor saxophone, and at age eighteen, he joined The Happy Boys, one of the only two rock 'n' roll bands in the country. Rivera soon moved on to work with Antonio Morel y su Orquesta, one of the country's best dance bands; this was Trujillo's daughter Angelita's favorite group, and it often performed at events that the dictator attended. Rivera moved on to work at La Voz Dominicana with Orquesta Angelita (named after the same daughter), led by Tavito Vásquez. This was a studio band that backed up singers on television; its basic lineup of five saxophones, four trumpets was sometimes augmented with a small violin section, a classical flutist, cello, and bassoon. Vásquez often improvised with the group, and Rivera later remembered that listening to Vásquez's solos was his "initiation into jazz." Rivera began studying jazz, for example transcribing Stan Getz's solo on "Pennies from Heaven." Already in this early period, Rivera experimented with merengue, adapting tambora beats to ¾ meter by playing along with Dave Brubeck's hit, "Take Five," just "for fun," as he told me.[56] As we shall see, later in his career, Rivera developed an acute penchant for multi-instrumental musical exploration.

Rivera moved to New York City after Trujillo was assassinated in 1961. Although many jazz recordings had been available in the Dominican Republic during Trujillo's reign, the fact that only certain labels were distributed there made for a lopsided musical education. When Rivera arrived in the States, he was already familiar with Sonny Rollins, Gerry Mulligan, Stan Getz, and Zoot Sims, but had never heard of Count Basie, Duke Ellingon, or Charlie Parker. He was soon hired as the baritone saxophonist for Tito Rodríguez's top-flight mambo band, working around the States as well as touring South America from 1963 to 1966. After that he worked with Tito Puente from 1966 to 1972, and then with groups such as Machito, Eddie Palmieri, and Típica '73. Working in this environment exposed him to great jazz players, but Rivera never consciously decided to specialize in jazz: he told me that he "just wanted to learn what it was, because I liked it. I didn't say that 'I want to have a career in jazz,' no, . . . it just happened naturally that the love of it took me to be in the right place."[57] He developed a friendship with tenor saxophonist George Coleman and joined Coleman's Octet, which rehearsed in Rivera's apartment. Coleman helped Rivera master jazz, and soon, Rivera was playing in Dizzy Gillespie's United Nations Band (an all-star Cubop organization) and doing stints with the likes of Roy Haynes, Reggie Workman, Sonny Stitt, and Roy Brooks.

While his principal instrument is the tenor saxophone, Rivera also plays the baritone and alto saxophones, flute, alto flute, trumpet, vibraphones, and tambora. Among jazz musicians in New York, he is known for his incessant practicing and the informal jam sessions that he holds in his Manhattan apartment during the wee hours. Rivera told me that he began his voracious doubling "for the fun of it":

Actually I am not really practicing, here, I'm *playing,* you know what I mean. I actually play more than seven hours [a night] usually, yeah. I might stay for a long time with one horn . . . , and then I stay with another one. I like to play at night mostly. I might start probably at six o'clock, or three or four o'clock, and go until six in the morning the next day, . . . on and off, you know, learning the tunes, practicing some of the book exercises whatever. Or I listen to videos you know. For me, it's like twenty-four hours, I would say; I just developed that discipline to be able to keep going.[58]

Like most jazz musicians, Rivera has wide-reaching tastes:

I listen to rap, I listen to Cuban music, I listen to Brazilian music, I listen to rock and roll too. You see, I listen to everything. . . . I listen to Beethoven, Bach, . . . all the great classical flute players, you know what I mean, James Galway, he's like my man, . . . [Jean Pierre] Rampal. It's all music, man.[59]

As mentioned, Rivera had been playing tambora for years, and as he became involved in jazz, he "saw that the tambora had possibilities to be a virtuoso instrument like the conga or timbales."[60] Rivera, in fact, played tambora as well as reeds with Dizzy Gillespie on tour in Europe, as documented on the Grammy Award–winning CD, *Live at Royal Festival Hall.*[61]

In the mid-1980s, a coterie of New York Latin musicians, led by trumpeter/conguero Jerry González and joined by his brother, bassist Andy González, began developing a new brand of Latin jazz and presenting informal jam-session performances at the Nuyorican Village and Soundscape clubs. These musicians worked in various configurations, with various leaders. Rivera was part of this scene and started his own Latin jazz group called the Salsa Refugees. He explained to me that while it might seem like it refers to immigration issues, the group's name actually refers to musicians' desire to move away from commercial salsa to develop new musical modes: the name "sounds like a political name, but . . . we [just] wanted to play more creative music than just having to play salsa."[62]

The Mariel boatlift brought many excellent Cuban musicians to the United States in the mid-1980s, including saxophonist/clarinetist Paquito d'Rivera and conguero Daniel Ponce. Their presence changed the climate of the New York Latin jazz scene, and it was in this atmosphere that Rivera became more interested in developing Dominican rather than Cuban rhythms. He told me that "there was like a [tension] between the Cubans and the Puerto Ricans about the music . . . [so] I said, no, I don't want to get into [this]; I'm Dominican so I'm going . . . [to develop] merengue-jazz."[63]

Featuring established Latin jazz players such as trombonist Steve Turré and pianist Hilton Ruiz and working mostly in New York City, the Salsa Refugees incorporated Cuban and Brazilian influences but its most original contribution was the use of Dominican rhythms; Rivera believed that "the tambora and the güira add . . . different colors."[64] His percussionists Julito Figueroa, Chinito Díaz, and Isidro Bobadilla instigated rhythmic experiments, using unconventional combinations such as two tamboras and conga. When Figueroa joined the group, he wanted to play congas, but Rivera asked him to double on tambora. Figueroa took Rivera's advice to heart, developing a unique style of tambora drumming as a solo improviser's art. He continues developing this idiom today in the Dominican Republic in spite of the paucity of performing venues.[65]

Bobadilla, who later became a steady member of Juan Luis Guerra's band, had studied Afro-Dominican drumming with folklorist Fradique Lizardo. He brought palos drums, which are usually used in Afro-Dominican religious ceremonies, into the group, using three palos on arrangements of tunes such as "Equinox" and "Spiritual." Rivera explained to me that he had been exposed to palos as a child. As we have seen, many Dominicans avoid talking openly about African-derived religious practices. Rivera, however, has no such compunctions; it is likely that his long-term participation in the Afro-Cuban musical scene in New York influenced his attitude. Rivera told me that his grandmother was a traditional healer devoted to "Dolorita," the Virgen de Dolores, a saint syncretized with the Afro-Dominican spirit Metresilí.[66] His grandmother had taken him to ceremonies where palos drumming was played:

[M]y grandmother was like a country doctor [who] used to prepare medicines. . . . They brought that saint, that Dolorita . . . in a procession. . . . I saw that when I was a kid. . . . I used to go and listen and we stayed up all night long and they were singing all those chants, and . . . the palos played.[67]

During the 1980s and 1990s, Rivera worked steadily with Tito Puente's Latin Jazz Ensemble, a small group that called upon Rivera's abilities as a jazz soloist; this group's first LP, *On Broadway,* won a Grammy and features Rivera playing a rhythmically distinctive Latin version of "Sophisticated Lady." Working steadily with Puente left little time to pursue his merengue-jazz projects. In 1994, however, Rivera recorded a CD entitled *El Comandante . . . the Merengue-Jazz,* which brings tenorist George Coleman and bassist Walter Booker together with Rivera, pianist Hilton Ruiz, and a Dominican percussion section in a recording that documents the brand of experimentation that he had begun with the Salsa Refugees. The CD includes straight-ahead bebop tunes, merengue-jazz, and arrangements that seamlessly alternate between bebop and merengue rhythms. Rivera's prodigious use of double-time eighth notes, integral to bebop as well as merengue, is equally planted in both traditions.[68]

Contradiction and Creativity

During the 1980s and 1990s many Dominican musicians and culture-watchers lamented Tavito Vásquez's lack of exposure and his isolation from the center of jazz happenings; this master of Dominican music had never received the recognition that he deserved. To make matters worse, there were few, if any, jazz musicians of his caliber living in the Dominican Republic, so Vásquez sorely lacked musical collaborators. Aiming to pay homage to this Dominican jazz innovator, Mario Rivera brought Vásquez together with first-rate New York City jazz musicians to do a recording. While it was never released, the recording session produced some excellent music. It featured merengue standards performed in jazz arrangements. Here, in addition to his assured solos on tenor saxophone, Mario Rivera demonstrates his technical mastery of, and inventive jazz voice on, trumpet and vibraphones. While it evinces the spontaneity of a live performance—most cuts were done in only one take—the recording also features Rivera's overdubbed jaleos for five saxophones, which evoke the accordion-inspired saxophone sound innovated by Orquesta Hermanos Vásquez and made famous by the 1950s merengue bands. Combined with the típico feel of the all-Dominican percussion section, this jazz recording is firmly rooted in traditional merengue. In the company of musicians who share his musical sophistication, and playing longer solos than on earlier recordings, Vásquez shines. Digging into his characteristic Charlie Parker–like flights, displaced diatonic triads, and diminished scale patterns, his musical imagination is as relaxed and creative as it was with accordion-based groups, except that instead of a static harmony and an accordion-dominated texture, the saxophone is bathed in piano, bass, and percussion timbres and underpinned by shifting jazz harmonies. This session occurred in Vásquez's last days, before his death in 1995. Dominican musicians lament his tragic passing in poverty and obscurity.

The Dominican medical doctor Federico Chan is a longtime friend and admirer of Tavito Vásquez and Mario Rivera and a self-styled champion and patron of Dominican jazz. His efforts to promote the music include producing the Rivera/Vásquez collaborative CD session with his own funds. Chan told me about his motivations: "Merengue has cultural value. It's the most authentic Dominican thing, just as jazz is the most authentic American contribution to the arts. We [Dominicans] don't have a painter, poet or novelist at the level of [the Colombian author] Gabriel García Marquez, but we have those merengues."[69] Chan's efforts to book the Rivera/Vásquez group in the Dominican Republic's prestigious National Theater were unsuccessful. He feels that the group's focus on merengue was behind the rejection; the National Theater customarily presents symphonies and concertos, not local Afro-Caribbean forms. Noting that performance in this prestigious venue would have meant much to Tavito Vásquez, he did not hide his bitterness when he told me that "the pseudo-intellectuals in the Dominican Republic still reject merengue."

Pianist Michel Camilo (a.k.a. Michael Camilo) emerged as the single most successful Dominican jazz musician of all time in the 1980s and 1990s. He studied classical music at the Dominican National Conservatory as a youth and performed with the Dominican National Symphony Orchestra at the age of sixteen. Camilo developed a love for jazz at a young age and moved to New York City to pursue this interest in 1979. Within several years he was a regular member of Cuban saxophone and clarinetist Paquito d'Rivera's band. In addition to being sought after for his virtuosic command of the piano, Camilo gained fame for the originality of his compositions. While most Latin jazz is based on Cuban rhythms, and experimenters such as Tavito Vásquez and Mario Rivera fuse merengue with jazz, Camilo developed a polished, idiosyncratic style that fuses generically Latin-sounding rhythms and melodies with jazz and funk in effervescently catchy tunes. Paquito D'Rivera used Camilo's "Why Not!" as the title tune for one of his albums, and Manhattan Transfer's subsequent recording of it won a Grammy Award in 1983.[70] Based in New York City, Camilo makes frequent visits to his home country, where his compatriots are justifiably proud of his accomplishments; he was even named Knight of the Heraldic Order of Christopher Colombus by the Dominican government in 1992. In the following year, Camilo was invited to perform Gershwin's *Piano Concerto in F* with the Dominican National Symphony Orchestra in the prestigious National Theater.[71]

Young Dominicans began to challenge their country's Eurocentrism during the post-Trujillo era. While many city dwellers associated Afro-Dominican drumming and religion with backward lifestyles that are best left behind, others, especially artists and intellectuals, embraced the philosophy that "black is beautiful."[72] The question of merengue's origin was central to a debate that developed between conservative Dominicans, who insisted on the republic's Hispanic identity, and those who promoted the country's African heritage. The traditionally minded faction claimed that merengue had little or no African influence, while progressive thinkers celebrated its African-derived aesthetic. Bandleader Juan Luis Guerra spoke eloquently about merengue's African roots without negating its syncretic nature: "Unequivocally, you can't take merengue out of Africa. No matter how much you may want to, you can't take it out of Africa. Forget it: the rhythms are African, period. Of course there are these influences, which are melodic: the melodies are European, the harmony, just like in jazz."[73]

Many urban youth, whose forebears had left the Dominican countryside and traditional arts behind, joined folk dance groups that performed stylized versions of Afro-Dominican ritual drumming and dance. Young artists formed bands that blended Afro-Dominican drumming with non-Dominican styles ranging from Peruvian music to rock and jazz. Guitarist/composers Luis Días and Tony Vicioso and singers José Duluc and Xiomara Fortuna spearheaded this musical movement. Vicioso told me that like most middle-class Latin Americans, his first musical loves were rock and jazz. Listening to McCoy Tyner while driving in the Dominican countryside one day, however, he encountered a band of musicians and dancers performing the processional one-note trumpet and percussion music called gagá. Vicioso immediately made a connection between the recorded African American music in his car and the living Afro-Dominican expression that surrounded him. After studying jazz in the United States, Vicioso realized that, as he told me, "there was a *Dominican* thing for me to get into." Returning to the republic, he began to conduct fieldwork on Afro-Dominican drumming and composing music that combined Dominican drumming with jazz. But as he says, "there's a resistance" to Afro-Dominican drumming in the republic; "people didn't appreciate this kind of thing."[74] Since 1991, Vicioso, along with other young Dominicans such as Bony Raposo, has been performing and conducting educational workshops on Afro-Dominican culture in New York City.[75]

Even though his compositions are unmistakenly Afro-Caribbean, Michel Camilo's background in classical music and his success on the international stage makes his music consonant with Dominican Europhilism; Camilo is heralded as a national treasure in the republic. Tavito Vásquez, on the other hand, never received the recognition he deserved; his background as working-class merengue musician contradicts conventional Dominican notions of "high culture." At the same time, merengue's status as a national symbol and its disassociation from Afro-Dominican religious rituals give it more cachet than Afro-Dominican ritual drumming has; in stark contrast to the media hype that surrounds pop merengue, genres such as palos, salve, and gagá and artists such as José Duluc, Tony Vicioso, and Bony Raposo, have no access to the Dominican music industry. It is ironic that the dominant classes in the Dominican Republic, who often pursue cosmopolitan connections, are so out of tune with the transnational pan-African movement. While there is a thriving music industry in the Dominican Republic, this industry promotes only commercial merengue and bachata, neglecting both traditional Afro-Dominican religious music and bold experiments in Dominican jazz and experimental popular music.

As an African American music, jazz embodies an alternative to hegemonic, Euro-American elements in the United States. At the same time, it represents connections to the hegemonic United States in the minds of many Dominican fans, who see it as a cosmopolitan marker of social status. Dominican musicians, on the other hand, created aesthetically integrated

merengue-jazz hybrids that stand as an affirmation of the shared foundations of African-influenced musics in the United States and the Dominican
Republic. The doubleness of jazz, its status as a generically U.S. form on
one hand and a specifically black form on the other, overlaid upon parallel
contradictions endemic to Dominican culture, lies behind the rich multi-
fariousness of Dominican jazz consciousness.

CHAPTER 5

"Rhythm-Music"
Jazz in Finland

~~~

As a graduate student, when putting together my first research project on Finnish music, I yearned for authenticity. My interest went beyond academic concerns: born in Finland but raised in the United States, I was ambivalent about my identity as an American and wanted to find roots in the country of my birth. I hoped to meet an elderly Finnish clarinet player and hole up with him in a rustic backwoods area to forge musico-ethnic bonds and receive the secrets of a tradition. I should have known better. Finland is no longer predominantly rural, and most Finns partake of the same transnational popular culture that is dished out worldwide. I was struck by the formidable African American influence on Finnish music. Instead of finding rustic horn players, I found artists who had revamped Finnish music through the lens of jazz. Their reality was uncannily similar to mine: my research, like their music, was motivated by a desire to bridge jazz and Finnishness.

The story of jazz in Finland complements our perspective by illustrating the impact of black music outside the African diaspora. The equivocal position of African American music, its double status as an art that is both central to and marginalized from dominant currents in the United States, affected the development of jazz in Finland. While the music's assimilation within the African diaspora, among Cubans and Dominicans, for example, builds upon shared African influences, the spread of jazz outside the African diaspora develops the music's Western basis: as an occidental art sharing much of the musical language of European music, jazz has a base upon which reinterpretations were built in Finland. Moreover, as we have seen, prevailing Western notions about African-influenced aesthetics developed in a cosmopolitan playing field spanning centers such as New

York City, Havana, and Paris. Certain aspects of the story of jazz in Finland are thus remarkably similar to jazz history in the United States. At the same time, of course, jazz was interpreted according to local attitudes and aesthetics.

In 1949, Finnish jazz musician Olli Häme wrote a book entitled *The Triumph of Rhythm* in which he coined the term "rhythm-music" as a moniker for jazz, arguing that this art was on a rising trajectory of success in Finland.[1] This African American musical influence came on the heels of other waves of foreign influence from Sweden, Germany, and Russia. Indeed, as a small nation, marginalized and periodically invaded, Finland did not have the luxury of remaining unaware of outside influences cultures. Finns thus developed their own brand of musical multiconsciousness.

Music and Finnishness

Finland, like other European countries, has a history of epic song whose heyday lasted from the Middle Ages and into the seventeenth century. This epic repertory was largely improvised. Melodies and tales were extemporized according to formulas—in the manner, for example, that Albert Lord describes for Yugoslavian epics[2]—and it was often accompanied by a five-string zither called the *kantele*. Starting in the seventeenth century, end-rhyming strophic songs and new dances arrived from western Europe, along with such imports as new agricultural technology and the potato. Instrumental dance music called *pelimanni* music (from the Swedish *spelman,* or "player," fiddler, musician) was performed for social dancing. Group dances such as the *polska* held sway until the mid-nineteenth century, when independent couple dances such as the waltz, *polkka* (the local version of the polka), and *jenkka* (a type of schottische) emerged.[3] The violin was the main instrument in pelimanni music.[4] While it never assumed a central position in the style, the clarinet began to be used in the second half of the nineteenth century.[5] Military bands, amateur brass groups,[6] and choirs also flourished in the nineteenth century, and the accordion became popular.[7] Also at midcentury, Russian melodic influence became paramount and is still present today: even midtempo dance tunes convey a Russian-tinged melancholia. Many local popular songs are actually Russian *waltz-romances* translated into Finnish. By the late nineteenth century a small but specifically urban musical culture took shape as central European and Russian influence came to the cities of Helsinki and Viipuri through Saint Petersburg. Central European salon orchestras, comprising piano, violin, and cello,[8] and often featuring foreign musicians, played in elite restaurants.[9]

The history of Finnish vernacular music can be divided into three rough periods: the period of epic song (approximately until the seventeenth century); the period of strophic vocal and dance music, which was marked by Russian and western European influences (from the seventeenth century); and the period of African American influence (the early twentieth century to today). These periods naturally overlap: the twentieth century, for example, was marked by European strophic song as well as African American influences and revivals of elements from the early, epic period. During all periods, of course, outside influences were domesticated; they were transformed into Finnish music.

Finland was part of the Kingdom of Sweden until 1809. The gulf separating elites from masses was exacerbated in small, nonsovereign entities such as Finland, where the upper classes spoke the languages of, and shared worldviews with, ruling powers.[10] Finland was, and still is, bilingual: the upper classes, as well as peasants in areas near Sweden, spoke Swedish, while the rest of the population (the vast majority) spoke Finnish. In 1809, Finland was incorporated into the Russian Empire. Russian imperial authorities, however, granted a great deal of sovereignty to Finland, whose status was that of an autonomous grand duchy. A nationalist movement took shape, and like romantic nationalism in other nineteenth-century European countries, Finnish nationalism was inspired by the ideas of Johann Gottfried Herder, who taught that discrete ethnic entities express their essences and highest manifestations in language and the arts. Some elites went so far as to abandon Swedish as their mother tongue and adopt the Finnish language while forging a Finnish, rather than a Swedish, identity. Russian moves to control the area included their encouragement of this emerging "Fennoman" cultural nationalist movement, which sought to replace Swedish with Finnish as the official language. The Russians supported this movement not because they supported Finnish nationalism but because they wanted to encourage any move away from Swedish identity. As part of their strategy, the Russians moved the capital of Finland from the old Swedish-speaking center of Turku to Helsinki.

Equally significant was the link between rural arts and national identity; Herder's embrace of rural, unlettered bards in his own land was singularly strategic. He saw rural storytellers and singers as purveyors of the German national soul, not because he believed that urban, literate poets were incapable of expressing the spirit of the *Volk;* on the contrary, he considered Homer and Shakespeare two of the greatest "folk" poets of all time. Because the nineteenth-century German upper classes had international (mostly French) tastes in the arts, however, there was nothing distinctly German about their literature.[11] Similarly, in Finland, bourgeois tastes ran generally to the elite arts emanating from larger countries. Uncorrupted by foreign influence, orally transmitted rural arts were attractive to bourgeois nationalists who found themselves immersed in cosmopolitan rather than local culture, and a vibrant trend of folklore research developed. Finnish folklorist Rantoja went so far as to assert that "folklore research is with us in Finland a national branch of science whose task it is . . . to create an ideological-historical foundation for our nation's independent life."[12]

In 1835, the Finnish medical doctor and folklorist Elias Lönnrot wove together a compilation of orally transmitted narratives that he had collected in rural areas into a Finnish epic, calling it the *Kalevala*. Lönnrot's *Kalevala* is a written text, but in traditional contexts, the "folk poetry" upon which it is based was actually improvisatory song in the old epic style. But by Lönnrot's time, epic singing was on the decline, and it was performed without instrumental accompaniment; Lönnrot saw "kanteles on the walls" of every house that he visited when collecting epic song in the early 1800s, but these kanteles were usually used to play the newer pelimanni music.[13] The kantele, however, figures prominently in the epic tales; the *Kalevala*'s central section (Poem 41), for example, describes the hero Väinämöinen charming the world with his virtuosity on this instrument. Along with the *Kalevala* itself, the kantele became an important symbol of Finnish nationalism. Although not so important as the kantele, herdsman's horns, played by the tragic hero Kullervo, also figure in the epic.[14] The *Kalevala* attracted international attention and boosted the Finnish nationalist movement.[15] Significantly, the Finnish-language *Kalevala* demonstrated the viability of local culture to upper-class Swedish-speaking Finns.

Both rustic rural arts and concert music played roles in Finnish cultural nationalism and, like the movement's philosophical base, the dominant influence was German. Although he rarely incorporated vernacular melodies, the Finnish composer Jean Sibelius was influenced by Wagner's use of Germanic mythology and looked to Finnish folklore for inspiration; many of his works, such as his *Kullervo Symphony*, were inspired by the *Kalevala*. Arnold Perris points out that musical nationalism was most important in "'little' countries, geographic/ethnic entities that were not sovereign nations. . . . For the tiny nation, so unequal to her conqueror, every cultural achievement which brought her international attention, as Sibelius's music had done, was a subtle act of resistance."[16]

Nationalists took advantage of unrest surrounding the October Revolution and declared the independence of Finland in 1917. In the early years of independence the ruling class, which was politically and culturally oriented to Germany, debated whether the new nation-state should be a monarchy or republic, going so far as to choose a German prince as king of Finland.

When Germany lost the Great War, however, the plans for monarchy were scrapped and a republican system was established; the new state was notable for immediately granting women's suffrage (the first in Europe). In 1918, however, a civil war ignited between "Reds" and "Whites," as peasants and workers tried to seize power. The situation resolved in favor of the Whites, but not peacefully; many Reds were killed or detained in camps. Although it continued to operate underground, the Communist Party was outlawed in the aftermath of the civil war. The Lapua Movement[17] sponsored paramilitary gangs that kidnapped and tortured leftists, enjoying tacit support from established politicians.

Its cosmopolitan connections notwithstanding, Finland remained overwhelmingly rural. As elsewhere in Europe, handmade clarinets, trumpets, and flutes made of animal horns, wood, and birch bark were essential to peasant culture. Cowherds blew them as signaling devices, to frighten away wild animals, and as magical means to drive away evil spirits (as ethnomusicologist Hannu Saha writes, boredom and loneliness were allied with these spirits).[18] Herdsman's horn and kantele player and builder Feodor Nikitin Safronoff (a.k.a. Teppo Repo) learned his art in traditional contexts at the turn of the century in his native Ingria, a region ethnically and linguistically kin to Finland and bordering Finland, Karelia, and Russia. He received instruction in musical notation and learned to play the baritone horn during a two-year stint in the Russian army. Moving to Helsinki, the capital of Russia's Grand Duchy of Finland, in the second decade of the twentieth century, Feodor Safronoff adapted to his new surroundings. He shed his Russian name in favor of the Ingrian-Finnish Teppo Repo, and shifted his tremendous musicality to instruments he considered consonant with his new urban surroundings: the violin, mandolin, balalaika, and baritone horn. As Saha masterly demonstrates, however, cultural nationalists saw Repo as an exponent of *Kalevala*-ish expression, and with their urging, he cultivated a style resonating with Finnishness.[19] Folk music scholar A. O. Väisänen played a crucial role in forging Repo's new persona as a tradition-bearer. Under Väisänen's tutelage, Repo stopped playing the baritone horn and balalaika, focusing on rustic herdsman's horns and taking up the kantele. He also added Finnish horns to his Ingrian instrumentarium. Repo stopped playing tunes that were obviously Russian, developing a repertory stressing newly composed melodies in the Ingrian style. Repo was soon performing as a concert soloist, on radio, and at patriotic assemblies; journalists portrayed him as a modern-day version of Kullervo, the Kalevalaic hero who played herdsman's horns. Like epic singers brought to cities by intellectuals to perform at patriotic rallies, Repo participated in forging the nascent national identity.[20]

Even as this new identity was being forged, a new wave of foreign influence was breaking across Finland. Teppo Repo, as a working-class artist alive to contemporary popular culture, would find his musical taste at odds with the cultural nationalists' agenda as he dabbled in a new art form soon known to Finns as "jatsi."[21]

Salon Noise Jazz

Because of the prevailing German influence, the first "jazz" in Finland was actually jazz-tinged German cabaret music. Suffering a severe economic depression at the time, Germany had developed a local form of ragtime-like music, associated with primitivist modernism and with noise as a prime mover. As in American "nut-jazz," musicians clowned around and produced bizarre sound effects. Novelty instruments such as the musical saw and lotus flute, as well as saxophones (which often produced laugh-like effects), were central to German "noise-jazz." The drummer was the main attraction; the drum set was actually called "a jazz." But instead of contributing to a melo-rhythmic flow of the kind described in chapter 2, drums and trappings such as bells and Tibetan woodblocks were used as noisemakers. Replete with a funny hat and cardboard nose, the drummer expressed the macabre anomie of depression-era Germany with his bizarre antics and racket.[22]

The tango had arrived in Finland in the early years of the second decade of the twentieth century, first danced at spectacles by professional dancers and later by the general public. Tangos were soon being played by brass septets and military bands as well as salon orchestras. A "tango fever" developed, with associated clothing styles and even candy.[23] As in the rest of the world, black music from the United States came to Finland after the Great War. The cakewalk, one- and two-step, and ragtime became available through sheet music and were incorporated into the salon orchestra and brass band repertoires. New instruments such as the saxophone, banjo, and drum set were added to salon groups in the 1920s. Despite these influences, repertoires often stayed the same: groups continued to play German popular songs, or *Schlagers* (literally, hits), but with the added attraction of the new instruments.

The first known use of the word "jazz" in Finland occurs in a 1919 newspaper article that compares the new music to the tango and the "tongara" (apparently, another dance) in an equivocal blend of racist epithets and laments about European adulteration of African American music. Finnish jazz historian Jukka Haavisto quotes the article in his monumental study on Finnish jazz:

It's coming, it's coming! Jazz is coming. And Tongara. Are they famous artists, or possibly apes or elephants . . . or some manner of metaphysical, theological beings? —They are the newest modish dances of our dead-serious times, which in their triumph from America to Europe have now arrived in Scandinavia and here. The inroads that jazz, especially, has made can be compared to those of the tango in its time. I can well understand that Jazz has provoked admiration in the larger civilized world, the senseless and clearly uglier jumping that dim-witted Negroes have invented. —Unfortunately, Jazz has lost much of its charm in the trip across the Atlantic. Experts say that the European version is like morning milk in comparison with the sulfuric acid of the original.[24]

In 1921 the first Finnish jazz band, Huttunen's Original King of Jazz Orchestra, began an almost yearlong engagement in an elite Helsinki restaurant. This was a salon trio to which a German drummer was added; interestingly, the drummer was called the "King of Jazz." Betraying cognizance of the American provenance of the form in spite of the German overlay is that the phrase "King of Jazz" was always used in the original English rather than translated to Finnish. Other similar bands were formed and the vogue's primitivist air was expressed by bass drums painted with images of African Americans, American Indians, or Hawaiians. Like the drum set, the exotic saxophone and banjo attracted attention. These instruments often figured in names of bands such as Jazz-Xaxofon-Band [*sic*] and the Jambo Jazz-Saksofoniorkesteri (Jambo Jazz-Saxophone Orchestra). Bands played German Schlagers in stock arrangements of new dance genres (such as the foxtrot), arranged in a style influenced by ragtime. Like Finnish tango fever, this vogue encompassed novel hair and clothing styles as well as music and dance.[25] Jalkanen's study of Finnish jazz shows that, as Germany was Finland's model in the years following independence, it is no coincidence that "while Finland was looking for a German king, the first 'continental jazz band sounds' were being played by the German Kings of Jazz" in Helsinki restaurants.[26]

But competition for the German brand of jazz was arriving; African American cosmopolitan modernism was broadening its reach to the corners of Europe.

Schoolboy Hot Jazz and the SS Andania Band

Class struggle remained central in the wake of the civil war, and jazz developed differently among workers and bourgeoisie. In the mid-1920s a group of Swedish-speaking upper-middle-class Helsinki youth became interested in the new music, listening to recordings and learning to play. These "schoolboy bands," as Jalkanen calls them, were different than the salon orchestras in that they looked to what they considered authentic

American jazz, rather than German music, as their model. Most older professional musicians looked askance at the young players; because the latter were self-taught, they were seen as amateurs.[27] The English *Melody Maker* magazine served as an instruction manual for many young Finnish musicians, providing nuts-and-bolts materials such as notated hot breaks.[28]

In 1926 the schoolboy take on jazz was bolstered by the arrival of the SS *Andania*, which had sailed from the United States, carrying upward of six hundred Finnish Americans to their mother country for an extended visit with family and friends. Among the travelers were several musicians who had formed a band called the Finnish Jazz Orchestra.[29] Consisting of alto and tenor saxophones, trumpet, trombone, sousaphone, piano, and drum set, the Andania band played in Helsinki restaurants, featuring tunes such as "Dinah" and "St. Louis Blues," which soon became local hits. The prevailing German-influenced style interpreted fox trots at fast tempos, and Finns were surprised that the Andania band played them slower. Even more striking was the Andania musicians' swing: they stressed beats 2 and 4 instead of 1 and 3. Although they played mainly from written arrangements, the Andania musicians occasionally improvised hot choruses, which caused a sensation: most Finns had never previously witnessed jazz improvisation. The star of the band was Finnish American alto saxophonist Wilfred "Tommy" Tuomikoski (who doubled on clarinet and violin), remembered both for his good tone quality and his ability as an improviser, seen as a "virtual miracle" by locals.[30] The band also featured saxophonist Freddy Martin, who had led a sweet band in the United States, and Merle Wilckin, a formidable tuba player.

Things went so well for the Andania musicians that several band members decided to stay in Finland. Tuomikoski joined a band called Zamba, giving it an air of jazz authenticity. He was happy to teach local musicians about the music, organizing band competitions and even authoring a saxophone method. He also became a cause célèbre among fans, spawning "Tuomikoski fever" as his clothing and dance style were imitated.[31] Jalkanen argues that the Andania musicians' role in influencing Finnish jazz has been exaggerated. Indeed, U.S. influences had already made a mark on the schoolboy bands prior to the Andania's arrival.[32] Still, it was largely due to the Andania musicians' influence that the bulk of Finnish musicians switched from German noise-jazz to African American concepts of swing and improvisation.

Workingman's Accordion Jazz

The working class, meanwhile, was developing a unique local take on a cosmopolitan style. In the years following independence, leftist political organizations often sponsored leisure activities for workers. The Border-hill Boys,[33] a workers' musical group led by songwriter and accordionist Masa Jäppilä, was active in Helsinki's workers' events in the early 1920s. They sang humorous political songs to the accompaniment of two accordions in community centers around the city, complementing their music with dramatic sketches and even athletic displays. With the growing popularity of German popular songs and jazz, the musicians augmented their ensemble to two five-row accordions, tenor banjo, and drum set and began to play for dances instead of communist political events. Fans sometimes called the musicians the "Dallapé boys," after the esteemed Dallapé Italian accordion brand. The name stuck, and the group came to be called the Dallapé Orchestra. The group experimented with various musicians, bringing in players who leaned toward jazz and could read music. By 1929 Dallapé was using written arrangements, and only Jäppilä was left from the original group. He had taken up drums and vocals in addition to the accordion, and sometimes even played bass drum and accordion at the same time. Many band members doubled on accordion; at one time the lineup was saxophone, accordion/saxophone double, saxophone/violin/accordion double, drums/accordion double, and sousaphone. Jäppilä wanted to promote accordion playing and Dallapé even sponsored an accordion school; at one time the band included ten accordions and was called the Dallapé Accordion Orchestra.[34] Many of their hits, such as "Säkkijärven polkka," are still popular today.[35] In 1932 Dallapé began a series of successful yearly summer tours, traveling across the Finnish countryside in their own bus. In 1933 the band was again remade, transforming from an accordion band to a jazz big band. Singer Georg Malmstén gained fame as director of the group in the 1930s.[36] Looking back on the early days of accordion jazz, he explained: "When the fashionable new dances, fox-trot and tango, became fashionable . . . young people would hum the melodies that they heard in the dance halls, but they did not know the titles of the songs, and the lyrics, if such existed, were foreign. . . . It was evident that there was a need for an indigenous popular music."[37] Local musicians responded to this demand by forging a fusion of local and imported styles. Significantly, they looked to Afro-diasporic music as a source of their own indigenous popular music.

Accordion jazz groups sprang up all over the country, playing at workers' organizations and temperance affairs.[38] Finnish ethnomusicologist Erkki Ala-Könni tells of a band that he led in the 1920s:

We founded [the region] Etela-Pohjanmaa's first, I guess I could call it, jazz band. We called it ZULU, because we played "African music," and the drums had a type of picture on them [*sic*]. We got modern arrangements from Helsinki. We played stuff like English fox trots. . . . I don't know whether you could call it a jazz band or not. For example, we didn't improvise, except every once in a while, kind of as a joke. But it was a lot more modern, it was something new.[39]

The lines between the schoolboy hot bands and the accordion bands blurred as working-class musicians became proficient in hotter jazz and bourgeois players gigged with accordion bands.[40] In 1928, Allan Teräsvuori started the Saxophon Jazz Band [sic], a quintet consisting of Teräsvuori doubling on clarinet/saxophone/trumpet, a violinist, pianist, bassist, and a banjo/drums doubler.[41] They played new tunes from the United States such as "Happy Days are Here Again" in simple arrangements. Having received instruction from Tuomikoski, the Andania alto saxophonist, Teräsvuori could improvise a bit, wowing fans with his clarinet glissandos and jazzy vibrato. The band's bassist Eero Lindroos employed a slap style, while drummer Ossi Aalto constructed his own high-hat according to a model from *Melody Maker*. Aalto's playing was clearly influenced by African American drumming, differing markedly from the marchlike style of the German "Kings of Jazz." The Saxophon Jazz Band sometimes played final choruses of songs in collective improvisation, the bandleader calling out "hotia!" (hot!) while musicians played "straight from their gut, from their own lives, letting anything happen," as they later remembered.[42]

Of all the new jazz-tinged music that emerged from Helsinki, though, Dallapé garnered the greatest favor among the rural masses.[43] On tour in 1938, the Dallapé musicians encountered a Finnish American saxophonist named Bruno Laakko whose playing was so good that he was immediately asked to join the band. That same year, Dallapé met up with Edgar Hayes and his Blue Rhythm Band, visiting from the United States. Hayes's group featured Kenny Clarke on drums and played two sold-out concerts rather than dances. After performing, Hayes's musicians jammed in a restaurant, and Bruno Laako joined them. The Saxophon Jazz Band's bassist remembers: "So then the gentlemen got on stage and began jamming in a way that was, to us, completely new. Those black guys played nonstop for an hour and a half! And what a feeling—it was totally unbelievable and taught us a lot."[44] Indeed, visits by foreign musicians greatly influenced the development of local jazz. The first visiting band to play New Orleans–style jazz without written arrangements in Finland was German clarinetist Erich Borchard's group, which came in 1929.[45] Josephine Baker visited in 1933.[46]

After working with Dallapé for a year, Laakko founded his own outfit in Helsinki, which worked steadily at Helsinki's Lepakko Restaurant under the name Laakko's Bats.[47] This group featured American hits sung in Finnish, including "Jeepers Creepers," which is still much loved in Finland today.[48]

Syncretism and the Accordion

In the 1930s Dallapé, led by singer Georg Malmstén, reigned in the countryside and among workers. The urban bourgeosie, on the other hand, favored a band led by none other than Georg's brother Eugen, a trumpeter. The Rhythm Radio Boys, also known simply as the Rhythm Boys, or Rytmi-pojat, started out by broadcasting live on a popular jazz radio program[49] inspired by the American "Let's Dance" radio show (which had catapulted Benny Goodman to fame).[50] Consisting of three trumpets, three saxophones, trombone, violin, and piano, bass, and drums, the band soon made a name for itself in live venues as well as on recordings. As leaders of the two top groups, Georg and Eugen Malmstén dominated the dance band scene.[51] The third top band, and the most jazz-influenced of them, was the Ramblers.[52] This group had developed from early school-boy jam sessions in 1929–30 and featured trombonist Karl Klaus Salmi, whose style was influenced by Tommy Dorsey.[53]

In spite of their commitment to African American jazz, the Ramblers had to cater to local taste, accompanying top singers such as Matti Jurva perfroming polkas and jenkkas, to keep working.[54] This demonstrates a cleavage between the musicians' and public tastes. Rytmi-pojat, too, strove to emulate American swing bands, taking its studies of African American music seriously; but it also catered to Finnish taste, playing local waltzes and popular songs.[55] The confluence of African American and local influences on these groups was a harbinger of the subsequent history of Finnish popular music; the rising new sound was a syncretic blend of African American, Finnish, German, and Russian elements. As Finns excelled in accordion playing, they naturally applied this skill in the emergent music. The accordion already traversed genre boundaries in Finnish music: it was used in rural folk music as well as all urban styles. It is thus perhaps no surprise that much of the most original jazz playing in Finland up to the 1950s was accordion playing; while local players of other instruments imitated African American models, accordionists forged a unique take on jazz.[56] Players such as Viljo Vesterinen (who played with Dallapé) recorded astonishing jazz recordings that evince understanding of jazz voicings and include interesting improvised solos. Players developed a typically Finnish manner of using the accordion's bellows to accent certain phrases or notes; Vesterinen, for example, used this effect to emphasize swing, stressing off-beat pulses. Although he was primarily a pianist and composer, Toivo Kärki was also an excellent accordionist in this style.[57]

While foreign melodies were popular ("The Yellow Rose of Texas" was a big hit), much of the dance band repertory consisted of Finnish folk songs.[58]

Bands sometimes renamed old Finnish tunes, trying to pass them off as new dance music, and some folk musicians resented this. One musician told me that it especially irked his father, Veikko Leino, a well-known fiddler:

Yrjö Saarnio's Polka Band used to try to pass off folk music as original compositions on radio broadcasts, and my father used to get really angry around the radio whenever Yrjö Saarnio played a jenkka or *polkka*, saying . . ."everyone in Finland knows that that [tune] isn't what they say it is. . . . " And he jumped up and played along with the record, to make his point.[59]

Even when dance bands played foreign tunes, the accordion-dominated timbre and predilection for minor keys branded the results as typically Finnish. This was clearly an emergent, syncretic "jatsi."[60]

Musical dialogue between the new dance music and old pelimanni music was bi-directional: while dance bands incorporated the older Finnish repertory, folk musicians gradually became influenced by the new sounds. Improvisation remained a rarity in the jazz-tinged bands, and it did not influence folk music. Still, a few traditional fiddlers did learn to improvise: Veikko Leino (quoted above), for example, occasionally played with dance bands and enjoyed soloing on jazz standards such as "All of Me."[61] More significant, while rural Finnish dance music was traditionally a solo fiddler's art, the jazz vogue influenced folk musicians to play in groups.[62] According to musicians, the bass was incorporated into pelimanni music in the 1950s to "strengthen the beat." Drums fulfilled this purpose in dance bands, but because they were so closely identified with urban music, they were deemed incompatible with the pelimanni style.[63] That the bass was used in a rhythmic manner, shows that its incorporation into folk music signaled the impact of African American "metronome sense" on Finnish taste.[64]

Reading and Riding Rytmi

In the late 1920s, a group of young Finnish intellectuals celebrated noise and jazz as carnivalesque manifestations of primitivism and futurism.[65] This trend corresponded to similar intellectual currents in Europe and the United States. Articles, short stories, and poems in the *Torchbearers*[66] magazine related jazz to both the wilds of Africa and the rhythmic churning of machines in modernistic urban centers. One *Torchbearers* article asked, "Do Negroes really need us?" answering, "Perhaps we are in greater need of them,"[67] while a writer associated with the *Torchbearers* wrote a book called *Searching for Today,* which stated that "Negroes have taught us to see that every-day Americanized life can be full of rhythm, color, and joy."[68]

Other magazines criticized jazz for the same reasons that the *Torchbearers* celebrated it, claiming that jazz can lead to "over-stimulation of shot nerves, and even nudity." One article warned that "Jazz-Girls Cannot Find Husbands" as they paint their faces and enjoy alcohol and sex, quoting a young woman saying that although she is a "jazz-girl" who enjoys "men, jazz, diversion, cigarettes," she has recently begun to strive for something more, something "higher."[69] These reactions to jazz came on the heels of a long-standing Finnish suspicion of dance, sexuality, and alcohol. One of the first actions taken by independent Finland in 1917 was the institution of the prohibition of alcohol. This was but one of a series of prohibitions against spirits. Finnish folk clarinetist Pilli Herman wrote a song commenting on the ban against making home brew in 1866:

> In the year of '66
> Came to Finland a new law
> Forbidding us to make home brew,
> Ending endless drinking days.[70]

Its association with alcohol earned dance a similar infamy. A suspicion of dance has often made itself felt throughout the entire Western world, as well as the Middle East. Across northern Europe in a belt stretching from Russia to Ireland, dance music and its prime medium, the fiddle, were seen as instruments of evil; couple dances and their associated musics were censured for their alleged lewdness, but flourished nevertheless. Stories went around of musicians learning to play from the devil, and in Finland, tunes such as "The Devil's Polska" were played. Dance was strongly discouraged by the Lutheran Church, and even curtailed or outlawed at various times. In spite of the restrictions, Finns continued to dance, often instigating hush-hush events called "corner dances."

As noted, much of the Finnish anti-jazz writing of the 1920s and 1930s played into the same discourse as did writing that considered the new music a cure for the ills of modern society. Similar attitudes were expressed in the United States, where jazz was linked to all manner of psychic illness on one hand and considered a life-giving power on the other. Both sides agreed on the efficacy of the new music; they only disagreed on whether it was good or bad.[71] One magazine organized a contest in which readers were invited to write short responses to the questions "Why do I dance? Why don't I dance?" While some of the entries criticized jazz, others referred to its therapeutic qualities, saying, for example, "Listening and dancing to jazz is the best medicine for life's ills," or "I cannot say that dancing is merely physically enjoyable; it also brings on a type of 'psychic enjoyment.'"[72]

The Finnish Musicians Union rejected jazz and the magazine that it published openly criticized the music; one article, clearly derived from a North American source, told of Nebraska farmers who had played recorded music in fields in efforts to increase production. When a large dose of jazz was played one year, crops failed.[73] Folklorist Ilmari Krohn demonstrated his formidable musicality in an astute rhythmic analysis of jazz, which he followed with a scathing attack on the music, recommending that it be violently purged from Finland in the same way that the Lapua Movement was attempting to do to communists.

> Jazz thus does not have, and cannot have, artistic worth. . . . We live in an age of great and increasingly critical spiritual antagonism in the arts and in other fields. . . . Jazz has undoubtedly contributed to the rotten swamps of the dark side, but in the light of the dawning day it is destroyed as reprehensible. We must especially pity the youth, which throws itself to the ecstasy of jazz hoping to find true happiness in life. Are we not in need of a storm not unlike the "Lapua movement" to sweep away the racket of this brazenly swollen swamp-music."[74]

My grandfather, an amateur violinist and prominent Finnish citizen at mid-century, considered Sibelius nearly a god but reacted with a combination of consternation and amusement when a Danish friend suggested that the two play Duke Ellington's "Mood Indigo" as a violin and saxophone duet. As one observer put it, "jazz was not music and the saxophone was not an instrument" to many members of the bourgeoisie.[75]

At the same time, others displayed serious interest in the new music. The German composer Ernst Krenek's opera *Jonny Spielt Auf,* which tells the story of a black fiddler in Germany, was well received in Helsinki when it was presented in 1928 and 1929, gaining enough attention to lure the country's president to the debut.[76] In 1931 a magazine published a series of articles presenting twenty-two Finnish composers' answers to the questions "Does jazz have artistic value?" and "Do you believe that jazz will have a lasting influence on music composition?" Twelve of the twenty-two composers expressed positive or neutral views about jazz, while ten criticized the new music.[77] Many of the surveyed composers admitted that they knew little about jazz, and the tone of the ten critical responses was less strident than that of journalists who criticized the music. A 1924 survey of prominent American musicians' opinions about jazz evidenced similarly varied opinions.[78] Only a handful of Finnish art music composers, however, were influenced by jazz. Composer Sulho Ranta wrote an article in *Torchbearers* on historical links between art music and dance music, suggesting that jazz could be a fruitful influence on classical music: "In my opinion, there are three truly contemporary trends in composition, and they are German influence, nationalist modernism, and conservatory jazz."[79] Ernst Pingoud composed a ragtime-influenced ballet called "The Face of the Big City,"[80] while Uno Klam wrote a chamber work called "Ragtime and Blues" and a jazz-tinged piano concerto called "Night on the

Montmartre,"[81] whose name betrays the Parisian influence on the Finnish jazz vogue.[82]

Interestingly, Finland had a jazz magazine earlier than did either the United States or France. *Downbeat* and the French *Jazz Hot* were both founded in 1935,[83] while *Rytmi* (*Rhythm*) was founded in 1934 in conjunction with the Rytmi-pojat radio program. *Rytmi* provided details on band memberships and accounts of musicians' experiences (often written by musicians themselves). Also including instructional articles on how to play jazz by leading musicians such as Tommy Tuomikoski, it served as an important educational tool.[84] *Rytmi* responded to the staunchly anti-jazz Musicians' Union with articles protesting the union's treatment of dance musicians. This led to the founding, in 1937, of the Rhythm Musicians Organization,[85] whose mandate was to promote dance musicians' concerns in cooperation with the Musicians' Union.[86] While other magazines criticized jazz, Rytmi criticized classical music: one article, for example, decried the concert repertoire for its promotion of dead men's music and its emphasis on musical scores rather than on musical sound: "Classical works consist of melodies that no one likes until the composer is dead. As soon as he has finally found his way to the grave people begin a search for and organization of his instruments [and] yellowed scores. . . . All they need is a piano and some manuscript paper. Oh, actually, the piano is not even necessary."[87]

In a 1934 *Rytmi* article called "What is Hot [Music], Really?" trumpeter Eugen Malmstén of Rytmi-pojat wrote that a song's theme is best considered cold, while solo improvisation is hot. He added that in this music one must "feel what one plays . . . play with a certain kind of warmth." He took a Louis Armstrong improvisation discussed in *Melody Maker* as an example. This chorus consists of only four pitches, but these four pitches are enough to convey to the listener that this is Armstrong and not another trumpeter. Malmstén was making an important point: African American vernacular music, as compared to European music, is a performer's art in which it is difficult to draw lines between composer and player.[88] Malmstén worked hard for his band to gain the nuances of jazz style, and the Rytmi-pojat rehearsed a great deal. In 1936 they traveled to England to record on Columbia-Gramophone records and also to learn about jazz from local musicians. *Rytmi*'s publisher, who accompanied the band on this trip, wrote, "We wanted to thoroughly acquaint ourselves with the local bands . . . naturally, we want to listen and learn as much as possible.[89]

The debates on jazz were similar around the world, but nuanced differently in different countries. In Japan, for example, the Japanese word meaning "noise," *sōon,* became practically synonymous with jazz, which, as in the United States and Finland, simultaneously epitomized the primitive and the modern, old and new, savage and civilized.[90] Significantly, primitivism was less appealing to the Japanese than to Europeans, as the Japanese had to counter the Western idea that they themselves were savages.[91] What is remarkable about the debates about jazz in Finland is the seriousness with which the music was taken on both sides. Behind most debates lurked the question of how to reconcile jazz, now ascendant, with Finnishness: how to assimilate this next level of cosmopolitan influence? Nationalists, meanwhile, continued their program of finding and promoting indigenous folk elements. The Kalevala Society's prestigious Celebration of 1937 featured performances of Sibelius's music as well as appearances by an epic singer, a kantele player, and Finnish folk instrumentalist Teppo Repo. The folk music scholar Väisänen, who had played such a large part in creating Repo's nationalist persona, introduced Repo thus: "Since the sublime melodies of the *Kullervo Symphony* have echoed from this stage, shouldn't we listen for a moment to the original herdsman's tunes, which have echoed on summer days in village lanes and in the forests of the Kullervo runes' original locale?"[92] And yet when it came to one of his most celebrated compositions, Repo explained that he considered it to be a type of "jazz." For his part, Väisänen insisted that it was a "scherzo":[93]

In '36 when I went to Germany, on the way, on the boat, the engine was making a lot of noise, and I couldn't sleep at all. In the morning, on the deck, Dr. Väisänen asked me if I had slept well.
    "I couldn't sleep at all."
    "How is that?"
    "The engine was sputtering, so I started composing."
    "And what kind of composition is it?"
    "Well, jazz."
    And then when he had heard it, he said that there is no jazz in it at all, that it is a scherzo. . . . Väisänen said right away that this is a good piece, and that I should play it at the dinner party in Lübeck.[94]

During this trip to Germany, Väisänen presented a contingent of folk musicians to the highest ranks of the Third Reich; Repo recalls that Hermann Göring even offered him a shot of whisky.[95] Repo's anecdote testifies that Finnish nationalists preferred to link local vernacular arts to Germanic concert music, not to African American popular music.

The War and the Dance Ban

World War II began in Finland in November 1939, when the Soviet Union attacked with the objective of obtaining a buffer zone to protect Leningrad. By March of the following year the Soviets had taken almost all of Finland's Karelia region. The devastating defeat of this Winter War, as

Finns call it, resulted in the majority of Finnish Karelians relocating to western Finland. Finland joined Germany's attack of the Soviet Union in 1941 in what Finns call the Continuation War, whose purpose was to regain lost territory as well as to take eastern Karelia, which had not previously belonged to Finland. Finland lost the war and, according to the 1944 truce, not only failed to regain any of Karelia but also gave up the area of Petsamo and was required to drive German troops from Lapland.

The war was a taxing, all-out effort. Dance was considered frivolous and unsuitable in these serious times; in 1939, the Ministry of the Interior decreed that patriotic parties, theater, and concerts were the only appropriate amusements. Dancing was banned.[96] At weddings, fiancés could dance one waltz only, while others watched. Fines were levied when police caught dancers.[97] Dancing in private homes did not stop, but one person was assigned the task of looking out for authorities; if the police appeared, musicians switched to non-dance music.[98] While dance was banned, teaching it was not, so dance schools were founded to serve as de facto dance halls.

In the United States, of course, the opposite view prevailed as amusements were considered a way to gain strength in wartime, and a similar attitude prevailed in the United Kingdom.[99] Finland, in fact, was the only country where dance was banned during World War II.[100] While the ban was purportedly instituted because festivity was unsuitable while the country fought for its survival, attitudes were also informed by religious movements' long-standing suspicion, and occasional proscription, of dance. Although the 1917 alcohol ban had been lifted in 1931, general wariness of drinking remained, and restrictions on dance had always had to do with the fact that, combined with alcohol, it was believed to lead to sexual activity. The dance ban was debated in newspapers, with religious leaders and rightist youth organizations supporting it and leftist Social Democrats opposing it—possibly because of the great popularity of dance among the working class.[101]

While the ban was on dancing and not on jazz, it implicated jazz directly, as jazz was the top urban dance music of the period. Restaurants either stopped presenting live music altogether or switched from jazz to light classics.[102] In Germany and occupied Europe, of course, jazz and all American culture was highly suspect. Nazi ideologue Goebbels argued that Americans had no indigenous culture and instead perverted traditional civilization; for example, by turning conventional language into slang and waltzes into "nigger-Jew jazz," performed by simian blacks and diffused by cunning Semites. Still, the Nazis were unable to curb jazz's popularity in Germany and pursued policies alternating between proscription and hesitant tolerance.[103] It is difficult to assess the degree to which Finnish attitudes were informed by anti-Americanism: U.S. films, for example, were shown during the beginning of the war, but were later banned.[104] The Finnish Army sponsored its own swing group, the Bunker Boys, which was led by Eugen Malmstén and enjoyed great popularity. Sweden still exerted considerable cultural influence in Finland, and swing was very big in Sweden in this period. The 1940 film *Swing it, magistern!* (Swing it, Teacher!), starring the vivacious Swedish singer Alice "Babs" Nilsson, had an element of tame youth rebellion that appealed to Finnish youth. Nilsson toured Finland in 1943 and a Finnish all-woman swing vocal group called the Harmony Sisters gained popularity in Sweden and even Germany.[105]

Finns did not participate in the virulent anti-Semitism endemic in Germany (or Russia and Poland, for that matter). Heinrich Himmler paid a "private holiday visit" to Finland in 1942 during which he pressured authorities to deport the more than two thousand Jews estimated to be in the country. Eight Jewish refugees were deported but, following protests from the Finnish Social Democrats and Lutheran leaders, no further deportations were made.[106] Still, the Finnish right wing leaned toward German thinking, and some Finnish rightists opposed African American music outright. One magazine article suggested, for example, that "Negro music should be abandoned" because although jazz "is suitable for Negroes and may be suitable for Anglo-Saxons, it is only stupefying to civilized Europeans."[107] As mentioned, the core of jazz fans and players were Swedish-speaking upper-middle-class youth. Several major movers of this jazz community, such as guitarist Herbert Katz and drummer Jaakko Vuormaa, were Jews.[108] *Rytmi* magazine stopped appearing during the war and Vuormaa put out a Swedish-language newsletter called *Yam* (jam) that featured articles on jazz and employed youthful, slang-laden language. Referring to *Yam* in Nazi-like tones, an article in another magazine reported: "The Jewish film and dance publication YAM recently organized a propaganda matinee. A series of jazz and step films, mainly from Hollywood, were shown. This particularly inferior, cheap art form (to be generous) was meant to cheer up the audience in these somber times."[109]

Still, outside of right-wing circles, the African American origins of jazz were not seen as cause to discredit the music, as the name of a 1943 radio talk show on jazz, "Black Music," shows.[110] It seems that the wartime dance ban had more to do with the deep-rooted suspicions of dance, alcohol, and sexuality. "Evening Shows"[111]—variety programs consisting of plays, poetic recitation, athletic demonstrations, song, instrumental music, and social dance—had long been popular in Finland. After the truce of August 1944, dance was allowed for one hour at the end of an Evening Show, but was still forbidden at political events and in restaurants (possibly because they served alcohol).[112] The postwar ban against dancing at political events may also have been an effort on the part of rightist elements to curtail leftist political activity; leftists could have benefited from the popularity of dance among workers. The ban on dance at political events was lifted in December 1944, but the ban on dancing in restaurants remained.[113]

Yet dance was more popular than ever. Often, "edifying," nondance events were put on merely to allow the one hour of dance, which, in practice, was stretched to a longer time.[114] Bandleader Olli Häme wrote that musicians capitalized on this, often doing several gigs in one night.[115] When arms were put down in 1944, Dallapé and other bands played in the open air in downtown Helsinki. Among other genres, they played the conga, the Cuban carvival dance that had become popular transnationally. As one musician remembers, "the conga made a surprise attack in Finland right after the war. It was the first modish dance in Helsinki after the war."[116] The most popular conga was an instrumental arrangement of a song called "Kerenski," named for the president of the postrevolutionary provisional government of Russia:

> Oh, stupid Keren-SKI,
> Vainly did you hope—PAM!
> Finland is a free coun-TRY,
> Free of all you Russians—PAM!

Because Finland had lost the war to the Soviets, this text could not be sung, but its meaning was known to most Finns and likely contributed to the conga's popularity.[117]

Some criticized postwar dancing as "dancing on graves." Others continued to oppose it on religious grounds. The tax on dance events remained, while, as mentioned, "edifying" Evening Shows stressing other activities could include one hour of dancing without being taxed.[118] Both rightists and leftists participated in the anti-dance and anti-alcohol discourse.[119] Religious organizations and the rightist Finnish Youth League[120] opposed dancing, while the leftist Finnish Democratic Youth League[121] taught that dance should not be banned but that dance and alcohol should not go together.[122] Alcohol was rationed after the war; each citizen had a card that permitted him or her to buy a prescribed amount of hard alcohol in liquor stores per month. Still in the early 1960s, many Finns considered dance an appropriate activity for youth, but suspect for others.[123]

Finns were fortunate that the Soviets neither incorporated their country into the USSR nor pulled it behind the Iron Curtain after the war. The country retained a multiparty, free market system, while granting concessions such as leasing the Soviets the Hanko and Porkkala peninsulas for use as military installations and allowing the Communist Party (which had been banned after independence) to operate within the multiparty system.[124] Urho Kekkonen became president in 1956, proving adept at appeasing the Soviets, and remained in power until 1981. Finland was successful in rebuilding after the war, gaining transnational recognition by hosting the Olympics in 1952 and through the rise of Finnish architecture and design of Alvar Aalto and others.

Influences from Britain and the United States grew as Finns turned away from German influence. Foreign popular culture made big inroads: prior to the war, 5 percent of records sold in Finland were foreign; this figure rose to more than 50 percent in the 1950s.[125] Increased ties to the outside world were also manifested in performances by jazz greats from the United States, performances that vitalized the Finnish jazz scene. Louis Armstrong came in 1949 and returned in 1953. In that year Lee Konitz, Dizzy Gillespie, and Norman Granz's Jazz at the Philharmonic tour, featuring Lester Young, Oscar Peterson, and Ella Fitzgerald, also came.[126] Bassist Slam Stewart, trumpeter "Peanuts" Holland, and tenor saxophonist Franz Jackson visited, recording with locals and instigating jam sessions that were fondly remembered.[127] Of course, American artists' visits were important educational experiences for Finnish musicians, but because these visits were rare, and also because Finnish musicians might have been intimidated by the Americans, ideas about jazz often came from Sweden. Visiting Swedish musicians thus exerted an important influence on the development of jazz in Finland. The Finnish jazz historian Jukka Haavisto opines that Swedish jazz was "digestible, clean, clearly arranged, and in good taste" but also that it was often "anemic and academic." He added: "Who has seen a Swedish jazz musician play with his eyes crossed, shaking to the beat?"[128] Perhaps exoticizing African American style, he wrote that Finnish musicians developed two schools: the Swedish hypercorrect style on one hand and an "eccentric, even ecstatic, black" style on the other.

Local dance band music became more popular than ever, and dance halls took over from restaurants as the prime contexts for dance.[129] Composer Toivo Kärki rose as an important pianist and dance music composer;[130] he was firmly committed to African American music, writing that "my soul is black and it sings the blues."[131] As compared to prewar sound, the postwar bands bore a greater African American influence, incorporating more jazz harmonies and swinging more.[132] Large international record companies placed little attention on small markets such as Finland in the postwar period, so a group of Finnish musicians and entrepreneurs, led by the Finnish Jew Harri Orvomaa (an enthusiastic jazz record collector and expert on Slavic and klezmer music),[133] founded the Scandia Record Company in 1953. Scandia produced several jazz hits, outselling established Finnish labels. Songs were either translated American hits or jazzed-up versions of traditional Finnish songs, many of which were actually Russian tunes translated into Finnish. " Bei mir bist du schoen," a Yiddish song that had been converted into a jazz hit in the United States, was released in Finland and translated into Finnish as "You are the Prettiest."[134] Interestingly, because Yiddish musical style has an Eastern European flavor similar to that of Russian music, it melded perfectly with Finnish taste. Contributing to the charm of the Finnish version are teenaged singer Brita Koivunen's voice, swinging clarinet playing, and the song's Finnish words, which employ informal spoken rather than standard Finnish, a practice that became more and more prevalent in Finland and likely developed as a result of African American influence.[135]

As we have seen in the cases of the *Rytmi* and *Yam* magazines, musicians themselves often took the driver's seat when it came to thinking and writing about jazz. No book-length study of jazz, however, had appeared in the Finnish language. To fill this void, bassist/bandleader Olli Häme wrote *The Triumph of Rhythm*[136] in 1949. This book not only traces the history of jazz in the United States and Finland, but includes musical analysis of bebop and an instructional chapter on jazz harmony and arranging. It thus served as an important practical guide for Finnish jazz musicians. Like some U.S. and French critics, Häme did not recognize an overarching category encompassing all the forms that we today consider jazz. He reserved this epithet for the New Orleans and Chicago styles, called dance-band music "swing," and considered bebop a genre in its own right.[137] This taxonomy was adopted by other Finns in the postwar years: for example, when the state radio station instituted a jazz program, it was called "From Jazz to Bebop." A concert series of the period was also called "From Jazz to Bebop," and band competitions had separate categories for traditional jazz, swing, and bop.[138] In contrast to the United States, where jazz has occasionally been claimed as a generically American form rather than a specifically African American one, there was no debate about the origins of jazz in Finland. Evidence suggests that Finns recognized the music's roots in black culture, and recognized that this influence was becoming pervasive in their own country: Häme, for example, wrote that "Afro-American dance music is the original Negroid dance music that is played in our dance halls." Along similar lines, he opined that the notion that Gershwin's music is a "bejewelled form of jazz" is "incorrect" because Gershwin's music has little to do with African American aesthetics.[139] He thus concurred with Ellington, who once said Gershwin failed to capture black style.[140]

As noted, Finnish musicians considered *rhythm* the characteristic element of African American music. Häme wrote: "The bases for evaluating Afro-American dance music and concert music are completely different. Rhythm never appears in concert music to the extent, or most importantly, in the same way as it appears in dance music."[141] *The Triumph of Rhythm* not only celebrates his adopted musical aesthetic, but was also prophetic: African American musical style *did* triumph in Finland, as it did on the larger world stage. Even today, the concept of *rytmimusiikki,* or "rhythm-music," is invoked in Finland to refer to Afro-diasporic forms such as jazz, rock, and hip-hop, as well as to other styles deemed "rhythmic," such as Middle Eastern and eastern European musics. But how exactly did Finnish musicians interpret the African American aesthetic (or "rhythm," as they called it)?

The editors of *Rytmi* magazine once asked the Swedish jazz critic Harry Nicolausson to attend and comment on a 1952 Finnish "Jazz-jamboree" concert. He obliged with his frank assessment that in many cases, bands did not swing: "Many soloists knew their instruments well enough, had style and ideas, and at least gave the feeling that they understood the question at hand. But they will not be all the way there until they have good rhythmic support."[142] After wounds healed, Finnish jazzmen began a lively discussion about the groove. Haavisto writes that swing depends on band members having the same idea of where the beat is, opining that Finnish musicians' problems with swing occurred when one player "slows down" while another "speeds up."[143] This perspective is similar to the perspective explicated in chapter 2; however, while Haavisto claims that the bassist and drummer should aspire to having the same idea of the beat's location, U.S. jazz musicians usually emphasize the importance of rapport, a willingness to enter into a *conversation* about the pulse.

Given Finland's limited exposure to African American music until the 1960s, one must marvel at local musicians' devotion to it, which indicates that the music had deep meaning for them. While some rhythm sections might have been a bit stilted, many others had a nice groove.[144] Growing contact with American culture beginning in the 1950s created a situation in which various Afro-diasporic musics, ranging from jazz to rock, salsa to hip-hop, came to dominate Finnish musical culture.

While rock 'n' roll was often considered in opposition to jazz in the United States in the 1950s, it was seen as a complement to jazz in Finland;

their common blues base was obvious. One Finnish critic wrote in 1956 that the new rhythm and blues "has influenced jazz as it is performed around the world, which in recent years has come to include more and more swing. In Finland there are [jazz-influenced] musicians who . . . get very close to the spirit of 'rock and roll.'"[145] The first Finnish rock record was jazz accordionist Matti Viljanen's version of "Rock Around the Clock," which appeared in 1955.[146] Viljanen continued in the line of Finnish accordionists who adapted the prevailing accordion style to African American musics.

Dallapé and other Finnish bands had included Cuban numbers, such as those popularized by Xavier Cugat, in their repertories since the 1930s.[147] As in the United States, Latin American dance music gained popularity in the 1950s. Afro-Cuban music aficionado and multi-instrumentalist Sacy Sand[148] rose to the fore of the Finnish Latin music scene, playing drums, bass, and tenor saxophone in various groups during the late 1940s. Sand was a many-faceted man who approached his interest in Afro-Cuban music from several angles. In addition to being a musician, he worked as a commercial artist and painted artworks. He wrote newspaper articles about Benny Moré and Tito Rodríguez, took Spanish classes, and studied Latin percussion on his own. Ossi Runne's group specialized in Latin music; the bandleader explained, "My own band's repertoire consisted of ⅓ tango, ⅓ jazz, and ⅓ Latin."[149] In 1953 Runne hired Sand to sing in Spanish and play percussion. Sand started his own band, the Rytmi-Veikot (loosely, the Rhythm Guys) in 1957, featuring himself singing and taking conga solos lasting up to seven minutes, à la Desi Arnaz.[150] The Finnish Latin music explosion even produced a film, *Rion Yöt* (A night in Rio), in 1951. This Finnish-language production reproduced the Hollywood style, with music and dance numbers featuring Sacy Sand.[151]

Significantly, it was after the assimilation of rock and Latin music in Finland in the 1960s that Finnish musicians truly internalized Afro-diasporic aesthetics and began to produce jazz on a world-class level. The Swedish critic Nicolasson's 1952 negative assessment of Finnish swing came at the turning point of the Finnish assimilation of African American aesthetics, at the beginning of the postwar era of increased contact with the United States. While rock displaced jazz as the dominant form of popular music, it also facilitated a better understanding of African American aesthetics, as we shall see.

Tango, Russia, and the Finnish Soul

Increased influences from Britain and the United States and the impact of television and youth culture began to be felt; in 1962 there were 336,000 television sets in Finland, and by 1966 there were 822,000.[152] As mentioned, rock 'n' roll had blended easily with Finnish jazz-tinged music in the 1950s. In the 1960s, however, rock met opposition from proponents of the now-traditional Finnish dance bands, who called it "steel-wire music."[153] The polemics surrounding the rise of the electric guitar paralleled the similarly generational and class-based polemics surrounding Finnish jazz in the 1920s.[154]

Because of its long-standing popularity among Finns, the tango had a special place among musical types in Finland and was considered a genre apart from "Latin" styles of Cuban and Brazilian origin. While the tango had long been part of the dance band repertory, it had not dominated in the early years. In the 1960s, however, older-generation rural and working Finns, who disliked the encroaching popularity of rock 'n' roll among urban bourgeois youth, adopted the tango in a search for Finnish authenticity. As Finnish ethnomusicologist Pekka Gronow writes, many agrarian and working-class Finns were "now looking for a music which would sound truly Finnish, and somewhat paradoxically . . . adopted the tango. Either you supported the Beatles or the tango. At the height of the Beatles' popularity, the only domestic records that made the top three on the record charts were tangos."[155] In the 1950s, tangos constituted approximately 10 percent of all records sold, but after the Beatles hit in 1963, it grew to 50 percent.[156] A local version of the tango which has been called "the only original Finnish musical genre of the twentieth century," emerged in the postwar era.[157] Jalkanen shows that the earlier style of Finnish music, based in the melancholy Russian-influenced melodies, survived in the tango (as well as other Finnish styles) in spite of changes in the surface level of Finnish music. Proclaiming it a "crystallization of Finnish soul," he writes that the Finnish tango is "shy and reserved" rather than "macho" like the Argentine original. Songs express the melancholy of "the quiet village road, on the one hand; the soothing escape of Fairyland and the Argentine pampas on the other."[158] Rhythms are less syncopated than in the Argentine version, and melodies conform to the Russian type so prevalent in Finnish dance-band music. At a dance during a 1988 field trip, I asked my partner, "What type of music are we dancing to?" Her answer: "Don't you know? This is the national dance of Finland, the tango!"[159]

Several simultaneous layers of musical taste are apparent in the music of violinist, vibraphonist, and vocalist Matti Heinivaho. Heinivaho gained fame in the early 1950s, singing with a group called the Pelimanni-Pojat, or Pelimanni Boys. This jazz-tinged dance band's name interestingly invokes links to the earlier pelimanni folk music style. In addition to gaining fame as a singer of hit dance tunes in the early 1950s, Heinivaho developed into a dedicated jazz man, taking up the vibraphones, which came into favor during this period (possibly due to the extraordinary popularity of George Shearing's quintet, which featured this instrument). Heinivaho was chosen as director of the Rhythm Musicians' Club[160] of Tampere, Finland's second largest city, in 1959. He is remembered today for instigating memorable jam sessions where he insisted that established bands not play together, mixing players together from various groups in order to force them to improvise rather than rely on arrangements. In 1963, a Finnish line dance (à la conga) called the *letka-jenkka* became popular, spreading to Sweden and beyond; Finnish letka-jenkka records were sold as far away as the United States and Japan. Heinivaho had a letka-jenkka hit that featured an improvised jazz solo on baritone saxophone.[161] Heinivaho currently serves as head of Tam-Jazz, a jazz musicians' organization in Tampere, where I taught on a Fulbright grant in 2001. I once participated in a jam session where Heinivaho held court on vibes. After we played a few jazz standards, Heinivaho began singing a medley of his hit songs from the 1950s. I was surprised and stopped to listen, because all of a sudden, instead of jazz, the band was playing what sounded like Finnish folk music. The tunes were obviously familiar to audience members, since almost everyone in the club began to sing along and clap to the (unsyncopated) beat. The musician in me felt left out, but the ethnomusicologist in me perked up. I decided to catch the eye of the only non-Finn in the small club, a visiting student from Russia who was attending my lectures at the university. I expected to exchange knowing glances with her, sharing befuddlement at all this Finnishness. When I located her in the crowd, however, I was surprised to see her happily singing and clapping along with the rest of the audience: the only difference was that while everyone else was singing in Finnish, she was singing in Russian! Many of the songs in the medley were, in fact, Russian songs. The following week I recounted this story to the band's bassist. He answered that, "no, I don't understand; those songs are Finnish, not Russ—wait a minute, you are right, many of them are translated from Russian songs." His hesitation reflected a basic Finnish ambivalence about Russianness. Because Finland gained its independence from Russia and protected itself valiantly againt Soviet incursions during World War II, Finnish national identity is largely articulated in opposition to Russia. At the same time, the infusion of Russian style in Finnish music indicates a closeness with Russian musical aesthetics.

The Music Is Dead—Long Live the Music!

Until the late 1950s, of course, jazz was only a spice in the brew of Finnish dance-band music. At this time, however, what Otto Donner calls a "paradigm shift" occurred as players increasingly wanted to pursue jazz as a profession and began injecting more improvisation into the dance-band repertoire.[162] At the same time, rock emerged as the top form of popular music, and jazz increasingly became music for listening rather than dancing.

Postwar Finland saw the rise of social-democratic policies supporting education, social programs, and the arts. As workers demanded rights, leading to institution of the welfare state in the 1960s, jazz musicians demanded that their art be taken seriously by the state. The League of Finnish Rhythm Clubs, established in 1947, had become inactive, and a group of the country's prominent musicians (joined by the grand man of Finnish ethnomusicology, Pekka Gronow) founded the Finnish Jazz League in 1966. In a statement of purpose written to announce its formation, the league explained that its purpose was to "demand an explanation and a solution to the problem that in Finland official support is given to the artistic endeavors of 'concert music' but not of jazz. The Finnish Jazz League demands that state and local government's arts policies support jazz and other forms of music in addition to 'concert music.'"[163] Beginning in the 1960s, various arms of the Finnish state began to actively support jazz, sponsoring grants that in some cases, fund musicians for years at a time.[164] The Finnish Broadcasting Company funded trips of Finnish jazz musicians to European Broadcasting Union (EBU) annual jazz concerts; the EBU sponsored jazz competitions, and Finns won several times.[165] By 1991, the Finnish Jazz League had a budget of more than 2.5 million Finn Marks annually, of which 40.3 percent came from the Ministry of Education.[166] The league took over *Rytmi* magazine in 1967, and beginning in 1971 it began to sponsor the "Georgie" Prize, awarded annually to a top jazz musician.[167] One of the major movers of postwar Finnish jazz, saxophonist Seppo Paakkunainen, made an astute tongue-in-cheek comment about the role of public funding in Finnish jazz: "Without resources, art will not develop these days. The myth that the blues was born only of suffering, persecution, and poverty does not hold in Finland."[168] While *Rytmi* magazine had long promoted jazz education, presenting instructional articles—and bands functioned as educational institutions in themselves—there were no formal educational programs for jazz in Finland until the establishment of a program in jazz performance at the University of Jyväskylä in 1970. The establishment of other programs followed. The Helsinki Pop/Jazz Conservatory was founded in 1972, and Finland's most prestigious conservatory, the Sibelius Academy, founded a jazz department in 1983.[169]

Urban youth participated in youth movements emanating in Paris and the United States. Leftist songsters expressed young people's views, and several innovative, progressive rock bands emerged that served as incubators for creative developments in jazz; many jazzers played in these groups.[170] Increasingly adept in African American aesthetics, young Finnish jazz musicians also supported African American social movements. While their stance against U.S. capitalism and imperialism distanced Finnish progressive youth from the United States on one hand, their affinity for the black rights struggle and their love of African American music linked them to the United States on the other. This double-edged situation was, of course, an outgrowth of jazz consciousness's inherent doubleness—paralleling the development of jazz in the Dominican Republic, where the music's doubleness was also important in the ways that it was reinterpreted. Because Finland is not in the African diaspora, however, there were different issues at stake. The African American strategy of inclusion resonated with Finns because, as citizens of a small country, they also needed to balance awareness of dominant trends with attendance to in-group needs.

The Radio Dance Band (later renamed the Radio Jazz Band) had been working since 1957. Members of this group formed UMO (Uuden Musiikin Orkesteri, or the New Music Orchestra) in 1975 and soon gained recognition with acclaimed performances in London and the United States. Successful in gaining financial support from the state and working consistently, the group developed into an important vehicle for new jazz compositions, regularly commissioning works from both Finnish and foreign composers.[171] UMO's recordings often premiere works by top-shelf guest musicians and composers who record with the band. Its list of American collaborators is thus a veritable Who's Who of contemporary jazz: Dizzy Gillespie, Gil Evans, McCoy Tyner, Muhal Richard Abrams, Thad Jones, Kenny Wheeler, John Scofield, Michael Brecker, Natalie Cole, Manhattan Transfer, Maria Schneider, and Dave Liebman.[172] In addition to playing cutting-edge jazz, UMO's domestic repertoire caters to the taste of non-jazz aficionados, featuring vocalists and swing-era hits.

Heikki Sarmanto and Edvard Vesala emerged as the major movers of postwar Finnish jazz.[173] A composer and pianist, Sarmanto is the best-known Finnish jazz musician internationally. He studied at the Sibelius Academy (with the noted composer Joonas Kokkonen) and at Boston's Berklee College of Music, developing into a skilled writer. After valuable experiences as a player in both Europe and the United States (notably, with Nils-Henning Østed Pederson in the Nordic All-Stars Band), Sarmanto began to gain recognition as a composer. His "New Hope Jazz Mass" brought him to the limelight with an auspicious premiere at Saint Peter's "jazz" Church in Manhattan.[174] Saint Peter's hosts funerals and other important events, and many consider it the religious home of the New York jazz community. The New Hope Jazz Mass received a favorable review in the *New York Times* and was recorded on the Finlandia record label, which specializes in Euro-classical music. In addition to other sacred works, Sarmanto composed a concert piece for Sonny Rollins that premiered in Japan and is the subject of a documentary film, as well as a large-scale symphonic work, *Suomi* (Finland), which premiered in Carnegie Hall in 1988. Stylistically, Sarmanto uses the harmonic palette of postromanticism associated with the national romantic school spearheaded by Sibelius; his lyrical style and interest in national themes thus inspired one journalist to call him a Finnish "national-romantic jazz-lyricist."[175]

Sarmanto takes a stance against musical categories, quoting Miles Davis as saying that "jazz is dead" but also affirming that much valuable music has emerged postmortem.[176] He proudly notes that while he is firmly grounded in classical music and is a member of the Finnish Composers' Guild he is also a member of the Finnish Entertainment Music Guild.[177] In fact, genre-blurring and an openness to the idea that jazz may as well be dead was perhaps the dominant trend in Finnish jazz during the 1970s and 1980s. Even the Finnish Jazz League expressed a holistic musical consciousness, its statement of purpose declaring: "Although the Finnish Jazz League's main purpose is to promote the position of jazz, the League's perspective is not to blindly drive the interests of one group, but to develop musical life in its totality. The Finnish Jazz League does not want our music politics to lead in any single direction."[178]

Drummer, bandleader, and composer Edward Vesala emerged as whom many consider the most original voice in Finnish jazz; along with colleagues from neighboring countries, he forged a specifically north European form of jazz.[179] Vesala studied percussion and theory for two years at the Sibelius Academy and went on to play in continental Europe with Peter Brötzmann and others, and in the United States with Chick Corea and Archie Shepp. He made a series of recordings on the ECM label that gained international recognition.[180] Vesala produced a distinctive, crystal tone on cymbals and developed an original voice as a composer; his group's name, Sound and Fury, aptly describes the fiery passion and acid timbres of his music. His compositions are often studies in timbre: "Sylvan Swizzle," for example, blends shimmering cymbals with similarly icy woodwind tones.[181] Vesala's music shows influence by Euro-classical music, evident in the long through-composed sections. His music-making, however, employs aural methods of transmission and rhythmic underpinnings derived from African American sources. Rhythmic underpinnings range from free jazz drumming to funky beats and Finnish tango. He often taught his music to players aurally, singing the parts to them, thus imparting nuances of interpretation in addition to pitches and rhythms. He also worked closely with his musicians, urging them to develop personal sounds as im-provisers.[182] Vesala once went so far as to flaunt his commitment to the aural tradition, saying that score paper is only "good for lighting fires."[183] Like Sarmanto, Vesala espoused genre-busting: while acknowledging his debt to African American music, he felt no allegiance to a reified jazz tradi-tion, going so far as to name one of his CDs *Ode to the Death of Jazz*.[184] Referring to jazz neoclassicists' re-creations of earlier styles, he said, "This empty echoing of old styles . . . I think it's tragic. If that's what the jazz tra-dition has become then I don't see my band as part of it any longer."[185]

Jazz and the Folk Music Vogue

Some of the most vital trends in Finnish jazz developed in tandem with a renewed interest in folk music. This "folk music vogue"[186] began as a grassroots rural movement but gained a following among urban youth when rural fiddlers wowed audiences at a 1971 "Ruisrock" rock festival, touted as the "Finnish Woodstock."[187] This trend reflected a need to ar-ticulate Finnish national identity in the transnational sphere; again, the need to define national identity, this time not in response against imperial-ism (as with Russia), but against homogenizing global mass culture. An ad-venturous new folk music movement took shape, as urban groups com-bined Finnish materials (often culled from archival sources) and traditional instruments with sundry cosmopolitan influences. From its inception, jazz musicians were instrumental in this burgeoning Finnish "world music" fu-sion movement.[188]

Inspired by the British folk-rock group Fairport Convention as well as jazz, baritone saxophonist Seppo Paakkunainen and Edward Vesala founded a band called Karelia in 1970. Karelia combined traditional Finnish instru-ments such as the kantele, *jouhikko* (a bowed lyre similar to the Welsh crwth), and fiddle with saxophones, electric bass, accordion, synthesizers, trap drums, and Latin percussion.[189] At main stage in the band's instrumentation are herdsman's instruments similar to those Teppo Repo played. Asked whether his music is jazz or Finnish folk music, Paakkunainen answers, "It's neither."[190] He expounds on his use of Finnish sources, crafting a new Finn-ish identity based in purported links to African American, rather than Euro-pean culture:

The meaning of Finnish folk music for jazz has been the same as its meaning for jazz in other countries. In my opinion there is a clear connection between African melodies and Finnish [Kalevalaic] poem melodies. [Finnish] laments are Finnish blues, where you can also hear a strong blue note . . .and a type of "neutral third" in which, for example, a rising third from C is sung between E and E♭, that is, purposefully off-pitch.[191]

He adds that "unless it is possible [for Finns] to create jazz on the highest international standards, we should build upon our own national resources."[192] Karelia and other similar groups foreshadowed the interest in "world music" fusion that rose internationally in ensuing decades.[193]

An interesting band variously called "Etnopojat" (The Ethnoboys), "the Urban Shepherds," or "the World Mänkeri Orchestra" emerged in the 1980s.[194] I shall discuss them at length in spite of their relatively low profile on the Finnish music scene, partly because of their musical worth, but also because their story brings up important issues. Pekka Westerholm played saxophone and clarinet in progressive rock groups and jazz-tinged dance bands as a teenager and university student, citing Charlie Parker, Eric Dolphy, and Jan Garbarek as major influences. He teaches in the same primary school as Heikki Syrjänen, who started playing clarinet, baritone horn, and alto saxophone as a child in local wind ensembles and jazz bands. In 1983, the two reed players started improvising on cowherd's horns such as the *mänkeri* and *liru,* which are similar to the instruments that Teppo Repo had played. An instrument-making course offered at the Kaustinen Folk Music Festival excited them about building as well as playing the old cowherds' instruments; Westerholm discovered a true talent for instrument making. Teaming up with bassist Olli Penttilä, Syrjänen and Westerholm started "The World Mänkeri Orchestra." They expressed a note of irony when telling me that the name was inspired by the innovative World Saxophone Quartet; Syrjänen and Westerholm feel that it is incongruous, almost comical, to pair the down-home rural Finnish word mänkeri with the cosmopolitan hipness of that group. While they utilize non-Finnish instruments such as the Irish *bodhran* and Turkish *darabuka* drums and electric bass, the World Mänkeri Orchestra's style centers on handmade Finnish instruments. Their improvisations and compositions are based on early Finnish melodies couched in rock and free-jazz idioms.

Syrjänen told me that he had always loved improvised music but felt that standard jazz instruments such as the saxophone carry stylistic baggage that impeded his early development as an improviser. For this reason he found playing Finnish cowherds' horns liberating: "Due to the nature of the instruments, so-called jazz clichés pretty much vanished from our music, and of course, we have probably striven for this." While Syrjänen and Westerholm are capable of playing bebop lines on the cowherd's horns (their chromatic facility on these keyless instruments is astounding), they rarely, if ever, do so in performance. Syrjänen told me that his primary jazz influences come from free improvisers rather than from bebop: "Proponents of the bebop school, straight-ahead, have not really interested me; they have always really been the free saxophonists, people like Pharaoh Sanders or someone. . . . The only style that I can personally say that has influenced me, at this point anyway, if anything, is, like, new music . . . free improvisation: I have gotten ideas from this." This influence is clear in their recording "Let's Dance," which features two horns improvising contrapuntally in a style evocative of Ornette Coleman's classic recording *Free Jazz,* overlain on funky electric bass lines.

The members of the World Mänkeri Orchestra feel that their originality stems largely from the fact that they play Finnish instruments, made by Finns from Finnish wood. Syrjänen affirms: "Yes, it is important to us that we can say that this [music] is Finnish. . . . We're not any proud nationalists, I don't mean that. What I mean is that . . . we are truly content that this style can be based on Finnish music."[195] The folk music vogue developed as a response to globalization and the concomitant inundation of transnational mass culture. Syrjänen sees the World Mänkeri Orchestra music as an avowedly Finnish alternative to what he considers capitalist cultural imperialism:

You shouldn't get involved in something just because some advertising executive is ingenious and shrewd enough to create a demand for rock and disco and these things. . . . We would like to . . . make it known that Finns should have the courage to understand that we have our own culture and our very own music, which is of value, and you can connect anything you want with it, and live contentedly.

Referring to some of his compatriots' interest in various non-Western styles, he asserts:

We aren't especially interested in the musics of other cultures, except to the extent that of course it's worthwhile to acquaint oneself with them. But in Finland there are a lot of musicians who have gone, for example, to Africa especially to fulfill their musical ambitions. In Finland, we have [one of] Havana's most popular Cuban groups [El Septeto, discussed below]. . . . Some people feel that they need to leave this country, but we don't have to leave. . . . This Finnish tradition is enough; we have nothing to be ashamed of here, and we don't need anything else.[196]

At the same time, however, the World Mänkeri Orchestra players derived much of their inspiration from black American musicians who had found their own roots in Africa. African American musicians' interest in non-European styles, and their use of African instruments in the 1960s, piques these Finnish musicians' fascination, as well as my own, with Finnish cowherd's horns. Syrjänen told me: "I have thought about the reed-playing idols that I used to have, and each of them has had this kind of ethnic image also; if you think about Pharaoh Sanders, or even Rahsaan Roland Kirk, they all had a certain type of ethnic image, so this has also naturally had an influence in this direction too."[197] Witness the photos of Teppo Repo, Rahsaan Roland Kirk, Heikki Syrjänen, and Pekka Wesserholm. The Ethno-Boys kaleidoscopically interweave local and Afro-diasporic tropes in their musical consciousness.

Cuban Music in Finland

The Finnish Left supported the Cuban Revolution, and musical as well as political ties with Cuba grew.[198] The innovative Cuban jazz group Irakere visited Finland in 1976, and Paquito d'Rivera's first recording outside of Cuba was recorded in Finland.[199] In 1979 Seppo Paakkunainen formed a twelve-man Machito-style group, using arrangements copied from Tito Puente and others. This band often translated Cuban songs into Finnish, and also performed Finnish tangos arranged into salsa. Helsinki's Hesperia Hotel instituted a Winter Carnival festival in 1979 that functioned off and on for twenty years. In addition to Finnish bands, it presented performers from abroad, including Machito and his Afro-Cubans.[200] Machito's son and bandmember Mario Grillo remembers that, upon arrival at a gig in Finland, musicians were shocked to see an audience of hippies:

The first time we played Finland we were supposed to play a music festival. We drove into a large field with a huge tent in the middle. We heard what we thought was hard rock blasting from that tent. My father looked at me and asked if this was the place at which we were to play. We saw a lot of long-haired youths wearing jeans. The scene looked like an indoor Woodstock. We started to set up after the rock band had left the stage. Everyone was asking what we should play. My father just told everybody, "Play violently because that's what these people like." So we played a hot set with everybody blasting their instruments on stage. You can imagine what an awesome sound a big band can generate with sixteen pieces going full speed. The crowd loved us and brought us back for an encore. We went back to Finland every year after that.[201]

Machito's Finnish fan base, however, consisted primarily of avid dancers rather than hippies; in fact, most of the Machito band's work in Finland was in dance venues; the traditional Finnish love of dancing, alive despite (or because of?) historical pressure to give it up, was at the heart of their interest in Latin music. Mario Grillo remembers Finns as exceptional dancers and told me that Machito liked to play for them because of their dance prowess. Many Finnish musicians developed a strong interest in Cuban music, founding excellent salsa and son bands; Oxford Open University's Cuban music researcher Michael McDonald-Ross goes so far as to argue that Finland has better Latin bands than London or Paris.[202]

The Pori Jazz Festival

Finland developed a vital festival culture beginning in the 1960s, possibly because of the auspiciousness of the Finnish summer with its short nights, long days, and long light, which contrast starkly with the cold, dark winter. Jazz performance in Finland thus came to center on festivals rather than clubs. The western Finnish town of Pori had had an active jazz scene since the 1940s; dance-band musicians looked forward to playing there because they knew that the local audiences enjoyed jazz. A group of local players organized a dance music festival there in 1957, attracting top jazz musicians from around the country. Possibly inspired by the film *Jazz on a Summer's Day*, which documents the 1958 Newport Jazz Festival, they suggested that a bona fide jazz festival be instituted, securing a modicum of state funding in 1966.[203] In addition to Finnish bands, the first festival presented trumpeter Ted Curson and composer George Russell, and the following year featured Ben Webster. The early years of the festival featured much open jamming in which Finnish musicians played with Americans. As time went on, however, this informality was lost. The festival grew fast, and by 1969 *Playboy* magazine had voted it and the Montreux Jazz Festival as the two best jazz events in Europe. Other jazz festivals sprang up in Finland; in 1964 George Wien presented the first annual Helsinki Jazz Festival, and by 1991 there were at least fifteen world-class jazz and blues festivals in the country.[204]

As a preeminent jazz event not only in Finland but also on the world stage, Pori Festival sparks debates about vital issues facing the music today—issues of genre, identity, cultural capital, and financial influence. Bassist Jyrki Kangas, managing director of the Pori event since its inception, is extraordinarily savvy about the jazz business. He explains that in the early period, festival organizers strove to expose non-jazz audiences to the music. Gradually, however, the festival began to cater to mass taste, attracting around fifty thousand people a year in the 1970s. Pori became a media event, advertised extensively and presented on television. The festival featured more and more non-jazz megastars to help draw people.[205] By the turn of the millennium, the festival was selling approximately 60,000 to 70,000 tickets per year. In addition to this an estimated 80,000 to 100,000 people customarily attend free concerts, producing a total attendance of approximately 150,000.[206] The vast majority of the festival's public consists of Finns; the event is not aggressively promoted outside of Finland because attracting visitors from abroad would benefit ancillary businesses such as hotels and airplane companies, but not the festival itself. Each year, Pori typically presents approximately 104 bands in 121 concerts, playing on thirteen stages.[207] This is truly a world-class event: in 2001, for example, it presented jazz artists such as Chick Corea, Bobby McFerrin, the Brecker Brothers, Ahmad Jamal, and Manhattan Transfer. It also features non-jazz performers such as John Hammond, John Mayall, Erykah Badu, and Big Bad Voodoo Daddy.

Festival organizers rely on what Kangas calls "businessmen" for economic support. For their part, the sponsoring "businessmen" come to Pori mainly to see and be seen, to make business deals.[208] As of 2001, the festival had a yearly budget of twelve million dollars, half of which came from ticket sales and advertising sponsors. Interestingly, so-called VIP tickets account for the full other half. "Businessmen" buy these high-priced VIP tickets to effect what Kangas calls "business-to-business opportunities," the chance to network.[209] VIPs attend private parties and receive souvenirs, and the festival's outdoor concert areas have a "VIP Village" that is set apart from the rest of the audience. This "Village" is farther away from the stage than is the area for normal ticket holders, but it has video monitors that allow VIPs to see and hear the performance: like conventional ticket holders, VIPs can walk around the grounds near the stage if they wish.[210]

The festival has what Kangas calls several audience "target groups." The economically least important sector consists of local people who attend the festival's many free concerts. The "normal jazz audience" attends paid events and consists of people who enjoy jazz but come to hear many types of music. Another sector consists of young people who come to see pop stars and attend few jazz events. Kangas explains that the inclusion of rock and other genres at the festival allows it to present many jazz acts at affordable prices. "Heavy jazz users" are the smallest fraction of the audience. Kangas says that while rock audiences react mainly to the promotion surrounding an artist, to the artist's "brand name," "jazz people know the history of the music, they analyze the music."

Kangas says that jazz cognoscenti often think that they are better than others, and that many of them come to Pori not only because they enjoy jazz, but also because they "want to be associated with" it. Rock fans go to "have a good time," while many jazz fans are "snobs." Kangas explains that this group is the most expensive per person, because of the jazz acts they demand, in proportion to their small numbers, but that the investment is worthwhile from a business standpoint because they have a disproportionate influence on the whole affair: they are "trendsetters of public taste." Jazz thus carries the most cultural capital of the various genres, cultural capital that readily converts into profit. Although the festival was unable to attract a non-jazz megastar in 2001, organizers were happily surprised when it turned out to be one of the festival's best years anyway. Kangas told me that he then realized that as much, or more, than its content, what sells the festival is its "brand name": people come because they want to be associated with the "reputation of the Pori Jazz Festival." Kangas estimates the price of the brand name of the festival, which could literally be sold on the open market, to be about ten million dollars. Kangas told me that he was not contemplating selling the name, but added that even if he did, the festival's fans would not have to worry: no new owner would likely change much, and certainly not the location of the event.

Kangas argues that musical genres express particular worldviews, that "people buy an experience" at festivals, going to them as an expression of their self-image or lifestyle. Audiences address the question, "Where do I belong, jazz or blues?" when they choose to attend a particular event. The difference, then, between jazz and rock audiences is essentially "a lifestyle question." Kangas makes an analogy with political parties in Italy, which, he says, are more important socially than ideologically, adding that audiences rarely "change sides after they choose." Nevertheless, he believes that genre "borders are changing all the time," that what is considered jazz today may not be considered jazz tomorrow.

Questions of genre and canon have been at the fore of debates about Pori. The neoclassical trend pushed by Wynton Marsalis in the United States did not find much popularity in Pori; its formality and lack of experimentation did not appeal to most Finnish jazz fans. One reviewer wrote: "Everyone agrees about Marsalis and his band, which are praised for their professionalism. Still, many people feel that it lacks the true spirit of jazz. Its over-confident, disciplined, and academic take on things is annoying."[211] One reason for this may be that Marsalis's battle for dignity and financial support for jazz is moot in Finland; this battle has already been won there. Some local musicians have complained that Finnish players rarely get top billing at the festival.[212] Many of Pori's policies are identical to policies at other top jazz festivals, all of whom belong to the International Jazz Festival Consortium (IJFC), which books acts for all the events.[213] Like other major jazz festivals, Pori began the policy of presenting a wide variety of musical types ranging from funk to Brazilian styles and rock in the 1980s. Chaka Khan and Youssou N'Dour played in 1988, Ringo Starr in 1992, and James Brown in 1995.[214] Many critics reacted disfavorably; one writer, for example, declared that including pop music at Pori amounts to "commercial pandering to the masses which is shameful to the name of jazz and its veritable tradition."[215] Another critic asserted: "The shine of money seems to be the main motivation of [festival] organizers, judging by this year's performers. B. B. King and James Brown, of course, have never had anything to do with jazz."[216] Festival organizers countered that "presenting only orthodox jazz will not bring bread to the table. Its friends would fit in the Finlandia House [concert hall]. That is why we have to present a wider variety of musical types. It is a matter of survival."[217]

In 1994, organizers resorted to the time-honored Finnish category of "rhythm-music" to describe the broad range of styles presented at the festival.[218] Critics of the Pori Festival criticize the inclusion of non-jazz styles in the program as crass commercialism, but most of the music presented at Pori shares a basis in the African diaspora. B. B. King and Youssou N'Dour's music *do* share much with jazz. Moreover, as we have seen, jazz musicians, both in Finland and elsewhere, tend to embrace a wide array of influences, eschewing stylistic categories. The New Jersey–based Spirit of Life Ensemble has played at Pori many times. After finishing its 2001 performance, the group's leader, Daood David Williams, spoke to the audience, saying that he enjoys the festival's wide range of programming and that he sees it as a reflection of the fact that "music is a universal language" whose purpose is to bring people together.[219]

Trumpeter Ted Curson has performed regularly at the Pori Jazz Festival since its inception, is married to a Finn, and spends most of his summers in Finland. When I asked him to assess the musicianship of young Finnish and other European players as compared to their American counterparts, Curson said that while the musicianship is the same, "it doesn't matter," because today's jazz is qualitatively different from the music of his formative period. Recalling his days as a young player, developing alongside Dexter Gordon, Eric Dolphy, and Bill Barron, he says that then the music was forged through personal relationships between a relatively small group of players. He goes so far as to say that the music that he came up playing no longer exists in the United States or Europe, because today's creativity is dominated by business concerns. He laments that today's jazz is marketed to the extent that the music business "could sell you my music even if you didn't like it."[220] Finnish jazz innovator Edward Vesala agrees, arguing that jazz marketing, like the marketing of other commodities, depends on offering consumers a plethora of styles to choose from. This "choice," however, denatures the endeavor:

Jazz has become a very cynical big business. Everywhere you turn you find everything from New Orleans to swing to bebop to fusion professionally played and it has no meaning, no brain, no spirit. All of the music's human values have been washed away. . . . It's becoming like something you buy at the supermarket, plastic-wrapped with everything good pumped out of it. But people eat anything, right?

And the groups you hear at the festivals now—it's boom-time for festivals in Finland—they play in this completely undiscriminating kind of "fast food" way.[221]

An even more important African American influence on European jazz than swing is the process by which music is conceived: improvisation and aural transmission.[222] As we saw, in tandem with their European aesthetics, Finnish jazz-makers embraced a process-oriented approach. As Finnish jazz composer Heikki Sarmanto said, while it may be true that "jazz is dead," the music continues to spawn much "post-mortem" creativity not only in the United States, but in Finland and around the world.[223]

Musician-scholar Jerome Harris points out that jazz players outside the United States often view the music's transnationalization as empowering: the music's process orientation affords possibilities for developing original and exciting forms of local creativity. African American musicians, on the other hand, may legitimately feel threatened by the rise of jazz around the world, especially when European players are able to gain substantial economic support from local governments.[224] Indeed, European arts institutions have supported jazz to a greater extent than have their counterparts in the United States, and the lack of support for jazz in the United States has, of course, been linked to endemic racism.[225] Harris also points out that players in large countries such as Germany and Japan are "strong enough economically and creatively" to be unconcerned with African American players' evaluation of them and that they consider their local jazz scenes to be separate from U.S. jazz.[226] In Japan, for example, local musicians felt that a new indigenous form of jazz had already developed by the 1960s, and that they no longer needed to catch up with the United States.[227] In a small country such as Finland, however, musicians have often felt the need to keep up with cosmopolitan currents. Moreover, rock, free jazz, fusion, and all manner of other trends arrived fast, almost at the same time, so while they were often seen as diametrically opposed in the United States, these styles dovetailed in Finland.

Finnish jazz pioneer Olli Häme's *The Triumph of Rhythm* was prophetic: as Afro-diasporic styles came to dominate musical taste around the world, a homegrown aesthetic of "rhythm-music" did triumph in Finland.[228] It grew in currency through the twentieth century, beginning with Häme's early usage and continuing with its application to rock, Afro-Cuban music, and later, other styles that were considered rhythmic, such as Balkan and Middle Eastern musics. Developing from Afro-diasporic responsorial, dance-based aesthetics, Finnish "rhythm-music" grew in its own cultural and political climate into a different flower. While local players struggled with swinging in 1952, Afro-diasporic musical aesthetics were eventually reinterpreted in Finnish ways. This process of assimilation came on the heels of a long history of the domestication of variegated influences. Indeed, interwoven layers of Finnic, Germanic, Russian, Latin American, and African-influenced musics, assimilated in the context of a dramatic political and cultural history, intertwined to form a mosaic of musical aesthetics that is authentically Finnish.

CHAPTER 6

"My Teacher Is the Human Heart"
The Human Music of Milford Graves

by Milford Graves, as told to Paul Austerlitz

—⁓⁓—

Prologue

As one reviewer recalls, an assemblage of instruments waited for Milford Graves at his solo performance in Tampere, Finland, as he began the event by vocalizing and playing a talking drum offstage:

> Trap drums, congas, *djembes,* bongós, timbales, gongs, and racks of industrial gears, springs, and pierced castings were ready as the first vocal callings and talking drum tones of Milford Graves danced into view out of the darkness.

After emerging, Graves began to play the drum set, "roaring like a giant throbbing *multicolored* plane." Not content to remain separated from the event's other participants—the listeners—Graves "transformed himself into a tumbling shaman at the stage edge. Suddenly he was discovered seated in the audience." He further obliterated borders by bringing members of the public onstage to play multilayered percussion patterns with him:

> Quickly, before there was time to indulge in self-consciousness, four audience members were drawn up onto the stage, each given a different percussion instrument and a different personal rhythm. With a little physical coaching from the Professor, they were soon really leaning into their parts, a multiple complex rhythm was emerging, and the great patterned plane was taking off again.

Everyone present became part of the event: "the audience itself was the engine roaring Forward (!!!) into a moment of undeniable Healing-Transformation-Happening time."[1]

Many critics have commented on the emphatically melodic color of Milford Graves's drumming. Nat Hentoff, for example, wrote that, like Ellington's drummer Sonny Greer, who "always played colors as well as time," Graves produces a "nearly infinite scope of percussive textures," an "almost hypnotic new world of colors and dynamics."[2] When asked about this, Graves said, "It's the tone that sets you straight, don't always pay attention to the rhythm."[3] Graves derives inspiration for his melodic rhythm from African-based drumming: "The music that I play is directly linked to African music and Afro-Cuban music that is used in Santería."[4] He also bases his music on diligent study of tone and timing in the human body, especially the human heart. In 2000, Graves was awarded a Guggenheim Fellowship to buy computers and other equipment to aid his research on the sound of the heart and to develop what he calls "biological" or "human" music. Graves told me that the "tone of the heart . . . is just as important as the rhythm, just as in music, the sound of the drum is just as important as the duration."[5] In addition to using computer technology, Graves calls upon internal psychobiological resources in his research: he has developed techniques to control his own cardiovascular system. At one performance, he demonstrated his internal mastery of biological multiple rhythm by asking an audience member to monitor the pulse on both his arms and report the resulting rhythms back to the audience. Soon, the surprised pulse-reader exclaimed that Graves's right arm was beating differently than his left![6] The "Professor," as Graves's students affectionately call him, has much to teach us about music, the African diaspora, and humanity.

Milford Graves was born in the Jamaica section of Queens, New York City, on August 20, 1941. Inspired by the vital pan-African links that were nourished during the mambo boom, he began his musical career playing Afro-Cuban music and acquired an acute interest in all forms of African-based drumming. He developed this background into a unique and influential style of freely improvised drumming, making his initial mark with Albert Ayler and the New York Art Quartet (which included Amiri Baraka) and gaining international recognition by the end of the 1960s.[7] In addition to performing with horn players such as Hugh Glover and David Murray, Graves has participated in many all-percussion projects. These range from his early recordings with pianist Don Pullen (who used his instrument as a percussion instrument); to "Dialogue of the Drums" concerts and recordings with Andrew Cyrille and Rashied Ali; and the all-star Pieces of Time group, which included Andrew Cyrille, Don Moye, and Kenny Clarke.[8] Graves is an accomplished martial artist as well as musician, and incorporates a unique language of body motion, along with idiosyncratic vocalization techniques, into his art.[9]

Milford Graves has an insatiable mind. In addition to performing internationally, he pursues tireless self-study of healing techniques based in African practices, acupuncture, herbalism, and Western medicine. Since 1973, Graves has taught at Bennington College, presenting courses on music's influence on the human mind and body. I studied with him there as an undergraduate, and many of the perspectives offered in this book are a result of my lifelong engagement with his philosophies. This chapter calls upon ten approximately four-hour research sessions that I conducted with Graves in 2001 and 2002.[10] These sessions consisted primarily of open-ended conversations, but also included playing music together as well as my informal participation, as a subject, in Graves's research on heart sounds. Rather than writing a chapter *about* Graves, I opted to present Graves's opinions in his own prose voice: he has his own vocabulary that is supremely suited to conveying his ideas. Moreover, my own academic stance requires a detachedness that does not do justice to Graves's thinking. Graves presents his philosophies on his own terms; he adapts techniques from the hard sciences, but he does so in a personal and creative way. He has abundant respect for Western medicine and scientific research, but as he says, "We need to put the guy who calculates together with the guy who wears feathers." His research on healing manifests not only in his work as an herbalist and acupuncturist, but every time he performs: Graves's listeners' experiences prove the efficacy of his work. —PAUL AUSTERLITZ

I was born in New York City, in the Jamaica section of Queens, on August 20, 1941. My grandparents influenced me a lot: my grandfather was from South Carolina, and he was a very self-reliant kind of person. He played the blues guitar, and also played the drums. He also knew a lot about roots and herbs, home remedies, and he cured people of various ailments; he was known in the community for this. As I got older I began to reflect back on the things that my grandfather used to say, only then realizing how big an influence he was on me. He used to make everything himself. He would go down to South Carolina and butcher hogs to make his own sausage, which he sold in a soda jerk shop he had with my grandmother. I was pretty wild as a kid, but when I was around my grandparents I would quiet down. I really respected them, and they had a lasting effect on me.

As a boy I was fascinated by Hollywood movies and TV. People criticize TV a lot, but if it had not been for TV I never would have been exposed to many of the things that I got involved in as an adult. I loved Tarzan movies, movies about cowboys and Indians, and a series of movies about a South Asian boy named Sabu. Whenever a Sabu movie came on TV, I dropped everything to watch it: Sabu, Tarzan, I went wild for them. Even if it was a western orchestra imitating music in the Sabu films, I just liked the way it sounded. The music in the Sabu movies just caught my attention, and this led to my later interest in Hindustani music. Of course, movies about Tarzan ruling the black people and whites killing Native Americans are terrible, but I was fascinated by them. When I played outside with my friends, if anyone fell down and got a scratch, I would find plants and rub them on their legs, imitating Native Americans using herbs in the movies. I was fascinated by movies about "voodoo," especially the ones that had people sticking pins into "voodoo dolls." Although this was a perverted Hollywood portrayal of Vodou, it fascinated me. I later became interested in BaKongo nail fetishes, which are Central African wood carvings with nails stuck in them. I used to get my friends to bang on pots and pans and make up signals, drum signals, like a Morse code, imitating the drumming that we had seen in Tarzan movies. So as stereotyped as these movies were, they exposed me to valuable practices that I eventually pursued as an adult.

My parents used to have boarders, and one man who rented a room in my house died in a fire. He left his drums in the house, and they were my toys. They were marching band drums, a bass and a snare, New Orleans–style. I used to play them for hours at a time. I also listened to a Latin music radio show hosted by Dick "Ricardo" Sugar. That really turned me on. I didn't know too much about Latin music at the time but I knew enough to see that this was something that I should pay attention to. Then I made friends with a Cuban kid in the neighborhood, whose father was a percussionist who played professionally. There was also a mambo band in the neighborhood called the Five Mambo Kings. I used to hang around them; they had made a record and they were heroes in the neighborhood. I used to go to the Palladium all the time, to hear all the greats: Machito, Tito Rodríguez, Tito Puente. My friends and I didn't dance; we went to watch the percussionists. There was a railing about five feet from the stage, and we used to make sure that we got there early so we could stand in front; we would fight to get a good spot! My friends and I always wanted to see which band could get the people out of their seats and make them dance; we wanted to see what would motivate the people, and when we saw everybody moving, we'd say, "Yeah, that's the beat!" There were three or more bands a night, and we would latch on to the band that got people out on the floor doing all the flashy dance steps.

I started playing conga when I was about nine years old. There was a school in my neighborhood for what was then called "interpretive dancing," which was actually African dancing. All the people in the neighborhood who were interested in drumming used to play for dance classes there. Soon I was playing timbales and bongó in addition to conga, mostly Afro-Cuban music but also calypso, merengue. I was also into the religious music coming out of Cuba, the music of Santería; the drummers on the scene used to talk about batá drumming. A black American drummer from New Haven, Bill Fitch, was a close friend of mine. He started playing with Cal Tjader when he was only nineteen years old, and through him I got to hang out and play with Tjader's band. I was attracted to these types of music because they use a lot of drums. It was great to have all these drums around me; I was stimulated by them. I was a drum guy; for me to be interested in any kind of music, it had to have a lot of drums. I didn't touch on jazz too much, because there weren't enough drums in it.

I never studied music in school. But the way I came up was great in a lot of ways. There are two ways you can learn: you can learn by somebody else teaching you, or you can learn by being self-taught. Things have become so commercialized and industrialized that we have forgotten how we function with our basic senses. If you learn from the outer part of yourself, depending on someone else to pump things into you, you will be under their control. You will be saying, "Well, I can't do it because I need somebody else to show me," instead of using keen observation where you just watch something and learn from it. Just using your basic senses is a great way to learn, but to do this, you need to trust yourself, relax, let things come in, and just pick them up using your basic common senses. If you pay attention to nature, especially to animals, you can learn a lot. Animals give their offspring a small introduction, and then leave them on their own. Humans have a way of trying to take charge of each other, and to try to clone each other. A dog or a cat doesn't say to their offspring, "OK, kitten or puppy, it's time for class now—I'm going to give you a test on how to do this or that." An animal will say: "Watch me." That's nature. Some of the dogs in my neighborhood were mean; they'd come out like they were going to attack you. Animals can tell whether they can overpower you or whether you can overpower them. Sometimes, two animals confront each other and they ward each other off by just using sound and body movements. They don't need to fight; they just walk away from each other. I learned this by being in the community as a teenager; when a dog would come up to me I could get rid of him by using sound and movement. I would get on all fours and try to bark louder than the dog, playing a game of frequency exchange. I started countering the posture and countering the sound; when the dog made a sound, I made a sound. When the dog made a movement, I made a movement. I would do different kinds of posturing and making sounds, and soon, the dog would move out, stop barking, stop dead in his tracks. He would go away after that. I didn't think of this as musical training when I did it as a teenager, but as I got older I realized that I had been reaching another level of sound. Talking to animals put me in touch with the power of sound. If you can do this, you know you are producing powerful vibrations. Because an untrained dog won't understand you if you say, "Stop it, or I'll hit you." When you get a dog coming after you with his teeth showing and his nose contracted, all hunched up with his muscles popping out, the scales you learned in music school will not do you any good; they are not the real vibrations! You can't learn the really powerful stuff in school.

I started practicing martial arts when I was a kid, but I never went to a school for that either. I studied martial arts in the streets. I also boxed at PAL.[11] In the streets we did not use any particular forms; we would just try to beat each other up! This was dirty stuff: we called it "sham battling." If we were playing basketball, someone might say, "Let's go, let's sham battle, let's box, man!" I learned a lot from this, a lot about the idea of contact, developing a sense of somebody coming at you hard. Most martial artists never learn this because they're always saying, "Well, in the event that this happens, this is what you do," but they haven't really experienced the real situation. There are a lot of lessons in life to be learned from fighting. You have to be alert; if you are not alert, you will get hurt.

Development

I got married and had children young, and I needed to support my family. So after graduating from high school, in addition to playing music, I went to college at night and worked a day job; I was taking business classes in college and working in the mailroom at a big corporation during the day. At that time people used to work their way up in the business world, starting in the mailroom and eventually getting jobs as executives. But I was not getting the promotions. Some of the white people on the job told me that this was not fair, that I deserved to be promoted. This racism made me angry. I finally lost the job. I was going to all these job interviews but I just wasn't getting hired. I was often told that the job had been filled, but once I eavesdropped on an interview with a white person, right after my interview. And he got the job. There was no doubt about what was going on.

I was walking around and walking around, looking for work, getting angry, I was getting really angry. What kind of society is this, if a person cannot even get a job? I needed money so badly that I swallowed my pride and did something that I thought I would never do: I went down to the welfare office. I said, "I got children, I need money or a job." They sent me on a lot of job interviews, but they were interviews for jobs that I was overqualified for. I told the welfare people that I refused to do work that was beneath me. I was fed up with the system, I was angry, and I got very loud: I said, "Give me some training." So they sent me to a local community college, New York Community College in Brooklyn, to study medical laboratory technology. I could not stand that school, because it was an inferior institution: the instructors were teaching subjects that they were not qualified in. I finished the first semester there and got an A in biology, but I was not learning anything. I found out about the Eastern School for Physicians' Aides, a one-year private school that had a good medical laboratory technology program, went back to the welfare office, and said that I knew where I wanted to go. I graduated in 1970 and went to work as a lab technician for one of the top veterinarians in New York, Dr. Katz.

All during this period, my music career was also developing. I started my own band, the Milford Graves Latin Jazz Quintet, in 1960. The instrumentation was usually vibraphone, piano, bass, congas, and bongó/timbales. At one point the band was called the McKinley-Graves Quintet, with Ray

McKinley, a piano player. We started by playing locally, playing Latin jazz in the black community. They loved to dance to Latin jazz, especially when we mixed our own funk stuff into it. Black folks in this country were deeply affected by Afro-Cuban music, because of the close links to Africa. But you also need to remember that Mario Bauzá and the other Latin musicians also got something out of the interchange with jazz; the jazz influence helped them arrange Cuban music in a different way. My quintet eventually began to get jobs in Manhattan and I started using musicians like Chick Corea on piano, Pete Yellin on alto, and Bill Fitch on congas. We played at a big concert in Town Hall in 1962, on the same bill with Cal Tjader and Herbie Mann. I also did studio work, recording a variety of percussion with people like Miriam Makeba and Montego Joe.

Musicians encouraged me to start playing trap drums. I was playing timbales in a Latin band, and one time, we decided to do some jazz things, so I would act like I was playing trap drums, with my right hand on the cymbal playing the ride rhythm and my left hand doing the offbeats. Some of the musicians commented on my left hand, saying that I had a good feel for jazz. This encouraged me, so I thought that maybe I should try playing trap drums. At first I did it for economic reasons: I wasn't getting enough gigs playing congas and timbales. It is interesting that sometimes you can be good at things that you don't think that you want to do, and other people lead you into them, they lead you into yourself.

In 1963 I was in Boston at a jam session, and Guiseppi Logan the alto player got up to play. Everyone got off the bandstand: no one wanted to play with him. I guess he had a reputation as an abstract kind of player, a free player. I got up there and played with him, and we hit it off, and started playing together regularly. He was already playing in the same free improvisational style that he eventually became known for, and I was also playing free—I wasn't playing straight time. In New York, Guiseppi took me to a rehearsal of the New York Art Quartet, which at that time had John Tchicai on alto, Roswell Rudd on trombone, a bassist, and J. C. Moses on drums. I sat in with them, and they liked it, so I started playing with the group, replacing J. C. Moses. This was before the group had recorded or was working, so I got in at a good time. I started making the rounds with a lot of the bands that were recording on Bernard Stollman's ESP label, which specialized in the new music, or what people call "free jazz." The first ESP LP that I did was with the New York Art Quartet. After that I recorded ESP LPs with Guiseppi Logan, Paul Bley, Lowell Davidson, and I also made my own album, *Milford Graves Percussion Ensemble*. I also put out my own records: two duos with pianist Don Pullen, a duo with percussionist Andrew Cyrille, a trio with saxophonists Hugh Glover and Arthur

Doyle. I also recorded *Love Cry* with Albert Ayler on Impulse and with Sonny Sharrock on Atlantic.

Ever since I had watched the Sabu movies as a kid, I had loved Indian music. So in 1965, when Ravi Shankar was really popular, I listened to him a lot, and I especially listened to his tabla player, Chatur Lal. There was a tabla record with him improvising with a string instrument accompanying him that I listened to a lot. So I decided that I needed to find somebody that can teach me tabla. I looked in the yellow pages under "Music Instruction" and found an ad for the "India School of Music." I called the number and made an appointment to go to the teacher's house in Manhattan; he had all the shades down, with a lot of sitars and tablas lying around. The teacher's name was Wasantha Singh, and taking lessons with him was the joy of my life. I would go up to his house for a one-hour lesson, and all of a sudden, three to five hours had passed, and I was still there. He used to tell me stories about being in India; being with this guy was just like being in another world. I bought my tablas from him, and I would woodshed and woodshed and woodshed. I was serious about tabla. He always liked my feeling. I think that the fact that I played bongó helped me out; since I already had a good idea of how to use my fingertips; I just needed to re-position them. Then I recorded "Tabla Suite" with Guiseppi Logan.

I have never been a person who waited for someone else to show me what to do; I have always relied on myself. And I have always been curious about things, so I have always just self-educated myself. In lab technician school they teach you how to run the electrocardiogram, but they never show you how to read it, or do diagnosis on patients. I was interested in these things, so I would just go and find books about these things. Through self-education, I eventually learned to run the whole veterinary lab on my own. Dr. Katz even once told me that I knew as much about the lab side of his practice as he did. His office was on 12th Street in Manhattan, in the Village. Bill Dixon lived on 13th Street. After I had worked there for two years, Dr. Katz decided to move his practice to Boston. I didn't want to relocate, and coincidentally, Bill asked me to go up to Bennington to teach in the Black Music Division that he had started there.

My courses at Bennington are an improvisation ensemble and a lecture course called "Music Healing with Computer Technology," which looks at the ways that music affects people psychologically and physiologically. I also teach at home: music, martial arts, and acupuncture. Some of my students are former students from Bennington, but most of them are drummers who read about me in magazines and want to see what makes me tick. I also have had a few students who studied music, martial arts, and healing with me who went on to go to medical school, and these guys have really hung in there, staying committed to the things I talk about for long periods of time.

Black Community and Black Creativity

As I mentioned, certain jobs were just not available to black folks when I was young; you just could not go for them It was really something, the things that black folks could not do. You could not get into certain schools, and down South, you could not even vote. There were lynchings, with burned-up bodies hanging from trees. That makes me sick, it just makes me sick. Black nationalism arose because black folks just got fed up with racism and started rebelling. I used to say that if they put a dog on me the way they put dogs on the Civil Rights demonstrators in the South, I'd kick their asses. I used to say that if you call me a nigger, I'll kick your ass.

The so-called free jazz, or new black music of the 1960s, was directly related to the social movements of that time. There was a lot of creative energy in the air; it was a volatile period. We felt that playing the same old tunes was the same as going only where the white man wanted us to go. A lot of the white critics were saying that black musicians did not know what they were doing, that they should not play the way they wanted to play. That's the same as white folks telling black folks where they can live and cannot live. The 1960s was a major turning point because the movement did not just touch black folks, it touched other groups in this country. And it touched people all over the world. When black groups like the Black Panthers started talking about coalition politics and working with radical white groups like the Students for a Democratic Society, the power structure really got nervous.

Young black folks do not have any understanding of the way that it was; they have no idea, they take so much for granted. I look around and see the jobs they have now. I see them walk around, getting high. They don't know what we fought for, they have no idea. Some white folks have spit on us and stepped on us. You have to say, "To hell with it, man," you've got to go deep down in yourself and have the confidence that you can do what you need to do; if you don't believe that you can do something, then you're going to fail.

In the past, some students told me that they took my class at Bennington because they were wondering, "What it would be like to take a class with a black teacher?" So I talk about politics and race a lot, in ways that will open them up. Some students told me that I was their first experience with a black person. Others explained that they had been brought up as racists, that their parents are bigots. I told them that when they go home, at the dinner table, they need to set their parents straight, that it is the young folks who are going to make this planet better: don't live your life the way your grandpop and grandmom did. You have to go out and make this a better planet. The only advantage I have had from being in a so-called deprived culture is that I have seen lots of difficulties, so certain things don't throw me off. Privileged people who have never been fired from a job do not know which way to turn when they have problems. They rely on rules to keep themselves straight, and there is always someone there to say "don't worry, we'll take care of you." Black folks did not get that. You could be fired from ten to twelve different jobs in ten years.

While it is true that black folks in this country were stripped from many of the direct links to African culture, we have preserved the inner workings of African culture. In a film called *Repercussions* there is a section where Max Roach talks about a time when he was late for a rehearsal with Charlie Parker. When he got there, Charlie Parker was playing complex polyrhythms on the drum set; the rhythms that he played are identical to many rhythms that are found in West Africa and the Caribbean. This is inspirational because Charlie Parker was coming from a very traditional thing.[12]

The music that I play is directly linked to African music and Afro-Cuban music that is used in Santería. Now, of course it is true that people like the Afro-Cubans have preserved closer links to Africa than we have in this country. We were stripped of many things, we were stripped of the drum. Being stripped of so much taught us to call upon our inner resources to survive. It is important to avoid looking at things negatively. People keep crying, crying, and crying; they complain too much. I look at things positively, and see that black folks in this country have become some of the greatest improvisers on the planet. In a way, they are naturally practicing a form of Zen: so much has been stripped away that they have been forced to go deep inside their inner selves and totally open themselves up to new levels of consciousness. When you do that, you are not regimented, and you piece things together creatively. I learned this a long time ago, by watching the old black folks that I grew up around. They might have no formal education, but they put things together in ways that are effective. The bourgeois blacks who have a lot of money are different: they can't improvise any better than whites, because they have been brought up in a system. When you come up as a part of a system, you are very well organized, everything is worked out, and you are not able to just jump into a situation and think freely. Most black folks in this country have been free thinkers; they had no choice in the matter.

BaKongo Acupuncture

During the 1960s I was also self-educating myself in the area of so-called alternative healing: herbalism, acupuncture, and so forth. I got into this because in the early '60s I started to get all these stress-related health problems. I was a typical hang-out musician, doing all the things that musicians do: drinking alcohol and staying out all night. Luckily, I never used drugs, because that would have totally messed me up. But I started getting all these digestive problems and I knew that something was not working right in my body. I had a lot of intestinal problems, you name it. I went to the authorized medical doctors and they could not diagnose my problem. I was astounded because although I knew something was wrong with me, they were saying I was fine. So I got into the whole herbal medicine thing: I started scouting around for books on herbalism, and also remembering things about roots and remedies that my grandfather used to talk about. So I started taking herbs, and it worked. I fixed myself up, I healed myself. I became a vegetarian; at first I stopped eating beef and salt. After that I stopped eating meat completely and reduced it down to vegetables. I started feeling good and realized that maybe this is what I should be doing. Guys who knew me started saying, "You used to look sick and complain about pains, but now you look good, man!" I had never thought about being a healer, but people started asking me to help them out with their health problems. This really changed my state of mind.

I was introduced to acupuncture at A. B. Spellman's house. I was really inspired by black intellectuals like A. B. Spellman, Larry Neal, and Amiri Baraka, or Leroi Jones as he was called at the time. So I used to go up to A.B.'s house just to hang out, and I liked to look at his books. One day I saw a book on acupuncture, and the word just caught my eye. It was a new word to me and I did not know what it meant, but I was fascinated by it. I started reading the book, and asked A.B. about it. He asked me if I wanted it, and I said, "Yes!" I don't really know why I was so attracted to acupuncture; I was just drawn to it. Life is like that sometimes—sometimes we don't really know why we get involved with certain things. At that time there were no formal schools in acupuncture, so I took a correspondence course with the Occidental Institute of Chinese Studies, which is based in Canada. Since it was based mainly in reading, the course focused on the theoretical aspects of acupuncture, but every so often they would sponsor a convention for the students and instructors in a rented hotel space. I got a diploma in acupuncture from them in 1978.

In places like Africa, people are in touch with nature. There is a book discussing African villages showing that local people know fractal geometry, that their villages are laid out in fractal patterns.[13] You also find fractals in basic drum rhythms and in the structures of African dance. In the rainforest, the so-called witch doctors have some of the most potent medicine that exists; these guys have a thorough, dynamic, working knowledge of healing plants, and poisons too. The scientists in their cubicles have botany and pharmacology, but they can still only elaborate off of basic chemical forms that are found in nature. They are only using a small percentage of the plant world for potential medicine, the tip of the iceberg. They have to go back to the guys who have a thorough knowledge of all the plants, to the so-called witch doctors. They've got to go back and find these guys, because if these guys die, if we don't learn from them, we will have no more knowledge of their medicine.

There is a limited amount of written material available about African healing practices. Also, the Africans do not stress the physiological stuff. They focus on the spiritual, you know, the psychic relationships. But these things are related. In places like the Kongo they have nail fetishes, which are wooden figures with pieces of metal or nails stuck into them. I have studied the locations of these metal objects, and if you make a parallel with acupuncture, it is very interesting. I had a student who had done a religious initiation in Ghana that included scarification rites. She had been given small cuts all over her body, and medicine had been inserted into them. Each cut was on a particular point on the body, and there were specific reasons for the placement of each cut. They had done a good job in the sense that the cuts healed perfectly, leaving no scars that you can see. When she came to my house and I gave her acupuncture treatment she said, "Wow, this is amazing, because the places where you inserted those needles in me are the exact places where they made the little cuts in Africa; they gave me a similar kind of diagnosis." I said, "Well, you know, this is very interesting. What does that tell you? What did they tell you about why they were putting medicine in those points; did they give you any reason what that cut on the skin was for?" She said that they had not made any explanation, that a deity had just told them to do it. So then I said, "I'll tell you this: I can't give you the African explanation, but I can tell you what the Chinese say about these points." That experience really got me interested in studying possible connections between acupuncture and African healing, although this was in Ghana, this was not in the Kongo. So I went down to Washington, D.C., to the African Museum and I was able to go downstairs into the scholars' section and they had a cabinet full of all these BaKongo nail fetishes. They opened the cabinet and let me inspect these things. I had them all out on the table and I was looking at these things, making my notes. So then they told me to go down the block to a little library where they have an article on these objects and what they represent written by Robert Farris Thompson.[14]

I am interested in work by the Chinese scholar Joseph Needham.[15] Some of his works deal with a relationship between the Chinese and Africans during the tenth century, what kind of exchange those guys had, how they influenced each other. Needham also clarifies a lot of stuff about the acupuncture meridians.[16] People are always trying to connect the acupuncture points with linear meridians, but it might not be a predictable situation: the meridians might not be as linear as people think. That's not the way it works. It is more like a city ghetto situation where people might be lurking in back alleys. Or like the bush: there's no direct path over there in the jungle. Looking at it from the martial arts standpoint, if you're involved in warfare in the bush, you won't find a direct path.

When everything is so calculated we end up fighting ourselves and we have a problem. People living in cities walk in straight lines; they almost know how many steps they need to take each block. Musicians use metronomes and tempered scales. We are taken out of our natural setting and everything is worked out, controlled. As a result, our biological clocks are all screwed up. If you go into the woods, you will not find a path, but you will be more in tune with yourself. We need order in the world, but we also need non-order. Our bodies have no sense of equal measured time; heartbeats change according to what the situation is. The arts can bring us into our inner selves.

I met this guy in the neighborhood once and we had a little conversation. He was kicking a soccer ball, working on his kicks, and I could tell he had a martial arts background. I said, "So you do martial arts, huh? I saw by the way you kicked the ball that you do some kind of martial arts." It turned out that he had quite a reputation as a martial artist. We sparred one time; he was a vicious kind of guy sparring. I came up to him with some kicks, and he said that my form is wrong. So I kicked again, and I could see him hesitating. He was used to linear motion, but I move a different way. I took my hand and popped it right on his chest and I could see him tighten up. After that he gave me the highest respect. Coming up as a fighter in the streets, I have always been into unpredictable moves, never straight stuff. If you are calculating your punches, you are just waiting for someone to get you in the throat. It is like you see in the movies: you don't know where the guy's gonna come from, and BAM!

Western science generally works in terms of constants, and I think that there are too many constants in European music, like tempered scales and fixed measures. Where are the variables? Mathematical equations should have more variables than constants. Constants are limited in that they do not go to deeper levels; they do not move. You do not get spiritual growth when your imagination is dampened. Then we cannot resolve the problems we have, the deep biological problems, like cancer and the major problems that medical science cannot solve right now. People go to universities and fix their minds on one great constant. But their mathematics are off; their beautiful-looking formulas are too straight-on. They want to make sure that they can keep reproducing things with particular formulas like a machine. But what happens when something goes wrong; how can you diagnose a machine? That type of math is not made for the human body.

Holism

They say that people use only 5 to 8 percent of their brain capacity, but ever since I was a kid, I have wondered, how can they know that? How can they know whether someone is using 8, 50, or 100 percent of his brain? They have to have a reference point. In essence, that statement about brain capacity doesn't mean anything. Scientists have a lot of fun; they love their research, but their experiments are less than absolute. Neuroscientists have the areas of the brain pretty well mapped out but their experiments are only built off a particular mind-set. All the testing that scientists do on the brain, lungs, and other organs is based off a limited sample of people; there are people on the planet who have developed themselves to a greater extent, like yogic breathers, who use much more inflation of their lower lungs than most people usually do. The researchers need to use samples from different kinds of people from all over the planet.

I am fascinated with quantum physics, quantum mechanics. In 1965 I did a film with Guiseppi Logan called *Improvisation*, which was produced by the owner of the ESP record label, Bernard Stollman. After the premiere showing of the film, a physicist in the audience said that some aspects of quantum mechanics are similar to the things that improvising musicians do. I went to the library and read up on quantum mechanics, and I could see that, from a philosophical perspective, there is a similarity. Then I went back to reading Einstein: this man is talking about space, time, the fourth dimension, and music too.[17]

Some Western musicians have a problem, because they separate things apart too much. They separate performers from composers; they are too segregated. They have no idea of how to integrate all the different disciplines. In jazz or black music, if you write a tune and make a record you are a composer. We have a different way of classifying things. All musicians should be able to compose and also know how to play an instrument. I always say to musicians that if you only deal with the tempered scale of the keyboard, you are not going to open yourself up very much. We need to take advantage of all our potential. If you are a right-handed person and you begin to do things with your left hand, it will create new nerve pathways. Anything that feels awkward for you: that's what you should do. The simple way is just open yourself up by studying things that seem like they have a lot of paradoxes and contradictions.

If we could just mix all these things together, we would really have something. I put together a twenty-first-century concert at Bennington in 1994. I had a physicist there, with his scientific equipment. There were drummers, and I was doing acupuncture. I had dancers and martial artists, all at the same time. It's too silent in the scientific laboratories; scientists are cut off from certain creative things. And artists are cut off from what the scientists do. We need to put the guy who calculates together with the guy who wears feathers; the three-piece-suit guy has got to meet the guy with the feathers and beads on. People come to my place in Queens and think it is weird, because they will see an acupuncture mannequin, and next to it, a lot of computer technology. Then they go to another part of the studio and see herb jars and my BaKongo fetish. Each of these things has to do with a different kind of mind-set. If you combine all those things, you really get something going. I have been blessed to get turned on by the real stuff from many different places. When you see the real deal, you're convinced.

Self-Cultivation

I believe that there are three different ways to play music that are totally different from each other. One way is to play for the regular people, to tune in to regular folks and play music that will touch them. Another way is to play for other musicians, for the in-group, the clique. There are also times when a musician doesn't play for other musicians or the regular people. He plays for himself, and he plays for a higher force. This is a form of self-cultivation for the musician: he stays at home or maybe you go out into the woods and he just plays. He gets deep enjoyment out of it and you develop yourself. This deals with cosmic forces, cosmic vibrations. To do this at the highest level, you have to have a commitment to the higher power, God, the natural forces, or whatever you want to call it. Once you have this, you can go into a state where you do not operate according to earthly laws any more. Then you can really stretch out.

Musicians who do not know how to self-cultivate have to play fixed licks and copy other styles, like clones. People like this have no internal ideas; all their ideas are external, they come from the outside. I hear rappers say, "Man, I know this rhyme," or jazz musicians say, "I know this or that tune." This is all external; it has got nothing to do with the inside. Once you deal with the internal music, or as they say, the music of the cosmos, you are on another level. A lot of people talk about cosmic music or the music of the spheres but I do not think they really understand it. They are still playing tunes that are structured from earth vibrations.

I am not interested in composing music in the sense that I would come to you and tell you what I want you to play. I don't want to do that. Maybe you can still call me a composer if I inspire people who work with me to play in a particular way. Many people write down music, saying, "Well I want four measures here, two measures there." To me, it does not work that way. Or people practice and practice, almost cloning them- selves in the image of some other player's licks. The only reason to do that is to develop yourself to a certain point. After you develop yourself to a certain point, if you have any confidence in yourself, if you have a high character, you do not need anyone to dictate to you any more. Music to me is an improvised, spontaneous event. I just do not see it any other way. Some musicians have admitted to me that the reason they do not like spontaneous improvisation is because that level of creativity is so de- manding: after one minute they run out of ideas! Before you knock spon- taneous improvisation, try it. Get up there and just start playing, and cap- tivate people's attention. Afterwards, if they say to you, "Oh man, that was a release, just what I needed; that was great!" then you did your job. People ask me what I played at a particular concert. In truth, there is no real answer to that question, because that music was for that event. Next time, it'll be different.

I'm not out doing a lot of gigs, so people sometimes ask me, "Are you still playing?" I answer, "Sure, I'm still playing!" Just because you do not see me out there does not mean anything. I once met a musician at a solo performance that I did in Italy. He told me that his approach was to stay in shape by playing all the time, to practice a lot and always be performing. He was surprised at my approach, saying, "Man, you hardly ever come out but when you do play it sounds like you've been playing every day!" I told him that I do not have to be on my instrument every day. I do other things to physically keep my body in good shape. I work on my house, and I work in my garden. I do martial arts, grapple techniques that keep my muscles and nervous system together. I am always doing things with my mind, stimulating my mind by solving problems. I stay open to what is happening in the world, not just the physical world but also the cosmic world. So I am always ready to play. By being involved in all these things, I maintain myself and I am always ready.

To do this, you have to have a strong belief system. You also have to have a little bit of ego; not ego in the competitive sense that you step down on people, but you have got to have a lot of self-pride. If something happens to destroy your pride, you cannot let it break you down. The difficult things that people go through, like some of the difficulties that black folks have gone through in this country, make you stronger. If you have it too easy, you will not have the strength to do certain things. The Buddhist Scriptures are not always interpreted properly. If you misinterpret these things, it could be dangerous. Take the old Eastern saying, "He who speaks does not know." If you take this literally and sew your lips up and never talk, you are off the mark. If you take the great master literally when he says, "He who speaks does not know" it will mean that this same master does not know, because he spoke. You cannot find intellectual answers to Zen koans. But by trying to solve that riddle you will keep moving on and on, and you will be exploring different areas of yourself. A lot of people do not understand that. The worst thing to do is to formulate yourself where everything is laid out, where you think you have all the answers. If you do that, there is nothing to further stimulate you. So you should always have something set up that you may not ever reach. You may say that, "Well, I want to fly to a cosmic body that is far beyond, to another planet." You may never get there, but you will be trying to lift off the ground. You'll be trying to lift off every chance you get, and though you may not ever overcome gravity, you just might overcome gravity in your mind-set. Everybody is looking at the physical set, but I say that you have got to get a spiritual and a mental workout as well as a physical one. And just by thinking certain ways you might achieve things that you thought were impossible. When the Buddhist Scriptures say that we need to remove ourselves from all earthly affairs, I think they are just teaching you not to collapse when things don't go your way. A lot of people have so much pride and so much ego that they cannot do anything because they are afraid to fail. They don't want to fail because they think they'll look bad. The Buddhists show that doing something that makes you look bad might bring you into a state of nothingness where you turn on another switch, and BOOM: nothing affects you anymore.

The Human Heart

Can music heal? Yes, it can. But I am disturbed by much of what I have read about music and healing: many of the books say that the best music for healing is European classical music. Some even say that blues and jazz are detrimental for the healing process. When you use music or sound to heal, the twelve-note tempered scale alone will not get to the deep-seated problems: you can use it, but you need more. About two years ago, during an acupuncture class that I was teaching in New York, one of my students got an asthma attack. I used the opportunity to show the class how acupuncture works, and I treated her. Two weeks later she had another attack in class. I started treating her with acupuncture and massage, but she started turning blue. The treatment was not working, and I got scared. I started shaking. Something in the back of my mind reminded me of my old days in the Baptist Church when the preacher used to shake and use a particular tone of voice. I don't know why I did it, but while I was shaking I said into her ear, using a particular tone of voice, "Do you want to live?" She snapped out of it and said, "I'm fine." It blew my mind: a simple shake and a simple sound did the trick. Trembling is a type of vibration; it worked because I wasn't jiving about wanting her to get better. I looked deep within myself and found the faith and the right vibration to help her. That was my lesson: a divine type of belief can heal.

Once, two drummers from Ghana came to my house, and I asked them, "What is the origin of the drum?" They said that the drum came from genies. I have a different view: I say that the origin of the drum is in the human body, in the human heart. Belief and faith are powerful, but there is also a biological basis to the power of music.

I do not deal with music that has any ethnic classification. I deal with what I call biological music, or human music. If you deal with that, you deal with everybody. Because we are all ethnically mixed. I always tell people that the blood from someone in your own ethnicity can kill you if it is not your blood type. The blood from a person of a different ethnicity might save your life, if it is your blood type. People always look on the outside to make things work, I say we need to look at what is inside. A massage therapist or acupuncturist is no different than a drummer; if a patient is sick and out of balance, the healer has to make him vibrate properly, the healer has to make him dance. The Chinese say there must be an uninterrupted flow of energy and blood; that is the whole meaning of ritual dance. When people come to a restaurant hungry, what they put in their mouths is important. And when people sit down to hear some music, you have got to make sure that you have them vibrating right. Certain music might have vibrations that set off bad reactions.

When I was doing lab technology I became interested in the heart because one of my fortes was hematology: I could take blood samples and diagnose them and do electrocardiograms. The simplest way for me to learn about how the body vibrates is to record as many heart sounds as possible. I have been collecting samples of people's heartbeats for many years, at Bennington, and in my studio in Queens. I collect frequencies from healthy people and from people with diseases, heart imbalances and other conditions. I am interested in the heartbeat, the rhythm of the heart, but also the pitch and the timbre.

The heart pump is the most basic thing we have. Many heartbeats are similar to drum rhythms: a common djembe pattern and the basic jazz ride cymbal beats are similar to what is going on in the heart. I was in Barnes and Noble bookstore in the medical section one time—I used to just go in there and browse around—and I saw this book called *The Guide to Heart Sounds: Normal and Abnormal* that came with a tape.[18] I said, "Hmm, I wonder what that's about?" and I bought it. It just knocked me out, because the heart rhythms were so similar to the Afro-Caribbean rhythms I was playing. I called up my musician friends and told them that these recordings of abnormal heartbeat sound just like batá drumming. The rhythmic patterns of Afro-Cuban batá drumming are so similar to cardiac rhythms that it is unbelievable. This is why they are so powerful. Each of the three drums in the batá ensemble plays a different normal or abnormal heart rhythm, with the difference that while the heart plays these rhythms in a linear fashion, one after another, the batá drums overlay them on top of each other. My research has shown that if someone has an arrhythmia, I can change it by overlaying a normal rhythm on top of it, the way the batá group does. This brings about a healing effect.

Also, batá music is used for putting people into possession trances, and if you take cardiac readings of people who have normal heartbeats the rest of the time, when they are in trance you will hear batá rhythms. When I wrote my Guggenheim grant application, I explained that I am doing research on what I am calling "Biological Music." This grant is funding my research now; I have bought computers that I use in my work. I make recordings of heartbeats and computer-aided spectral analyses of each sound, analyzing the harmonics.

The tone of the heart rhythm is just as important as the rhythm, just as in music, the sound of the drum is just as important as the duration. A lot of musicians do not realize that they should listen to the drum tonally; they think of it as a rhythm thing. You cannot separate rhythm from melody, time from the tone. If you try to separate these things, you cause a lot of problems. If you get too deductive about the situation it screws things up because you lose the integrative process, you lose continuity. The Western thought process is very analytical, using deductive logic to extract and put a particular value on things. The same thing happens socially. They have segregated people by ethnicity, determining which ethnicity has a greater advantage and which ethnicity has lesser advantage. We are raised in a society that has a lot of bias, taking the whole and separating it, giving greater and lesser value to things. This has entered many disciplines. When it comes to the human body, they'll say that there are more important organs and less important organs, but like the Chinese say you have to look at everything; even the spleen has its function. If you separate these things you lose the real motive force that is behind everything, the force that keeps things constantly moving, constantly turning. When things are integrated you will not be in a rut when you come across an unknown factor, the question-mark factor. So we need to throw out this kind of segregative process, we've got to learn how to integrate everything together. The same goes for music: time and tone go together. The pitches or frequencies of the heart are just as important as their durations because they indicate what kind of tension is being put on the neuromuscular system. This tension dictates the way the heart valves close. So the tone of the heart is a response to the type of stress factor, or the type of tension, that was put on the total heart muscle itself. It is an indicator of what kind of stress factors are at play, showing whether there are high amplitudes, high voltage, low voltage, or no juice at all going in certain areas. So the pitch of the heart is very important.

In the mid-'70s, I started reading a journal called *Circulation*, which discusses frequencies of the heartbeat. At that time heart sound research looked only at single pitches, never harmonics. And the pitch that they looked at was not even the fundamental, because the filters they used to listen to heart sounds at that time were not as sophisticated as today; they could only hear as low as 40 cycles per second. Now we know that the fundamental frequencies of heart sounds are as low as nine or ten Hertz. My computer programs can also tell me what frequencies are coming out in terms of music, what notes they are, if it's A-flat minus 100 cents or whatever. The pitch of your heartbeat is not static; it keeps changing. One heartbeat might hit at a frequency of 11 Hertz, and after that it might up to 32, then maybe as high as 56, and drop down to 11. The pitch is constantly changing, and of course, it never comes out to a whole number; it is always a fraction. The heart only beats for a short period of time, so it does not sound melodic—the duration is too short—but I can slow each frequency down from 300 or 150 milliseconds to one whole second. At this speed it sounds like a melody, so I can actually hear the melodies that are being played on the hearts of each of the people who come down to my studio to record their heartbeats. I also use computer programs that create different shapes by punching in numbers to create squares, circles, or other designs. But instead of using fixed numbers, I use the frequencies of heart sounds. I put these frequencies in the program, which generates a design based on them. Once I get it standardized I will be able to compare the designs for people who have various conditions; since people who have diabetes, leukemia, or other conditions will have their own shapes.

I am also interested in the harmonics or overtones of heart sounds, and the new technology is good for studying them. The timbres of heart sounds are important for the same reason that timbres of musical instruments are important: a flute is different from an oboe because it has a different timbre. Timbre expresses the *quality* of the vibration. Every sound has many vibrations going at once, bouncing off each other, blending together, creating a larger sound. Also, pure tones don't stimulate human cells as much as tones with more harmonics; they are fuller, richer. Each vibration stimulates something else to vibrate, and that starts to vibrate something else. All these combinations come together to create what are called beats, or tones in between two sounds. This keeps going on until you have a big array of frequencies going on. The spectral analyses that I do of heart sounds express the timbres of the heart sounds and tell a lot about each subject.

I let people hear their own heart sounds, and when people have diseased hearts they can usually intuitively hear that something is wrong with the sound. It is similar to taking rancid food in your mouth: you feel nauseous immediately and instinctively you know that you should not eat it. It is the same with sounds: when you hear certain ones, you can tell if something is off, especially if you are a person that is tuned in to sound. We can learn a lot if we pay attention to our intuitions.

It's the People Who Decide

If you want to find out whether something works, you have got to go to the uneducated people, the common folk. And you have to try it on a multitude of people, from different cultures. If they go for it, then you know you have something that is integral to the human body and nothing to do with where you are from, what language you speak, what religion you believe in. This is part of the body structure. Regardless of where you are from, sodium is an integral part and a necessary part of your body. Potassium, calcium—without these ions we wouldn't be able to do anything, we couldn't function; they belong in the body.

Most people do not intellectualize things. The regular people come up with things that do the trick. Each culture develops foods that are simple and nutritious, like rice and beans, or tofu. These foods are in touch with the body. The same is true for folk music. It is the regular folk who decide whether my music is working or not; if I get positive reactions from people I know I'm on the right track. A true musician should be able to get through to all kinds of audiences, to walk among all kinds of people, all ethnicities, all religions, both genders, the young and the old. Music should transcend all that. Vibration should function just like water, just like sugar, just like salt. These are vital, essential constituents of the body. I might cook an ethnic meal that will appeal to a particular ethnicity. But what about cooking a meal that cuts across all ethnicities? That's a human meal. That meal will have the tastes and substances that all human beings need. All of our hearts function the same way, regardless of ethnicity. That is the kind of music I am looking for.

I have played for audiences in the black community and I have played for whites. I have played in Europe, Japan, and Africa. I always try to open myself up to the energy of the audience, to get into a comfort zone where I am completely in tune with myself but also totally open to the people's vibrations. It is similar to what people talk about when they talk about clairvoyance or telepathy. Sometimes it is best to play something simple, really simple, to pull the people in. I use my voice, I dance, and I also use a little humor sometimes. The first thing I do is that I try to learn what are the basic things I can do to turn people on. If I am playing and the audience does not seem to be tuning in I get on my trap set with my mallets and play basic rhythms based off certain djembe parts or batá rhythms, which are also similar to the jazz ride cymbal beat. As I mentioned, these are all similar to heart sounds, and they grab people right away.

Thurston Moore, a guitar player and the music director in the rock group Sonic Youth, really loves improvisation. Sonic Youth wants to get into improvised music, so they ask improvising musicians to play on the same bill with them. Thurston Moore came to my studio and played a little bit, and then I played on the bill with Sonic Youth in the Empty Bottle in Chicago, which is basically a rock bar. And people were really receptive. To me, this really proves something; people are ready to receive loud, wild stuff, and soft quiet stuff too, if it is done in the right way on the biological level. And when it is humor-related, people respond. I had all my bells hanging off my body, and went through all my vocal stuff. At the Empty Bottle they said they had never seen anything like that before. They said that what was amazing was that nobody was drinking; everybody was quiet for the whole length of my concert. The jazz scene has gotten so cool, so educated, so intellectual that they have lost touch with something. A lot of the young people are looking for something else, and the rock fans are getting hip. Thurston says that rock needs more substance, and he gets this from freely improvised music. Many of the rock fans are really opening themselves up. I see a certain kind of response and openness, all these faces smiling and moving; it is inspirational. I am glad that I can give people this deep kind of feeling. This is my motivation to just keep checking things out.

Ethnicity and Humanness

The basic stuff of life is solely of one family. Music is something that is a part of us as human folks; no one can claim ethnic ownership of music. The great thing about science is that it breaks things down to the fundamental stuff that we are made out of. And at least as far as the physical self goes, it all comes down to certain constituent elements that make us up. There is no getting around the fact that we all have sodium molecules, and phosphate molecules, and calcium.

If you do not really accept yourself and what you are, you might want to be a member of another ethnic group. Some Americans get into Chinese culture and want to be Chinese, or they want to be Japanese. If you do this, you might lose your connection to your deep self, you might lose conviction, you might be in denial of yourself. And the information you get about the other culture will be superficial. I have seen a lot of black cats try to get into a European spirit, changing their whole lifestyles. I think that you should not do that because you cannot really know what other people are thinking; you are not in their environment. At one time I was involved with some of the so-called black classical musicians. But it was only when I went to Europe, and I saw where this music had come from, that I said to myself, "Hmm, *now* I think I understand what classical music is all about."

Ethnicity is not as important as experience. If we can understand the experiences that have motivated people to make music in particular ways, then we can get deeply involved in it. This will not work if you are outside of yourself, dealing with things superficially, talking the talk, trying to being hip. If we understand another culture experientially, accepting who we are, we can really get involved in it. I call this cultural transmutation. In alchemy, transmutation is the process of transforming one substance to another, like turning lead into gold. Cultural transmutation is when a person immerses himself in another culture to the extent that he becomes adept at certain aspects of it. An American musician can learn to play music from the Dominican Republic to the extent that people will listen to him and think he is Dominican. Transmutation also works with plants: I can take a plant from any place in the planet and replant it, and if I treat it right it will adapt; it will grow right along with the rest of the family. But if you do not know the internal formula, you can't transmute. For cultural transmutation to work, you have to be in tune with both yourself and others.

It's about experience more than how people look. A lot of white people listen to the blues or rap, but they have not experienced the meaning of these styles. The old blues singers in the backwoods were involved in a particular lifestyle; blue notes have particular meanings. A lot of people play bebop, but few people know what bebop is. Bebop is not just a musical style, a particular way of putting notes together. During its period, bebop was a way of talking, a way of walking, a worldview.

Ethnicity is something that people adopt later in life. You don't see small children identifying with any particular ethnic group; white children approach black folks completely openly, with no racism. To get to the human level, you have got to go to the fundamental essence of what satisfies the human system. I am not talking about the cultural system that has adapted to things, that has been acquired. I am talking about the general system that is given to all human beings, that exists no matter where a person comes from. You can only contact this system if you have cleansed yourself of the blockages that you have acquired, because every culture has certain prejudices built into it. You have to cleanse yourself of these and be completely open, and get into a comfort zone where you can really appreciate people, where you can really tune into people's vibrations. If you have a people hang-up, this will not work, and if you are out of touch with yourself, it also will not work.

I had to replace my attic windows, and I redid them with colorful rockwork frames. It was a lot of work, but the feedback made it worthwhile. I get comments from crackhead prostitutes and straight-up drunk folks. I have many ethnicities coming through here, from Guyanese people to Indians, to Jamaicans, policemen and firemen. White folks that pass through make comments, and some old Italian contractors who were working on the roadway and had recently come over from Italy, speaking Italian. I even see little kids, eight- and nine-year-old kids, discussing it. When I saw this wide array of different people have the same reaction I had to reflect back and study this. I enjoy different kinds of architecture, looking at pictures of architecture from around the world. And I have paid a lot of attention to buildings that I have seen in my travels around the world, like all the old churches in Florence. I design my windows by spontaneously improvising on all these influences. When Spanish people see my windows they say,

"This is Spanish!" Africans come by and say, "It's African!" One guy came by and said, "I am from Trinidad, man. This is a carnival house, man, from Trinidad!" Muslims pass by and say "That's Islamic, brother." And we've got a few Moors around here who said that it is Moorish. I just say that I guess it is everybody, I guess it has a little bit of everyone.

That is on the visual level, but the same principles work on the level of food. I gave a few little performances in my house: I took away the tables in my studio and put pillows on the floor for people to sit down on. I played with Charles Gayle on tenor saxophone and William Parker on bass. Andrew Cyrille and I also did a percussion duo. I had about sixty folks in my studio. People loved it, and I think that a big reason they loved it so much is that the night before, my wife and I were in the kitchen cooking. I made soups in big soup pots, and different kinds of breads. Now, this is a really mixed audience of Europeans, Asians, you name it. And everybody commented on my peanut soup, regardless of their ethnic background; the soup's a hit, it's a winner! I use special ingredients, seasonings from every culture I can think of in the world; my soup pot has the whole world in it. There's one seed I use, a black caraway seed, and when I tell Muslims about it they go ape because the Prophet Mohammed used a black seed. I just use it because it tastes good! And it opens something up. I mix that in with some tofu. I also make a mock duck, like the Chinese do: imitation duck or chicken. I have all these different things in the right proportions.

What is important to me is that people from so many different backgrounds respond. It is the regular people who make the decision, right? Experts should not decide what works and what does not. I watch the reaction of the regular people and then study it, take it apart. I try to find the common element to see what it is that makes us human, that makes us vibrate a certain way. Being open to all of these different cultures has been very advantageous to me. Respecting people, not having hang-ups about people. Studying people's ideas and accepting them, saying, "Wow, that's pretty good; I can see how that works over there." If you take all these ideas and incorporate them into what you do it loosens you up, and once you are loose you become sensitive to what all humans share.

People have always been observing nature and then creatively expressing what they found. They have always been tuning into the cosmos, and also tuning into their own bodies, their own hearts. There is something very essential in all of us. On a musical level it is based in basic vibrations. That's how the blues and gospel music came about. People naturally tuned into themselves, and these musics came out. They hooked in to certain inner tones within the biological system. When music or food or architecture is based on these principles, people all over the world accept it. So-called

Latin music, salsa or Afro-Cuban music is very popular now; people are starting to gravitate toward it all over the world. Before that, Afro-American music from this country was already cutting across boundaries, getting into other cultures: everybody was affected by it. The blues touches a common type of thing, a fundamental. If you elaborate on it to the point of getting intellectual or academic, it loses its power.

Physics is all about vibration, so if you are a musician, you've got to study vibration: the first thing you should study is what causes us to bounce, what causes the body to bounce, what makes it move. When I played timbales my feet wanted to move; I used to dance while I played. So when I switched to drum set, I transferred my dance steps to the high-hat and bass drum pedals. African-influenced music is based in dance; it makes people move, it makes them bounce. If you are a drummer and you cannot dance you have a problem, and if you are a musician and you cannot dance, you have a problem. I'll go even farther and say that if you are alive and you cannot dance, you have a problem. The human body responds to drumming by moving, by dancing. And the most fundamental drum is the human heart.

Sounds can inspire people; a person can be down, and music can lift his spirits, make him feel good. So music is beyond just chord changes and tunes. It is about basic movements; you have got to go back to the music of how we vibrate, how we bounce, how we create sound within ourselves. The way a saxophonist plays, the way he blows breath across the reed, creates a particular sound that expresses his inner self. When people have asthma, you can hear that the whole respiratory system is off; there is something wrong with the sound! It all has to do with the way things move, airflow and pressure, that creates sound. People take certain things for granted; they don't think about certain things, but we all have the ability to make fine discernments about people's inner states based on sound. If you hear somebody talk in a particular tone of voice you might say, "Are you okay? You just sound a little down or something." You don't even realize that you are using sound as a method of diagnosis. Certain basic things have been given to us as human beings. If we just sit back, we can really discern a lot.

You know who my music teacher is? My teacher is everybody that comes through my studio, who lies down on my table and has their heart sound recorded. I didn't do all this research on heart sound just to check it out: my computer research on heart sounds has had a huge influence on my playing, on the way I can hear, hit, and blend when I play the drums. After spending days and days listening to these heart sounds, they really get into me; I sit down and listen to these wave forms and internalize them, and now I have a multitude of wave forms in me, which I express in my music. The human heart is my teacher.

A Human Vibration

If there's an expansion, there has to be a contraction. History books teach about the European explorers like Columbus, but there was an even bigger exploration that took place way before that time. In those early days there was a *big* expansion. In the beginning, all the people in the world were in the same place, we all started in one common place. People looked like they were cloned, they were look-alikes. All of us were together, multiple dimensions all connected. At some point, we just got blown apart from each other, and everything was expanding. We were spreading all over the planet. This continued into the times of the Italian, Spanish, and Portuguese explorers who went all over the world in their little boats. Today, with what they call multiculturalism, we are going back into a state of compression or contraction; we are coming together again. When I was growing up, my neighborhood was not nearly as ethnically diverse as it is now. I look at the neighborhood now and I see Dominicans, Haitians; the multitude of ethnicities that I see in the neighborhood now is amazing! Sometimes there are ethnic festivals on weekends, and I can hear all kinds of music, it is like traveling without going anywhere. This is a major change. You can see all this information and knowledge starting to condense; everybody's coming together.

We're at a crossroads, as they say in the Yorùbá religion, at the intersection where the Yorùbá deity Ẹlẹ́gbá rules. Being at a crossroads means making decisions. We are at a junction point, so what are we going to do? Some people might say, "I am going in this particular direction." Someone else says, "No, no, I am staying right here, in the midst of all this change, and I am going to let it all come right in." We are getting so close that a new kind of energy is being generated. If you are sitting next to somebody who you don't know in a crowded area, the electrical charge around his body will be in contact with your own electrical charge. His charge will affect your charge and the two of you will form a big ring of energy. It is coming back in, it is condensing, and when this happens, we have to regroup. We need to learn from this, it should make us wiser. Everybody starts inspiring each other, not just from the intellectual mind, but from a deep level. We are all coming together in a human vibration.

Conclusion

⁓⁓⁓

This book is the fruit of my "coming together in a human vibration" with jazz consciousness around the world. Now that we have looked at various manifestations of the music in separate contexts, let us consider the big picture.

Jazz consciousness, as discussed in this book, is a musical manifestation of what W. E. B. Du Bois called "double consciousness," the simultaneous African American affiliation with the black in-group and the larger mainstream.[1] Jazz—and the whole mind-set or consciousness that surrounds it—is based in African American culture and evinces parallels with other Afro-diasporic musics. At the same time, it is integral to the larger mainstream of the United States and exhibits an extraordinary openness to all manner of influences and ideas. This inclusivity is based in the syncretic nature of all Afro-diasporic culture: jazz fuses African-derived responsorial melo-rhythms with European modes of musical organization to forge a new whole that is eminently modern and eminently Western. As a cosmopolitan music, jazz has engendered variegated reinterpretations around the world. It is also essential, however, to note that the inclusivity of the jazz community has not been absolute: women have often been marginalized, and exclusionist black nationalist tendencies have been present. Still, the ethos of the music has generally been one of inclusivity.

Jazz is not alone in its doubleness: other African American musics, ranging from spirituals to ragtime, gospel to hip-hop, configure their own forms of multiconsciousness. Many of this book's paradigms, in fact, could be fruitfully applied to other African American musics. Like jazz, hip-hop developed from its African American base to be embraced by people of all ethnicities in the United States and around the world. Unlike hip-hop, however, jazz developed under the shadow of legalized segregation and was inextricable from the social movements that struggled against it. The forward-looking spirit of the Harlem Renaissance and civil rights eras is a powerful motivating factor behind jazz consciousness. In spite of many important gains, however, the utopian promises of the Harlem Renaissance and the civil rights movement did not materialize. Disillusionment with lost expectations may well lie behind both the nihilism of "gangsta rap" and the black nationalism of politicized rappers who advocate turning inward to the African American community rather than outward to the mainstream. But hip-hop culture nevertheless evinces a sense of racial inclusivity that parallels jazz consciousness: all nationalities and ethnicities participate in hip-hop while acknowledging its Afro-diasporic base.

Machito and his Afro-Cubans were maximum exponents of jazz consciousness. Disillusioned with the Cuban myth of racial democracy and inspired by the promises of the Harlem Renaissance, they were committed to blackness, melding Afro-Cuban and black North American elements in a supremely pan-African offering. At the same time, the Machito band spanned boundaries. The group's director, Mario Bauzá, as well as its top arrangers, René Hernández and Chico O'Farrill, were firmly based in Euro-classical music. Moreover, the band's fan base was multicultural: Jewish mamboniks and other whites were just as important to the Machito family as were Harlemites. The Machito band was "American" in the largest, hemispheric sense of the word: for all its excellence as a Latin American dance band, its most lasting contribution was in a North American form: jazz. This New York–bred brand of Afro-Cuban music had a major impact on the development of many forms of popular dance music throughout the Americas and around the world. Machito and his Afro-Cubans, then, was at once pan-African, pan-American, and transnational.

Machito and his Afro-Cubans made the dynamic of stereotype and reappropriation work in their favor: while gaining popularity by riding the waves of Latino and black stereotypes, they surpassed them, presenting Afro-diasporic creativity on their own terms. Milford Graves employed similar strategies: for example, by developing his early exposure to media stereotypes about Vodou dolls into serious study of African healing and acupuncture. Like many African Americans of his generation, Graves was directly inspired by the Afro-diasporic links forged by Machito, Mario Bauzá, Dizzy Gillespie, and Chano Pozo; he developed his innovative style of freely improvised drumming primarily from Afro-Cuban and African influences rather than from straight-ahead jazz. Building on this background, he took the inclusiveness of jazz consciousness to new heights, imbibing further influences from Asia and Europe to develop a unique approach combining African-based musics with Eastern healing practices, computers, and Western medicine. In addition to reaching outward to all manner of influences, Graves reaches inward, studying his own psychobio-logical self. He overcomes duality by looking inside for what connects us all as humans.

As we have seen, ideologies of nationalism unite disparate groups of people under socially constructed banners of "fictive identity."[2] At the same time, national identities can reflect genuine lifeways and shared histo-ries. Black nationalism, for example, celebrates real Africanisms, real par-allels between black cultures that were once obfuscated by the "myth of the Negro past."[3] Like other forms of nationalism, black nationalism and pan-Africanism unite peoples that, despite many links, also diverge in many ways. This paradox became apparent in Charlie Parker's collaboration with Machito and his Afro-Cubans. Mario Bauzá opined that Parker refused to record "El manicero" with Machito specifically because this song outlines Afro-Cuban rhythms in a way that is difficult to blend with bebop. At the same time, the Machito/Parker collaboration produced some of the most exciting music of the twentieth century. Recorded at the same session, "Mango mangüé" successfully blends Afro-Cuban music and bop; as Mario Bauzá put it, it imparts the feeling that you get when "you put your key in your door" and "you [are] . . . home."[4]

We define the self in relation to the other. An infant, for example, de-velops a personal identity as she experiences separation from her mother. Similarly, national identity is articulated in the transnational arena: Finns see themselves in silhouette with Russians and Swedes, while Domini-cans contrast themselves to Haitians. Similarly, jazz was only embraced as "America's music" *after* it became popular abroad. Jazz and other forms of Afro-diasporic music spread worldwide as U.S. influence grew during the twentieth century to the extent that various forms of black music stand as a musical lingua franca today. The variegated reinterpretations of jazz that developed around the world reflect the music's doubleness, its simultaneous links to the African American in-group and the mainstream United States. Within the African diaspora, among Cubans, for example, jazz offshoots build upon shared African influences. In other areas, such as Finland, people reinterpret jazz aesthetics in local ways, building upon its ecumenicity and process-oriented nature. On one hand, jazz propa-gates U.S. influence around the world. On the other hand, it often serves as a counterforce to U.S. hegemony, spreading through pan-African net-works and appealing to people of all ethnicities who have been inspired by black people's struggle for social equity. The hallmark, then, of trans-national jazz consciousness is that it simultaneously promotes U.S. inter-ests around the world and motivates resistance to certain elements of U.S. policy and culture.

As we have seen, in spite of the strong African influences on Dominican culture, Dominican national identity is largely Eurocentric. Rooted in colonialism, Dominican "socialized ambivalence"[5] had a second life when the United States emerged as a neo-colonial power in the Dominican Republic. While Dominicans were fiercely patriotic in the face of North American domination and valiantly resisted both U.S. invasions of their land, they were also attracted to the wealth and might of their northern neighbor. On the one hand, Dominican musicians developed pan-African links by cultivating local forms of jazz and progressive Dominicans embraced African American culture as an index of resistance to U.S. hegemony. On the other hand, many bourgeois Dominican jazz fans associated the music with the wealth and power of the United States and distanced it from other Afro-diasporic musics. It is important to remember that while this ambivalence may be lamentable, it never denatured the creativity of Dominican musicians; neither did it prevent them from developing pan-African links. The extremity of Dominican socialized ambivalence is a reminder that such feelings are part and parcel to the "war" of unequal power relations, and that they are endemic to all parts of the African diaspora, including the United States. Ambivalence, in fact, is a natural by-product of sensitive engagement with the complex realities of life for all people. Instead of running away from contradiction, instead of denying our own internal incongruities or blaming others for theirs, I believe that it is by honestly confronting ambivalence and learning from it that we can grow.

The Genius of Humanity

Diffused around the world almost since its inception, jazz has long been a cosmopolitan music revolving around two axes: the United States and the larger African diaspora. Machito and his Afro-Cubans situated themselves in multiple ways: as a musical expression of pan-Africanism, as exponents of Latin American culture, and as jazz musicians based in the United States. Dominican musicians, like the Cuboppers, created vibrant fusions based in aesthetic links between jazz and Dominican music, but many members of the Dominican jazz community preferred to see jazz as an index of the United States in general than as black music.

African American musicians have expressed their ethos of universalism by embracing all manner of influences; musicians like Eric Dolphy created an aesthetic space of inclusivity that counteracts the exculsionism endemic to American life. Milford Graves champions a profoundly universalist musical vision; he states, "I do not deal with music that has any ethnic classification; I deal . . . with human music." I will not scientifically evaluate

Graves's views on the relations between human heart sounds and music. I will instead discuss the relation between cultural relativism and the inclusive universalism of jazz consciousness. The truism that jazz is "America's music" and appeals for musical "color-blindness" may be naive because they deracialize the music, ignoring fundamental differences in power that, in the United States, are often drawn along lines of color. African American artist-intellectuals such as Milford Graves, however, are not naive: they have confronted the injustice of the world—its "war"—and developed their musical philosophies precisely as a result of an acute awareness of it.

Indeed, the inclusiveness of jazz consciousness developed as a response to racial exclusionism. Jazz musicians have sought out all manner of influences; Eric Dolphy, for example, said that "Everything affects you. Every musician I've ever heard has influenced me."[6] On one hand, this sentiment expresses a natural human proclivity for taking advantage of multifarious resources. But nurturing their art in a context of marginalization and inspired by the utopianism of the Harlem Renaissance and civil rights movements, African American musicians had a special incentive to cast a wide net, a special incentive to focus on the things that people share all over the world. Struggling to survive in contexts that denied their humanity, people of color have articulated "strategic universalism" and "planetary humanism."[7] Invoking all of humanity may be a grandiose gesture, but it may be a necessary gesture to make in the face of inhumanity.

Cultural relativism is a valuable tool: considering musical types in their specific cultural contexts unlocks their particular secrets. The lessons of relativism, however, should not blind us to other valuable perspectives. Graves's belief that there is such a thing as "human music," for example, contradicts neither his grounding in the African diaspora nor his identity as an American. Moreover, it does not undermine his understanding that music must be understood in cultural context: with regard to Euro-classical music he said that "it was only when I went to Europe, and I saw where this music had come from, that I said to myself, 'Hmm, *now* I think I understand what classical music is all about.'" We rarely dissect the fine points of cultural relativism. Franz Boas elaborated this in opposition to the racist evolutionism that prevailed during the nineteenth century. He turned away from comparative studies, which dominated the anthropology of his day, in favor of detailed ethnographic descriptions of individual cultures on their own terms. The conclusion that Boas drew from his studies of Native American peoples was that non-European cultures are equally sophisticated as European cultures. Although this may not come as a surprise today, it was indeed groundbreaking in academic circles when he proposed it. The ethnographies that Boas and his students completed demonstrated that there is no evidence to support racist and hierarchical models that taught that some people more "civilized" than others.[8] A universalistic assumption thus underlies cultural relativism: by demonstrating that no culture is superior to another, Boas showed that there is an underlying unity to humanity.

Boas was strongly influenced by the eighteenth-century German philosopher Johann Gottfried Herder. As noted, Herder was a prime architect of romantic or cultural nationalism, which focuses on links between culture (ethnicity, nation), language, and the arts. Herder has been unfairly blamed for the excesses of German nationalism as it developed in the nineteenth and twentieth centuries: although he may have influenced German chauvinism, it was actually antithetical to his thinking in many ways. Herder articulated the relativist idea that no culture is superior to another. He also believed that each culture has a contribution to make to the larger whole. Herder proposed that each culture has its own particular spirit or "genius," which it contributes to a larger "genius of humanity":

Above all, let one be *unbiased* like the *genius of humanity* itself; let one have no pet tribe, no favorite people on the earth. Such preference often seduces one into ascribing too much good to the favored nation and too much bad to the others.[9]

Du Bois studied in Berlin from 1892 to 1894 and was influenced by German nationalism and Herder's thinking. Even prior to going to Germany he had been fascinated by Bismarck's ability to unite the German-speaking peoples.[10]

Wilson Moses shows that black nationalism was "one of the earliest expressions of nationalism." While it was certainly "not an imitation of North American or European nationalism," black nationalism developed "in unison" with European thinking.[11] The Herderian idea of *Volksgeist,* or "the spirit of the folk," for example, corresponds to the ideas expressed in Du Bois's *The Souls of Black Folk;* the book's title translates to German as *Der Schwarze Volksgeist.*[12] This congruity, of course, negates neither Du Bois's originality nor the African American influences on his development. Links between Du Bois's ideas and German thinking instead point to the fact that African American thought, like the African diaspora as a whole, developed in a milieu shared with other Western peoples.

Both Boas and Du Bois elucidated the Herderian idea that each culture has a unique creative spirit to contribute to the larger "genius of humanity." Boas advised: "We must bow to the genius of all, whatever race they may represent: Hamitic, Semitic, Aryan, or Mongol."[13] Meanwhile, Du Bois suggested that "it [is] the duty of the Americans of Negro descent, as a body, to maintain their race identity until . . . the ideal of human brotherhood has become a practical possibility."[14] The pairing of the in-group and mainstream, the particular and the ecumenical, lies at the bedrock of both Boasian relativism and Du Boisian doubleness and thus behind major currents in both ethnomusicology and Africana studies.[15] It is also, of course, basic to jazz consciousness, which embodies the genius of Afro-diasporic culture in a superlatively (pan-)American and cosmopolitan configuration.

Music gives voice to unspoken sentiments. In Finland, for example, a love of Russian musical style persisted in spite of a persistent western European orientation in most other areas of life. Similarly, in the Dominican Republic, musicians remained alive to pan-African links in spite of prevalent Eurocentrism. In the United States, racial barriers could not stop African Americans from contributing to the development of European-influenced musical traditions, nor did they stop whites from adopting Africanisms. While the process of creolization takes place on an unequal playing field, musical consciousness elides the dualism of verbal discourse. As Christopher Small writes, the musical experience "can deal with many concerns, even contradictory ones, while words can deal with only one at a time."[16] And because the musical experience is eminently social, musical mind-sets inevitably influence public life. Inclusive jazz consciousness is a utopian space, but it is a real utopian space, a lived mode of expansiveness that enacts a step in awareness, moving from ambivalence to multivalence, from doubleness to all-ness.

It is my hope that these thoughts begin to address the provocative question that my professor of ethnomusicology, David McAllester, posed when I began graduate school: What is musical truth? In-depth studies of specific musical cultures are valuable in pursuing this question. But, as Milford Graves says, expansion always follows contraction, not only in the human heart, but also in human thought. Inspired by the transcendent thinking of the artist-intellectuals with whom I have sojourned on my musico-scholarly journey, I want to end in a more poetic mode:

Charlie Parker once said that they "teach you there's a boundary line to music. But, man, there's no boundary line to art."[17]

I want to say this:

All-consciousness reveals that while social boundaries are real, there is no boundary to humanity.

Notes

Introduction (pp. ix–xxii)

1. Taylor 1986.
2. Ellington 1976 [1973]: 436.
3. See Gerard 1998: 36; Monson 1996: 202–3.
4. Du Bois 1961 [1903]: 16–17; my emphasis.
5. See Early's anthology in which several black thinkers present widely divergent views of what doubleness means to them (1993). Adolph Reed argues that today's African Americanists develop personalized interpretations of double consciousness that resonate with their own predicament as middle-class blacks, but that they ignore its historical context and exaggerate its importance in Du Bois's thinking (1997: 95–127, 165). Reed's scholarship is compelling, but it does not invalidate interpretations of what doubleness might mean today. While many of the ideas presented here are *inspired* by Du Bois's thinking, this book is not a treatise on Du Bois's ideas.
6. Du Bois himself discussed African American music, in *The Souls of Black Folk* as well as in *The Gift of Black Folk* (1924), but he was interested in spirituals, and looked down on jazz; see Lutz (1991).
7. Herndon and McCleod 1980.
8. I wrote most of these essays for publication elsewhere but rewrote them, conceiving them anew, to form this book.
9. I developed the concept of jazz consciousness under the influence of Ingrid Monson's insightful application of Du Boisian doubleness to jazz studies (1996: 99–100) and also through many stimulating conversations with Scott Currie and Katherine Brucher (see Currie forthcoming and Brucher 1999).
10. I use the adjective "American" when referring to the Western Hemisphere as a whole, but also when referring to the United States in contexts that do not preclude application to other parts of the hemisphere. I use the term "black" when referring to people of African descent primarily in the United States, but also in contexts that do not preclude its application to people of African descent elsewhere in the world. I use the term "African American" to refer to black North Americans.
11. John Storm Roberts coined this valuable term (1979).
12. Gilroy 1993b.
13. Ibid., 9.
14. This is from an oration that Ellington made as part of his composition *My People* (quoted in Lock 1999: 115).

15. Du Bois 1961 [1903]: 16.

16. Marley 1999 [1962–80].

17. Herskovits 1958 (1941): 10ff.

18. Herskovits 1937: 295–96. In my experience, this is much more prevalent among the Haitian middle classes than among the majority of Haitians. In the Dominican Republic, however, ambivalence about African-influenced religion runs across class lines (see Austeritz 1997a).

19. Bourguignon 1951: 173; also see Bourguignon 1969.

20. Fanon 1967: 18, 83. Gilroy also sees ambivalence as a central predicament of the African diaspora (Gilroy 1993b; also see Moses in Early 1993). I have previously argued that racial ambivalence is central to national identity in the Dominican Republic (Austerlitz 1997a). On ambivalence, see also Miller 2000 and Wilcken 1992b. On internalized racism, see Fanon 1967 and Cross 1991: 142, 150, 181ff.

21. Emerson 1986: 105.

22. Goethe 1990 [1961]: 145.

23. As James noted, *Principles of Psychology* was written "in connection with the author's class-room instruction in Psychology" precisely during the period that Du Bois studied with him (1890: v). Several Du Bois scholars have argued that James exerted a strong influence on Du Bois (Rampersad 1976: 73–74, Sundquist 1993: 571–72, Bruce 1992, Bell 1987, and Lutz 1991). Du Bois's biographer David Levering Lewis acknowledges that Du Bois was influenced by James's discussion of "split" personalities, but points out that there is no direct evidence showing that James's work had a major impact on his thinking, and, moreover, that African American realities themselves were enough, on their own, to inspire Du Bois's thinking about doubleness. He therefore deemphasizes James's possible influence on Du Bois (Lewis 1993: 96, 603). Reed shows that during the period in which *Souls of Black Folk* was written, it was commonly believed that a condition of "overcivilization" could cause feelings of alienation and a state of "fragmented consciousness;" like Lewis, Reed therefore downplays James's impact on Du Bois (1997: 95–127, 165). Regardless of the extent of actual influence, considering Du Bois's thinking in relation to James illuminates the application of the concept of double consciousness to the study of jazz.

24. James 1890: 227ff., 329ff.

25. James 1997: 81, 143.

26. Ibid., 147–48.

27. Ibid., 160.

28. Lewis 1993: 281–83.

29. See Damasio 1999 and Varela and Shear 2000.

30. See Damasio 1999 and Varela and Shear 2000. Judith Becker has done groundbreaking work wedding ethnomusicology with neuroscientific consciousness studies (Becker 2004).

31. Small 1998: 221. Small provocatively argues that music is better understood as a process rather than an entity and calls the musical experience—playing, listening, dancing, or even cleaning a concert hall—*musicking* (1998; see also Small 1987).

32. Lock focuses on Duke Ellington, Sun Ra, and Anthony Braxton, but his perspective is applicable to many other jazz musicians (1999).

33. 1993 [1959]: xlii.

34. Small goes so far as to say that African American music is "a central contribution . . . to the very mainstream of human culture" (1987: 1).

35. See Atkins 2003.

36. Turino 2000: 7.

37. Ibid., 8.

38. Ibid., 10.

39. Ibid., 11.

40. Quoted in Monson 1996: 201.

41. Boas 1887: 588, quoted and discussed by Stocking in Boas 1982: 5.

42. Becker 2004: 73 and 1, 29, 72–73, 129–30. See Lévi-Strauss 1963, Leach 1970, Chomsky 1972, McAllester 1971, and Nettl 1983: 36–43.

43. Gilroy 2000: 327–56.

44. Ibid., 330.

45. Ibid., 330.

46. Fanon 1967 [1952]: 231–32. Gilroy adds that one of Fanon's greatest contributions was showing that the worst thing about European colonialism and racism is "not merely that European powers wrongfully deprived colonial subjects of their humanity, but that Europe has perpetrated the still greater crime of despoiling humanity of its elemental unity as a species" (Gilroy 2000: 71, Fanon 1963: 316). See also Gordon 1995.

47. Du Bois 1961 [1903]: 16–17.

48. In addition to reexamining the ethnographic endeavor, the current academic mood of self-examination has resulted in an autobiographical approach—what Geertz calls a "confessional" stance, which allays "authorial uneasiness" issuing from acute sensitivity to the unequal power relationships that are integral to humanistic scholarship (1988: 15). He notes that many ethnographies have resultingly moved from "Participant Observation" to "Participant Description," becoming "I-witness accounts" (1988: 79; see Rabinow 1977). This trend strikes some observers as solipsistic (e.g., Bourdieu and Wacquant 1992: 40–41), and even Roland Barthes, whose own work is often reflexive, wrestles with what he calls "diary disease," noting that in Freud's and Foucault's aftermath it is naive to take "confession" and "sincerity" at face value (1982). As Geertz puts it, "'I' is indeed very hard to write" (1988: 99).

49. See Austerlitz 1986, 1993, 1997a, 1999.

50. See Kluckhohn 1940; Vidich 1955.

51. See Chernoff 1979; Austerlitz 1997a: xii–xiii.

52. Hood 1971: 40.

53. Gramsci 1971.

54. In recent years, I have concentrated on developing as an improviser on the bass and contrabass clarinets and composing music based in Afro-Dominican rhythms; see the recordings Austerlitz 1998 and 2003; Austerlitz and Harper 2004a and 2004b, Brooks 1979; Lowe 1992, 1993, 1996; Elisha 1997; and Obeng 2002 and 2003.

55. For example, Monson 1996, and Berliner 1994.

56. For example, De Veaux 1997, and Porter 1998.

57. Gabbard 1995a and 1995b, and Tucker 2000.

58. A growing body of literature documents jazz as a transnational music (Acosta 2003, Atkins 2001 and 2003, Harris 2000, Jackson 2003, Kater 1992, Starr 1983, Zwerin 1985).

59. Porter 2002, Braxton 1985, Taylor 1977, Lewis 2004a and 2004b, Iyer 2004a and 2004b, Modirzadeh 2000.

60. Coplan 1985, Manuel 1988, Guilbault 1993, Pacini 1995, Waterman 1990, Turino 2000.

61. Hebdige 1979, Hall 1991, Williams 1964.

62. This chapter is based on an earlier article (Austerlitz forthcoming a).

63. This chapter is based on an earlier study that treats Caribbean and African musics, but not jazz (Austerlitz 2003).

64. This chapter is based on an article that was conceived as part of a critical edition of arrangements and transcriptions of Machito's music (Austerlitz forthcoming b).

65. This chapter is based on an earlier article, which is more limited in scope (Austerlitz 1998).

66. This chapter incorporates material from my study of the influence of jazz on the Finnish folk music revival (Austerlitz 2000), but most of the material presented here is new.

Chapter 1. Jazz Consciousness in the United States (pp. 1–24)

1. On Mingus 1960 in "Filmography and Discography."

2. I borrowed this turn of phrase, which riffs on the jazz standard "What Is this Thing Called Love?" from the title of Eric Porter's insightful study of jazz musicians as critics (2002).

3. Lock 1999: 125.

4. Ellington 1976: 452.

5. Jauss 1982.

6. Handy 1941: 122–36.

7. De Veaux 1991; also see Gennari 1991. While this etymology is not conclusive, speculation points to a Ki-Kongo (Central African) source for the word "jazz"; it may come from "jizz," an American word for semen that likely derives from the Ki-Kongo *dinza*, to ejaculate (Merriam and Garner in Clark 2001). Although it is of course interesting to note the word's etymology, I am more concerned with the ways that the word has been used than in its source.

8. Bechet 1960: 3; quoted in Peretti 1993: 133.

9. Panassié 1960: 73–74, cited in De Veaux 1991: 538. Parker quoted in De Veaux 1991: 556.

10. De Veaux 1991: 541.

11. I have previously argued that several Dominican bandleaders tried to market stylistic innovations as new genres but were unsuccessful: the time-tested category of merengue had a momentum whose usefulness overshadowed their claims to innovating new genres (Austerlitz 1997a; see Kallberg 1988; Averill 1989a: 122, Waterman 1990: 17).

12. Parker made this comment during an on-air radio interview with emcee Symphony Sid:

> ss: "That new thing that you did with Machito was one of the most sensational things yet."
> cp: "Mango Mangüé?"
> ss: "Mango Mangüé was one of the most sensational things . . ."
> cp: "I enjoyed working with Machito, I mean, extremely."
> ss: "Well, it more or less puts bop in a more or less commercial sort of a groove, don't you think?"
> cp: "Well, if you want to think of it that way, I mean, but bop is just a title. I mean, it's all still music."
> ss: "Still gone music." (Parker 1999 [1949] in "Videography and Discography")

13. De Veaux 1991: 525, 552.

14. Sarmanto Finnish Jazz Archive interview.

15. In Wilmer 1992 [1977]: 23.

16. Personal communication with the author.

17. In Wilmer 1992 [1977]: 23.

18. Gerald Shapiro, personal communication with the author.

19. Taylor 1986 and Sales 1984.

20. Walser 1999: 327.

21. De Veaux 1991: 545ff.; Hodeir 1956.

22. Similarly, Grout's standard European music history text, *A History of Western Music,* treats popular and dance forms in diminishing perspective as the book moves forward in time: while they are discussed in the sections on medieval and Renaissance music, they are minimized or absent in the sections on later periods (Grout and Palisca 2001).

23. In Wilmer 1992 [1977]: 23.

24. Hobsbawm and Ranger 1983.

25. Quoted in Waterman 1990: 377; Hobsbawn and Ranger 1983. See also Handler and Linnekin 1984.

26. "The chances of two people who are both 'Caucasoid' differing in genetic constitution at one site on a given chromosome are about 14.3 percent, while, for any two people taken at random from the human population, they are about 14.8 percent" (Appiah 1992: 36, citing and interpreting Nei and Roychoudhury 1972 and 1983).

27. Omi and Winant 1986.

28. Gilroy 2000: 57.

29. Gilroy 2000: 2, 327–56.

30. Anderson 1983. Smith (1971: 168–69) draws a useful distinction between nationalism, which refers to political movements, and patriotism, which he calls "national sentiment." See also Turino 2000:12–17.

31. Hobsbawm points out that the "proper and original" meaning of the word "nation" did not allude to bounded territories or sovereignty (1990: 14–18).

32. Colonel Piłsudski and Massimo d'Azeglio, quoted in Hobsbawm 1990: 44–45.

33. Balibar 1991: 96.

34. Flores 1993: 199–224; O'Gorman 1961.

35. Stocking 1968.

36. Jazz critic Winthrop Sargeant expressed a middlebrow view when he wrote that in spite of Paul Whiteman and Benny Goodman's attempts to fuse European classical music with jazz, the two idioms "act like oil and water": while jazz is a "simple, direct, emotional . . . folk music," art music is "as complicated as architecture," the "result of centuries of musical thinking" (in Gottlieb 1996: 766, 767). Savran (2003) shows that similar attitudes are still prevalent today, for example, in *New York Times* coverage of the theater.

37. Quoted in Tibbetts 1993: 129.

38. Steinberg 1995: 150–51.

39. Levine 1989.

40. In Merriam 1964: 242.

41. See Ogren 1989 and Radano 2000. Mechanistic theories linking music's efficacy to the body go as far back as Plato and extend into both Christian and Islamic thought. See Rouget 1985: 187–226; Radano 2000; Agawu 2003: 55–56.

42. Public Enemy 1990.

43. Tuttle 1999: 1212. Lynching had originated as a way of executing criminals during the colonial period, when many areas lacked courts and jails. After Reconstruction, however, lynching became a method of terrorizing blacks in the Southern states. See Tolnay and Beck 1995 and Brundage 1997.

44. See Lott 1988; Tucker 2000: 233–34.

45. Gillespie and Fraser 1979: 120.

46. There is a tradition in the United States of pathologizing African American behavior; during the period of slavery medical professionals even suggested that slaves who wished to escape were mentally ill (Lock 1999:56).

47. In Walser 1999: 240–41.

48. Gillespie and Fraser 1979: 120.

49. Armstrong in Burns film 2000. Charles Mingus called Faubus the "first second or third all-American hero." See the words to his song "Fables of Faubus" (as sung by himself and drummer Danny Richmond on the CD Mingus 1960).

50. Moses 1996: 35.

51. Ibid., 5.

52. Wolters 2002: 143; King 1999.

53. Garvey 1969 [1923]: 44; also see Wolters 2002: 148.

54. Six Pan-African Congresses were held, the last one in 1974.

55. In Kofsky 1970: 63.

56. This led to the establishment of the musicians' self-help organizations called the Jazz Composers Guild and the Jazz Composers Orchestra.

57. Muhal Richard Abrams and the Art Ensemble of Chicago are prominent in the AACM.

58. Radano 1993: 89–104.

59. Gilroy 2000: 224, 231f., 236, 237; see also Monson 2000.

60. This melody became known as "Goin' Home"; see Steinberg 1995: 151. Mastering unusual instruments such as the manzello and stritch was one of Kirk's significant innovations. The manzello bears similarity to the B-flat soprano saxophone, while the stritch is a straight version of the E-flat alto saxophone.

61. On the recording Kirk 1993 [1970].

62. On the recording Kirk 2002.

63. Ellison 1998 [1970], in Roediger 1998: 162.

64. The fact that this stipulation actually limited the power of slave states by lowering their de jure populations does not temper its inhumanity.

65. Ellison 1998 [1970] in Roediger 1998: 165.

66. See Flores 1993: 185, 192.

67. Murray 1983: 22; see also Toomer 1993: 105–14.

68. Murray 1983: 3.

69. Ibid., 21.

70. See Hobsbawn 1993: 190.

71. I have heard this anecdote from several sources, but because I do not have the musician's permission to recount it, I shall keep his identity anonymous.

72. Lott 1993.

73. Because of discrepancies in their philosophies, Baraka and Ellison are rarely invoked in the same breath. I, however, believe that both have much to offer, and in fact, that their perspectives complement each other. Baraka discussed the role that white musicians such as Bix Beiderbecke played in the history of jazz, arguing that white jazz players developed into a "new class" of Americans whose participation in black music surpassed the legacy of minstrelsy (1963: 149–50).

74. Baraka 1963: 220, 1987: 328–32.

75. Keil did groundbreaking work in elucidating this dynamic in relation to social class as well as race (1985). Jackson points out that Keil's thinking on this matter was strongly influenced by Baraka (T. Jackson 2000: 72).

76. Mailer 1994 [1957]: 155, 156, 157.

77. Lipsitz 1994: 54–55.

78. See Lott 1993 and Roediger 1999.

79. Reprinted in Roediger 1998: 178.

80. Malcolm X 1966: 399, discussed in Roediger 1998: 19. Roediger shows that the fact that this anecdote is often repeated demonstrates its importance (1998: 19).

81. See Otis 1993.

82. Du Bois 1975 [1921]: 29–56. Du Bois went so far as to write that blacks are "clairvoyant" when it comes to the souls of white folks because they see whites more clearly than whites see blacks (1975 [1921]: 29).

83. Fanon 1967 [1952]: 150.

84. Ibid.

85. hooks 1989: ix, 11.

86. Charles 2002.

87. See Coltrane's comments on Third Stream in Kofsky 1970: 230. In addition to his background in black vernacular and Euro-classical musics, Coltrane was interested in African and Indian, as well as Chinese musics. See Modirzadeh's fascinating study of the latter (2000).

88. hooks 1989: 11.

89. hooks 1989: 11.

90. Baba Wande Abimbola, personal communication with the author.

91. Herskovits 1958 (1941): 15ff.

92. See Dahl 1984; Tucker 1993.

93. Frazier 1962 [1957]: 27.

94. Lutz 1991: 147–50.

95. Among middle-class jazz musicians, some of those who attended college were Benny Carter, Duke Ellington, Coleman Hawkins, Jimmy Lunceford, Sy Oliver, and Don Redman (Baraka 1963: 160; Hsio 1959: 174).

96. Quoted in Tucker 1993 and Lock 1999: 133.

97. Ruff 1991: 227.

98. Ibid., 227–31.

99. In Woideck 1996: 30.

100. Appel 2002: 60.

101. See Moore 1992.

102. In Gottlieb 1996: 748.

103. Thayer 1967 [1921]: 87; discussed in Gottlieb 1996: 749. Subsequent research suggests that this might not be based in fact. However, even if it is merely an anecdote, the fact that this story has entered the folklore about Mozart and Beethoven demonstrates the importance of improvisation in Euro-classical music.

104. Whitehead 1993.

105. See, for example, the recordings Dolphy 1964 and 1999.

106. Simosko and Tepperman 1996 [1974].

107. In Williams 1964: 282; my emphasis.

108. Simosko and Tepperman 1996 [1974]: 27–30.

109. In Williams 1964: 283.

110. In Simosko and Tepperman 1996 [1974]: 34.

111. Jost 1994 [1975]: 41.

112. In Priestly 1982: 110.

113. In ibid., 110.

114. Simosko and Tepperman 1996 [1974]: 22.

115. Ibid., 68; Kernfeld 2001.

116. Simosko and Tepperman 1996 [1974]: 53.

117. Quoted in ibid., 13.

118. In DeMichael 1962: 21.

119. Ibid.

120. In "Reedman Eric Dolphy" 1964.

121. Tynan, quoted in DeMichael 1962: 20.

122. In Simosko and Tepperman 1996 [1974]: 86.

123. Ibid.

124. Braxton 1985, vol. 1: 79ff.; also see Lock 1988 and 1999; Radano 1993.
125. See Braxton 1985; Lock 1988 and 1999; Radano 1993.
126. Du Bois 2000 [1897]

Chapter 2. Kente Cloth to Jazz: A Matrix of Sound (pp. 25–41)

1. In M. Tucker 1993: 255–57; quoted and discussed in Lock 1999: 132.
2. My Ghanaian drumming teachers, whose teachings are expressed in this chapter, were Freeman Donkor, Abraham Adzinyah, and Kwaku Kwaakye Obeng.
3. Gilroy 1993a: 80.
4. Ibid., 102.
5. While it is important to note that ideas about cultural authenticity are socially constructed, after we have made this observation, we must move on. Taking a clue from musicians such as Eric Dolphy, we need to take a rounded view that admits multiple perspectives. We can look at both strategic moves in the construction of identity and empirical links between cultures at the same time. In fact, these ingredients work together. Italian tourists in the Dominican Republic often speak Italian to Dominicans, and Dominicans respond in Spanish. Combined with an improvised sign language and many smiles, the resulting pidgin is sufficiently intelligible to effect purchases in shops and communicate taxi fares. The strategy works both because all parties involved have an interest in communicating, and also because these Romance languages share many qualities. Finnish tourists in the Dominican Republic, however, cannot use their native tongue with the local population. No matter how they might wish to meld Finnish and Spanish, it will not work, because Finno-Ugric and Romance languages share next to nothing.
6. Nketia 1974: 4; also see Agawu 1995: 1.
7. See Merriam 1964: 85–101 and Hornbostel 1927 on synesthesia. As we saw in chapter 1, ethnomusicologists seek to evaluate musical cultures on their own terms, and to the extent that this is possible, this is what I aim to do here. As we also saw, however, we can never escape power plays in which the dominant culture imposes standards by which the world is understood and judged, and my work is no exception. This chapter, then, like all ethnomusicological work, represents an individual scholar's interpretation of a music culture.
8. Feld points out that Seeger's musicological predicament refers to language as literal referent, not to language as metaphor (Keil and Feld 1994: 93; see Seeger 1977: 16, 7). In studies of African art and music, Thompson and Chernoff paved the way in presenting perspectives that convey the feeling of African arts through metaphorical language. In jazz studies, Monson and Berliner have produced masterly studies that look at musicians' metaphorical language (Chernoff 1979, Thompson 1983, Monson 1996, Berliner 1994).
9. Seeger 1977: 168–81.
10. Agawu charges that ethnomusicologists who utilize new notational systems deny that all types of musical notation are exercises in interpretation as well as description. While this may be true for some ethnomusicologists, I am presenting several notational systems precisely because I want to interpret the music in various ways: each notational system highlights a different aspect of a sound (2003: 64–65).
11. This chapter concentrates on West African from the Guinea coast (Ghana and Nigeria) rather than Central African, or Kongo, music largely because I have studied Ghanaian but not Central African styles. This does not mean that Kongo cultures did not come to the African diaspora. On the contrary, they had a strong impact in the United States, Haiti, Cuba, the Dominican Republic, and Brazil. By the same token, my absence of attention to the music of the Savannah region of

West Africa (Mali, the Gambia, Senegal, Guinea) does not imply that these areas did not influence music in the diaspora. On the contrary, as Oliver (1970) and Kubik (1999) show, Savannah music had an enormous impact in the United States, especially on the blues.

12. Nzewi 1997: 41. The fact that Agawu coincidentally quotes the same passage from Nzewi is a testament to the importance of Nzewi's thinking on this matter (Agawu 2003: 85, 92–93).

13. Koetting 1970.

14. Koetting himself once used this system, although he used the same color to represent all the sounds (1980: 179).

15. Thompson 1984: 207.

16. Ibid., 208.

17. Nzewi 1997: 32–33, 34, my emphasis; also see Nzewi 1974. Ghanaian musicologist Kofi Agawu goes so far as to assert that the notion "African rhythm" is a European-based "invention" (2003: 55–70).

18. Koetting uses the term sonority to refer to the aggregate of pitch, loudness, tone quality, and carrying power of drums, noting their importance in West African drumming (1970: 120; see Jones 1959: 67, 68).

19. By fixed-pitchness, I do not mean that the sounds produced on these instruments cannot be bent. Instead, I mean to distinguish them from instruments, like many (though not all) percussion instruments, whose sonorities are so rich that they cannot be fixed on one single pitch.

20. Austerlitz 1986: 3.

21. Soucous is Congolese popular music.

22. In Monson 1996: 62.

23. The resulting transcription is found in Austerlitz 1997a: 138, and the recording is on Austerlitz 1997 in "Videography and Discography."

24. Chernoff 1979: 55; emphasis in original.

25. Nzewi 1997: 39, my emphasis.

26. On hockets, see Nketia 1962.

27. This appellation may derive from the fact that hockets are basic to Western bell playing.

28. Ortiz [n.d.] in "Videography and Discography."

29. Chernoff 1979: 164.

30. In recent years, similar exoticist discourse has surfaced in discussions about hip-hop (Rose 1994).

31. Advocates of black creativity have also invoked the metaphor of contagion. Ishmael Reed uses it as a central trope of his novel, *Mumbo Jumbo*, an Afrocentric story about the mysterious life-giving power of African-based creativity that "jes' grew" (1972). In *Contagious Rhythm*, Barbara Browning points out that the metaphor of African-influenced culture as an infectious agent can be presented in a positive or negative light (1998). I have noticed that in the Dominican Republic people often say that merengue is "contagious" without exoticizing the music in any way.

32. Ágawu 2003: 73.

33. Maxwell Amoh, personal communication with the author; Agawu 2003: 21. Hornbostel also noted the relation of African music to body motion (1928).

34. Schuller 1989: 223.

35. Chernoff 1979: 50. Sometimes it is performed aurally, in which case it can be called a "guiding pulse sense" (Meki Nzewi, personal communication with the author).

36. Koetting 1970: 134.

37. See the recording *Angels in the Mirror*, track 3: 1997; and Amira 1992.

38. Personal communication with the author.

39. Stone 1985: 140, 142. Kubik has done groundbreaking work elucidating the ways African music plays with aural gestalt (1962, 1979).

40. While this roll consists of four strokes, it can give the impression of having five, as the ear easily misinterprets the bass slap preceding the roll as an open tone.

41. Austerlitz 1997a: 57–58.

42. Austerlitz 1986: 163, 165.

43. While African-based improvisatory traditions often employ great feats of musical mastery, their focus often stresses the collectivity. Soloistic virtuosity, however, is not absent from sub-Saharan Africa: Savannah vocal improvisation, for example, is supremely virtuosic.

44. Chernoff 1979.

45. Thompson 1966. Also see Nzewi on an aesthetic of the "hot" (1974).

46. Henderson 1983: 113.

47. See Monson 1996: 70.

48. Gillespie and Fraser 1979: 177, 232; De Veaux 1997: 260–69. "Mango Mangüé" can be heard on *Original Mambo Kings* 1992 (in "Videography and Discography").

49. Mbiti 1970: 24, 21; cited in Merriam 1982: 456.

50. Nzewi 1997: 33.

51. Seeger 1977: 169.

52. For examples of circular notation of African as well as Javanese and Indian musics, see Rycroft 1967; Nzewi 1997: 46–48; Locke 1996: 87, 89, 90; Becker, 1979; and Nelson 1991: 6–27.

53. The cinquillo (quintuplet) Caribbean rhythm, in spite of its name, is a syncopated duple rhythm (consisting of two pulses with off-beat accents) rather than a true quintuplet (which would have five equal durations). This rhythm is extremely common in Afro-Cuban, Dominican, and Haitian music. Alén notes that Dahomey-influenced Cuban Tumba Francesa drummers stretch two cycles of the cinquillo pattern to create a pattern of varied subdivisions (1995: 60–61). Haitian Vodou drummers sometimes stretch the rhythm to approach a true quintuplet, especially at points in the music when the lead drummer plays patterns of five laying over a larger time frame (David Yih, personal communication with the author). *Pri-prí* drum and accordion music of the Dominican Republic switches back and forth between $^{12}/_8$ and $^4/_4$ meters; like the jazz eighth note, this music would thus be impossible to express in TUBS or kente notation.

54. Dave Liebman, personal communication with the author. On microrhythmic push-push aesthetics in jazz, see Keil 1966; Keil 1995; Prögler 1995; Mingus 1971: 251–52; and Priestley 1982: 124–25.

55. Mingus 1971: 251–52; Priestly 1982: 124–25.

56. Washburne 1997: 174, 175–77.

57. Ibid., 175.

58. *Rock & Roll* 1995 (in "Videography and Discography").

59. Chamber music in the European classical tradition also employs a variegated push-pull feeling, but in a style that does not rely on the responsorial aesthetic of Afro-diasporic musics.

60. On Davis 1992 in "Videography and Discography." Keil's engagement with this issue began with his early work and continued with the instigation of Prögler and Alén's important studies (Keil 1966 and 1995; Prögler 1995; Alén 1995).

61. In the original Latin, "Si nemo me quaerat, scio, si quaerenti explicare velim, nescio" (in Husserl 1964: 21).

62. Langer 1953: 104, 19. Also see De Selincourt 1958: 152–60, 287.

63. Schutz 1970: 104; see also Schutz 1962: 230 and Skarda 1989: 50, 57.

64. Schutz 1970: 170; cited in Merriam 1982: 373.

65. Schutz 1976: 37.

66. Many observers of African-influenced musics have discussed virtual time (Blacking 1971: 37; Merriam 1982; Stone 1982: 72, 1985; Averill 1989a: 20; Austerlitz 1997a: 96).

67. Music theorist Jonathan Kramer argues that increased European and Euro-American contact with African and Asian cultures has brought about an ascendance of nonlinear time in twentieth-century Euro-classical music (1988: 387). Arguing that "time exists primarily within us" as "a relationship between people and the events they perceive," he notes that "events, not time, are in flux. And music is a series of events, events that not only contain time but shape it." Asserting that music has "the power to distort or even destroy time," he maintains that both linear and nonlinear time exist in music. He identifies linear time with left brain thinking, defining it as "the determination of some characteristic[s] of music in accordance with principles that arise from earlier events," and nonlinearity with right brain thinking, defining it as "the determination of some characteristic[s] of music in accordance with principles governing an entire piece or section" (1988: xiii, 5, 20). Kramer draws an analogy between the architectural structures of Euro-classical music (e.g., sonata form) and notions of linear time as expressed in Christian doctrine (e.g., the Last Coming) or the nineteenth-century novel (plot with climax). McClary makes similar connections, while relating goal orientation to masculinity and nonteleological modes to femininity (1991: 119, 146–47, 155).

68. Stone 1982: 72.

69. Ibid., 72.

70. Austerlitz 1997a: 96–97.

71. See Chernoff 1979: 115.

72. Brown 1991.

73. In Monson 1996: 68.

74. Kenny Washington in Monson 1996: 68.

75. In Monson 1996: 27.

76. In Monson 1996: 68.

77. Ethnomusicologist Travis Jackson discusses jazz in relation to Csikzentmihalyi's provocative theories about psychological "flow" states (T. Jackson 2000; Csikszentmihalyi 1991).

Chapter 3. Machito and Mario Bauzá: Latin Jazz in the U.S. Mainstream (pp. 42 – 97)

1. J. Roberts 1979: 38 and 1999: 2ff.

2. The figure comes from the 2000 U.S. census. The category is "Hispanic or Latino," and the exact number of 35,305,818, of course, omits many undocumented residents. This figure also includes many people of African descent.

3. Flores 1993: 185, 199–200.

4. Ibid., 185, 192.

5. Gillespie and Fraser 1979: 318; see the recording Gillespie 1993.

6. Machito/Salazar interview.

7. In Ortiz 1987 (film).

8. Acosta 1986: 16.

9. Machito/Salazar interview.

10. See Thompson 1983.

11. These included singer María Teresa Vera and bandleader Antonio María Romeu.

12. Bauzá/Roberts interview.

13. See Gerard and Sheller 1989.

14. In Ortiz 1987 (film).

15. Raúl Fernánadez, personal communication with the author.

16. Salazar 1991a: 26.

17. Machito/Salazar interview.

18. Borneman 1969: 102.

19. Tannenbaum 1947: 43–82, 153.

20. Hoetink 1967: 22.

21. Frazier 1939 [1966]: 15; also see Herskovits 1958 [1941]: 3–4.

22. Hoetink 1967: 6–28; Du Bois 1961 [1903].

23. Graciela/Brown and Fernández interview.

24. Salazar 1991a: 25.

25. Bauzá/Brown interview.

26. Bauzá interviews.

27. Machito/Salazar interview.

28. Bauzá/Brown interview.

29. Moore 1997: 27–30.

30. Ruiz Suárez 1922: 67–71.

31. Ruiz Suárez 1922: 22–28; see Brock and Castañeda Fuertes 1998: 10, 105.

32. Ruiz Suárez 1922: 67–71.

33. Bauzá/Glasser interview.

34. Still, it is not clear how much of Bauzá's racial stance was developed in the United States and how much was intact before he left Cuba. He claimed to have told his godfather about his decision to move to New York by saying that "I only got one plan: . . . I want to be with the people like me. I want to know what it is to be a black man" (Bauzá/Glasser interview). In another interview Bauzá expressed distaste for Martin Luther King's ideology, going so far as to say that "integration is degradation" (Bauzá/Brown interview).

35. Bauzá interviews.

36. Bauzá/Brown interview.

37. The notion of a jazz tinge in Latin music was suggested to me by the Dominican saxophonist Crispín Fernández (personal communication with the author).

38. Moore 1997: 141–43.

39. *Afro-sones* often use rhythms derived from *Wardo*, a Santería rhythm dedicated to the òrìsà Obàtálá. The song "El ciboney" is a well-known example (Bobby Sanabria, personal communication with the author).

40. Moore 1997: 78–79, 94–96.

41. Herrera/Austerlitz interview; Acosta 1986: 16.

42. Bauzá/Roberts interview.

43. Machito/Salazar and Herrera/Austerlitz interviews.

44. Handy 1941: 122.

45. Cugat, quoted in J. Roberts 1979: 87.

46. Glasser 1995.

47. Bauzá/Roberts interview.

48. Bauzá interviews.

49. Bauzá/Roberts interview.

50. Bauzá/Brown interview; also see Bauzá/Berger interview.

51. Bauzá/Berger interview.

52. Bauzá/Roberts interview; my punctuation.

53. Bauzá/Brown interview; also see Bauzá/Berger interview.

54. Glasser 1995.

55. In J. Roberts 1999: 37, 55–56.

56. Bauzá/Brown interview.

57. Bauzá/Roberts interview.

58. Many of Webb's arrangements, in fact, were written by Fletcher Henderson.

59. Bauzá/Roberts interview.

60. Bauzá claimed that his pay with Webb was about eighty dollars per week and that he made an additional several hundred a week doing studio work (Bauzá/Brown interview).

61. Salazar 1991a: 26.

62. Bauzá interviews. Bauzá said that the two musicians remained on good terms nevertheless.

63. Bauzá/Brown interview.

64. Gillespie and Fraser 1979: 107–8.

65. Gillespie and Fraser 1979: 64.

66. Bauzá/Brown interview.

67. Gillespie and Fraser 1979: 96.

68. Bauzá/Roberts interview.

69. Gillespie and Fraser 1979: 96.

70. Bauzá/Brown and Bauzá/Berger interviews.

71. Gillespie and Fraser 1979: 115.

72. Bauzá/Berger interview.

73. Salazar 1991a: 26.

74. Quoted in Glasser 1995: 78.

75. In Ortiz 1987 (film).

76. Salazar 1991a: 26, Acosta 1986: 17.

77. Salazar 1991a: 27.

78. Ibid.

79. Johnakins/Carp interview.

80. Machito/Salazar interview.

81. Brown/Bauzá interview.

82. Brown/Bauzá interview.

83. Data on personnel are hard to verify and are thus tentative. According to available information the lineup was as follows. Along with Bauzá, Doc Cheatham played trumpet. The saxophone section consisted of Johnny Nieto and Freddy Skerrit on altos and José "Pin" Madera on tenor. Bauzá switched from trumpet to lead alto saxophone when the band played slow tunes, or boleros. The pianist was Gilberto "Frank" Ayala (later replaced by Luis Varona and then Joe Loco), and the bassist was Julio Andino. Machito's first bongó player was José "Bilingüe" García, who played for six months, was replaced for a short period by Chino Pozo (not Chano Pozo) until the great José "Buyú" Mangual joined, staying until around 1960. The band's first timbales player was Tony "Cojito" Escolies. Known for his swinging style, Escolies was a top-rated drummer, but he was not able to read music, and for this reason was soon replaced by a seventeen-year-old Tito Puente for a short period of time until Ubaldo Nieto joined, staying until about 1960. A master of traps as well as timbales, Nieto developed a hybrid setup in which he augmented the two timbales with the bass drum of the trap set. In performances at jazz clubs and other venues, he developed a style in which he hit the bass drum on the clave beat, making the bandstand (and listeners) jump (Santos/Carp; Machito/Salazar; Bauzá/Roberts; Santos/Austerlitz; Madera/Austerlitz interviews).

84. José "Pin" Madera was born in Guayama, Puerto Rico, on May 11, 1911, into a well-known and respected family of musicians. His grandfather was a music teacher and his father, Simon Madera (1875–1957), was a violinist and the composer of a well-known *danza* called "Mis amores." As a young man, Madera studied arranging and solfège with his father, developing into a fine reed

doubler on saxophone, clarinet, and flute. Like Mario Bauzá, the Madera family was versed in both European classical music and local popular music. José Madera moved to New York City in November 1930, settling in East Harlem and working as a reed doubler in pit orchestras, Latin bands (notably, those of Xavier Cugat and Noro Morales), as well as jazz groups, including that of Noble Sissle (Carp 2001).

85. Bauzá/Roberts interview.

86. Bauzá/Brown interview; Grillo/Austerlitz interview.

87. In Medina n.d.:16.

88. The Park Plaza and the Park Palace were adjacent clubs that may have been affiliated. Because they are often confused with each other in oral testimony, I refer to the two as an aggregate (this approach was suggested to me by David Carp).

89. Salazar 1991a: 27–28.

90. Berrios/Carp interview.

91. Machito and his Afro-Cubans 1993.

92. Salazar/Machito interview.

93. Ibid.; my punctuation.

94. Ibid.; my emphasis and punctuation.

95. Ibid.; my punctuation.

96. Glasser 1995: 81.

97. Brown/Bauzá interview.

98. Bauzá/Roberts interview.

99. Harlemites called the midtown section of Manhattan "downtown."

100. Bauzá/Roberts interview.

101. Machito/Salazar interview; Bauzá/Roberts interview.

102. Machito/Salazar interview; Bauzá/Roberts interview.

103. David Carp, personal communication with the author.

104. Bauzá/Roberts interview; Graciela/Brown and Fernández interview.

105. Tentative data on Machito's conga players are as follows: Carlos Vidal was the band's first conguero and he stayed with Machito until joining Stan Kenton. Later top congueros in the Afro-Cubans were Luis Miranda, Carlos "Patato" Valdéz, and occasionally, Candido Camero (Bauzá/ Roberts interview).

106. Graciela/Brown and Fernández; Salazar/Austerlitz; and Grillo/Austerlitz interviews. Galíndez stayed on as a back-up singer (Henry Medina, personal communication with author, 2005).

107. She meant that her head felt cold, not that she had a head cold.

108. Graciela/Brown and Fernández interview; Graciela/WKCR-FM interview.

109. Tentative information on the Second Afro-Cubans's personnel is as follows: the band was directed by Machito's former pianist Luis Varona and included Rogelio Valdéz on bass, José "Bilingüe" García on bongó, and Ubaldo Nieto or Steve Berrios on timbales (Berrios/Carp interview; Brown/Bauzá interview).

110. La Conga was open seven days a week, and each band had one night off. The Second Afro-Cubans played on Machito and Curbelo's free nights and also did Sunday matinees and Saturday gigs at other venues (Berrios/Carp interview; Brown/Bauzá interview; Delannoy 2000: 71).

111. Brown/Bauzá interview.

112. Machito/Salazar interview, Bauzá/Roberts interview.

113. Villar/Austerlitz interview.

114. Machito/Salazar interview.

115. Salazar 1991a.

116. Woll 1980: 55.

117. Woll 1980: 56–69; Pérez Firmat 1994.

118. S. Roberts 1993; see Keller 1994: 124.

119. Bauzá/Roberts interview.

120. Johnakins/Carp interview.

121. Roberts/Machito interview.

122. Berger/Bauzá interview.

123. Grillo/Austerlitz interview.

124. Bauzá/Roberts interview.

125. Mario Grillo, personal communication with the author.

126. Delannoy n.d.

127. Carp 2001; Machito/Salazar interview.

128. Machito/Salazar; Bauzá/Roberts; Brown/Bauzá interviews; Bauzá/WKCR-FM interview.

129. Johnakins/Carp interview.

130. Bauzá/WKCR-FM interview; Macho/Salazar interview.

131. Santos/Carp interview.

132. Ibid.

133. Santos/Austerlitz interview.

134. Santos/Carp interview.

135. Ibid.

136. These included Orquesta Casino de la Playa and Julio Cueva's group.

137. Santos/Carp interview.

138. Ibid.

139. Ibid.

140. Bauzá/Brown interview.

141. Santos/Carp interview.

142. Ibid.

143. Santos compares Hernández's collaboration with Vicentico Valdés to Nelson Riddle's collaboration with Frank Sinatra (Santos/Carp; Carp 2001).

144. Bauzá/WKCR-FM interview; my punctuation. Tito Rodríguez's early hits for his three-trumpet conjunto were arranged by Hernández, who worked with Rodríguez until 1977 (Santos/Austerlitz; Santos/Carp interviews). Hernández also arranged much of Eddie Palmieri's *White Album* and *The Sun of Latin Music*, which won a Grammy Award (Graciela/Brown and Fernández interview, Carlos de León, personal communication with the author).

145. Santos/Carp interview; Bauzá/WKCR-FM interview.

146. Santos/Carp interview.

147. Santos/Carp interview; O'Farrill/Austerlitz interview.

148. In Puerto Rico, Hernández played in Rodríguez's big band and in duo settings with the singer. He also worked in the San Juan Caribe Hilton House show orchestra and led his own band (Santos/Austerlitz interview; Santos/Carp interview).

149. Santos/Austerlitz interview; Santos/Carp interview.

150. Johnakins in Ortiz 1987 (film).

151. Johnakins/Carp interview.

152. Santos/Carp interview.

153. Johnakins/Carp interview.

154. Johnakins/Carp; Santos/Carp interviews.

155. Austerlitz/Villar interview.

156. Medina n.d.: 16.

157. Salazar 1991a. See the recording *Original Mambo Kings* 1992.

158. Machito/Salazar interview.

159. Clearly, this folk etymology has only anecdotal value. I have been unable to trace a reliable etymology for the word (Salazar/Austerlitz interview).

160. The phrase's literal meaning is "the sacrifice that is carried becomes the sacrifice that is suitable" (Mason 1997: 397).

161. Delannoy 2000: 70.

162. Johnny Nieto was timbalero Ubaldo Nieto's brother (anonymous, personal communication with the author).

163. Santos/Carp interview; my punctuation.

164. Johnakins/Carp interview.

165. Johnakins/Carp interview; my spelling and punctuation.

166. J. Roberts 1999: 67.

167. Recognizing the commercial viability as well as artistic merit of Cuban bebop, as it was sometimes called, impresario Norman Granz signed Machito and his Afro-Cubans to Mercury Records. The first studio recording of "Tanga, Parts One and Two," of 1948, features Flip Phillips as guest tenor saxophone soloist. In 1949, Granz again recorded "Tanga," this time on Verve Records. While the "Tanga" studio recordings featured guest jazz soloists, band members, especially baritone saxophonist Leslie Johnakins, were featured at performances. Emcee Symphony Sid was impressed when he heard Machito play "Tanga" with jazz soloists trumpeter Howard McGee and tenorist Brew Moore at the Apollo in 1948. He arranged for the band to record a new tune, "Cubop City," arranged by René Hernández and based on the same idea, on Roost Records. Due to contractual conflicts, the band recorded under the name Howard McGee and his Cuboppers. More bop-oriented than "Tanga," "Cubop City" signals a true innovation in jazz (Machito/Salazar interview; J. Roberts 1999: 78; Delannoy 2000: 75–76).

168. Gillespie and Fraser 1979: 115–16, 317.

169. Gillespie and Fraser 1979: 348–49; Stearns 1956.

170. Delannoy 2000:100–107; Bauzá/Brown interview.

171. Berrios/Carp interview; Luis Chacón and Victor Rendón, personal communication with the author.

172. Machito/Salazar interview.

173. Bauzá/Brown interview.

174. The Gillespie big band recorded this piece with Pozo in Paris on a European tour (Delannoy 2000: 151; see Gillespie and Fraser 1979: 317–25; J. Roberts 1999: 76).

175. Delannoy 2000: 151; Gillespie and Fraser 1979.

176. Because this composition's heart was created by Pozo, some have accused Gillespie and Fuller of unrightfully claiming authorship (anonymous, personal communication with the author).

177. Chambers 1983–85, Monson 2000.

178. Stearns 1956: 243.

179. Gillespie and Fraser 1979: 319.

180. Ibid., 171.

181. Ibid., 483.

182. Bauzá/Roberts interview; Delannoy 2000; Stearns 1956: 244; on Cubop see J. Roberts 1979: 13–21, Stearns 1956: 243–56, Gitler 1985: 291–93, Gillespie and Fraser 1979: 317–25, 347–49.

183. "Band of the Year: Stan Kenton," 1947: 46.

184. Bauzá/Roberts interview.

185. J. Roberts 1999: 74.

186. Santos/Carp interview.

187. Bauzá/Roberts interview.

188. Austerlitz/Santos interview; Santos/Carp interview; J. Roberts 1999: 81.

189. Santos/Carp interview.

190. Bauzá interviews.

191. Machito/Salazar interview.

192. Machito/Salazar interview.

193. Bartee explained that he got the idea for the "No Noise" title because his baby kept crying while he prepared the score (Machito/Salazar interview, Bauzá/Roberts interview).

194. Chino Pozo is not related to Chano Pozo.

195. Bauzá/Roberts interview.

196. Machito/Salazar interview.

197. O'Farrill/López interview; Delannoy 2000: 136–39.

198. O'Farrill/López interview.

199. O'Farrill quoted in Delannoy 2000: 145, Delannoy 2000: 143–45, 149.

200. Delannoy 2000: 140.

201. Delannoy 2000: 136–39.

202. Delannoy 2000: 140.

203. Luc Delannoy, personal communication with the author.

204. O'Farrill/López interview.

205. Delannoy 2000: 143–45, 149.

206. O'Farrill in Ortiz 1987 (film).

207. O'Farrill/López interview.

208. Graciela/López interview.

209. Santos/Carp interview.

210. See the recording *Original Mambo Kings* 1992.

211. Delannoy 2000: 145–50.

212. O'Farrill/López interview.

213. O'Farrill studied harmony with Hal Overton and Juilliard professor Bernard Wagenaar and analyzed Bartók's quartets under Stephan Wolpe. During his stay in Mexico, O'Farrill studied the twelve-tone technique with Radolfo Halffter, as he later said, "till it was coming out of my ears" (O'Farrill/López interview). O'Farrill's extended works include the twelve-tone "Six Jazz Moods," a symphony and a clarinet fantasy. These have not been recorded, while "Three Cuban Dances," was recorded by the Cuban saxophonist/clarinetist Paquito d'Rivera (O'Farrill/López interview; Delannoy 2000: 150–51, 157; Luc Delannoy, personal communication with the author).

214. Machito and his Orchestra 1989 [1957].

215. Santos/Carp interview; Madera/Austerlitz interview.

216. Bauzá/Roberts interview.

217. Brown/Bauzá interview.

218. Ibid.

219. J. Roberts 1999: 79, 91.

220. Santos/Austerlitz interview. See the recording Parker 1995.

221. Bauzá/Roberts interview.

222. Ibid.

223. Ibid.

224. Santos/Austerlitz interview; J. Roberts 1999: 79, 91.

225. O'Farrill/Austerlitz interview; my emphasis.

226. Ortiz 1952–55: 232–33, 241, 246; Thompson 1983: 110–11; Pérez Firmat 1994: 82.

227. Orestes López cites this as the date of the recording in his interview with Adrianna Orejuela (Lise Waxer, personal communication with the author). Giró, however, cites Arcaño stating that the year was 1939, while others claim that it was as early as 1935 (Giró 1995: 215).

228. Odilio Urfé in Giró 1995: 215.

229. Giró 1995: 211.

230. Robbins 1989.
231. See Austerlitz 1997a.
232. Giró 1995: 216.
233. Acosta 1986: 69.
234. Giró 1995 [1988]: 220–21.
235. J. Roberts 1999: 71.
236. Pérez Firmat 1994: 91–92.
237. Delannoy 2000: 89.
238. Because of the English-language convention that the last name is the primary surname, Dámaso Pérez Prado is sometimes erroneously referred to as Prado in the United States. His first name, however, is Dámaso, and his two surnames are Pérez and Prado.
239. Giró 1995: 213; Pérez Firmat 1994: 84.
240. Pérez Firmat 1994: 92; Delannoy 2000: 160.
241. Cited in Pérez Firmat 1994: 90.
242. Ibid.
243. Ibid.
244. Interestingly, some Congolese covers of Pérez Prado's tunes also feature this distinctive grunt.
245. Pérez Firmat 1994: 97.
246. Delannoy 2000: 164.
247. J. Roberts 1992: 220; J. Roberts 1979: 11; Boggs 1992: 156, 220; Waxer 1994: 156; J. Roberts 1979: 11.
248. Machito/Salazar interview; Graciela/Brown and Fernández interview.
249. In Ortiz 1987 (film).
250. Rondón 1980: 30.
251. Boggs 1992: 130.
252. Waxer 1994: 159; Garcia, personal communication with the author.
253. Boggs 1992: 129, 147; Salazar/Austerlitz interview.
254. Salazar/Austerlitz interview.
255. Santos/Carp interview.
256. Salazar/Austerlitz interview.
257. In Boggs 1992: 148.
258. In Ortiz 1987 (film).
259. Santos/Austerlitz interview.
260. Andrew Jerritt, personal communication with the author.
261. Santo/Austerlitz interview.
262. Quoted in J. Roberts 1979.
263. David García, personal communication with the author.
264. Santos/Carp interview.
265. Johnakins/Carp interview.
266. Santos/Carp interview.
267. Johnakins/Carp interview.
268. Poirier 1965: 25.
269. In the 1960s, Killer Joe switched to promoting the Twist and the Frug, developing a lucrative business teaching these dances to socialites (Santos/Carp interview; Poirier 1965).
270. Santos/Austerlitz interview.
271. See Manuel 1985.
272. Santos/Carp interview.
273. Johnakins/Carp interview; Angolero in Boggs 1992: 252.
274. Grillo/Austerlitz interview; José Madera, Jr./Austerlitz interview.
275. René López in Graciela/Brown and Fernandez interview.

276. Santos/Carp interview.

277. Johnakins/Carp interview.

278. Machito/Salazar interview; my punctuation.

279. Machito/Salazar interview.

280. Bernabé and Glissant 1990.

281. Other than Harlow, prominent whites in the New York Latin music scene have included trombonist Barry Rogers and trumpeter Marty Sheller.

282. Quintana/WKCR-FM interview; my emphasis.

283. Boggs 1992: 149–52.

284. Santos/Austerlitz interview.

285. Anonymous, personal communication with the author. Another longtime musical associate of both Puente and Machito went so far as to tell me that his friends "very often kiddingly say that Tito Puente and Tito Rodríguez are two poor copies of Machito's band. You know, Tito Puente has his own frenetic style and Tito Rodríguez was a more laidback melodic style" (anonymous interview).

286. It was rumored that magnates at a particular record company had black-listed Machito; while the other top mambo bandleaders worked with this company, Machito did not. Significantly, after Machito signed with them, he was again booked at the Palladium (anonymous, personal communication with the author).

287. Machito/Salazar interview.

288. Villar/Austerlitz interview.

289. Raúl Fernández, personal communication with the author.

290. Santos/Austerlitz interview.

291. Santos/Carp interview.

292. Johnakins/Carp interview; my spelling.

293. Grillo/Austerlitz interview.

294. Mario Grillo, personal comunication.

295. O'Farrill/Austerlitz interview.

296. Machito/Salazar interview; Graciela/Brown and Fernández interview.

297. Grillo/Austerlitz interview.

298. Armanteros had joined already in 1957 (Raúl Fernández, personal communication with the author).

299. Machito/Salazar interview.

300. Salazar 1991b.

301. Salazar 1991b; Medina n.d.: 62.

302. It was rumored that there were additional, personal reasons for the split.

303. The band included trumpeter Victor Paz, tenor saxophonist Mario Rivera, pianist Jorge Dalto, bassist Victor Venegas, conguero Julito Collazo, and Machito's son, timbalero Mario Grillo. Dalto, a brilliant Argentine pianist, arranged the band's regular repertoire, such as "Mambo Inn" and "Cuban Fantasy," for the small group (Grillo/Austerlitz interview).

304. Grillo/Austerlitz interview.

305. Salazar 1991b.

306. Ibid.

307. Ibid.

308. Medina n.d.: 62.

309. See Salazar 1991b.

310. O'Farrill/Austerlitz interview.

311. Machito/Salazar interview; Stearns 1956: 250–51; Roberts 1999: 37.

312. In Ortiz 1987 (film).

313. Gillespie and Fraser 1979; Herskovits 1958 [1941].

314. Moreover, "Mambo Inn's" authorship has been contested (anonymous, personal communication with the author).

315. Several of the recorded versions of "Tanga," for example, feature essentially the same solo by Bauzá, consisting of a repeated altissimo motive.

316. Glasser 1995.

317. Bauzá/Roberts interview, my punctuation.

318. Bauzá/Brown interview.

319. Machito/Salazar interview.

320. Delannoy 2000: 96, 164; Lipsitz 1994: 81.

321. Washburne notes that one of Basie's "signature" rhythms, the "Wood-chopper's Ball" riff, is extremely clave-like (1997: 68).

322. Elvin Jones, personal communication with the author.

323. Coltrane 1974, 1995; note especially the cymbal rhythm (see L. Porter 1998: 238). *The Africa Brass Sessions* also present reworkings of Afro-Cuban rhythms (Coltrane 1974).

324. Byron 1995, Hargrove 1997, Coleman et al. 1996.

325. See Laukkanen 2000 (in "Videography and Discography").

326. Santos/Carp interview.

327. Thompson, personal communication with the author.

Chapter 4. Ambivalence and Creativity: The Jazz Tinge in Dominican Music (pp. 98 – 118)

1. Herskovits 1937: 295–960.

2. Pérez Cabral 1967: 75.

3. M. E. Davis 1976: 2.

4. Fanon 1967: 83.

5. Dominican palos drumming is separate from, although similar to, the music of the Cuban Palos religion.

6. Gagá was mentioned in chapter 2 in relation to hockets and Haitian rara.

7. See Austerlitz 1997a, M. E. Davis 1976 and 1981, Fernández and Sánchez 1997, Pacini Hernández 1995.

8. Pichardo interview. This style of saxophone playing can be heard on the CD Austerlitz 1997a.

9. Hoetink 1982: 206, Rodríguez-Demorizi 1971: 87, Pichardo n.d.b.

10. "Nació el jazz en Santo Domingo?" 1931.

11. Alberti 1975: 87.

12. Hernández interview.

13. Lora interview.

14. Hernández interview.

15. Calder 1984: 241.

16. Incháustegui 1974.

17. Tolentino interview.

18. Later, this group went under the names of Orquesta Lira de Yaque, Orquesta Presidente Trujillo, Orquesta Generalísimo Trujillo and Orquesta Santa Cecilia.

19. Incháustegui 1973.

20. Alberti 1975: 30.

21. Incháustegui 1973.

22. These orquestas used piano accordions instead of the harmonically limited button accordions used in típico merengue.

23. Alberti 1975: 29, Tolentino interview.

24. Hernández 1969: 61.

25. Both of these are still played today, although the paseo is now usually dropped from the sectional form. See the recording Austerlitz 1997 (in "Videography and Discography").

26. Alberti 1971: 79.

27. This story is still often recounted, perhaps because the Dominican Republic is still subjected to neocolonial domination by the United States (the United States occupied the Dominican Republic again in 1965 and continues to exert behind-the-scenes influence on Dominican politics). As mentioned, the pambiche is still performed today as a musical form, but merengue estilo yanqui dance has fallen into disuse, and I have been unable to find any specific information on its choreography.

28. Estimates of the number vary from twelve thousand to forty thousand.

29. Crassweiler 1966: 78 and 358.

30. Nolasco in M. E. Davis 1976: 22.

31. Alberti 1975: 71.

32. See the recording Austerlitz 1997 (in "Videography and Discography").

33. Mateo interview.

34. Arístides Incháustegui interview.

35. Rivera/Austerlitz interview.

36. Ibid.

37. Solano 1992: 105.

38. Other respected jazz players were pianist Guillo Carias and saxophonist Betico Payan, who played in a style influenced by Stan Getz (Rivera/Austerlitz interview).

39. See the recording de León 1981.

40. In South Africa, the word "Skokiaan" refers to illicit spirits that were sold in townships (Turino 2000: 141).

41. Coplan 1985: 270, 154.

42. Turino 2000: 141.

43. See the recording Vásquez [no date] and Austerlitz 1997.

44. Vásquez interview.

45. Ibid.

46. Vásquez on a videotaped Dominican television program; more detailed information about the source is not available.

47. Vásquez CD n.d.

48. Vásquez can be heard on Austerlitz CD 1997b.

49. Tejeda 1993: 114.

50. Guerra interview.

51. This album was later released under the name El Original 4:40 (Guerra 1991 [1984]).

52. Cassette recordings made on nightclubs' sound systems do exist.

53. McLane 1991: 28.

54. Pianist/composer Dario Estrella has also conducted bold experiments in Dominican jazz. After performing in the Dominican Republic as a youth, Estrella moved to Puerto Rico and New York City, playing with Latin jazz greats such as Mario Bauzá and Tito Puente. He composes idiosyncratic small-group compositions displaying a blend of funk, bebop, and free-jazz with merengue and other Dominican forms such as the mangulina and salve.

55. Also of note in the Santiago jazz scene are guitarist Edwin Lora, saxophonist Sandy Gabriel, percussionist Felle Vega, and bassist Quico del Rosario.

56. Rivera/Austerlitz interview.

57. Ibid.

58. Ibid.

59. Ibid.

60. Ibid.

61. Gillespie 1993 CD.

62. Rivera/Austerlitz interview.

63. Ibid.

64. Ibid.

65. Figueroa's playing can be heard on Austerlitz 1997 (in "Videography and Discography").

66. Metresilí is the same as the Haitian Vodou *lwa* (or spirit) Metres Ezili.

67. Rivera/Austerlitz interview.

68. Rivera 1994.

69. Chan, personal communication with the author.

70. Camilo 1992.

71. "Michel Camilo" n.d.

72. Castillo and Murphy 1987–88: 62.

73. Guerra/Austerlitz interview.

74. Vicioso/Austerlitz interview.

75. Raposo's excellent group can be heard on the CD *Quisqueya en el Hudson: Dominican Music in New York* 2004.

Chapter 5. "Rhythm-Music": Jazz in Finland (pp. 119–156)

1. Häme 1949.

2. The stylistic characteristics of this art displayed great variation: it was performed sometimes with instrumental accompaniment, sometimes a cappella; sometimes in groups, sometimes by solo singers. The first-ever study of Finnish folk music, dating from 1778, describes a Kalevalaic ensemble consisting of a lead singer (*laulaja*), a supporting singer (*puoltaja*), and a kantele player. Surrounded by attentive listeners, the singers sat on a bench, clasped right hands, and touched knees. Assuming serious facial expressions and swaying back and forth gently while they sang, the bards rose to their feet when the story reached climax points (Porthan in Lönnrot 1963: 381; also see Asplund 1981a and R. Austerlitz n.d.). "Singing went on for hours," and like some modern musicians, people "rarely start[ed] singing before their spirits have been aroused by the gifts of Bacchus" (Porthan in Lönnrot 1963: 381).

3. Rausmaa 1981.

4. The kantele was adapted to the new style, and musicians added strings as pelimanni music developed; models with as many as thirty-six strings were eventually made.

5. Entering Finland with military bands from the west, the clarinet made inroads into popular expression especially in the west and south, the areas closest to Sweden. There the clarinet was solicited at large functions, where it increased pelimanni music's dynamic level: it was often used in outdoor processions, and weddings often featured two fiddles and a clarinet. As elsewhere in eastern Europe, peasant weddings were elaborate and often lasted several days; acting as masters of ceremony, musicians played important roles in local ritual life. Clarinetists generally played seven-keyed models of the type invented by the German instrument-maker Jacob Denner. Clarinetist Herman Saxberg (1830–1909) is remarkable for having capitalized on the Finnish penchant for woodworking by building clarinets with wooden keys (Helistö 1988: 148–49 and 1989; Leisiö 1983: 252; Asplund 1981b).

6. The amateur groups were usually septets consisting of E-flat cornet, two B-flat cornets, alto, tenor, and bass horns.

7. Jalkanen 1996.
8. These groups could be augmented with more players.
9. Jalkanen 1989: 48.
10. Hroch 1985: 8–9, 131.
11. Wilson 1973: 826.
12. Quoted and translated in Wilson 1978: 53.
13. In Asplund 1983: 79.
14. Lönnrot 1963, Poems 31–36.
15. Lönnrot 1963.
16. Perris 1985: 25, 38; also see P. Austerlitz 1997b: 30–51, 151.
17. This was named after the town of Lapua.
18. Saha n.d.; Leisiö 1983.
19. Saha 1982.
20. Ibid.
21. This is pronounced "yatsi."
22. Kater 1992: 14–15, Jalkanen 1989: 355.
23. Häme 1949: 136.
24. In Haavisto 1991: 34.
25. Henttonen 1983: 129.
26. Sources on Finnish noise jazz are Jalkanen 1989: 74–78, 90, 391–92, 391; Haavisto 1991: 30–31; Häme 1949: 137–38.
27. Jalkanen 1989: 104, 393, 395.
28. Ibid., 33–34.
29. In Finnish, Suomi-orkesteri (the Finnish word for Finland is *Suomi*).
30. Häme 1949; Haavisto 1991: 38–42.
31. The Ramblers' 1932 recording "Muistan su Elaine" features a good solo by Tuomikoski and solid rhythm section, led by the Andania band's tubist Merle Wilkin.
32. Jalkanen 1989: 393.
33. In Finnish, Rajamäen Pojat.
34. Gronow and Bruun 1968: 39–40.
35. See the recording Dallaepé Orkesteri 2000.
36. Häme 1949.
37. In Gronow 1973: 59.
38. Jalkanen 1989: 120–22.
39. In Saha 1981: 3–4.
40. Jalkanen 1989: 208.
41. The band was first called first called Pajazzo.
42. In Finnish, "peräsuoli ulkona omasta elämästä mitä sattuu" (quoted in Haavisto 1991: 49–51); Jalkanen 1989: 101–104.
43. Haavisto 1991: 74.
44. Eero Lindroos quoted in Haavisto 1991: 82–83.
45. This was a racially mixed band including a South African, an Englishman, an American, and a black American (Jalkanen 1989: 105; Häme 1949: 143; Haavisto 1991: 47). Häme gives the years of Borchard's visit as 1927–29 (1949: 143).
46. Haavisto 1991: 82.
47. In Finnish, Laakon Lepakot.
48. Haavisto 1991: 76–77.
49. In Finnish, Rytmin Radio-pojat.
50. Haavisto 1991: 68.
51. Jalkanen 1989: 64.
52. Henttonen 1983.
53. Haavisto 1991: 63–66. There was also a famed Dutch band called the Ramblers, formed in 1926 (Kernfeld 2001: 347).

54. Gronow and Bruun 1968.

55. Ibid., 39.

56. A similar accordion jazz tradition developed in Sweden. The accordion was also used in the United States; in fact, hundreds of thousands were sold during the swing era (Robert Walser, personal communication with the author).

57. Jalkanen 1989: 112 ff.

58. Raimo Leino interview; Konttinen 1987: 24.

59. Raimo Leino interveiw.

60. See the CD set *Suomijazzin Svengaava Historia* 2000.

61. Raimo Leino interveiw.

62. The most enduring of the folk music ensembles, Kaustisen Puppuripeli-mannit (Kaustinen's Potpourri Fiddlers) is still active today and consists of violins, portative organ, and double bass. The organ entered the music via Lutheran influence.

63. Westerholm 1976.

64. Waterman 1952; Timo Leisiö, personal communication with the author.

65. I am indebted to Jalkanen (1989) for his rigorous and thoughtful treatment of early twentieth-century debates about jazz, as well as for his summaries and quotations of the primary source literature.

66. In Finnish, *Tulenkantajat*.

67. Hällström in Jalkanen 1989: 339–41.

68. Paavolainen in Jalkanen 1989: 339–41.

69. Jensen in Jalkanen 1989: 343–45.

70. The translation is mine. The original is: "Vuonna kuusikymmentäkuus / tuli Suomeen laki uus / Viinaa kiellettiin keittämäst, / Juomapäiviä viettämäst" (in Gronow and Bruun 1968: 25).

71. Henttonen 1983: 65.

72. Quoted in Henttonen 1983: 64–65.

73. Quoted in Haavisto 1991: 87–88.

74. Quoted in Jalkanen 1996: 336.

75. Nevanlinna 1994: 75, 107.

76. Henttonen 1983: 58–59.

77. Ibid., 73–74.

78. In Walser 1999: 41–54.

79. Emphasis in the original; quoted and discussed in Jalkanen 1989: 336–37.

80. In Finnish, "Suurkaupungin kasvot." Pingoud, who had arranged the hit "Asfalttikukka" under the pseudonym Johnny Loke, lamented that "Asfalttikukka" was his best-known work (Jalkanen 1989: 338).

81. In Finnish, "Yö Montmartrella."

82. Jalkanen 1989: 357.

83. The English *Melody Maker* magazine began featuring jazz in 1930, becoming a "bible" for local jazz fans (Hobsbawm 1993: 214; Harris 2000: 113).

84. Henttonen 1983: 76–77.

85. In Finnish, *Rytmimusikeeri-yhdistys*.

86. Many dance musicians were members of the Musicians' Union as well as the Rhythm Musicians' organization (Henttonen 1983: 79).

87. In Henttonen 1983: 78.

88. Malmstén in Haavisto 1991: 69–70.

89. Backmansson in Haavisto 1991: 72.

90. Atkins 2001: 102–13.

91. Atkins 2001: 123.

92. In Saha 1982: 44.

93. On the recording Repo 1994.

94. Interview on the CD Repo 1994.

95. Saha 1982: 43.

96. Haavisto 1991: 97.

97. On rare occasions, people were arrested for dancing; for example, two women were arrested in 1943, one for arranging a dance and another for dancing. In September 1944 a man was shot and killed by police while fleeing from a dance that had been raided (Pesola 1996: 100, 108).

98. Haavisto 1991: 97.

99. Ibid., 96.

100. Pesola 1996: 108.

101. Ibid., 110.

102. Haavisto 1991: 95–97.

103. Kater 1992: 33.

104. Gronow and Bruun 1968: 46.

105. Haavisto 1991: 115–17; Gronow and Bruun 1968: 48.

106. Gilbert 1985: 534. One of them was a German Jew who fought in the Finnish Winter War (Gilbert 1985: 715).

107. In Gronow and Bruun 1969: 46.

108. Haavisto 1991:105.

109. Quoted in Gronow and Bruun 1968: 46.

110. Haavisto 1991: 142.

111. In Finnish, *iltamat*.

112. Pesola 1996: 110–11.

113. Ibid., 112.

114. Ibid., 121.

115. Häme 1949: 163.

116. Luhtala 1997: 361–62.

117. Ibid., 363.

118. Pesola 1996: 114, 117.

119. Ibid., 122–24.

120. Suomen Nuoriso Liitto.

121. Suomen Demokraattinen Nuorisoliitto.

122. Kurkela 1989: 186–209.

123. During most of the 1960s, alcohol consumption outside the home was controlled by requiring restaurant patrons to eat while drinking: customers had to buy one sandwich for every three beers. This was liberalized at the end of the decade, and by the 1970s, most restrictions on alcohol were lifted.

124. Klinge 1994: 106–13.

125. Gronow and Bruun 1968: 75.

126. Haavisto 1991: 244–45.

127. Stewart, Holland, and Jackson recorded and jammed with local musicians (Haavisto 1991: 153–54).

128. Haavisto 1991: 247–48.

129. Häme 1949:160. The Finnish jazz scene saw a small "traditional" (or New Orleans–style) revival, foremost in which was the band called the Downtown Dixie Tigers, or DDT. A seminal member of this group was Rick Wahlstein, who had lived in the United States as a child. Wahlstein thus continued the tradition of Finnish Americans such as Tommy Tuomikoski, Bruno Laakko, and, later, guitarist Raoul Bjorkenheim, who made major impacts on jazz in Finland (Haavisto 1991: 250–53).

130. Kärki developed a personal style as a popular song composer, touring Finland with singer Henry Theel and incorporating elements from Russian and African American music (Gronow and Bruun 1968: 50–53; Häme 1949: 165).

131. Kärki quoted in Haavisto 1991: 78.

132. Erkki Aho's big band, under the direction of drummer Ossi Aalto (of earlier Saxophon Jazz Band fame), used arrangements from Benny Goodman's and other American bands, experimenting with instrumentation; for example, he occasionally used a violin section. (Haavisto 1991: 149–52).

133. Jari Muikku, personal communication with the author.

134. In Finnish, "Sä kaunehin oot."

135. Jari Muikku, personal communication with the author; Haavisto 1991: 231.

136. *Rytmin Voittokulku.*

137. Häme 1949; Haavisto 1991: 135.

138. Haavisto 1991: 135, 144.

139. Häme 1949: 34.

140. In Watkins 1994.

141. Häme 1949: 5.

142. This is my English translation from Haavisto's Finnish translation of the original Swedish (in Haavisto 1991: 228).

143. Haavisto 1991: 229. It is unclear from Haavisto's text whether he is relating his own views or relaying opinions expressed by Finnish musicians in the 1950s. The question may be moot as he might have participated in those debates himself.

144. Ossi Aalto's band featured the bandleader's swinging drums and in-the-pocket bass playing by Erik Lindström, which nicely support tasty arrangements and solos. Female singers such as The Harmony Sisters and Brita Koivunen sang soulfully, accompanied by various bands.

145. Paavo Einiö quoted in Haavisto 1991: 179.

146. Translated to Finnish as "Tunnista tuntiin"; Haavisto 1991: 178–79.

147. Luhtala 1997: 360.

148. His given name was Rolf Rainer Sigurd Sandqvist.

149. Luhtala 1997: 370–71.

150. Ibid., 371–76.

151. Ibid., 368.

152. Gronow and Bruun 1968: 76.

153. In Finnish, *rautalankamusiikki;* The Shadows and The Ventures were major influences on this trend (Jari Muikku, personal communication with the author).

154. Jalkanen 1996: 219.

155. Gronow 1987b: 29.

156. Gronow and Bruun 1968: 115.

157. Ibid., 113.

158. Jalkanen 1996: 227.

159. In more recent years, the tango has diminished in popularity, but its importance in the Finnish soundscape is still acknowledged.

160. In Finnish, Rytmimuusikot.

161. The hit's name was "Jonojenkka" ("Line-jenkka") (Haavisto 1991: 191–92, 283).

162. Donner interview.

163. Quoted in Haavisto 1991: 299.

164. The Finnish Ministry of Education provides artists' grants, paid tax-free as monthly salaries for half a year or more. Originally, the longest grant period was fifteen years, and later it was reduced to five years. Recipients work full-time on their art and are not permitted to earn money from other sources. The most prestigious, fifteen-year grants, were awarded to five jazz musicians: Esa Pethman in 1967, Eero Koivistoinen and DDT in 1969, the Tuohi Quartet in 1971, and Edward Vesala in 1972 (Haavisto 1991: 345–46).

165. The Finns who won the EBU jazz competitions are Esa Pethman in 1967, Eero Koivistoinen and DDT in 1969, the Tuohi Quartet in 1971, and Edward Vesala in 1972 (Haavisto 1991: 345–46).

166. In the early years of support, jazz received 7.5 percent of the total amount that the state allocated to music, and most of this was given to the Finnish Jazz League. Jazz musicians began to receive these grants in 1970; as early as the following year, the amount awarded to jazz musicians equaled 10 percent of the total. The league's largest expense was the support of musicians' concerts and tours (67.2 percent of their budget). Administrative costs and support for jazz education were the league's other main expenses (17.7 percent and 7.6 percent, respectively) (Haavisto 1991: 367).

167. In Finnish, *Yrjö Palkinto*. The league published *Rytmi* until 1984; after this it became a private enterprise and turned away from a focus on jazz. The Finnish Music Information Center became active in promoting jazz in 1981, publishing an English-language informational book on Finnish jazz as well as a series of yearly sampler CDs with examples from the top Finnish jazz records.

168. It is estimated that several European governments spend three to five times more per capita on the arts than does the United States (Haavisto 1991: 311; Harris 2000: 114).

169. The Helsinki Pop/Jazz Conservatory was originally called the Oulunkylän Pop/Jazz School. It adopted its current name in 1986. See Haavisto 1991: 312, 315–19, 331–33; 336–37. The Sibelius Academy's jazz department is directed by Jukkis Uotila, an excellent drummer who plays in a style similar to many funk-jazz drummers in the United States.

170. These include Blues Section, Soulset, Wigwam, and Tasavallan Presidentti (The President of the Republic).

171. Haavisto 1991: 294, 326–30.

172. Notable domestic projects include performances of Edward Vesala's works arranged by Iro Haarla, and Heikki Sarmanto's "Kalevala Fantasy." Of particular note is the CD *Electrifying Miles,* arranged by Eero Koivistoinen, one of Finland's top saxophonists (UMO Jazz Orchestra 1998). Eero Koivistoineen studied classical saxophone and composition at the Sibelius Academy in the 1960s. His professional activities in the 1960s included work with the Hendrix–influenced progressive rock band Blues Section and a group featuring Edward Vesala and bassist Pekka Sarmanto (Heikki's brother). As mentioned, in 1969, Koivistoinen's own group was awarded the European Broadcasting Union's prize for the best European jazz group at the Montreaux Jazz Festival. Koivistoinen has worked steadily with UMO since it was founded as saxophonist, composer, and at times, as its artistic director. He has undertaken various innovative projects through the years with both Finnish musicians and Americans such as John Scofield and Jack DeJohnnette. He has also been active as a composer, writing works based on poetry and children's stories, a ballet, and a suite (Haaviisto 1996: 266–67; Muikku 2000: 21). *Electrifying Miles* features the American trumpeter Tim Hagans and brilliant post-Hendrix guitar work by a rising soul of Finnish jazz, Raoul Björkenheim. Björkenheim worked regularly with Vesala as well as with his own group, Krakatow. He moved to the United States in 2001. UMO performs from sixty to eighty times a year, and 80 percent of these are in the Helsinki area. It commands a yearly budget of approximately six million Finn Marks, 75 percent of which comes from various types of governmental support ("UMO" n.d.).

173. Trumpeter and composer Otto Donner has also been a significant mover and shaker of new musical trends in late twentieth-century Finland. Associating with the likes of György Ligeti and Terry Riley in the 1960s, Donner went on to

collaborate with progressive rock musicians and leftist songwriters, while remaining firmly rooted in jazz. In addition to forming a band, the Otto Donner Treatment, which included many top musicians, Donner was active as a composer, writing suites (some based on Finnish poetry), big band music for the UMO big band, film scores, and a piece that combines top Finnish players with four Moroccan Gnawa musicians (Jalkanen 1996: 216, 235; Haavisto 1991: 272–73; Muikku 2000: 12.) Donner has also been active promoting other musicians' projects, for example, founding Love Records in 1966 with collaborators. Love's catalogue, a rich mix of leftist songs, rock, children's music, and jazz, was a harbinger of a catholic vision that was growing among Finnish musicians, giving rise to all manner of fusion among jazz, classical, Finnish folk, and non-Finnish musics (Donner interview; Jalkanen 1996: 216, 235; Haavisto 1991: 272–73; Muikku 2000: 12).

174. Heikki Sarmanto Ensemble 1979 (in "Videography and Discography").

175. Muikku 2000: 47.

176. Sarmanto interview; Muikku 2000: 47.

177. Suomen Säveltäjät.; Säveltäjät ja Sanoittajat ELVIS.

178. In Haavisto 1991: 329.

179. Colleagues include the Englishman John Surman, Norwegian Jan Garbarek, and Dutchman Wilhelm Breuker.

180. Muikku 2000.

181. On the CD Vesala 1990.

182. Tenor saxophonist Juhani Aaltonen is notable among the musicians that have worked with Vesala. Aaltonen studied briefly at the Sibelius Academy and Berklee Schools but is primarily self taught. A founding member of UMO, he has worked with Tasavallan Presidentti, Heikki Sarmanto, Otto Donner, and Peter Brötzman (Muikku 2000: 9).

183. Lake 2001 [1989]: 6, 10.

184. Vesala 1990.

185. Vesala in Lake 2001 [1989]: 4. Vesala was an exacting bandleader who commanded the dedication of a coterie of fiercely loyal sidemen, including his wife, pianist Iro Haarla, tenor saxophonist Jorma Tapio, and bassist Uffe Krokfors. These three combined forces after Vesala's passing to form a strong aggregation, a major shaper of Finnish music. The pianist/bandleader Jarmo Savolainen also stands out among established Finnish jazz musicians, while among younger players, altoist Mikko Innanen and pianist Riitta Paakki follow trends of international jazz with great inspiration. See the recordings Jarmo Savolainen Quintet 1997, Mr. Fonebone 1997, Paakki 2000.

186. Folkmusikvågen 1984.

187. Hannu Saha, personal communication with the author.

188. The first fusion of jazz and Finnish folk music was Esa Pethman's "Shepherd's Song," recorded in 1964. Other early works in this vein were Vesala's "Joiku" of 1970, Paakkunainen's "Tuohiklangi" (Birch-bark Klang) of 1971, and Sakari Kukko's "Uusi laulu paimenelle" of 1975 (Haavisto 1991: 270–71).

189. See the recording Paakkunainen and Karelia 1993.

190. Konttinen 1987: 32–35.

191. Haavisto 1991: 277.

192. "[E]llei ole mahdollista tuottaa huipputason kansanvälisiä jazzsävellyksiä, on rakennattava kansalliseen varaan]" (Haavisto 1991:277).

193. The groups Tuohi and Piirpauke were also important in this trend. Tuohi (Birch-Bark), named for a ubiquitous substance in Finland and a material used in many herdsman's horns, won the European Broadcasting Union's Prize at the Montreux Jazz Festival in 1971. Saxophonist, bandleader, and composer Sakari Kukko

founded Piirpauke in 1974. Piirpauke, which is still active today, clothes traditional Finnish melodies in jazz garb while adding African, Arabic, and Latin tinges.

194. See the recording World Mänkeri Orchestra 1996.

195. Syrjänen interview.

196. Ibid.

197. Ibid.

198. In 1974, a group of Finnish jazz musicians visited Havana, meeting and jamming with local musicians. Prior to this, few foreign jazz players had visited Cuba in the postrevolutionary period. The Finnish Broadcasting Company invited Cuban musicians to Finland, and in 1977 the Love Record Company went to Cuba to record artists such as Compay Segundo and Omara Portuando (Donner interview).

199. D'Rivera's first recording made outside Cuba was on Love Records and featured Finnish players along with the Danish bassist Nils-Henning Østed-Pedersen (Luhtala 1997: 378, 380).

200. Luhtala 1997: 378–80, 386, 401f.

201. Quoted in Medina n.d.: 62.

202. Luhtala 1997: 358. When I visited Cuba in 1991, several local musicians spoke favorably about a Finnish group called El Septeto, founded in 1982 and originally called El Septeto Son, which plays the Cuban son and had visited Cuba. The band's leader, tres player Tero Toivanen, moved to the birthplace of the son, Santiago de Cuba, in 1992, marrying and settling there. He was appointed musical director of a state-supported band called Guitarras y Trovadores, which made several successful tours of Europe (Luhtala 1997: 382–85). The Finnish salsa band Salsamania began recording and performing in the early 1980s and is notable for its hot arrangements and clave-soaked Finnish-language singing (Luhtala 1997: 386–90). Arranger Jere Laukkanen developed an original arranging style influenced by René Hernández and Chico O'Farrill. Another Finnish Latin band, Mambo Sampo, plays *timba,* the new Cuban dance music of the turn of the century. The Nuyorican bassist and bandleader Julio Romero, who resides in Finland, became another major mover of Latin music there.

203. Ennekari 1996: 10–16.

204. Haavisto 1991: 261, 288–95, 343–44.

205. Kangas interview.

206. This many people, of course, are not present in the same place at the same time. The largest number of individuals in one place at the one time is approximately between fifteen thousand and twenty thousand.

207. These figures refer to the 2000 event (Pori Jazz website).

208. Kangas interview.

209. Corporations sponsoring the festival through advertising receive conventional tickets as promotion. They also, however, buy VIP tickets at higher prices than conventional tickets without receiving advertising in return.

210. Kangas interview. Subsequent Kangas quotes are from this interview.

211. In Eerola 1999.

212. Donner interview

213. Kangas interview, Harris 2000: 107.

214. Eerola 1999.

215. Turpeinen quoted in Eerola 1999.

216. In Eerola 1999.

217. In Eerola 1999.

218. Ennekari 1996: 273–76, cited in Eerola 1999.

219. Personal communication with the author.

220. Personal communication with the author.

221. Harris 2000: 121–22.

222. Finnish trumpeter and music promoter Otto Donner believes that, despite many legitimate aspects of the anti-globalization movement, globalization is necessary. Instead of benefiting a few multinational corporations, however, globalization should benefit local music scenes. Serving as chairman of the European Music Office, Donner hopes to develop channels through which local players from various parts of the union gain access to world markets (interview). Finland's support of local jazz—both its development and information about it—resulted in a situation in which the *New Grove Dictionary of Jazz* includes much more information on jazz in Finland than in the Dominican Republic for the simple reason that Finns have devoted a great deal of effort and resources to promoting all their arts.

223. T. Jackson 2000: 122; Atkins 2001: 37.

224. Atkins 2001: 255. Japanese musicians have incorporated deep structural aspects of Japanese aesthetics: for example, the use of *ma*, an indigenous concept roughly translatable to English as " space," in Japanese jazz (Atkins 2001: 39–40).

225. Vesala in Lake 2001: 4.

226. Harris 2000: 121.

227. Sarmanto interview.

228. Häme 1949: 204

Chapter 6. "My Teacher Is the Human Heart": The Human Music of Milford Graves (pp. 157–183)

1. Schlanger 2002; my spelling and emphasis.

2. Hentoff 1974. Similarly, Whitney Balliett wrote that the "chaos" of Graves's music "makes sense . . . tonally" (1965). A critic who admittedly had never previously been exposed to freely improvised drumming wrote: "Each drum was meticulously tuned to a compatible pitch" (Richard 1981). Another review of the same concert stated: "While many drummers pay lip service to playing melody . . . Graves plays a melody as naturally as he kicks a bass drum" (Bliss 1981).

3. Bliss 1981.

4. Graves/Austerlitz interview.

5. Graves/Austerlitz interview.

6. Corbett 1994: 74. Graves also performed this technique at a lecture-demonstration at Brown University.

7. In 1967, Graves won *Downbeat*'s Critics Poll for "Talent Deserving Wider Recognition" on drums and came in third, after Elvin Jones and Tony Williams, in a drummers' poll in the Dutch Jazz Magazine ("International Critics Poll" 1967 and *Jazz Magazine* 1967).

8. Clarke was replaced by Philly Joe Jones at one point.

9. See the recordings Graves 1964, 1997, 1992, 2000; Graves and Pullen 1966; Graves and Cyrille 1974; Graves and Murray 1991; Graves, Clarke, Cyrille, Moye 1983; Ayler 1991; Logan 1965 and 2000; New York Art Quartet 1964 and 2000.

10. Although several articles about and interviews with Graves have appeared, this chapter presents the most complete explication of his thinking in the literature (see Corbett 1994: 74–87; Micallef 2000; Gross and Graves 1999).

11. PAL is the Police Athletic League, a program for urban children.

12. Roach's testimony about this incident bears quoting because it speaks directly to the pan-African comparisons that I have been making throughout the book, and also because it shows both Parker's supreme talent and Roach's humility: "I was getting to be the number one drummer on 52nd Street: Kenny Clarke was in Europe, and Shadow Wilson was in the, you know [*sic*]. So . . . [I was getting a] big

head. So I'd come to the rehearsals a little late. And I remember coming to one rehearsal at the Three Deuces and Charlie Parker was sitting on the drums, and this was the first time I was exposed to what drummers now call 'separation.' . . . And he was sitting behind my drums and he said . . . 'Can you do this?' And he did a quarter note on the bass drum, a Charleston beat on the sock cymbal, a shuffle rhythm on the left hand, and . . . the jazz beat—chang-she-she-chang—on the right, all at the same time, comfortably, with the saxophone across his lap. It's impossible to do [this] unless you practice it. . . . He got up and I walked over to the stage and I attempted to do it, and I knew that I needed to practice it. . . . [This was how] he put me back where I should be, [where] I had been all the time" (in the film *Repercussions*).

13. Eglash 1999.
14. Thompson and Cornet 1981.
15. Needham 1995, Chang 1995.
16. Lu and Needham 1980.
17. See Capra 1975.
18. Novey, Pencak, and Stang 1988.

Conclusion (pp. 184 – 190)

1. Du Bois 1961 [1903]: 16–17.
2. Balibar 1991: 96.
3. Herskovits 1958 [1941].
4. Bauzá/Roberts interview
5. Herskovits 1937: 295–96.
6. Quoted in Simosko and Tepperman 1996 [1974]: 12.
7. Gilroy 2000.
8. Boas 1901, quoted and discussed in Helbling 1999: 21. Moses and Helbling provide important insights on relations between Herder, Boas, and Du Bois's thinking (Moses 1996 and 1998; Helbling 1999).
9. Herder 2002 [1793–97]: 394. The emphasis of "unbiased" is his, while the emphasis of "genius of humanity" is mine. Herder's position on Africans was remarkably enlightened; he implored: "let no one put into the hands of any people on earth on grounds of 'innate superiority' the scepter over other peoples—much less the sword and the slave ship" (394). Herder added: "The negro has as much right to consider the white man a degenerate, a born albino freak, as when the white man considers him a beast, a black animal" (394–95).
10. Gilroy 1993b; Lewis 1993.
11. Moses 1996: 5.
12. Moses 1998: 152.
13. In Helbling 1999: 21.
14. Du Bois 1887, reprinted in Bernasconi and Lott 2000: 116.
15. Like Du Bois, Franz Boas and his students were public intellectuals who were openly engaged in social issues of the early and mid-twentieth century. Boas was a Jew and had emigrated to the United States from Germany, in part to avoid anti-Semitism. He encouraged his students Melville Herskovits and Zora Neale Hurston to study African American culture, seeing a parallel between American racism and European anti-Semitism. With so much in common, it is not surprising that there are parallels between Du Bois's and Boas's work. In 1906, Du Bois invited Boas to deliver a commencement address at Atlanta University, a historically black institution. Boas spoke about the accomplishments of African civilizations, noting that "at a time when the European was still satisfied with rude stone tools, the

African had invented or adopted the art of smelting iron." He continued by discussing African kingdoms and artistic creativity, telling the graduating class, "To those who stoutly maintain a material inferiority of the Negro race . . . you may confidently reply that the burden of proof rests with them, that the past history of your race does not sustain their statement" (Boas in Stocking 1982: 311).

16. Small 1998: 184. William James asserts that music is more eloquent than speech in describing the heights of "cosmic or mystic consciousness[;] . . . not conceptual speech, but music rather, is the element through which we are best spoken to by mystical truth. . . . Music gives us ontological messages which non-musical criticism is unable to contradict" (1997: 313, 330). Milford Graves is adamant about the efficacy of the experiential mode of musical knowing. When I conducted research with him he insisted we play music together in addition to talking, saying that musical praxis is the only real clue to his philosophy. Today, most jazz players pursue their art despite the fact that performing opportunities are few: many musicians even feel that there is no real place for them in this world. Still, the experience is so compelling that they cannot stop playing. Musical praxis—playing, listening, and dancing—creates an experiential "high," but this high is not an escape from reality. Instead, it is the actualization of another reality, a nonverbal place where we negotiate psychic and social contradictions.

17. Shapiro and Hentoff 1966 [1955]: 405.

Videography and Discography

mm

Film/Videography

Burns, Ken. 2000. *Jazz*. Florentine Films.

Haydon, Geoffrey, and Dennis Marks. 1984. *Repercussions: A Celebration of African-American Music*. Third Eye Productions.

Ortiz, Carlos. 1987. *Machito, a Latin Jazz Legacy*. Icarus Films.

Rock & Roll, Vol. 2. 1995. WGBH.

Discography

Amira, John. 1992. *The Music of Santería: The Oru del Igbodu*. White Cliffs Media Company. Accompanying cassette to the book of the same name.

Angels in the Mirror: Vodou Music of Haiti. 1997. Ellipsis Arts CD 4120.

Austerlitz, Paul, ed. 1997. *Merengue: Dominican Music and Dominican Identity*. Rounder CD 1130.

Austerlitz, Paul, and Real People. 1998. *A Bass Clarinet in Santo Domingo and Detroit*. X Dot 25.

———. 2003. *Dominican Dreams, American Dreams*. Engine Studios.

Austerlitz, Paul, and Michael Harper. 2004a. *Double-Take*. Innova CD 604.

———. 2004b. *Our Book on Trane*. Z & S. CD.

Ayler, Albert. 1991. *Love Cry*. Impulse GRD-108.

Brooks, Art, and Ensemble V. 1979. *Nightcaller*. Institute for Black Music IBM LP 001.

Brown, James. 1991. *Star Time*. Polygram CD 849 108–2 to 849 112–2.

Byron, Don. 1995. *Music for Six Musicians*. Nonesuch 79354–2.

Camilo, Michel. 1992. *Why not?* Evidence ECD 22002–2.

Caribbean Revels: Hatian Rara and Dominican Gaga. 1991. Smithsonian/Folkways CD 2-4531.

Charles, Ray. 2002. *Ray Charles Sings for America*. Rhino.

Coleman, Steve, and the Mystic Rhythm Society, with Afro-Cuba de Matanzas. 1996. *The Sign and the Seal: Transmissions of the Metaphysics of a Culture*. RCA 74321–40727–2.

Coltrane, John. 1974. *Africa Brass*. Vols. 1 and 2. MCA Records MCAD-42001.

———. 1986. *A Love Supreme*. MCA MCAD-5660.

———. 1995. *The Heavyweight Champion: The Complete Atlantic Recordings*. Rhino R2 71984.

Dallapé Orkesteri. 2000. *Dallapé Orkesteri Solisteinen.* F Records 8573–81–392–2.

Davis, Miles. 1992. *Relaxin'.* Prestige 7129.

de León, Choco. 1981. *San Cristóbal: Merengues Instrumental* [*sic*]. Quisqueya.

Dolphy, Eric. 1964. *Last Date.* Fontana 822 226–2.

——. 1999. *Out to Lunch.* Blue Note 7243 4 98793 2 4.

Elisha, Ehran. 1997. *Shoresh.* Eye Tone 001.

Gillespie, Dizzy. 1993. *Dizzy Gillespie and his Big Band in Concert, featuring Chano Pozo.* GNP/Crescendo GNPD 23.

Graves, Milford. 1964. *Percussion Duo with Sunny Morgan* . ESP 1015.

——. 1992. *Meditation among Us.* DIW R-270383.

——. 1997. *Grand Unification* . Tzadik 7030.

——. 2000. *Stories.* Tzadik. TZ 7062.

Graves, Milford, with Kenny Clarke, Andrew Cyrille, and Don Moye. 1983. *Pieces of Time.* SN 1078.

Graves, Milford, with Andrew Cyrille. 1974. *Dialogue of the Drums.* IPS 001.

Graves, Milford, with David Murray. 1991. *The Real Deal.* DIW 867.

Graves, Milford, and Don Pullen. 1966. *Nommo.* SRP 286.

Guerra, Juan Luis, and 4:40. 1991 [1984]. *El original 4:40.* Wea Latina (no number).

Hargrove, Roy, and Crisol. 1997. *Habana.* Verve 314 537 563–2.

Heikki Sarmanto Ensemble. 1979. With Maija Hapuoja, soprano, the Gregg Smith Vocal Quartet, and the Long Island Symphonic Choral Association. *New Hope Jazz Mass.* Finlandia 1576-52201-2.

Jarmo Savolainen Quintet. 1997. *Another Story.* A-Records AL 73112.

Kirk, Rahsaan Roland. 1993 [1962–1976]. *Does Your House Have Lions: the Rahsaan Roland Kirk Anthology.* Rhino CD R271406.

——. 2002. *Blacknuss.* Collectables, COL-CD-6345.

Laukkanen, Jere. 2000. *Jere Laukkanen's Finnish Afro-Cuban Jazz Orchestra.* Naxos Jazz CD 860562 FW.

Logan, Giuseppi. 1965. *The Giuseppe Logan Quartet.* ESP 1007.

——. 2000. *More.* ESP Calibre CD 1013.

Lowe, Alan, and Orchestra X, featuring Julius Hemphill. 1992. *New Tango, '92.* Fairhaven 003.

Lowe, Alan, and Orchestra X, featuring Doc Cheatham and David Murray. 1993. *A Modern Tribute to Louis Armstrong.* Stash ST 563.

Lowe, Alan, and the American Song Project, featuring Roswell Rudd. 1996. *Dark Was the Night—Cold Was the Ground.* Music and Arts 811.

Machito and his Afro-Cubans. 1993. *Greatest Hits.* Fania FA 73.

Machito and his Orchestra. 1989. *Kenya.* Palladium PCD-104.

Marley, Bob. 1999 [1962–80]. *Songs of Freedom.* Tuff Gong/Island CD3 314 512 283-2.

Mingus, Charles. 1960. *Charles Mingus Presents Charles Mingus.* Candid CD 9005.

Mingus, Charles. 1994. *The Complete Town Hall Concert.* Blue Note CDP 7243 8 28353 2 5.

Mr. Fonebone [with Mikko Innanen]. 1997. Mr Fonebone. ARFCD-463.

New York Art Quartet. *New York Art Quartet* . 1964. ESP 1004.

——. 2000. *35th Reunion.* DIW DIW-936.

Obeng, KK. 2002. *Sum Sum (Spirit).* KK Obeng. KKO CD1.

——. 2003. *Afrijazz.* Innova 583.

O'Farrill, Chico, with Machito and Dizzy Gillespie. 1976. *Afro-Cuban Jazz Moods.* Pablo OJCCD 447–2.

Original Mambo Kings: An Afro Cubop Anthology, The. 1992. Verve 314-513-876-2.

Ortiz, Luis "Perico." No date. *El Astro.* New Generation Records LP NG 725.

Paakki, Riitta. 2000. *Riitta Paakki Trio.* Impala/Texicalli 004.

Paakkunainen, Baron, and Karelia Group. 1993. *The Sound of Birchbark Flute*. Blue-bird BBCD 1013.

Parker, Charlie. 1995. *South of the Border*. Verve 314 527 779-2.

———. 1999 [1949]. *Live Performances*. Vol. 2. ESP CD 3001.

Public Enemy. 1990. *Fear of a Black Planet*. Def Jam 314 523 446-2.

Quis queya en el Hudson: Dominican Music in New York City. 2004. Smithsonian Folkways CD 40495.

Repo, Teppo. 1994. *Paimensoittaja Teppo Repo: Herdsman's Music from Ingria*. Kansanmusiikki-instituutti, KICD 7.

Rivera, Mario. 1994. *"El Comandante"—the Merengue-Jazz*. Groovin' High 1011-2.

Roland Kirk Anthology. Rhino R2 71406. Reprint, Impala 004.

Suomijazzin svengaava historia: Suomalaista jazzia/Finnish Jazz. 2000. Vols. 1–6. Suomen Jazz & Pop Arkisto JAPACD 001-008. With liner notes by Jukka Haavisto.

Titon, Jeff Todd, ed. 1996. Accompanying CD to the book *Worlds of Music*, 3rd ed. New York: Schirmer Books.

UMO Jazz Orchestra. 1998. *Electrifying Miles*. A-Records AL 73153.

Vásquez, Tavito. N.d. *Merengues Instrumentales*. Cassette tape; no label, no number.

Vesala, Edward. 1990 . *Ode to the Death of Jazz*. ECM 1413.

World Mänkeri Orchestra. 1996. *EkÉ*. ETCD 003.

Bibliography

~~~~

Primary Sources

INTERVIEWS WITH THE AUTHOR

Donner, Otto (trumpeter and bandleader). 2001. Helisinki, Finland.

Grillo, Mario (bandleader). 2000. New York, N.Y.

Guerra, Juan Luis (bandleader). 1985. Santo Domingo, Dominican Republic.

Hänninen, Eino (clarinetist). 1988. Oulu, Finland.

Heikkinen, Jaakko (clarinetist). 1988. Vantaa, Finland.

Helistö, Paavo (clarinetist, radio journalist, and music scholar). 1988. Helsinki, Finland.

Hernández, Julio Alberto (composer). 1985. Santo Domingo, Dominican Republic.

Herrera, Lazaro (trumpeter). 2000. Havana, Cuba.

Incháustegui, Arístides (singer and music historian). 1985. Santo Domingo, Dominican Republic.

Junno, Sauli (clarinetist, saxophonist, and arranger). 1988. Joensuu, Finland.

Kangas, Jyrki (music promoter). 2001. Telephone interview. Helsinki/Pori Finland.

Leino, Raumo (clarinetist, bassist). 1988. Finland.

Lora, Antonio (accordionist). 1985. Santiago, Dominican Republic.

Madera, José, Jr. (arranger and percussionist). 2000. New York.

Mateo, Joseíto (singer). 1985. Santo Domingo, Dominican Republic.

O'Farrill, Chico. 2000. New York, NY.

Pichardo, Agustín (merengue dancer and connoisseur). 1985. Santiago, Dominican Republic.

Rivera, Mario (multi-instrumentalist). 2001. New York, N.Y.

Salazar, Max (journalist). 2001. New York, N.Y.

Santos, Ray (saxophonist and arranger). 2001. New York, N.Y.

Syrjänen, Heikki (musician). 1988. Nakkila, Finland.

Tikkanen, Oren (guitarist). 1988. Telephone interview. Calumet, Michigan/Providence, Rhode Island.

Tolentino, Pavín (bandleader). 1985. Santiago, Dominican Republic.

Vásquez, Tavito (saxophonist). 1985. Santo Domingo, Dominican Republic.

Vicioso, Tony (guitarist and bandleader). 1994. New York, N.Y.

Villar , Manuel (deejay). 2001. Havana, Cuba.

Westerholm, Pekka (musician, and instrument builder). 1988. Nakkila, Finland.

Westerholm, Simo (ethnomusicologist and amateur clarinetist). 1988. Kaustinen, Finland.

Bauzá, Mario (trumpeter, saxophonist, and bandleader). By Ira Berger.
———. By John Storm Roberts.
———. On WKCR-FM.
———. By Ruth Glasser.
———. By Anthony Brown.
Berrios, Steve (timbales player). By David Carp.
Graciela (singer). By Anthony Brown and Raul Fernández.
———. On WKCR-FM.
Johnakins, Leslie (baritone saxophonist). By David Carp.
Machito (singer and bandleader). By Max Salazar.
O'Farrill, Chico. By René López.
Quintana, Miguel. On WKCR-FM.
Santos, Ray (arranger and tenor saxophonist). By David Carp.
Sarmanto, Heikki. (composer and pianist). By the Finnish Jazz Archive. Helsinki, Finland.

Secondary Sources

Acosta, Leonardo. 1983. *Del tambor al sintetizador.* Havana: Editorial Letras Cubanas.
———. 1986. "Machito: Padre del jazz latino y la salsa." *Revolución y Cultura* 5 (May): 16–23.
———. 2003. *Cubano Be, Cubano Bop: One Hundred Years of Jazz in Cuba.* Translated by Daniel S. Whitesell. Washington, D.C.: Smithsonian Books.
Adler, Barbara Squire. 1951. "The Mambo and the Mood." *New York Times Magazine,* September 16.
Agawu, V. Kofi. 1995. *African Rhythm: A Northern Ewe Perspective.* New York: Cambridge University Press.
———. 2003. *Representing African Music: Postcolonial Notes, Queries, Positions.* New York: Routledge.
Alberti, Luis. 1975. *De música y orquestas bailables dominicanas, 1910–1959.* Santo Domingo, Dominican Republic: Taller.
Alén, Olavo. 1995. "Rhythm as Duration of Sounds in Tumba Francesa." *Ethnomusicology* 39/1: 1–20.
American Fact Finder. U.S. Census Bureau web page: http://factfinder.census.gov/servlet/BasicFactsServlet
Amira, John, and Stephen Cornelius. 1992. *The Music of Santería: The Traditional Rhythms of the Batá Drums.* Tempe, Ariz.: White Cliffs Media Company.
Anderson, Benedict. 1983. *Imagined Communities.* London: Verso.
Anku, Willie. N.d. "Principles of Rhythmic Integration in African Drumming." *New Directions: Readings in African Diaspora Music* 1/1. Wilmington, Del.: Adama Publications.
Appadurai, Arjun. 1996. "Modernity at Large: Cultural Dimensions of Globalization." In *Public Worlds,* vol. 1. Minneapolis: University of Minnesota Press.
Appel, Alfred. 2002. *Jazz Modernism: From Ellington and Armstrong to Matisse and Joyce.* New York: Random House.
Appiah, Anthony. 1992. *In My Father's House: Africa in the Philosophy of Culture.* New York: Oxford University Press.
Asplund, Anneli. 1981a. "Kalevalaiset laulut." In *Kansanmusiikki,* edited by Anneli Asplund. Helsinki: Suomalaisen Kirjallisuuden Seura.

———. 1981b. "Pelimannimusiikki ja uudet soittimet." In *Kansanmusiikki,* edited by Anneli Asplund. Helsinki: Suomalaisen Kirjallisuuden Seura.

———. 1983. *Kantele.* Helsinki: Suomalaisen Kirjallisuuden Seura.

Atkins, Taylor. 2001. *Blue Nippon: Authenticating Jazz in Japan.* Durham, N.C.: Duke University Press.

———. ed. 2003. *Jazz Planet.* Jackson: University Press of Mississippi.

Austerlitz, Paul. 1986. "A History of Dominican Merengue Highlighting the Role of the Saxophone." M.A. thesis, Wesleyan University.

———. 1992. "Dominican Merengue in Regional, National, and International Perspectives." Ph.D. diss. Wesleyan University.

———. 1993. "Local and International Trends in Dominican Merengue." *World of Music* 35: 270–89.

———. 1997a. *Merengue: Dominican Music and Dominican Identity.* Philadelphia: Temple University Press.

———. 1997b. "Merengue in New York." In *Island Sounds in the Global City: Caribbean Popular Music and Identity in New York.* New York: New York Folklore Society.

———. 1998. "The Jazz Tinge in Dominican Music." *Black Music Research Journal* 18/1–2: 1–21.

———. 1999. "Popular Music and National Identity Dominican Merengue." In *Africana: The Encyclopedia of the African and African American Experience,* edited by Kwame Anthony Appiah and Henry Louis Gates, Jr. New York: Basic Civitas Books.

———. 2000. "Birchbark Horns and Jazz in the National Imagination: The Finnish Folk Music Vogue in Historical Perspective." *Ethnomusicology* 44/2: 183–213.

———. 2003. "Mambo Kings to West African Textiles: A Synesthetic Approach to Black Atlantic Aesthetics." In *Musical Migrations,* edited by Frances Aparicio and Candida Jaquez. New York: Palgrave Macmillan.

———. Forthcoming a. "Jazz Consciousness." In *A Companion to African American Studies,* edited and with an introduction by Lewis R. Gordon and Jane Anna Gordon. Malden, Mass.: Blackwell Publishers.

———. Forthcoming b. *Machito and his Afro-Cubans: Transcriptions and Arrangements.* Madison, Wisc.: A & R Editions and the American Musicological Society.

Austerlitz, Robert. N.d. "The Poetics of the Kalevala." In *Kalevala, 1835–1935: The National Epic of Finland.* Helsinki: Helsinki University Library.

Averill, Gage. 1989a. "Haitian Dance Band Music: The Political Economy of Exuberance." Ph.D. diss., University of Washington.

———. 1989b. "Haitian Dance Bands 1915–70: Class, Race, and Authenticity." *Latin American Music Review* 10/2: 203–35.

Balibar, Etienne. 1991. "The Nation Form: History and Ideology." In *Race, Nation, Class: Ambiguous Identities,* edited by Etienne Balibar and Immanuel Wallerstein, translated by Chris Turner. London: Routledge, Chapman & Hall.

Balliett, Whitney. 1965. "Jazz Concerts: Comes the Revolution." *New Yorker,* February 27.

"Band of the Year: Stan Kenton." 1947. *Metronome* 63 (January): 17–19, 44–46.

Baraka, Amiri. 1963. *Blues People: Negro Music in White America.* New York: Morrow.

Baraka, Amiri, and Amina Baraka. 1987. *The Music: Reflections of Jazz and Blues.* New York: William Morrow.

Barthes, Roland. 1982. "Deliberation." In *A Barthes Reader,* edited by Susan Sontag. New York: Hill and Wang.

Basch, Linda, Nina Glick Schiller, and Cristina Szanton Blanc. *Nations Unbound: Transnational Projects, Postcolonial Predicaments, and Deterritorialized Nation-States*. Basel: Gordon and Breach.

Bassani, Ezio, and William B. Fagg. 1988. *Africa and the Renaissance: Art in Ivory*. Edited by Susan Vogel, assisted by Carol Thompson. With an essay by Peter Mark. New York: Center for African Art.

Bechet, Sidney. 1960. *Treat it Gentle: An Autobiography*, edited by D. Flower. New York: Hill and Wang.

Becker, Judith. 1979. "Time and Tune in Java." In *The Imagination of Reality: Essays in Southeast Asian Coherence Systems*, edited by A. L. Becker and Aram A. Yengoyan. Norwood, N.J.: ABLEX.

———. 2004. *Deep Listeners*. Bloomington: Indiana University Press.

Bell, Bernard W. 1987. *The Afro-American Novel and its Tradition*. Amherst: University of Massachusetts Press.

Berlin, Isaiah. 1976. *Vico and Herder: Two Studies in the History of Ideas*. New York: Viking.

Berliner, Paul. 1994. *Thinking in Jazz: The Infinite Art of Improvisation*. Chicago: University of Chicago Press.

Bernabé, J., and E. Glissant. 1990. "In Praise of Creoleness." *Callaloo* 13/14: 886–909.

Bernasconi, Robert, and Tommy Lott, eds. 2000. *The Idea of Race*. Indianapolis, Ind.: Hackett.

Blacking, John. 1971. "The Value of Music in Human Experience." *Yearbook of the Folk Music Council* 1: 33–71.

Bliss, Robert E. 1981. "Drummer Milford Graves: A Percussion Technique That's Hard to Beat." *Evening Gazette* (Worcester, Mass.), June 30.

Boas, Franz. 1887. "Museums of Ethnology and their Classification." *Science* 9: 587–89.

———. 1901. "The Mind of Primitive Man." *Journal of the American Folklore Society*, January–March.

———. 1940. *Race, Language, and Culture*. Chicago: University of Chicago Press.

———. 1982. *A Franz Boas Reader: The Shaping of American Anthropology, 1833–1911*, edited by George W. Stocking, Jr. Chicago: University of Chicago Press.

Boggs, Vernon, ed. 1992. *Salsiology*. New York: Greenwood.

Borneman, Ernest. 1969. "Jazz and the Creole Tradition." *Jazzforschung/Jazz Research* 1: 99–112.

Bourdieu, Pierre, and Loïc J. D. Wacquant. 1992. *An Invitation to Reflexive Sociology*. Chicago: University of Chicago Press.

Bourguignon, Erika. 1951. "Syncretism and Ambivalence: An Ethnohistorical Study." Ph.D. diss., Northwestern University.

———. 1969. "Haiti el l'ambivilence socialisée: une reconsidération." *Journal de la Société des Americanistes* 58: 173–205.

Bourne, Randolph. 1916. "Trans-national America." *Atlantic Monthly* 118: 86–97.

Braxton, Anthony. 1985. *Tri-Axium Writings*. San Francisco, Calif.: Synthesis Music.

Brock, Lisa, and Digna Castañeda Fuertes, eds. 1998. *Between Race and Empire: African Americans and Cubans before the Cuban Revolution*. Philadelphia: Temple University Press.

Browning, Barbara. 1998. *Infectious Rhythm: Metaphors of Contagion and the Spread of African Culture*. New York: Routledge.

Bruce, Dickson D., Jr. 1992. "W. E. B. Du Bois and the Idea of Double Consciousness." *American Literature* 64/2: 299–309.

Brucher, Katherine. 1999. "African-American Concert Music in the Early Twentieth Century: Duke Ellington's Creole Rhapsody." BA Honors Thesis. Brown
University.

Brundage, W. Fitzhugh, ed. 1997. *Under Sentence of Death: Lynching in the South.*
Chapel Hill: University of North Carolina Press.

Calder, Bruce. 1984. *The Impact of Intervention: The Dominican Republic during
the U.S. Occupation of 1916–1924.* Austin: University of Texas Press.

Capra, Fritjof. 1975. *The Tao of Physics: An Exploration of the Parallels between Modern Physics and Eastern Mysticism.* Berkeley, Calif.: Shambhala.

Carp, David. 2001. "José Madera." In *Baker's Biographical Dictionary of Musicians,*
Centennial ed. New York: Schirmer Books.

Carpentier, Alejo. 1946. *La Música en Cuba.* Havana: Editorial Letras Cubanas.

Chambers, Jack. 1983–85. *Milestones.* Vols. 1 and 2. Toronto: University of Toronto
Press.

Chang, Kuei-Sheng. 1995. "The Ming Maritime Enterprise and China's Knowledge
of Africa Prior to the Age of Great Discoveries." In *The Global Opportunity,* edited by Felipe Fernández-Armesto. Brookfield, Vt.: Variorum.

Chernoff, John Miller. 1979. *African Rhythm and African Sensibility: Aesthetics
and Social Action in African Musical Idioms.* Chicago: University of Chicago
Press.

———. 1985. "The Artistic Challenge of African Music." *Black Music Research Journal* 5/1: 1–20.

Chomsky, Noam. 1972. *Language and Mind.* New York: Harcourt Brace Jovanovich.

Clark, Andrew, ed. 2001. *Riffs and Choruses: A New Jazz Anthology.* New York:
Continuum.

Condon, Eddie. 1947. *We Called it Music: A Generation of Jazz.* New York: H. Holt.

Coplan, David B. 1985. *In Township Tonight! South Africa's Black City Music and
Theater.* London: Longman.

Corbett, John. 1994. *Extended Play: Sounding off from John Cage to Dr. Funken-
stein.* Durham, N.C.: Duke University Press.

Cowdery, James, Dane Harwood, James Kippen, et al. "Responses." *Ethnomusicology* 39/1: 1–20.

Crassweiler, Robert D. 1966. *Trujillo: Life and Times of a Caribbean Dictator.* New
York: Macmillan.

Cross, W. E., Jr. 1991. *Shades of Black: Diversity in African-American Identity.*
Philadelphia: Temple University Press.

Csiksentmihaly, Mihaly. 1991. *Flow: The Psychology of Optimal Experience.* New
York: Harper Perennial.

Curtin, Philip D. 1969. *The Atlantic Slave Trade.* Madison: University of Wiscon-
sin Press.

Currie, Scott. Forthcoming. "Sound Visions/Free Initiatives: A Comparative Ethnographic Study of Improvised Music in New York and Berlin." Ph.D. diss.,
New York University.

Dahl, Linda. 1984. *Stormy Weather: The Music and Lives of a Century of Jazz
Women.* New York: Pantheon.

Damasio, Antonio. 1999. *The Feeling of What Happens: Body and Emotion in the
Making of Consciousness.* New York: Harcourt Brace.

Dance, Stanley. 1977. *The World of Earl Hines.* New York: Scribner.

Davis, Martha Ellen. 1976. "Afro-Dominican Brotherhoods: Structure, Ritual,
Music." Ph.D. diss., University of Illinois.

———. 1981. *Vozes del purgatorio: Estudio de la salve dominicana.* Santo Domingo,
Dominican Republic: Ediciones Museo del Hombre.

Davis, Miles, with Quincy Troupe. 1989. *Miles: The Autobiography*. New York: Simon and Schuster.

de la Fuente, Alejandro. 1999. "Myths of Racial Democracy: Cuba, 1900–1912." *Latin American Research Review* 34/3: 39–73.

De Veaux, Scott. 1997. *The Birth of Bebop: A Social and Musical History*. Berkeley and Los Angeles: University of California Press.

del Castillo, José, and Martin Murphy. 1987–88. "Migration, National Identity, and Cultural Policy in the Dominican Republic." *Journal of Ethnic Studies* 15/3: 49–69.

Delannoy, Luc. N.d. "The Autumn of the Patriarch." Manuscript.

———. 2000. *¡Caliente! Une histoire du latin jazz*. Paris: Editions Denoël.

DeMichael, Don. 1962. "John Coltrane and Eric Dolphy Answer the Jazz Critics." *Downbeat*, April 12, pp. 20–30.

"La Descarga Cubana." 1985. *Latin New York* 13 (June): 42–47.

De Selincourt, Basil. 1958. "Music and Duration." Translated by Suzanne Langer. In *Reflections on Art*, edited by Suzanne Langer. London: Oxford University Press.

De Veaux, Scott. 1991. "Constructing the Jazz Tradition: Jazz Historiography." *Black American Literature Forum* 25: 525–60.

———. 1997. *The Birth of Bebop: A Social and Musical History*. Berkeley and Los Angeles: University of California Press.

Díaz Ayala, Cristóbal. 1981. *Música cubana del areyto a la nueva trova*. San Juan, Puerto Rico: Editorial Cubanacan.

Du Bois, W. E. B. 1924. *The Gift of Black Folk: The Negroes in the Making of America*. Boston: The Stratford Co.

———. 1961 [1903]. *The Souls of Black Folk*. Greenwich, Conn.: Fawcett.

———. 1975 [1921]. *Darkwater: Voices from within the Veil*. Millwood, N.Y.: Kraus-Thomson Organization.

———. 2000 [1897]. "The Conservation of Races." In *The Idea of Race*, edited by Robert Bernasconi and Tommy Lott. Indianapolis, Ind.: Hackett.

Early, Gerald, ed. 1993. *Lure and Loathing: Essays on Race, Identity, and the Ambivalence of Assimilation*. New York: A. Lane/Penguin Press.

Eerola, Jari. 1999. "Pori-Jazz-festivaalien musiikki päivälehdissä 1967–1995." Master's thesis, University of Tampere (Finland).

Eglash, Ron. 1999. *African Fractals: Modern Computing and Indigenous Design*. New Brunswick, N.J.: Rutgers University Press.

Ellington, Duke. 1976 [1973]. *Music is My Mistress*. New York: Da Capo.

Ellison, Ralph. 1998 [1970]. "What America Would Be Like Without Blacks." In *Black on White: Black Writers on What it Means to be White*, edited by David Roediger. New York: Schocken.

Emerson, Ralph Waldo. 1986. *Emerson on Transcendentalism*. Edited by Edward L. Ericson. New York: Unger.

"Eric Dolphy, Jazz Star, Succumbs." 1964. *Los Angeles Sentinel*, July 9, p. 6B.

Fanon, Frantz. 1963. *The Wretched of the Earth*. New York: Grove.

———. 1967 [1952]. *Black Skin, White Masks*. New York: Grove.

Fernández Soto, Carlos, and Edis Sánchez. 1997. "Los Congos de Villa Mella." *Latin American Music Review* 18/2: 297–316.

Fischlin, Daniel, and Ajay Heble, eds. *The Other Side of Nowhere: Jazz, Improvisation, and Communities in Dialogue*. Middletown, Conn.: Wesleyan University Press.

Fiske, John. 1989. *Understanding Popular Culture*. Boston: Unwin Hyman.

Flores, Juan. 1993. *Divided Borders: Essays on Puerto Rican Identity*. Houston: Arte Público.

Folkmusikvågen. 1984. Stockholm: Swedish Rikskonserter.

Forward, Ian. 1997. "The Music of Finnish Migrants in Canberra and Melbourne." Master's thesis, Department of Music, Monash University.

Frazier, E. Franklin. 1939 [1966]. *The Negro Family in the United States.* Chicago: University of Chicago Press.

———. 1962 [1957]. *Black Bourgeoisie.* New York: Collier.

Gabbard, Krin, ed. 1995a. *Jazz among the Discourses.* Durham: Duke University Press.

———, ed. 1995b. *Representing Jazz.* Durham: Duke University Press.

Garvey, Marcus. 1969. *Philosophy and Opinions of Marcus Garvey.* Vols. 1 and 2. Edited by Amy Jacques-Garvey. New York: Atheneum.

Geertz, Clifford. 1980. "Blurred Genres: The Refiguration of Social Thought." *American Scholar* 49: 125–59.

———. 1988. *Works and Lives: The Anthropologist as Author.* Stanford: Stanford University Press.

Gennari, John. 1991. "Jazz Criticism: Its Development and Ideologies." *Black American Literature Forum* 25: 440–523.

Gerard, Charley. 1988. *Jazz in Black and White: Race, Culture, and Identity in the Jazz Community.* Westport, Conn.: Praeger.

Gerard, Charley, with Marty Sheller. 1989. *Salsa! the Rhythm of Latin Music.* Crown Point, Ind.: White Cliffs Media.

Gilbert, Martin. 1985. *The Holocaust: A History of the Jews of Europe during the Second World War.* New York: Henry Holt.

Gillespie, Dizzy, with Al Fraser. 1979. *To Be . . . or Not to Bop: Memoirs.* Garden City, N.Y.: Doubleday.

Gilroy, Paul. 1993a. *The Black Atlantic.* Cambridge, Mass.: Harvard University Press.

———. 1993b. *Small Acts.* London: Serpent's Tail.

———. 2000. *Against Race: Imagining Political Culture Beyond the Color Line.* Cambridge. Mass.: The Belknap Press of Harvard University Press.

Giró, Radamés. 1995. "Todo lo que Ud. quiso saber sobre el mambo." In *Panorama de la música popular cubana,* edited by Radamés Giró, Havana: Editorial Letras Cubanas.

Gitler, Ira. 1985. *From Swing to Bop: An Oral History of the Transition of Jazz in the 1940s.* New York: Oxford University Press.

Glasser, Ruth. 1995. *My Music is My Flag: Puerto Rican Musicians and their New York Communities, 1917–1940.* Berkeley and Los Angeles: University of California Press.

Glick Schiller, Nina, Linda Basch, and Cristina Blanc-Szanton, eds. 1992. *Towards A Transnational Perspective on Migration.* New York: New York Academy of Sciences.

Goethe, Johann Wolfgang von. 1990 [1961]. *Faust.* Translated by Walter Kaufman. New York: Anchor Books, Doubleday.

Goodman, Benny. 1979. *Benny, King of Swing: A Pictorial Biography Based on Benny Goodman's Personal Archives.* London: Thames and Hudson.

Gordon, Lewis R. 1995. *Fanon and the Crisis of European Man: An Essay on Philosophy and the Human Sciences.* New York: Routledge.

Gottlieb, Robert. 1996. *Reading Jazz: A Gathering of Autobiography, Reportage, and Criticism from 1919 to Now.* New York: Pantheon Books.

Gramsci, Antonio. 1971. *Selections from the Prison Notebooks.* New York: International Publishers.

Gronow, Pekka. 1973. "Popular Music in Finland: A Preliminary Survey." *Ethnomusicology.* 17/1: 52–71.

———. 1987a. "Afro-Ameriikkalaisen musiikin diffuusio vuosina 1900–1945." In *Etnomusikologian Vousikirja 1986.* Jyväskylä: Suomen Etnomusikologian Seura.

———. 1987b. "The Last Refuge of the Tango." *Finnish Music Quarterly* 3–4: 26–31.

Gronow, Pekka, and Seppo Bruun. 1968. *Popmusiikin vuosisata.* Helsinki: Tammi.

Gross, Josh, and Milford Graves. 1999. "Music Medicine: Josh Gross and Milford Graves Talk about Music Therapy." *Signal to Noise* 11 (May–June): 16–17, 19–20.

Grout, Donald, and Claude Palisca. 2001. *A History of Western Music.* New York: Norton.

Guilbault, Jocelyne. 1993. *Zouk: World Music in the West Indies.* Chicago: University of Chicago Press.

Haavisto, Jukka. 1991. *Puuvillapelloilta kaskimaille: Jatsin ja Jazzin vaiheita Suomessa.* Helsinki: Otava.

Hall, Stuart. 1991. "The Local and the Global: Globalization and Ethnicity." In *Culture, Globalization, and the World System: Contemporary Conditions for the Representation of Identity,* edited by Anthony D. King. Current Debates in Art History, vol. 3. Binghamton, N.Y.: Department of Art and Art History, State University of New York at Binghamton.

Häme, Olli. 1949. *Rytmin voittokulku: Kirja Tanssimusiikista.* Helsinki: Fazer.

Handler, Richard, and Jocelyn Linnekin. 1984. "Tradition, Genuine or Spurious." *Journal of the American Folklore Society* 97: 273–90.

Handy, W. C. 1941. *Father of the Blues: An Autobiography.* New York: Macmillan.

Harris, Jerome. 2000. "Jazz on the Global Stage." In *The African Diaspora: A Musical Perspective,* edited by Ingrid Monson. New York: Garland.

Hebdige, Dick. 1979. *Subculture: The Meaning of Style.* London: Methuen.

———. 1995 "Fabulous confusion! Pop before pop?" In *Visual Culture,* edited by Chris Jenks, 96–122. London: Routledge.

Helbling, Mark. 1999. *The Harlem Renaissance: The One and the Many.* Westport, Conn.: Greenwood.

Helistö, Paavo. 1972. *Konstan parempi valssi: Konsta Jylhä ja suomalainen kansanmusiikki.* Helsinki: Tammi.

———. 1985. *Klaneetti: Kansansävelmiä klarinetille.* Kaustinen: Kansanmusiikki-instituutti.

———. 1988. *Klaneetti: Suomalaisen kansanklarinetin vaiheita.* Kaustinen: Kansanmusiikki-instiutuutti.

———. 1989. "The Clarinet in Finnish Folk Music." *Finnish Music Quarterly* 1: 30–33.

———. 1997. *Konsta: Pelimannin ja kansansäveltäjan tarina.* Kaustinen: Kansanmusiikki-Insituutti.

Henderson, David. 1983. *'Scuse Me While I Kiss the Sky: The Life of Jimi Hendrix.* New York: Bantam Books.

Hentoff, Nat. 1974. "Sounding the Colors." *Village Voice,* May 16.

Henttonen, Veli-Matti. 1983. "Jazz musiikkina ja kulttuuri-ilmiönä Suomessa ennen toista maailman sotaa: tutkimus 'mustan' musiikin ensimmaisista vuosikymmenista Suomessa." Master's thesis. University of Helsinki.

Herder, Johann Gottfried von. 2002. *Philosophical Writings.* Translated and edited by Michael Forster. Cambridge: Cambridge University Press.

Hernández, Julio Alberto. 1969. *Música tradicional dominicana.* Santo Domingo, Dominican Republic: Julio D. Postigo.

Herndon, Marcia, and Norma McLeod. 1980. *Music as Culture.* Norwood, Pa.: Norwood Editions.

Herskovits, Melville. 1937. *Life in a Haitian Valley.* New York: Knopf.

———. 1958 [1941]. *The Myth of the Negro Past.* Boston: Beacon.

Hobsbawm, Eric. 1990. *Nations and Nationalism since 1780: Programme, Myth, Reality.* New York: Cambridge University Press.

———. 1993 [1959]. *The Jazz Scene.* New York: Da Capo.

Hobsbawm, Eric, and Terence Ranger, eds. 1983. *The Invention of Tradition*. Cambridge: Cambridge University Press.

Hodeir, André. 1956. *Jazz: Its Evolution and Essence*. Translated by David Noakes. New York: Grove.

Hoetink, H. 1967. *Caribbean Race Relations: A Study of Two Variants*. Translated by Eva M. Hooykaas. London: Oxford University Press.

———. 1982. *The Dominican People, 1850–1900: Notes for a Historical Sociology*. Baltimore: Johns Hopkins University Press.

Hood, Mantle. 1971. *The Ethnomusicologist*. New York: McGraw-Hill.

hooks, bell. 1989. *Talking Back: Thinking Feminist, Thinking Black*. Boston: South End.

———. 2000. *Feminism is for Everybody: Passionate Politics*. Cambridge, Mass.: South End.

Hornbostel, Erich M. von. 1927. "The Unity of the Senses." *Psyche* 7: 83–89.

———. 1928. "African Negro Music." *Africa* 1: 30–62.

Hroch, Miroslav. 1985. *Social Preconditions of National Revival in Europe*. Translated by Ben Fowkes. New York: Cambridge University Press.

Hsio, Wen Shih. 1959. "The Spread of Jazz and the Big Bands." In *Jazz*. Edited by Nat Hentoff and Albert J. McCarthy. New York: Rinehart and Company.

Husserl, Edmund. 1964. *The Phenomenology of Time-Consciousness*. Edited by Martin Heidegger and translated by James S. Churchill. Bloomington: Indiana University Press.

"In Tribute: Eric Dolphy, 1928–1964." *Downbeat*, August 27, p. 10.

Incháustegui, Arístides. 1973. "Luis Alberti (1906)." *Listín Diario*, March 27, p. 24.

———. 1974. "Juan Bautista Espínola Reyes (1894–1923). *Listín Diario*, September 27, p. 20.

"International Critics Poll: Talent Deserving Wider Recognition." 1967. *Downbeat*, August 24, p. 16.

Iyer, Vijay. 2004a. "Exploding the Narrative in Jazz Improvisation." In *Uptown Conversation: The New Jazz Studies*. Edited by Robert O'Meally, et al. New York: Columbia University Press.

———. 2004b. "Improvisation, Temporality, and Embodied Experience." *Journal of Consciousness Studies* 11/3–4: 159–73.

Jackson, Jeffrey. 2003. *Making Jazz French: Music and Modern Life in Interwar Paris*. Durham, N.C.: Duke University Press.

Jackson, Travis. 2000. "Jazz Performance as Ritual: The Blues Aesthetic and the African Diaspora." In *The African Diaspora: A Musical Perspective*, edited by Ingrid Monson. New York: Garland.

Jalkanen, Pekka. 1989. *Alaska, Bombay ja Billy Boy: Jazz kultturin murros Helsingissä 1920-luvulla*. Helsinki: Suomen Etnomusikologian Seura.

———. 1996. "Popular Music." In *Finnish Music*. Edited by Kalevi Aho. Helsinki: Otava.

James, William. 1890. *Principles of Psychology*. New York: Dover.

———. 1997. *The Varieties of Religious Experience*. New York: Touchstone.

Järviluoma, Helmi. 1997. "Musiikki, identtieetti, ja ruohonjuuritaso: Amatööri-muussikkoryhmän kategoriatyöskentelyn analyysi" (in Finnish and English). Ph.D. diss., University of Tampere.

Jauss, Hans Robert. 1982. *Toward an Aesthetic of Reception*. Translated by Timothy Bahti. Minneapolis: University of Minnesota Press,

Järviluoma, Helmi, and Airi Mäki-Kulmala. 1992. "Folk Music and Political Song Movements in Finland: Remarks on 'Symbolic Homecoming.'" In *1789–1989: Musique, Histoire, Démocratie*, vol. 3. Paris: Editions de la Maison des Sciences de l'Homme.

Jones, A. M. 1959. *Studies in African Music*. Vol. 1. London: Oxford University Press.

Jones-Bamman, Richard Wiren. 1993. "As long as we continue to joik, we'll remember who we are: negotiating identity and the culture of the Saami joik." Ph.D. diss., University of Washington.

Jost, Ekkehard. 1994 [1975]. *Free Jazz*. New York: Da Capo.

Kallberg, Jeffrey. 1988. "The Rhetoric of Genre." *Nineteenth Century Music* 11/3: 238–60.

Kater, Michael H. 1992. *Different Drummers: Jazz in the Culture of Nazi Germany*. New York: Oxford University Press.

Keil, Charles. 1966. "Motion and Feeling through Music." *Journal of Aesthetics and Art Criticism* 24/3: 337–51.

——. 1985. "People's Music Comparatively: Style and Stereotypes, Class and Hegemony." *Dialectical Anthropology* 10:119–30.

——. 1995. "The Theory of Participant Discrepancies: A Progress Report." *Ethnomusicology* 39/1: 1–20.

Keil, Charles, and Steven Feld. 1994. *Music Grooves*. Chicago: University of Chicago Press.

Keil, Charles, and Angeliki V. Keil. 1992. *Polka Happiness*. Philadelphia: Temple University Press.

Keller, Gary. 1994. *Hispanics and United States Film: An Overview and Handbook*. Tempe, Ariz.: Bilingual Press/Editorial Bilingüe.

Kernfeld, Barry, ed. 2001. *The New Grove Dictionary of Jazz*, 2nd ed. London: Macmillan Reference.

King, Martha. 1999. "Garvey, Marcus Mosiah." In *Africana: The Encyclopedia of the African and African American Experience*, edited by Kwame Anthony Appiah and Henry Louis Gates, Jr. New York: Basic Civitas Books.

Klinge, Matti. 1994. *A Brief History of Finland*. Translated by David Mitchell. Helsinki: Otava.

Kluckhohn, Florence. 1940. "The Participant-Observation Technique in Small Communities." *American Journal of Sociology* 46: 331–43.

Koetting, James. 1970. "Analysis and Notation of West African Drum Ensemble Music." *Selected Reports* 1/3: 116–46.

——. 1980. *Continuity and Change in Ghanaian Kasena Flute and Drum Music*. Ph.D. diss., University of California at Los Angeles.

Kofsky, Frank. 1970. *Black Nationalism and the Revolution in Music*. New York: Pathfinder.

Konttinen, Matti. 1985. "The Folk Tradition in Finnish Jazz and Light Music." *Finnish Music Quarterly*, 32–35.

——. 1987. "The Jazz Invasion." *Finnish Music Quarterly* 3–4: 21–25.

Kramer, Jonathan. 1988. *The Time of Music: New Meanings, New Temporalities, New Listening Strategies*. New York: Schirmer.

Kubik, Gerhard. 1962. "The Phenomenon of Inherent Rhythms in East and Central African Instrumental Music." *African Music* 3/1: 33–42.

——. 1979. "Pattern Perception and Recognition in African Music." In *The Performing Arts: Music and Dance*, edited by John Blacking and Joann W. Kealiinohomoku. The Hague: Mouton.

——. 1999. *Africa and the Blues*. Jackson: University Press of Mississippi.

Kurkela, Vesa. 1989. *Musiikkifolklorismi ja järjestökulttuuri: Kansanmusiikin ideolooginen ja taiteellinen hyödyntäminen suomalaisessa musiikki- ja nuorisojärjestöissä*. Helsinki: Suomen Etnomusikologisen Seura.

Laitinen, Heikki. 1977. "'Kaustislaisuuden' synty: kaustisen ensimmäiset kansanmusiikkijuhlat ja maaseutukulttuurin paluu 1960-luvun lopun Suomessa." Master's thesis, University of Helsinki.

Lake, Steve, 2001 [1989]. Liner notes to the CD by Edward Vesala, *Ode to the Death of Jazz*. ECM 4228431962.

Langer, Suzanne. 1953. *Feeling and Form*. New York: Scribner.

Leach, Edmund. 1970. *Claude Lévi-Strauss*. New York: Viking Press.

Ledang. Ola Kai. 1986. "Revival and Innovation: The Case of the Norwegian Seljefløte." *Yearbook for Traditional Music* 18: 145–56.

Leisiö, Timo. 1983. *Suomen ja Karjalan vanhakantaiset torvi-ja pilli soittimet*, Vol. 1, *Nimistö, rakenteet, ja historia*. Kaustinen: Kansanmusiikki-instituutti.

León, Argeliers. 1974. *Del canto y tiempo*. Havana: Editorial Letras Cubanas.

Lévi-Strauss, Claude. 1963. *Structural Anthropology*. Translated by Claire Jacobson and Brooke Grunfest Schoepf. New York: Basic Books.

Levine, Lawrence. 1989. "Jazz and American Culture." *Journal of American Folklore* 102/403: 6–21.

Lewis, David L. 1993. *W. E. B. Du Bois: Biography of a Race, 1868–1919*. New York: H. Holt.

Lewis, George, 2004a. "Experimental Music in Black and White: The AACM in New York, 1970–1985." In *Uptown Conversation; The New Jazz Studies,* edited by Robert G. O'Meally, Brent Hayes Edwards, and Farah Jasmine Griffin. New York: Columbia University Press.

———. 2004b. "Improvised Music after 1950: Afrological and Eurological Perspectives." In *The Other Side of Nowhere: Jazz, Improvisation, and Communities in Dialogue*, edited by Daniel Fischlin and Ajay Heble. Middletown, Conn.: Wesleyan University Press.

Lewis, Jan Ellen, and Peter S. Onuf, eds. 1999. *Sally Hemings and Thomas Jefferson: History, Memory, and Civic Culture*. Charlottesville: University Press of Virginia.

Lipsitz, George. 1994. *Dangerous Crossroads: Popular Music, Postmodernism, and the Poetics of Place*. London: Verso.

Lock, Graham. 1988. *Forces in Motion: The Music and Thoughts of Anthony Braxton*. New York, N.Y.: Da Capo.

———. 1999. *Blutopia: Visions of the Future and Revisions of the Past in the Work of Sun Ra, Duke Ellington, and Anthony Braxton*. Durham, N.C.: Duke University Press.

Locke, David. 1990. *Drum Damba: Talking Drum Lessons*. Tempe, Ariz.: White Cliffs Media.

———. 1996. "Africa/Ewe, Mande Dagbamba, Shona, BaAka." In *Worlds of Music: An Introduction to the Music of the World's Peoples*, 3rd ed. Edited by Jeff Todd Titon. New York: Schirmer Books.

Lomax, Alan. 1973. *Mister Jelly Roll: The Fortunes of Jelly Roll Morton, New Orleans Creole and "Inventor of Jazz,"* 2nd ed. Berkeley and Los Angeles: University of California Press.

Lönnrot, Elias. 1963. *The Kalevala; or, Poems of the Kalevala District*. Compiled by Elias Lönnrot and translated by Francis Peabody McGoun. Cambridge, Mass.: Harvard University Press.

———. 1980. *Matkat: 1848–1844*. Espoo, Finland: Weilin and Göössin.

Lord, Albert Bates. 1965. *The Singer of Tales*. New York: Atheneum.

Lott, Eric. 1988. "Double-V, Double-Time: Bebop's Politics of Style." *Callaloo* 11/3: 597–605.

———. 1993. *Love and Theft: Blackface Minstrelsy and the American Working Class*. New York: Oxford University Press.

Lu, Gwei-Djen, and Joseph Needham. 1980. *Celestial Lancets: A History and Rationale of Acupuncture and Moxa*. New York: Cambridge University Press.

Luhtala. Pepe. 1997. *Rumbakuningkaista salsatähtiin*. Helsinki: WSOY.

Luke Richard. 1981. "Graves, His Drums—Superb" *Worcester Telegram*, June 30.

Lutz, Tom. 1991. "Curing the Blues: W. E. B. Du Bois, Fashionable Diseases, and Degraded Music." *Black Music Research Journal* 11/2: 137–56.

Lyons, John. 1970. *Noam Chomsky*. New York: Penguin Books.

Mailer, Norman. 1994 [1957]. *The White Negro*. In *Legacy of Dissent: 40 Years of Writing from Dissent Magazine*. Edited by Nicolaus Mills. New York: Touchstone.

Malcolm X, with Alex Haley. 1966. *The Autobiography of Malcolm X*. New York: Grove.

Manuel, Peter. 1985. "The Anticipated Bass in Cuban Popular Music." *Latin American Music Review* 6/2: 250–61.

———. 1988. *Popular Musics of the Non-Western World: An Introductory Survey*. New York: Oxford University Press.

———. 1991b. "Latin Music in the United States: Salsa and the Mass Media."

———, ed. 1991a. *Essays on Cuban Music*. Lanham, Md.: University Press of America.

Mark, Peter. 1988. "European Perceptions of Black Africans in the Renaissance." In *Africa and the Renaissance: Art in Ivory*, edited by Ezio Bassani and William B. Fagg. New York: Center for African Art.

Mason, John. 1992. *Orin Òrìsà : Songs for Selected Heads*. 2nd ed. Brooklyn, N.Y.: Yorùbá Theological Archministry.

Mbiti, John S. 1970. *African Religions and Philosophy*. Garden City, N.Y.: Doubleday.

McAllester, David. 1971. "Some Thoughts on 'Universals' in World Music." *Ethnomusicology* 15: 379–80.

McClary, Susan. 1991. *Feminine Endings: Music, Gender, and Sexuality*. Minneapolis: University of Minnesota Press.

———. 2000. *Conventional Wisdom: The Content of Musical Form*. Berkeley and Los Angeles: University of California Press.

McGoun, Francis Peabody, trans. 1963. *The Kalevala; or, Poems of the Kalevala District*. Compiled by Elias Lönnrot. Cambridge, Mass.: Harvard University Press.

McLane, Daisanne. 1991. "Dance-Till-You-Drop Merengue," *New York Times*, January 6, pp. 28 and 38.

Medina, Luís. N.d. "Machito." *Avance* 14–16: 62.

Meier, August. 1963. *Negro Thought in America, 1880–1915; Racial Ideologies in the Age of Booker T. Washington*. Ann Arbor: University of Michigan Press.

Melnick, Jeffrey Paul. 1999. *A Right to Sing the Blues: African Americans, Jews, and American Popular Song*. Cambridge, Mass.: Harvard University Press.

Merriam, Alan. P. 1964. *The Anthropology of Music*. Evanston, Ill.: Northwestern University Press.

———. 1982. *African Music in Perspective*. New York: Garland.

Micallef, Ken. 2000. "Milford Graves: Drumming beyond Borders with the Father of Free Jazz." *Modern Drummer* 24/3 (March): 84–88, 90, 94, 96, 98, 100.

"Michel Camilo." N.d. Press release.

Miller, Rebecca Susan. 2000. "'The People like Melée': The Parang Festival of Carriacou, Grenada." Ph.D. diss., Brown University.

Mingus, Charles. 1971. *Beneath the Underdog*. New York: Vintage Books.

Modirzadeh, Hafez. 2000. "Spiraling Chinese Cycle Theory and Model Jazz Practice Across Millennia: Proposed Sources and New Perceptions for John Coltrane's Late Musical Conceptions." *Journal of Music in China* 2/2: 235–64.

Monson, Ingrid. 1996. *Saying Something: Jazz Improvisation and Interaction*. Chicago: University of Chicago Press.

———, ed. 2000. *The African Diaspora: A Musical Perspective*. New York: Garland.

Moore, Robin. 1992. "The Decline of Improvisation in Western Art Music: An Interpretation of Change." *International Review of the Aesthetics and Sociology of Music* 23/1: 61–84.

———. 1997. *Nationalizing Blackness: Afrocubanismo and Artistic Revolution in Havana, 1920–1940*. Pittsburgh: University of Pittsburgh Press.

Moses, Wilson Jeremiah. 1975. "The Poetics of Ethiopianism: W. E. B. Du Bois and Literary Black Nationalism." *American Literature* 47: 411–26.

———, ed. 1996. *Classical Black Nationalism: From the American Revolution to Marcus Garvey*. New York: New York University Press.

———. 1998. *Afrotopia: The Roots of African American Popular History*. Cambridge: Cambridge University Press.

Muikku, Jari, ed. 2000. *Finnish Jazz*. Helsinki: Finnish Music Information Centre.

Murray, A. 1954. "What the Heck is the Mambo?" *Downbeat*, December 1.

Murray, Albert. 1983 [1970]. *The Omni-Americans: Some Alternatives to the Folklore of White Supremacy*. New York: Vintage.

"Nació el jazz en Santo Domingo?" 1931. *Listín Diario*, March 26.

Nader, Laura. "Up the Anthropologist—Perspectives Gained from Studying Up." In *Anthropology for the Nineties*, edited by Johnetta Cole. New York: Free Press.

Needham, Joseph. 1995. "China, Europe and the Seas Between." In *The Global Opportunity*, edited by Felipe Fernández-Armesto. Aldershot, Great Britain, and Brookfield, Vt.: Variorum.

Nei, M., and A. K. Roychaudhury. 1983. "Genetic Relationship and Evolution of Human Races." *Evolutionary Biology* 14: 1–59.

Nelson, David Paul. 1991. "Mrdangam Mind: The Tani Avartanam in Karnatak Music." Ph.D. diss., Wesleyan University.

Nettl, Bruno. 1983. *The Study of Ethnomusicology: Twenty-nine Issues and Concepts*. Urbana, Ill.: University of Illinois Press.

Nevanlinna, Arne. 1994. *Isän Maa*. Porvoo, Finland: Werner Söderström Osakeyhtiö.

Nketia, J. H. Kwabena. 1962. "The Hocket Technique in African Music." *Journal of the International Folk Music Council* 14: 44–52.

———. 1974. *The Music of Africa*. New York: Norton.

Notes to the LP *Pohjantahti*. 1986. Polydor 829 497-1.

Novey, Donald, Marcia Pencak, and John M. Stang. 1988. *The Guide to Heart Sounds: Normal and Abnormal*. Boca Raton, Fla: CRC Press.

Nzewi, Meki. 1974. "Melo-Rhythmic Essence and Hot Rhythm in Nigerian Folk Music." *Black Perspective in Music* 2/1: 23–38.

———. 1997. *African Music: Theoretical Content and Creative Continuum, The Culture-Exponent's Definition*. Institut für Didaktik populärer Musik. Olderhausen, Germany: W. D. Lugert.

O'Gorman, Edmundo. 1961. *The Invention of America: An Inquiry into the Historical Nature of the New World and the Meaning of its History*. Bloomington: Indiana University Press.

Ogren, Kathy J. 1989. *The Jazz Revolution: Twenties America and the Meaning of Jazz*. New York: Oxford University Press.

Oliver, Paul. 1970. *Savannah Syncopators: African Retentions in the Blues*. New York: Stein and Day.

O'Meally, Robert, ed. 1998. *The Jazz Cadence of American Culture*. New York: Columbia University Press.

———, et al. 2004. *Uptown Conversation; The New Jazz Studies*. New York: Columbia University Press.

Omi, Michael, and Howard Winant. 1986. *Racial Formation in the United States: From the 1960s to the 1980s*. New York: Routledge and Kegan Paul.

Ortiz, Fernando. 1952–55. *Los instrumentos de la música afrocubana*. Vols. 1–5. Havana: Dirección de Cultura del Ministerio de Educación.

Östör, Akos. 1993. *Vessels of Time: An Essay on Temporal Change and Social Trans-formation*. New York: Oxford University Press.

Otis, Johnny. 1993. *Upside Your Head: Rhythm and Blues on Central Avenue*. Han-over, N.H.: University Press of New England.

Pacini Hernandez, Deborah. 1995. *Bachata: A Social History of a Dominican Popu-lar Music*. Philadelphia: Temple University Press.

Panassié, Hughes. 1960. *The Real Jazz*. Revised edition. New York: Barnes.

Peretti, Burton W. 1992. *The Creation of Jazz: Music, Race, and Culture in Urban America*. Urbana: University of Illinois Press.

Pérez Cabral, Pedro Andrés. 1967. *La comunidad mulata*. Caracas: Gráfica Americana.

Pérez Firmat. 1994. *Life on the Hyphen: The Cuban-American Way*. Austin: Univer-sity of Texas Press.

Perris, Arnold. 1985. *Music as Propaganda: Art to Persuade and to Control*. West-port, Conn.: Greenwood.

Pichardo, Agustín. N.d.A. "Retrospectiva del merengue." Photocopy of typewrit-ten manuscript.

———. N.d.B. Untitled. Photocopy of typewritten manuscript.

Poirier, Normand. 1965. "Discothèque: Go Go Madness Stikes and the Nation Gyres in a Frenzy of Swim, Surf, and Frug." *Saturday Evening Post*, March 27, pp. 21–27.

Pori Jazz web site, *www.porijazz.fi.*

Porte, Joel. 1968. "Emerson, Thoreau, and the Double Consciousness." *New En-gland Quarterly* 41: 40–50.

Porter, Eric. 2002. *What is this Thing called Jazz? African American Musicians as Artists, Critics, and Activists*. Berkeley and Los Angeles: University of Califor-nia Press.

Porter, Lewis. 1998. *John Coltrane: His Life and Music*. Ann Arbor: University of Michigan Press.

Prögler, J. A. 1995. "Searching for Swing: Participatory Discrepencies in the Jazz Rhythm Section." *Ethnomusicology* 39/1: 21–54.

Priestley, Brian. 1982. *Mingus: A Critical Biography*. New York: Quartet Books.

Rabinow, Paul. 1977. *Reflections on Fieldwork in Morocco*. Berkeley and Los An-geles: University of California Press.

Radano, Ronald M. 1993. *New Musical Figurations: Anthony Braxton's Cultural Critique*. Chicago: University of Chicago Press.

———. 2000. "Hot Fantasies: American Modernism and The Idea of Black Rhythm." In *Music and the Racial Imagination*, edited by Ronald Radano and Philip V. Bohlman. Chicago: University of Chicago Press.

Rahkonen, Carl John. 1989. "The Kantele traditions of Finland." Ph.D. diss., Indi-ana University.

Rampersad, Arnold. 1976. *The Art and Imagination of W. E. B. Du Bois*. Cam-bridge, Mass.: Harvard University Press.

Rausmaa, Pirkko-Liisa. 1981. "Kansantanssit." In *Kansanmusiikki*, edited by Anneli Asplund. Helsinki: Suomalaisen Kirjallisuuden Seura.

Reed, Adolph L. 1997. *W. E. B. Du Bois and American Political Thought: Fabian-ism and the Color Line*. New York: Oxford University Press.

Reed, Ishmael. 1972. *Mumbo Jumbo*. Garden City, N.Y.: Doubleday.

"Reedman Eric Dolphy Dies in Berlin." 1964. *Downbeat*, August 13, p. 8.

Reich, Howard. 1992. "Wynton's Decade/Creating a Canon." *Downbeat*, Decem-ber, pp. 16–20.

Richard, Luke. 1981. "Graves, His Drums—Superb." *Worcester Telegram*, June 30.

Robbins, James. 1989. "Practical and Abstract Taxonomy in Cuban Music." *Ethno-musicology* 33/3: 379–89.

Roberts, John Storm. 1979. *The Latin Tinge*. New York: Oxford University Press.

———. 1999. *Latin Jazz: The First of the Fusions, 1880s to Today*. New York: Schirmer Books.

Roberts, Shari. 1993. "'The Lady in the Tutti-Frutti Hat': Carmen Miranda, a Spectacle of Ethnicity," *Cinema Journal* 32/3: 3–23

Rodríguez Demorizi, Emilio. 1971. *Música y baile en Santo Domingo*. Santo Domingo, Dominican Republic: Colección Pensamiento.

Roediger, David, ed. 1998. *Black on White: Black Writers on What it Means to be White*. New York: Schocken Books.

———. 1999. *The Wages of Whiteness: Race and the Making of the American Working Class*. London: Verso.

Rondón, César Miguel. 1980. *El libro de la salsa: crónico de la música del Caribe urbano*. Caracas: Editorial Arte.

Rönström, Owe. 1989. "Making Use of History: The Revival of the Bagpipe in Sweden in the 1980s." *Yearbook for Traditional Music*, pp. 95–108.

Rose, Tricia. 1994. *Black Noise: Rap Music and Black Culture in Contemporary America*. Middletown, Conn.: Wesleyan University Press.

Rouget, Gilbert. 1985. *Music and Trance: A Theory of the Relations between Music and Possession,* translated by Derek Coltman. Chicago: University of Chicago Press.

Ruff, Willie. 1991. *A Call to Assembly: The Autobiography of a Musical Storyteller*. New York: Viking.

Ruiz Suárez, Bernardo. 1922. *The Color Question in the Two Americas,* translated by John Crosby Gordon. New York: Hunt.

Rycroft, David. 1967. "Nguni Vocal Polyphony." *Journal of the International Folk Music Council* 19: 88–103.

Saha, Hannu. N.d. Notes to the LP *Paimensoittaja Teppo Repo*. Kansanmusiikki-instituutin äänilevyja 7.

———. 1981. "Erkki Ala-Könni—suomalaisen kansanperinteen pioneeri." *Kansanmusiikki* 1: 2–21.

———. 1982. *Teppo Repo: Repertoaari ja asema suomalaisessa musiikkikultturissa.* Tampere: Tampereen Yliopiston Kansanperinteen Laitoksen Moniste 3.

———. 1992. "Viljo S. Määttälä 25-juhlista: Kaustinen pinnallisuutta vastaan." *Uusi kansanmusiikki* 3/4–7: 20–23.

———. 1996. "Kansanmusiikin tyyli ja muuttelu." Ph.D. diss. Kaustinen: Kansanmusiiki-intituuttin julkaisuja 39.

Salazar, Max. 1984. "Latin Music: The Perseverance of a Culture." In *The Puerto Rican Struggle: Essays on Survival in the U.S.,* edited by Clara E. Rodríguez, Virginia Sánchez-Korrol, and José Oscar Alers. Maplewood, N.J.: Waterfront.

———. 1991a. "Machito, Mario, and Graciela: Destined for Greatness, Part One." *Latin Beat* 1/6 (June): 25–29.

———. 1991b. "Machito, Mario, and Graciela: Destined for Greatness, Part Two" *Latin Beat* 1/7 (August): 9–13.

Sales, Grover. 1984. *Jazz: America's Classical Music*. Englewood Cliffs, N.J.: Prentice-Hall.

Savran, David. 2003. *A Queer Sort of Materialism: Recontextualizing American Theatre*. Ann Arbor: University of Michigan Press.

Schlanger, Jeff. 2002. "RAUHA (PEACE): Music Witness at the 20th Tampere, Finland Jazz Happening." *One Final Note* 11 (Summer/Fall). On-line journal: http://www.onefinalnote.com/issue9/

Schuller, Gunther. 1968. *Early Jazz: Its Roots and Musical Development*. New York: Oxford University Press.

———. 1989. *The Swing Era: The Development of Jazz, 1930–1945*. New York: Oxford University Press.

Schutz, Alfred. 1962. *Multiple Realities.* In *Collected Papers,* vol. 1. The Hague: Martinus Nijhoff.

———. 1970. *Reflections on the Problem of Relevance.* Edited by Richard M. Zaner. New Haven: Yale University Press.

———. 1976. "Fragments on the Phenomenology of Music." *Music and Man* 2/1: 5–72.

Seeger, Charles. 1977. *Studies in Musicology, 1953–1975.* Berkeley and Los Angeles: University of California Press.

Shapiro, Nat, and Nat Hentoff, eds. 1966 [1955]. *Hear Me Talkin' To Ya: the Story of Jazz as Told by the Men who Made It.* New York: Dover.

Sheehan, Elizabeth A. 1993. "The Academic as Informant: Methodological and Theoretical Issues in the Ethnography of Intellectuals." *Human Organization* 52/3: 252–59.

Simosko, Vladimir, and Barry Tepperman. 1996 [1974]. *Eric Dolphy: A Musical Biography and Discography.* Rev. ed. Washington, D.C.: Smithsonian Institution Press.

Skarda, Christine A. 1989. "Alfred Schutz's Phenomenology of Music." In *Understanding the Musical Experience,* edited by F. Joseph Smith. New York: Gordon and Breach.

Small, Christopher. 1987. *Music of the Common Tongue: Survival and Celebration in Afro-American Music.* New York: John Calder and Riverrun Press.

———. 1998. *Musicking: The Meanings of Performing and Listening.* Middletown, Conn.: Wesleyan University Press.

Smith, Anthony D. 1971. *Theories of Nationalism.* London: Duckworth.

Solano, Rafael. 1992. *Letra y música: Relatos autobiográficos de un músico dominicano.* Santo Domingo, Dominican Republic: Taller.

Southern, Eileen. 1983. *The Music of Black Americans: A History.* 2nd ed. New York: Norton.

Starr, Frederick. 1983. *Red and Hot: The Fate of Jazz in the Soviet Union, 1917–1980.* New York: Oxford University Press.

Stearns, Marshall W. 1956. *The Story of Jazz.* New York: Oxford University Press.

Steinberg, Michael. 1995. *The Symphony.* New York: Oxford University Press.

Stocking, George W. 1968. *Race, Culture, and Evolution: Essays in the History of Anthropology.* New York: Free Press.

Stone, Ruth 1982. *Let The Inside Be Sweet: The Interpretation of Music Event Among the Kpelle of Liberia.* Bloomington: Indiana University Press.

———. 1985. "In Search of Time in African Music." *Music Theory Spectrum* 7: 139–48.

Suhor, Charles. 1986. "Jazz Improvisation and Language Performance: Parallel Competencies." *Etc.* 43/2: 133–40.

Sundquist, Eric. 1993. *To Wake the Nations: Race in the Making of American Literature.* Cambridge, Mass.: Belknap Press of Harvard University Press.

"Suomalaisen Kansanmusiikin ensimäinen vuosikymmenen." 1987. *Kansanmusiikki* 1: 12–16.

Tannenbaum, Frank. 1947. *Slave and Citizen: The Negro in the Americas.* New York: Knopf.

Taylor, Arthur. 1977. *Notes and Tones: Musician to Musician Interviews.* Liège, Belgium: A. Taylor.

Taylor, Billy. 1986. "Jazz: America's Classical Music." *Black Perspective in Music* 14/1: 21–25.

Tejeda, Darío. 1993. *La historia escondida de Juan Luis Guerra y los 4:40.* Santo Domingo, Dominican Republic: Ediciones MSC, Amigos del Hogar.

Thayer, Alexander Wheelock. 1967 [1921]. *Thayer's Life of Beethoven*. Revised and edited by Elliot Forbes. Princeton, N.J.: Princeton University Press.

Thompson, Robert Farris. 1966. "The Aesthetic of the Cool: West African Dance." *African Forum* 2/2: 85–102.

———. 1984. *Flash of the Spirit : African and Afro-American Art and Philosophy*. New York: Random House.

Thompson, Robert Farris, and J. A. Cornet. 1981. *The Four Moments of the Sun: Kongo Art in Two Worlds*. Washington, D.C.: National Gallery of Art.

Tibbetts, John C., ed. 1993. *Dvořák in America, 1892–1895*. Portland, Ore.: Amadeus.

Tolnay, Stewart, and E. M. Beck. 1995. *A Festival of Violence: An Analysis of Southern Lynchings, 1882–1930*. Urbana: University of Illinois Press.

Toomer, Jean. 1993. *A Jean Toomer Reader: Selected Unpublished Writings*. Edited by Frederik L. Rusah. New York: Oxford University Press.

Tucker, Mark. 1993. *The Duke Ellington Reader*. New York: Oxford University Press.

———. 1996. "In Search of Will Vodery." *Black Music Research Journal* 16/1: 123–82.

Tucker, Sherrie. 2000. *Swing Shift: "All-Girl" Bands of the 1940s*. Durham, N.C.: Duke University Press.

Turino, Thomas. 2000. *Nationalists, Cosmopolitans, and Popular Music in Zimbabwe*. Chicago: University of Chicago Press.

Tuttle, Kate. 1999. "Lynching." In *Africana: The Encyclopedia of the African and African American Experience*, edited by Kwame Anthony Appiah and Henry Louis Gates, Jr. New York: Basic Civitas Books.

"UMO." N.d. Press release.

Van Elderin, P. Louis. 1993. "Värttinä: Between Tradition and Modernity: In Search of the Meaning of Finnish Folk Music." In *On the Borders of Semiosis: Acta Semiotica II*, edited by Eero Tarasti. Imatra: Publications of the International Semiotics Institute at Imatra, no. 4.

Varela, Francisco J., and Jonathan Shear, eds. 2000. *The View from Within: First-person Approaches to the Study of Consciousness*. Thorverton, Great Britain, and Bowling Green, Ohio: Imprint Academic.

Vidich, Arthur J. 1955. "Participant Observation and the Collection and Interpretation of Data." *American Journal of Sociology* 60: 354–60.

Walser, Robert, ed. 1999. *Keeping Time: Readings in Jazz History*. New York: Oxford University Press.

Waltham, Walter. 1952. "Mambo: The Afro-Cuban Dance Craze" *American Mercury* 74 (January): 17.

Washburne, Christopher. 1997. "The Clave of Jazz: A Caribbean Contribution to the Rhythmic Foundation of an African-American Music." *Black Music Research Journal* 17/1: 59–80.

Waterman, Christoper. 1990. "'Our Tradition is a Very Modern Tradition': Popular Music and the Construction of Pan-Yoruba Identity." *Ethnomusicology* 34/3: 367–79.

Waterman, Richard. 1952. "African Influence on the Music of the Americas." In *Acculturation in the Americas*, edited by Sol Tax. Chicago: University of Chicago Press.

———. 1990 [1952]. "African Influence on the Music of the Americas." In *Music as Culture*, edited by Kay Kaufman Shelemay. New York: Garland.

Watkins, Glenn. 1994. *Pyramids at the Louvre: Music, Culture, and Collage from Stravinsky to the Postmodernists*. Cambridge, Mass.: Harvard University Press.

Waxer, Lise. 1994. "Of Mambo Kings and Songs of Love." *Latin American Music Review* 15/2: 139–76.

Weir, Rob. 1994. "Rush to the Finnish: A Beginner's Guide to the Finnish Folk Music Revival." *Sing Out! The Folk Music Magazine* 39/1: 31–39.

West, Cornel. 1998. *Prophetic Fragments: Illuminations of the Crisis in American Religion and Culture*. Grand Rapids, Mich.: Eerdman.

Westerholm, Simo. 1976. "Kuinka kontrabasso tuli kansnamusiikkiin." *Kansanmusiikki* 4/5: 8–9.

———. 1992. "A Living Tradition: The Story of Finnish-American Music." *Finnish Music Quarterly* 4: 30–36.

Whitehead, Kevin. 1993. "Jazz Rebels: Lester Bowie and Greg Osby." *Downbeat*, August, pp. 17–20.

Wilcken, Lois. 1992a. *The Drums of Vodou*. Tempe, Ariz.: White Cliffs Media.

———. 1992b. "Power, Ambivalence, and the Remaking of Haitian Vodoun Music in New York." *Latin American Music Review* 13/1: 2–32.

Williams, Martin. 1964. "Introducing Eric Dolphy." In *Jazz Panorama*. New York: Collier.

Williams, Raymond. 1994. "Base and Superstructure in Marxist Cultural Theory." In *Contemporary Literary Criticism: Literary and Cultural Studies*. New York: Longman.

Wilmer, Valerie. 1992 [1977]. *As Serious as Your Life: John Coltrane and Beyond*. London: Serpent's Tail.

Wilson, William A. 1973. "Herder, Folklore, and Romantic Nationalism." *Journal of Popular Culture*. 4: 819–35.

———. 1976. *Folklore and Nationalism in Modern Finland*. Bloomington: Indiana University Press.

———. 1978. "The Kalevala and Finnish Politics." In *Folklore, Nationalism, and Politics,* edited by Felix Oinas. Columbus, Ohio: Slavica.

Woideck, Carl 1996. *Charlie Parker: His Music and Life*. Ann Arbor: University of Michigan Press.

Woll, Allen. 1980. *The Latin Image in American Film*. Los Angeles: UCLA Latin American Center Publications.

Wolters, Raymond. 2002. *Du Bois and his Rivals*. Columbia: University of Missouri Press.

Yih, Yuen-Ming David. 1995. "Music and Dance of Haitian Vodou: Diversity and Unity in Regional Repertoires." Ph.D. diss., Wesleyan University.

Zwerin, Mike. 1985. *La Tristesse de Saint Louis: Jazz under the Nazis*. New York: Beach Tree Books.

Index

~~~

Page numbers in **bold** indicate illustrations.

AACM (Association for the Advancement of Creative Music), 3, 11
Aalto, Ossi, 128, 216n144
Abacuá secret society, 44, 73
Abdulai, Ibrahim, 33
Academia: and boundaries of musical genres, 3; Graves's drumming courses, 164–65; and jazz in Finland, 144, 217n169; reluctance to generalize ethnically, 25. *See also* Ethnomusicology
Accordion: in Dominican musics, 100, 101, 105, 109; in Finnish musics, 120, 126–29, 141
Acosta, Leonardo, 82
Acupuncture, 167–70
Adzinyah, Abraham, 31
Aesthetics of music: bebop collectivism, 33; and class in Dominican Republic, 99–100, 102–3; holism of jazz, xix, 146–47; hot vs. cool jazz, 33, 133; and jazz consciousness, 16–20, 24; lack of research focus on, 26; Vodou and jazz, 98. *See also* African-influenced cultures/musics
African American influences (North America): aesthetic overview, 17; on dominant culture, 12–16; in Dominican Republic, 101–2; European appreciation of, 7–8; in Finland, 119, 121, 126, 127–28, 145, 149–50; international diffusion of, xiv, 9; and jazz as genre, 3; and musical creation process, 155; musical ecumenism of, 16–17. *See also* Jazz consciousness; Jazz genre

African Americans: Bauzá's hiring of, 58–59; contagion metaphor in black creativity analysis, 199n31; and creative tensions in modernity, xvi; Finnish support for civil rights movement, 145; as having second sight, xii, 197n82; identity and self-unification, xii; as mambo dancers, 88; marginalization of, 7; and middlebrow view of black music, 195n36; multiple aspects of, ix–xi; variations in double consciousness, 191n5. *See also* Black nationalism; Harlem Renaissance; Race and racism
African-influenced cultures/musics: aesthetics of, 81; and dance, 31–35, 182; diffusion of, xiv; and exoticization of blacks, 8, 14, 31, 138, 199n30; inclusivity of, 17; introduction, 25–26; and multiple perspectives on culture, 198n5; and music as conversation, 29–30, 37–39; notational transformations, 26–29, 35–37, 198n10; and pan-Africanism, 9–12, 43, 95, 186; and reappropriation of stereotypes, 74; relationship of Spanish culture to, 45–47; and time sensibilities, 40–41; U.S. development of, 18; West African vs. Central African music, 198–99n11. *See also* Afro-Cuban music; Dominican musics; Finnish cultures/musics; Percussion/drumming; Religion and spirituality
African Latino culture, 43
"Afro-Cuban Drum Suite" (Pozo), 73

Parker, 75–76; on Pozo, 73; on racial issues, 202n34; split with Machito, 91–92; and "Tanga" theme song, 70–71
Beachcomber nightclub, 61
Beat (pulse) and jazz conversation, 38. *See also* Rhythm
Bebop: Afro-Cuban contributions, 87–88, 93, 94; and black nationalism, 11; collectivist aesthetic in, 33; Cubop, 73–74, 75–76, 77, 80, 81, 206n167; in Finland, 139, 148–49; and free jazz development, 22; Graves on, 180; lack of popularity in Cuba, 90; and leaps in time experience, 41; and merengue, 114; O'Farrill's introduction, 78; vs. swing, 2, 14
Bechet, Sidney, 2, 53
Becker, Judith, xv
Beethoven, Ludwig van, 20
"Bei mir bist du schoen," 139
Bernabé, J., 88
Big band music: Afro-Cuban fusion, 43; and appropriation of mambo, 84; and bebop, 94; and Finnish jazz, 127; and Machito spin-offs, 89; merengue-jazz fusions, 105; swing, 2, 14, 38, 129, 139. *See also* Machito and his Afro-Cubans
Biological music of human heart, 158, 174–77
Biological vs. cultural origins of race, 4–5, 25
Birdland jazz club, 19–20, 90
Bitonality, Dolphy's use of, 22
Black Arts movement, 3, 4, 11
Black Atlantic: Modernity and Double Consciousness, The (Gilroy), x
Black nationalism: benefits of, 186; and double consciousness tensions, xiii; and Du Bois, 189–90; and exclusion of white jazz musicians, 18; Graves on, 165–67; and U.S. cultural identities, 9–12
Blacks. *See* African American influences (North America); African Americans; African-influenced cultures/musics
Blake, Eubie, 54
Blakey, Art, 95
Blen Blen Blen Club, 84
Blue Rhythm Band, 128
Blues: conversation in, 34; as counter-force to minstrelsy, 14; Du Bois' criticism of, 18; Latin influences on, 52; transnational appeal of, 182; utopian projects in, xiii

Blutopia (Lock), xiii
Boas, Franz, xv, 188–89, 221–22n15
Bobadilla, Isidro, 113, 114
Body/kinesthetic aspects of music, **30**, 31–35, **36**, 41, 68. *See also* Dance
Bolden, Buddy, 2
Boleros, 62, 79, 89
Bongó drums, 61
Booker, Walter, 114
Bop. *See* Bebop
Borchard, Erich, 128
Borderhill Boys, 127
Bounce-off effect in African ensemble music, 29, 31, 40
Boundaries of musical genres, 3. *See also* Inclusivity
Bourguignon, Erika, xi
Bowie, Lester, 20
Braxton, Anthony, 3, 24
Bridge, musical, 41
Brown, James, 41, 95
"Bucabú," 76
Buddhism, 173
Bunker Boys, 136
Business aspects of jazz festivals, 152, 154–55

Cabral, Pérez, 98
Calbo, José, 109
Call-and-response singing, 29
"Calle Alegría, La," 102–3
Calloway, Cab, 56
Camilo, Michel, 115–16, 117
Carambola (O'Farrill), 80
Caribbean cultures. *See* Afro-Cuban music; Dominican musics
Carnegie Hall, 72, 76
Carnival bands (*comparsas*), 44, 72
Carpentier, Alejo, 83
Carter, Ron, 23
Catskill resorts and Afro-Cuban music, 66
Caturla, Alejandro García, 77
Cha-cha-chá dance, 84
Challenges, value of personal, 173
Chan, Federico, 115
Charangas francescas, 47, 48
Charles, Ray, 16
Chernoff, John, 29, 30
Cibao region of Dominican Republic, 100–101, 101–3, 109
Ciego de Nagua, El (Bartólo Alvarado), 109
Cinquillo rhythm, 75–76, 200n53

Civic vs. cultural nationalism in United States, 5–9
Clapton, Eric, 33
Clarinet, 22–23, 48, 78, 120, 212n5
Clarke, Kenny, 128
Class, social: as basis for invented national identity, 7; and Finnish paths into jazz, 120–23, 122–23, 125–28, 129, 132; and Haitian vs. Dominican ambivalence about African religion, 192n18; and middlebrow judgments of black music, 7, 14, 18, 195n36; middle-class blacks' loss of ethnic identity, 166–67; and musical aesthetics in Dominican Republic, 99–100, 101, 102–3
Classical music. *See* European art music
Clave rhythm: and Dominican musics, 105; and jazz/Afro-Cuban integration, 57, 59, 67, 68; jazz musicians' difficulties with, 75–76, 81; origins, 45
Clef Club, 53
Clef record label, 79
Clock vs. virtual time, 40–41
Cloth patterns and musical notation, African, 27
Club Cuba, 58
Cole, Cozy, 56–57
Coleman, George, 112, 114
Coleman, Ornette, 2, 21–22, 23
Collaborative musical creation method, 71, 96
Collectivist philosophy in African-influenced musics, 29–30, 33–34. *See also* Conversation, music as
Colón, Juan, 110, 111
Colonialism, xi–xii, 7, 99, 102, 193n46
Color Question in the Two Americas, The (Ruiz Suárez), 49–50
Coltrane, John, 17, 21–22, 39
Columbia-Gramophone records, 133
Comandante . . . the Merengue-Jazz, El (Rivera), 114
Communal function of West African music, 33
Comparsas (carnival bands), 44, 72
Composers and composition: Afro-Cuban music, 60–61; aural method, 71–72, 146, 147, 155; Bauzá, 55; Camilo, 116, 117; Antonín Dvořák, 7, 11–12; Finnish jazz, 132–33, 145, 146–47; Hernández, 68–69; O'Farrill, 77, 78, 80; Ornette Coleman, 2, 21–22, 23; Pozo/Gillespie collaborations, 73–74;

Sibelius, 122; Stravinsky, 19–20, 77, 78. *See also* Arrangers and arranging
Concert performance: and Afro-Cuban music, 62, 76, 79, 80; arranging music for, 67; and Finnish jazz, 144
Conga dance: African origins of, 44; expansion from Cuba to United States, 51; in Finland, 137; stereotyping of, 52–53, 61, 62
Conga drums: African origins of, 44; in Dominican musics, 109; expansion of use, 74–75; Graves's introduction to, 160; Machito and his Afro-Cubans, 62, 204n105; and mambo, 87; Pozo's playing of, 73
Conga venue, La, 61–62, 63, 64, 204n110
Conjunto Azul, El, 72
Conjunto band format in Dominican Republic, 108
Consciousness: academic study of, xii–xiii; cultural consciousness raising, 15–16; musical, xiii, 170–77, 182; and music studies, xii–xiii. *See also* Double consciousness; Jazz consciousness
"Constructing the Jazz Tradition" (DeVeaux), 2
Contagion metaphor in black creativity analysis, 199n31
Contradanza, 48, 99
Conversation, music as: African origins of, 29–30, 37–39; in Afro-Cuban music, 96; and collectivist aesthetic, 33–34; in Dominican musics, 105; Finnish vs. American attitudes, 140; and improvisation, 1; notational limitations, 37–38
Cool vs. hot in aesthetics of music, 33, 133
Coplan, David, 105
Cosmopolitanism: and Dominican musics, 104, 106; and ethnomusicologist as performer, xviii; in jazz, xiv–xv, 119–20, 125, 184
Cowherds' horns in Finnish jazz, 148
Creative music and jazz as genre, 3
Creative tension and double consciousness, xvi
Creolization of U.S. culture, 12–15, 88
Critics, music: on Cubop, 81; on jazz as genre, 2, 3; on Machito's jazz forays, 75; and middlebrow view of black music, 195n36; rejection of Dolphy's innovations, 23–24
Cross-rhythm, 29

Crummell, Alexander, 10
Cuba: Afro-Cuban recorded music in, 64; and classical music training for people of color, 55; and influx of musicians to United States in 1980s, 113; lack of recognition for Afro-Cuban music, 43–44; and Machito's background, 44–48; and Machito's band, 89–91; O'Farrill's musical upbringing in, 77–78; race relations vs. United States, 45–47, 48–52; stereotyping of Afro-Cuban culture, 59. *See also* Afro-Cuban music
"Cubano Be, Cubano Bop" (Pozo/Gillespie/Fuller/Russell), 74, 96
Cubop, 73–74, 75–76, 77, 80, 81, 206n167
Cueva, Julio, 66, 82
Cugat, Xavier, 53, 58, 64
Cultural capital for jazz music, 2, 152–53
Cultural nationalism: vs. civic nationalism in United States, 5–9; in Dominican Republic, 101, 102, 104; in Finland, 121–22, 123–24; and focus on folk music, 134; and Herder, 189; and pan-Africanism, 186; and stereotyping of marginalized groups, 51. *See also* Black nationalism
Cultural perspectives: and American jazz development, 7–9; cultural consciousness raising, 15–16; cultural vs. biological origins of race, 4–5, 25; and Finnish multicultural influences, 120, 121, 122–23, 124, 134, 135, 136, 138, 142, 143; importance of, x, 188–89, 198n5, 198n8; and invented traditions, 4, 24; rural vs. urban artistic cultures, 99–100, 121–22, 123, 147; syncretism in Latino cultural mix, 45–47. *See also* Class, social; Dominant culture; Identity; Multiculturalism; Race and racism; Stereotyping; Transnational culture
Cultural relativism and jazz universalism, xvi, 188–89
Cultural transmutation, 179–80
Curbelo, Célido, 51
Curbelo, José, 62, 82–83
Curson, Ted, 154

Dallapé Orchestra, 127, 128, 129
Dance: and African-influenced musics, 31–35, 182; Afro-Cuban, 43–45, 48, 51–53, 61, 62, 67, 73, 79, 85–89, 96; and cyclical timing, 35, **36**, 37; dancers' rhythmic

role, **30**, 31, **32**, 32–33, **34**; Dominican, 99, 100–101, 103; drumming's importance in, 160; Finnish, 120, 124, 125, 127, 129–30, 131, 134–39, 141–43, 150, 215n97; fractal patterns in African, 168; vs. improvisation music, 90; jazz-influenced, 31, 50, 124; mambo, 81–91, 95, 112; and music as healing technique, 174; and origins of jazz, 4; and virtual time in music, 41. *See also* Conga dance
Dandys de Belén, Los, 72
Danzón/danza, 48, 82, 99, 100–101
Davis, Martha Ellen, 98–99
Davis, Miles, 2–3
Davis, Richard, 23
Decca Records, 63
Delannoy, Luc, 78
Delayed backbeat, 38
De León, Choco, 105
De León, Hector, 104–5
Del Rosario, Félix, 105
Descriptive vs. prescriptive musical notation, 26–27
DeVeaux, Scott, 2, 94
Días, Luis, 116–17
Diaspora, African: and Afro-Cuban music expansion, 43, 80–81, 93; in Dominican musics, 105; and repatriation to Africa, 10; social ambivalence as central to, 192n20; transnationalism of, x. *See also* African-influenced cultures/ musics
Díaz, Chinito, 113
Diffusion of jazz, international, xiv, 9. *See also* Transnational culture
Disco, Afro-Cuban rhythms in, 95
Discrimination, ethnic. *See* Race and racism
Divided self, xii. *See also* Double consciousness
Dixon, Bill, 3, 11, 164
Dolphy, Eric, 1, 20–24
Dominant culture: African American influences on, 12–16; as creator of fictive ethnic identity, 6–7; fears of cultural infection from jazz, 7–8; and power relations, 4, 5, 12–15, 24; unmarked vs. marked categories of music, 3, 4, 5, 24; and U.S. international influence, xiv. *See also* Euro-Americans
Dominican musics: contemporary expansion of, 108–18; and dancers' rhythmic

Dominican musics *(continued)*
  role, 32–33, **34;** historical overview, 98–103, 192n18; and hockets, 30; influence on Austerlitz, xvii–xviii; and mandala time notation, 35, **36,** 37; merengue jazz development, 103–8; and moment time, 41; and musical consciousness, 187. *See also* Merengue
Donkor, Freeman, 31
Donner, Otto, 143–44, 217–18n173
Double consciousness: and black nationalism, xiii, 11–12; and colonial hegemony, xi–xii; and creative tension, xvi; in Dominican musics, 117–18; Du Bois and James on, xi, 191n5, 192n23; and essence of jazz, 184, 186; for Finns, 145; and improvisation, 1; and musical movements, xiii; overview, ix–xi, xxi; second sight consequence of, xii, 14, 18–19, 197n82; and uniqueness of African North American culture, 46; variations in African American, 191n5
D'Rivera, Paquito, 113, 116, 150
Drumming. *See* Percussion/drumming
Dual identity. *See* Double consciousness
Du Bois, W. E. B.: author's reliance on thinking of, xii–xiii; and black nationalism, 189–90; and Boas, 221–22n15; criticism of jazz and blues, 18; on double consciousness, ix, x, xi, 191n5, 197n82; and James, xii, 192n23; and pan-Africanism, 10
Duluc, José, 116–17
Duration vs. pitch in rhythm, 28–29, 157–58, 175–77, 199nn18–19
Dvořák, Antonín, 7, 11–12

Eastern musics, 23, 27, 96, 159, 164
Eckstein, Billy, 94
Ecumenicity in jazz community, xiii–xvi, xxi, 16–17
Edison, Harry "Sweets," 81
Electric bass in Dominican musics, 109
Electric guitar, Finnish debate over, 142
Ellington, Duke: and aural composition, 71; and black nationalism, 10; on classical vs. improvisational training, 18–19; on essentialism, 25; on Gershwin, 140; and multiple identities, x–xi; universalism of, ix, 1
Ellison, Ralph, 12, 16, 196n73
Enlightenment nationalism, 5–9
Ensemble philosophy in African-

influenced musics, 29–30, 33–34. *See also* Conversation, music as
Ensley, Ernest, 85, 86, 89
Epic song in Finland, 120, 121, 122
Espínola, Juan, 101
ESP record label, 163
Essentialism, ethnic, 5–6, 7, 8
Estrada, Carlito, 110, 111
Estrella, Dario, 211n54
Ethnicity: academia's reluctance to generalize on, 25; dominant culture as creator of fictive identity, 6–7; essentialism in analyzing, 5–6, 7, 8; vs. experience as guide to life, 179–80; Graves on, 179–82; middle-class blacks' loss of identity, 166–67; and mixed-race Dominican community, 99; and nationalism, 5–6; and origins of music, ix; and uniqueness of Latino experience in United States, 42–43. *See also* Cultural nationalism; Race and racism
Ethnomusicology: and cultural context approach to music, 188–89, 198n8; and lack of focus on aesthetics and style, 26; metaphorical approach, 198n7; musical vs. verbal knowing, 26; and music as culture, x; overview, xix–xxi; participant-observer approach, xviii–xix, 193n48; scope of African music study, 198–99n11
Etnopojat (World Mänkeri Orchestra), 148–50
Euro-Americans: adoption of Cuban rhythms, 70; appropriation of black musics, 2, 13–14, 51, 84, 102; as carriers of dominant culture, 6–7; half-consciousness of, 15; and international diffusion of jazz, 9; and mambo craze, 83–84, 88; reluctance to acknowledge black cultural contribution, 7–8. *See also* Race and racism
Eurocentrism in Dominican Republic, 99–100, 102, 103–4, 116
Europe, James Reese, 53, 55
Europe, jazz's role in, 155. *See also* Finnish cultures/musics
European art music: and Afro-Cuban music, 48, 77, 78; appreciation for jazz, 7; in Dominican Republic, 99, 101, 108, 115–16; and Finnish musics, 132, 133, 146; improvisation in, 20, 197n103; integration in jazz consciousness, 3–4, 20–24; linear version of

Finnish musics, 120, 122, 126, 128, 129, 143, 148–49; Graves on, 110, 163, 165; in merengue-jazz, 107–8, 109–10; and Moore's Sonic Youth performances, 178–79; and quantum physics, 170; and rhythmic conversation, 1, 38; and self-cultivation, 172

Improvisation (film), 170

Inclusivity: in Afro-Cuban music, 93, 96–97; and Dominican jazz fusions, 112–13; in jazz community, xiii–xvi, 16–17, 19, 184; and jazz consciousness, xxi, 18–19, 185; and mambo, 88–89. *See also* Universalism, musical

Independent record production, 11

Ingrian musical style, 123

In-group focus, xiii, 9–12, 56. *See also* Black nationalism; Harlem Renaissance

Inner vs. outer time, 40–41

Inspiraciones (improvised lyrics), 60

Instrumentation: clarinet, 22–23, 48, 78, 120, 212n5; in Dominican musics, 102; electric, 109, 142; in Finnish musics, 120, 123, 125, 130, 131, 143, 148, 149; flute innovations, 22–23; horns, 51, 54, 100–101; maracas and Machito, 45; oboe in Afro-Cuban music, 70; piano, 52, 53, 66, 69, 116; solfège, 47–48; tabla, 164. *See also* Accordion; Percussion/drumming; Saxophone

Interdisciplinary approach to music studies, xix–xx, 26, 170–71

International Jazz Festival Consortium (IJFC), 153

Invented tradition, 4, 24

Islam, 11, 46

Jaleo riffs, 100, 102–3, 105

Jalkanen, Pekka, 125, 142

James, William, xii, 192n23, 222n16

Japan and jazz, 91, 133–34, 155, 220n224

Jäppilä, Masa, 127

"Jatsi" (Finnish jazz), 130

Jauss, Hans, 2

Jazz Band-Alberti, 102

Jazz consciousness: Afro-Cuban contributions, 43, 50–51, 69–72, 185; as counterpoint to Eurocentrism, 117–18; definition, x; Dominican complexities, 98; Finnish adoption of, 145; improvisation as central to, 155, 158, 185; inclusivity and ecumenicity of, xxi, 18–19, 185; and microrhythms, 38–39; relation to civil rights movement, 11; summary overview, 184–90; universalism of, ix, 1–5; and U.S. cultural identity, 16–24

Jazz genre: American cultural development of, 7–9; and black nationalism, xiii; as counterforce to minstrelsy, 14; as dance music, 31; and Dominican musics, 100, 102, 105; etymology of, 194n7; and Finnish musics, 124–25; fluidity of, 2–5; inclusivity and ecumenicity of, xiii–xvi, 16–17, 19, 184; intellectualizing of, 179; Jewish-influenced in Finland, 136; universalism of, xvi. *See also* Bebop

Jazz Scene, The (compilation album), 76

Jazz tinge vs. jazz fusion with other musics, 50

Jerritt, Andrew, 85

Jews, Finnish attitudes toward, 136, 139

Jitterbugs and mambo dance, 87

Johnakins, Leslie, 67, 69, 71, 88

Jones, Elvin, 95

Jonny Spielt Auf (Krenek) (opera), 132

Kalevala (Finnish epic), 122

Kangas, Jyrki, 151, 152

Kantele (Finnish zither), 120, 122, 212n4

Karelia, 147

Kärki, Toivo, 129, 138, 215n130

Kaustinen Puppuripelimannit (Kaustinen's Potpourri Fiddlers), 214n62

Keil, Charles, 13, 39

Kekkonen, Urho, 138

Kente musical notation, 26–29

Kenton, Stan, 75, 78

Kenya (Machito), 80–81

"Kerenski," 137

Kinesthetic aspects of music, **30**, 31–35, **36**, 41, 68. *See also* Dance

Kirk, Rahsaan Roland, 11–12

Klam, Uno, 132

Koetting, James, 27

Kofsky, Frank, 17

Koivistoinen, Eero, 217n172

Koivunen, Brita, 139

Kongo religions, 82

Konitz, Lee, 81, 138

Kpelle people of Liberia, 40–41

Krenek, Ernst, 132

Krohn, Ilmari, 132

Kukko, Sakari, 218–19n193

Laakko, Bruno, 128
Laakko's Bats, 128
Lal, Chatur, 164
Lander, Phil, 65
Langer, Suzanne, 40
Latin Jazz Ensemble, 114
Latin Jazz Quintet, 21
Latino cultures/musics: Cuban music in
    Finland, 150; early jazz/Latino collabo-
    rations, 42; and Graves, 160, 162–63;
    influence on Austerlitz, xvii, xviii;
    overview of jazz and, x; recent jazz de-
    velopments, 95–96. See also Afro-
    Cuban music; Dominican musics
Leap transitions in time experience, 40, 41
Learning as inner journey, 160–61
Lecuona, Ernesto, 44
Leino, Veikko, 130
Leinsdorf, Erich, 19
Lepakko Restaurant, Helsinki, 128
"Let's Dance," 149
Levine, Lawrence, 7–8
Lewis, David Levering, xii, 192n23
Liberia, 10
Licuado, 111
Liebman, David, 38
Lindroos, Eero, 128
Lindy Hop and Cuban music, 86, 87
Lipsitz, George, 14
Lock, Graham, xiii
Loco, Joe, 70
Logan, Guiseppi, 163, 164, 170
"Lona" (Bauzá), 55
Lönrot, Elias, 122
López, Orestes, 82
Lora, Antonio, 101
Lora, Pedro "Cacú," 101
Lord, Albert, 120
Los Angeles, California, Machito in, 65–
    66
Lott, Eric, 13
Love Cry (Graves), 164
Lucumí religion, 44
Lutheran Church and opposition to
    dance, 131, 135
Lyrics/singing, 29, 60, 73, 89

Machín, Antonio, 54
"Machito," 75
Machito and his Afro-Cubans: early de-
    velopment of, 58–61; Finnish fans of,
    150; jazz consciousness of, 185; lack of
    exposure in Cuba, 43–44; later years

of, 91–97; lineup of musicians in,
    203n83, 204n105; and mambo, 87–91;
    NYC expansion of, 61–66; Parker re-
    cording session, 75–76
Machito and his Big Band Salsa (Ma-
    chito), 92
Machito Orchestra, 92
Machito's Latin Jazz Octet, 92, 209n303
McAllester, David, xvii, 190
McBee, Cecil, 41
McCann, Les, 4
McDonald-Ross, Michael, 150
McKinley, Ray, 162–63
McKinley-Graves Quintet, 162–63
Madera, José "Pin," 59, 70, 82, 203–5n84
Mailer, Norman, 14
Malcolm X, 14
Malmstén, Eugen, 129, 133, 136
Malmstén, Georg, 127, 129
"Mambo" (López), 82
Mambo dance, 81–91, 95, 112
Mambo Devils, 83, 89
"Mambo Inn" (Bauzá/Sampson), 87
Mambo is Here to Stay (Machito), 83
Mandala musical notation, 35–37
"Mango mangüé" (Parker), 34, **35,** 76
Mangual, José, 75
Manhattan Transfer, 108, 116
"Manicero, El," 75–76
"Manteca" (Pozo/Gillespie), 73–74
Maracas and Machito, 45
Marginalization, cultural, 5, 7, 14, 18, 51.
    See also Race and racism; Stereotyping
Maria Teresa Vera's Sexteto, 45
Marked vs. unmarked categories of
    music, 3, 4, 5, 24
Marketing of jazz, 154–55
Marsalis, Wynton, 20
Martial arts and Graves, 158, 161–62, 169
Martin, Freddy, 126
Martin, Tommy, 84
Mateo, Joseito, 104
Mbiti, John, 35
Melodies: in drumming, 28, 157–58,
    220n2; in heartbeats, 176–77; and
    hockets, 30; in Parker's music, 34
Melo-rhythms in African-influence mu-
    sics, 28, 30, 32–33, 37, 41
Merengue: and dancers' rhythmic role,
    32–33, **34;** definitional issues, 194n11;
    development of merengue-jazz, 98–
    118; and mandala time notation, 35, **36,**
    37; and moment time, 41

Metaphor and music, 130–31, 198nn7–8, 199n31
Metered musical time, 27
Miami Beach, Florida, Machito in, 65
Microrhythms, 37–39
Middlebrow culture and attitudes toward jazz, 7, 14, 18, 195n36
Middle class, 121–22, 132, 166–67
Middle Eastern musics, 27
"Midnight Hour" (Pickett), 38
Miguel Zavalle sextet, 45
Milford Graves Latin Jazz Quintet, 162–63
Milford Graves Percussion Ensemble (Graves), 163
Mingus, Charles, 1, 21, 22, 38
Minstrelsy, 13–14
Mirabel, Rafaelito, 111
Miranda, Carmen, 64, 65
Mitchell, Ivory, 19
Mitchell, Mitch, 70
Mocambo Club, 65
Modal improvisation, 74, 96
Modernity, jazz's creative role in, x, xvi
Moment time, 40–41
Monk, Thelonius, 2
Montuno and riff structures in mambo, 82
Moore, Robin, 51
Moore, Thurston, 178–79
Morales, Noro, 58, 78
Moral issues for jazz, 131, 135, 136–37, 215n123. *See also* Sexuality
Moré, Benny, 90
Morton, Jelly Roll, 42, 52
Mosaic approach to sound, 32, 34, 156
Moses, Wilson, 189
Motorbeat, dancers', **30**, 31, **32**, 32–33, **34**
Mozart, Wolfgang Amadeus, 20
Multiculturalism: in Finland, 120–24; Graves on, 183; and immigrants' adoption of American culture, 12–13, 14; and jazz consciousness, 185; and spirituality tensions, xi. *See also* Ambivalence, multicultural
Murray, Albert, 12–13
Murray, Mrs. Arthur, 86
Musical consciousness, xiii, 170–77, 182. *See also* Jazz consciousness
Music as healing force, 158, 195n41
Music studies and book's focus, xii–xiii. *See also* Ethnomusicology

"Nagüe," 70
Nail fetishes, 168, 169

National Association for the Advancement of Colored People (NAACP), 10
Nationalism, 5–9, 195n30. *See also* Cultural nationalism
Natural sounds, Dolphy's innovations with, 23
Nature as guide to healing, 168
Navarro, Fats, 78
Nazi dislike of jazz, 135
Needham, Joseph, 169
"New Hope Jazz Mass" (Sarmanto), 145–46
New Orleans, Louisiana, race relations in, 52
New York Art Quartet, 163
New York City: Bauzá's introduction to, 48–50, 53–55; as center of Afro-Cuban music, 93; Dominican influx, 108; expansion of Afro-Cuban music in, 61–66; musicians' union discrimination in, 57; Puerto Rico influx, 87. *See also* Harlem Renaissance
Nicolausson, Harry, 140, 141
Nieto, Johnny, 71
Nieto, Ubaldo, 70
"Night in Tunisia, A" (Gillespie), 73
Nilsson, Alice "Babs," 136
Nketia, Kwabena, 26
"Noise jazz" in Europe, 124–25
Non-racialism as racial project, 5
North American African culture. *See* African American influences (North America)
Notation, musical, African-influenced, 26–29, 198n10
Novelty songs in Afro-Cuban repertoire, 70
"Nut jazz" in the United States, 124
Nuyorican Village, 113
Nzewi, Meki, 27, 28, 29

Obeng, Kwaku Kwaakye, 38
Oboe in Afro-Cuban music, 70
October Revolution in Jazz, 11
O'Farrill Theye, Arturo "Chico": background and musical development, 77–80, 207n213; on Bauzá, 92; compositional accomplishments, 91; concert performance specialization, 67; on lack of recognition for arrangers, 66; and mambo, 82
"Oleo" (Coltrane), 39
Omi, Michael, 5

"On Being 'White' . . . and Other Lies" (Baldwin), 14
On Broadway (Latin Jazz Ensemble), 114
Organic intellectuals, xviii
"Oro, Incienso, y Mirra" (O'Farrill), 91
Orquesta Angelita, 111
Orquesta Bohemia, 102
Orquesta los Hermanos Castro, 50–51
Orquesta los Hermanos Vásquez, 102
Orquesta Presidente Trujillo, 104
Orquesta Siboney, 58
Orquestas típicas, 48
Ortiz, Perico, 30
Orvomaa, Harri, 139
Osby, Greg, 20
Otis, Johnny, 15, 95
Outer vs. inner time, 40–41

Paakunainen, Seppo, 144, 147, 150
Pagani, Federico, 61, 84
Palladium, 84–85, 86, 90, 160
Palmieri, Eddie, 38, 66
Palo religion, 44, 82
Palos drumming, 99, 114
Pambiche form of merengue, 103
Pan-Africanism, 9–12, 43, 95, 186
Panassié, Hughes, 2
Parker, Charlie: Afro-Cuban collaboration, 75–76; on bebop vs. swing, 2; conversation in solo music, 34, **35**; difficulties of Cubop for, 81; and Dolphy, 21; and internalizing of African rhythms, 165, 220–21n12; and Stravinsky, 19–20
Park Palace/Park Plaza Ballroom, 60
Participant Discrepancies (PDs), 39
Participant-observation approach, xviii–xix, 194n48
Patriotism vs. nationalism, 195n30
PDs (Participant Discrepancies), 39
"Peanut Vendor, The," 52–53, 75
Pelimanni music, 120, 130, 212n4
Pelimanni-Pojat, 142
Peña, Oscar, 109–10
Peña-Morell, Estéban, 100
Penttilä, Olli, 148
Pepper, Art, 105
Percussion/drumming: African-influenced cultures/musics, 28, 29, 52, 165, 220–21n12; Afro-Cuban, 44, 61, 62, 69–70, 76, 95; and bassist/drummer conversation, 38, 39; as collective activity, 33; Dominican, 99, 100, 113,

114, 116; engaging audience in, 157; Finnish, 125, 128, 130; fractal patterns in African rhythms, 168; freely improvised, 158; and Graves, 157–58, 159–60, 162–65, 175; and healing vibrations, 174; and kinesthetic rhythms, **30**, 31–32; melodies in, 28, 157–58, 220n2; and noise jazz, 124; rhythm vs. tone, 28–29, 157–58, 175–77, 199nn18–19. *See also* Conga drums
Pérez, Francisco (Macho/Machito Grillo), 43, 44–48, 75, 94, 96. *See also* Machito and his Afro-Cubans
Pérez, Isidro, 77–78
Pérez, Luis, 108
Pérez, Rogelio, 44
Pérez Prado, Dámaso, 81–82, 83, 84, 89
"Perico lo tiene" (Ortiz), 30
Perris, Arnold, 122
Phillips, Flip, 75, 76
Philosophy and Opinions of Marcus Garvey (Garvey), 10
Piano, 52, 53, 66, 69, 116
Picadilly Boys, 89
Pickett, Wilson, 38
Pingoud, Ernst, 132
Piñiero, Ignacio, 45
Piro, Frank "Killer Joe," 86, 87
Pitch and duration in percussion, 28–29, 157–58, 175–77, 199nn18–19
Planetary humanism: in Dolphy's innovations, 24; in jazz community, xiv–xvi, 1–5; and race, xv–xvi, 20, 188
Polymetric musics, 27, 29, 32
Ponce, Daniel, 113
Pop music at jazz festivals, debate over, 153–54
Pori Jazz Festival, 150–54
Postromanticism in Finnish jazz, 146
Power relations, 4, 5, 12–15, 24. *See also* Dominant culture
Pozo y González, Luciano "Chano," 43, 70, 72–75, 76
Prescriptive vs. descriptive musical notation, 26–27
Principles of Psychology (James), 192n23
Process, national identity as, 6
Progressive jazz, 78
Puente, Tito, 83, 89, 114
Puerto Rico, 42–43, 87, 89, 91
Pulse (beat) and jazz conversation, 38. *See also* Rhythm
Push-pull rhythmic conversation, 38–39

Romeo, Antonio María, 48
Rotary perception in jazz groove, 38
Ruff, Willie, 19
Ruiz, Hilton, 114
Ruiz Suárez, Bernardo, 49–50
Rumba (drumming and dance), 44
Runne, Ossi, 141
Rural vs. urban artistic cultures, 99–100, 121–22, 123, 147
Russell, George, 74, 96
Russian influences on Finland, 120, 121, 142, 143
Rytmi (magazine), 133, 136, 144, 217n167
Rytmimusikki (rhythm-music) in Finland, 140, 154, 155–56. *See also* Finnish cultures/musics
Rytmi-pojat (Rhythm Boys), 129
Rytmi-Veikot (Rhythm Guys), 141

Sacassas, Anselmo, 61
Safronoff, Feodor Nikitin (Teppo Repo), 123–124, 134
Saha, Hannu, 123
Saint Patrick's Cathedral, 91
Saint Peter's Church in Manhattan, 145–46
Salazar, Max, 85
Salim, A. K., 80
Salmi, Karl Klaus, 129
Salon orchestras, European, 120, 124
Salon orquestas in Dominican Republic, 100, 101–2
Salsa in Dominican musics, 108
Salsa Refugees, 113
Salve drumming, 99
Salves sagradas, 99
Sampson, Edgar, 87
Santería religion, 44, 158, 160, 165, 202n39
Santiago de los Caballeros, Dominican Republic, 101–3, 109, 111
Santo Domingo, Dominican Republic, 99
Santos, Ray, 67, 68, 81, 85, 87, 89, 96
Sargeant, Winthrop, 195n36
Sarmanto, Heikki, 145–46
Savoy Ballroom, 54, 88
Saxophone: in Afro-Cuban music, 50, 67, 68, 69, 82; Bird's time, **35;** and Coltrane, 17, 21–22, 39; and cyclical timing, 35, **36**, 37; in Dominican musics, 100, 101, 102–3, 105, 108, 109, 110–15; rhythmic role of, 32–33, **34**. *See also* Parker, Charlie
Saxophon Jazz Band, 128

Scandia Record Company, 139
Schlagers (German popular songs), 124
"Schoolboy" bands in Finland, 125–26, 128, 129
Schools of dance and Afro-Cuban music, 86, 87
Schuller, Gunther, 16, 22, 23, 31
Schutz, Alfred, 40
Second Afro-Cubans, The, 63
Second sight from double consciousness, xii, 14, 18–19, 197n82
Seeger, Charles, 26
Segregationist thinking and Western rationalism, 170–71, 176. *See also* Race and racism
Self-cultivation, importance of, 171–73
Self-teaching, value of, 160–61, 164
Separatism, black, 10. *See also* Black nationalism
Septeto Nacional, 45
Sexteto Aguabama, 45
Sexteto Ancoaona, 47
Sexuality: and Afro-Cuban music, 63; Finnish attitudes, 130–31, 135, 136–37; and jazz, 8, 31
Shankar, Ravi, 23, 164
Shepp, Archie, 3, 11
Sibelius, Jean, 122
Siboney, Orquesta, 58
Silver, Horace, 96
Singh, Wasantha, 164
Singing/lyrics, 29, 60, 73, 89
Sissle, Noble, 53
"Skokiaan," 105, **106**
Slavery, Spanish vs. North American versions, 46
Small, Christopher, xiii, 190
Smith, Leroy "Stuff," 53
Socarrás, Alberto, 53, 92–93
Social class. *See* Class, social
Social Darwinism, 7
Socialized ambivalence in Dominican Republic, 187. *See also* Ambivalence, multicultural
Social movements of black consciousness, 11, 145, 165, 185
Social purpose of jazz consciousness, 24. *See also* Cultural perspectives
Solfège, 47–48
Solo performances, 22–23, 33. *See also* Improvisation
Son dance, 45, 51, 52–53, 61. *See also* Conga dance

Unification of self, xii, xiii, xvi. *See also* Inclusivity

Unions, 53, 57, 131–32, 133

United Nations Band, 112

United States: ambivalence about jazz, 186; and black nationalism, 9–12; cultural creolization of, 12–15, 88; cultural influence of, xiv, 9; cultural vs. civic nationalism in, 5–9; Finnish wartime attitudes toward, 136; and jazz consciousness, 16–24; vs. Latino race relations, 42–43, 45–47, 48–52; and musical consciousness raising, 15–16; occupation of Dominican Republic, 101, 102, 103; stereotyping for international influence, 64; strategic universalism and jazz in, 1–5, 12. *See also* African American influences (North America); African Americans

Universalism, musical: and cultural relativism, xvi, 188–89; and humanness, 179–82; in jazz, ix–x, xxi, 1–5, 12, 154, 187–89. *See also* Cosmopolitanism; Inclusivity; Planetary humanism

Universal Negro Improvement Association (UNIA), 10

Unmarked vs. marked categories of music, 3, 4, 5, 24

Urban vs. rural artistic cultures, 99–100, 121–22, 123, 147

Utopian space, jazz consciousness as, 190

Uuden Musiikin Orkesteri (UMO), 145

Väisänen, A. O., 123, 134

Valdés, Bebo, 82, 83

Valdés, Miguelito, 51, 63

Vargas, Wilfrido, 108

Varieties of Religious Experience, The (James), xii

Vásquez, Avelino, 101, 102

Vásquez, Cacha and Pepe, 73

Vásquez, Chachí, 109

Vásquez, Tavito, 106–8, 109, 111, 114–15, 117

Vaughan, Sarah, 19

Ventura, Johnny, 108

Verbal discourse on music, limitations of, 26–27

Vesala, Edvard, 145, 146–47, 154–55, 218n185

Vesterinen, Viljo, 129

Vibraphones in Finnish musics, 143

Vibration: healing nature of, 174, 177–79, 183; importance in music, 182

Vicioso, Tony, 116–17

Victor Talking Machine Company, 48

Vidal, Carlos, 75

Viljanen, Matti, 141

Villar, Manuel, 89

Violins in pelimanni music, 120

Virtual time, music as being in, 40, 201n67

Vodou rituals/religion, 98, 103–4, 159

Voz Dominicana, La, 104–5, 111

Waill, Victor, 41

Walser, Robert, 4

Washburne, Chris, 38

Webb, Chick, 54–55

West Africa, 27, 31, 44, 198–99n11

Westerholm, Pekka, 148

Western culture: and cultural relativism, xv; limitations of, 168, 169–71, 176

Whiteman, Paul, 2

Whiteness, study of, 14–15. *See also* Euro-Americans

Wien, George, 91

Wilckin, Merle, 126

"Wild Jungle" (Hernández), 81

Winant, Howard, 5

Winter Carnival festival, 150

Witch doctors, wisdom of, 168

Working class, 126–28, 142

World Mänkeri Orchestra (Etnopojat), 148–50

World music, Finnish contribution to, 147–48

World War II, 62–63, 66

Yam (newsletter), 136

Yiddish and Finnish musical styles, 139

Yorùbá religion, 44, 65, 71, 183

Zamba, 126

MUSIC/CULTURE

A series from Wesleyan University Press

Edited by Robert Walser and Susan Fast

Originating editors, George Lipsitz, Susan McClary, and Robert Walser

My Music
by Susan D. Crafts, Daniel Cavicchi,
Charles Keil, and the Music in Daily
Life Project

*Running with the Devil: Power, Gender,
and Madness in Heavy Metal Music*
by Robert Walser

*Subcultural Sounds: Micromusics
of the West*
by Mark Slobin

*Upside Your Head! Rhythm and Blues
on Central Avenue*
by Johnny Otis

*Dissonant Identities: The Rock 'n' Roll
Scene in Austin, Texas*
by Barry Shank

*Black Noise: Rap Music and Black Cul-
ture in Contemporary America*
by Tricia Rose

*Club Cultures: Music, Media and Sub-
cultural Capital*
by Sarah Thornton

Music, Society, Education
by Christopher Small

Popular Music in Theory
by Keith Negus

*Any Sound You Can Imagine: Making
Music/Consuming Technology*
by Paul Théberge

*Listening to Salsa: Gender, Latin Popu-
lar Music, and Puerto Rican Cultures*
by Frances Aparicio

*A Thousand Honey Creeks Later: My
Life in Music from Basie to Motown—
and Beyond*
by Preston Love

*Voices in Bali: Energies and Perceptions
in Vocal Music and Dance Theater*
by Edward Herbst

*Musicking: The Meanings of Performing
and Listening*
by Christopher Small

*Singing Archaeology: Philip Glass's
Akhnaten*
by John Richardson

*Music of the Common Tongue: Survival
and Celebration in African American
Music*
by Christopher Small

*Metal, Rock, and Jazz: Perception and
Phenomenology Music Experience*
by Harris M. Berger

Music and Cinema
edited by James Buhler, Caryl Flinn,
and David Neumeyer

*"You Better Work!" Underground
Dance Music in New York City*
by Kai Fikentscher

Singing Our Way to Victory: French Cultural Politics and Music During the Great War
by Regina M. Sweeney

The Book of Music and Nature: An Anthology of Sounds, Words, Thoughts
edited by David Rothenberg and Marta Ulvaeus

Recollecting from the Past: Musical Practice and Spirit Possession on the East Coast of Madagascar
by Ron Emoff

Banda: Mexican Musical Life across Borders
by Helena Simonett

Global Noise: Rap and Hip-Hop outside the USA
edited by Tony Mitchell

The 'Hood Comes First: Race, Space, and Place in Rap and Hip-Hop
by Murray Forman

Manufacturing the Muse: Estey Organs and Consumer Culture in Victorian America
by Dennis Waring

The City of Musical Memory: Salsa, Record Grooves, and Popular Culture in Cali, Colombia
by Lise A. Waxer

Symphonic Metamorphoses: Subjectivity and Alienation in Mahler's Re-Cycled Songs
by Raymond Knapp

Music and Technoculture
edited by René T. A. Lysloff and Leslie C. Gay, Jr.

Angora Matta: Fatal Acts of North-South Translation
by Marta Elena Savigliano

False Prophet: Fieldnotes from the Punk Underground
by Steven Taylor

Phat Beats, Dope Rhymes: Hip Hop Down Under Comin' Upper
by Ian Maxwell

Locating East Asia in Western Art Music
edited by Yayoi Uno Everett and Frederick Lau

Making Beats: The Art of Sample-Based Hip-Hop
by Joseph G. Schloss

Identity and Everyday Life: Essays in the Study of Folklore, Music, and Popular Culture
by Harris M. Berger and Giovanna P. Del Negro

The Other Side of Nowhere: Jazz, Improvisation, and Communities in Dialogue
edited by Daniel Fischlin and Ajay Heble

Setting the Record Straight: A Material History of Classical Recording
by Colin Symes

Wired for Sound: Engineering and Technologies in Sonic Cultures
edited by Paul D. Greene and Thomas Porcello

ABOUT THE AUTHOR

Paul Austerlitz is Assistant Professor of Music and Africana Studies at Brown University and author of *Merengue: Dominican Music and Dominican Identity* (Temple University Press, 1997). His articles have been published in *Ethnomusicology, Journal for Black Music Research, World of Music,* and *General Music Today.* He has recorded numerous CDs as a jazz bass clarinetist.